FROM THE ESOTERIC SCHOOL

ESOTERIC LESSONS

1913 and 1914

1920–1923

RUDOLF STEINER (1923)

ESOTERIC LESSONS
1913 and 1914
1920–1923

Notes Written from Memory by the Participants
and Meditation Verses by Rudolf Steiner

VOLUME 3

TRANSLATED BY MARSHA POST
INTRODUCTION BY CHRISTOPHER BAMFORD

RUDOLF STEINER

SteinerBooks
CW 266/3

Copyright © 2011 by SteinerBooks

SteinerBooks
Anthroposophic Press

610 Main Street
Great Barrington, Massachusetts 01230
www.steinerbooks.org

Original translation from the German by Marsha Post

This book is volume 266/3 in the Collected Works (CW) of Rudolf Steiner, published by SteinerBooks, 2011. It is a translation of the German *Aus den Inhalten der esoterischen Stunden, Band III, Gedächtnisaufzeichnungen von Teilnehmern und Meditationstexte nach Niederschriften Rudolf Steiners 1913 and 1914; 1920-1923*, published by Rudolf Steiner Verlag, Dornach, Switzerland, 1998.

Library of Congress Cataloging-in-Publication Data is available.
ISBN 978-0-88010-618-4

All rights reserved.
No part of this book may be reproduced in any form without written permission from the publisher, except for brief quotations embodied in critical articles for review.

CONTENTS

Introduction by Christopher Bamford ix
Preliminary Words from the Editor of the German Edition xx

PART I
NOTES OF THE ESOTERIC LESSONS
1913 and 1914

Written from Memory by the Participants

Meditation Verses used repeatedly in the Esoteric Lessons from 1913-1914......1

1913

JANUARY 2, 1913, COLOGNE..23
Separation from the direction represented by Mrs. Besant. Proper attitude regarding her as a personality and her deeds. Two rules of the Essene Order and their use today in connection with the Rosicrucian mantra: going to sleep with the consciousness of *Ex Deo nascimur* (love). Maintaining consciousness at transition moments. Visualizing the body in sleep as a preparation for imaginative seeing (house with door, corpse in the coffin, angel with chalice). Taking *In Christo morimur* (humility) with us into the time after death. The nature of spiritual substance after death, before and after the Mystery of Golgotha. Self-consciousness after death through *Per Spiritum Sanctum reviviscimus*.

JANUARY 4, 1913, COLOGNE..35
The esoteric processes around Mrs. Besant are no longer a matter of Western or Eastern esotericism but of truth and of untruth. The perception of thoughts disturbing meditation as progress. The experience of *It thinks me, It weaves me, It works me* connected with the feelings of devoutness, reverence and awe, gratitude. Living out karmic connections within the blood ties before the Mystery of Golgotha. Christ as the second Adam.

JANUARY 6, 1913, BERLIN...43
Falling asleep with the evening meditation: continuation of the meditation in the disembodied state. Symbolic dream images before awakening. Two rules of the Essene Order in connection with the Rosicrucian mantra. The spiritual substance after death before and after the Mystery of Golgotha.

FEBRUARY 8, 1913, BERLIN..49
Concerning proper meditation. The world of knowledge and the world of experience. The world of the Blessed. Example of dangers in the ascent into the spiritual worlds. Function of enjoyment. God in the *maya*. The mantras: *It thinks me, It weaves me, It works me*. Spiritual secrets in the sounds of these mantras. Two rules of the Essene Order in connection with the Rosicrucian mantra.

February 17-20, 1913, STUTTGART..58
About the continued working of the exercise, also when the student falls asleep during the exercise. The truth of the four statements: I am; I think; I feel; I will. The meaning and significance of the sounds of the Rosicrucian mantra.

MARCH 12, 1913, MUNICH..63
About the continued working of the exercise, also when the student falls asleep during the exercise. The truth of the four statements: *I am*; *I think*; *I feel*; *I will*. The meaning and significance of the sounds of the Rosicrucian mantra.

MARCH 16, 1913, BERLIN..69
The death of Oda Waller. Falling asleep during meditation. The truth of the statements: *I am*; *I think*; *I feel*; *I will*. The meaning of the sounds of the Rosicrucian mantra.

MARCH 21, 1913, THE HAGUE..77
Two possible experiences with meditating: 1. Being lifted up, expansion; the approach of yellow-red beings (archangels); bliss and fear. 2. Sinking down, contraction; the approach of blue-violet beings (angels); trembling, seeing oneself. Unification of these figures: conflict and temptation from Lucifer. Rosicrucian mantra.

MARCH 25, 1913, THE HAGUE..82
The four statements: *I am*; *I think*; *I feel*; *I will*. The sounds of the three mantras (*It thinks me*; *It weaves me*; *It works me*.) and the Rosicrucian mantra.

APRIL 11, 1913, BERLIN..86
Experiences during meditating and helpful advice: about thoughts disturbing meditation; headaches; the appearance of particular characteristics; reasons for the appearance of the double. Imaginations: the etheric body becoming mobile.

MAY 14, 1913, STRASSBURG..95
About the moral world and the natural world: the esotericists must unite them (examples: Sun, Moon, Mercury, Venus). Separated, the natural world contains forces that cause illness. Matter as concentrated sin. Lucifer's influence: egotism. Pain as a remedy against egotism. The necessity for morality with the ascent into the spiritual worlds. The Rosicrucian mantra.

MAY 18, 1913, STUTTGART..100
The task of the esotericists: read the outer manifestations as esoteric script. The three Suns (physical, spiritual, and Christ-Sun). Julian the Apostate. Direct working of planets below the Sun; indirect working of the planets above the Sun. The seven planets as the seven light-roses of the Rose Cross. The Rosicrucian mantra.

JUNE 1, 1913, HELSINGFORS (HELSINKI)..122
About the prayers to the spirits of the days. The "I"-begetting force of the Sun, and the reproductive force of the Moon. Mercury as messenger. The three Suns.

JUNE 5, 1913, HELSINGFORS (HELSINKI)..124
Thoughts disturbing meditation. Unfortunate results of the events in Adyar.

JUNE 8, 1913, STOCKHOLM..125
Difficulties of self-knowledge; three discoveries thereby: wanting to deny the spirit; fear before the spirit; hatred toward the spirit. About love and its connection with karmic bonds and egotism. Concerning the effect of Lucifer and Ahriman in the thoughts disturbing one.

SEPTEMBER 3, 1913, MUNICH...129
The difference between exotericism and esotericism. About the plurality and unity in philosophy and in esotericism. Recognizing only the unity is succumbing to Lucifer; acknowledging only the plurality is succumbing to Ahriman. System as dogma: ahrimanic. Forcing or imposing of a spiritual truth: luciferic. The book *Theosophy*, without the necessary effort of thinking would be luciferic. Concerning the so-called "vibrations." Effects of meditation.

SEPTEMBER 4, 1913, MUNICH...140
Effect of Lucifer and Ahriman. Lucifer and the mystics; Lucifer's inclination to become pious. Ahriman: in everything having to do with the will, gestures, writing, listening, and everything mediumistic. Swedenborg. The harmonizing of both forces. Non-use of esoteric capacities in physical life. About Maeterlinck's demand for proof of the spiritual. The Gospel of John as help to find a middle way.

OCTOBER 5, 1913, CHRISTIANIA (OSLO)..150
Lack of "robustness" in the thought life of esotericists. Pain through thoughts that are not in conformity with the laws of world existence, for instance, Crookes' microscopic human being. Feelings of cold and of warmth with various thoughts and philosophies. Example: oil-filled bowl in which a flame burns (image of the four members of the human being). The change of the etheric body at various places: North: expansion; South: compression.

OCTOBER 6, 1913, CHRISTIANIA (OSLO)..158
Justified and unjustified working of Lucifer and Ahriman. Ahriman: Lord of Death, his working through fear (materialism). Being satisfied as protection. Lucifer: promoter and stimulator of art and free science; temptation to arrogance; his working in naturalistic-realistic dramas (G. Hauptmann). Humility and modesty as protection. Lucifer and Ahriman carry their "I" onto the physical plane. Every being has its world in which it must experience its "I." About fainting at the sight of blood. Changes in the etheric body: North: expansion; South: compression; East: becoming small.

OCTOBER 11, 1913, BERGEN..159
Typical experiences in connection with meditating: tingling, prickling, buzzing or roaring in the blood (becoming conscious of egotism). Shortness of breath (lack of sense of truth). Weakness and breaking into a sweat (experiencing the physical body as hindrance). A kind of pleasant dream-state (lack of sociability). Remedy against egotism (example: Gospel of John). Cultivation of devotion.

OCTOBER 15, 1913, COPENHAGEN...162
Contact with Lucifer and Ahriman upon entering the spiritual world. Ahriman: works in all sounds and words. Lucifer: in visions. The result of the Fall. The human aura as a shell to be broken through in order to achieve access to the spiritual world. The Rosicrucian mantra. Temptation by Lucifer through voices; by Ahriman through images. Producing concentrated attention without an object in the meditation: overcoming Lucifer. The experience of being outside of oneself (image of the lightning). The nature of the mantra in relation to the concept. The result of the Fall. Duties and experiences of esotericists.

NOVEMBER 9, 1913, NUREMBURG..171
Esotericists must pay attention to the subtlest processes. Imaginations are given. Esotericists objectify their *other human being*. Lucifer's temptation approaches from within; Ahriman's from outside. Examples are given. Learn to draw conclusions about earlier experiences. Reproach works strongly in the subconscious.

NOVEMBER 10, 1913, NUREMBURG..173
Our behavior in relation to the spiritual world. The spiritual teacher as educator: esotericists must be treated as developing, becoming beings. Even if we do not enter into the spiritual world consciously it is important to devote ourselves to the esoteric life. What matters is the prevailing mood of soul. The human aura is described as a shell to be broken through in order to achieve access to the spiritual world. Imaginations are given. The Sun as the center of our "I".

NOVEMBER 17, 1913, BERLIN..175
Before the Mystery of Golgotha on the Sun, Christ is found on the Sun; now in the aura of the Earth. What would be the result if human beings received their "I"-consciousness in the second seven-year period of life? Life in eight dream-like states with the image of death beside them. Cowardice today before the spiritual world. Results of rejecting the Christ impulse: the soul becomes desolate and sclerotic; feeling the death forces. Weariness of life, suicide epidemics.

NOVEMBER 23, 1913, STUTTGART..185
Flighty thoughts revealing the life of desires as a hindrance to spiritual progress, but also as a means of attaining self-knowledge. The connection between desire (interest) and memory. Love for Lucifer and Ahriman. The work of Ahriman as shown by two examples: in the seeking of excuses in self-knowledge; in false philosophical ideas (conversation of Deussen and Nietzsche about denial of the will and ennoblement of the will). Knowledge of Lucifer and Ahriman in all of our doing and not-doing. The increasing of the spiritual and the dying away of the material in connection with the Rosicrucian mantra.

DECEMBER 9, 1913, MUNICH..191
Results of the progressive sensitizing of esotericists through meditation: noticing disturbing thoughts, bodily pain during meditation. The appearance of peculiar experiences that were imprinted earlier, consciously or unconsciously, into the etheric body (visions of violent scenes, and so on). Improvement and refining of the good side; independence of the ugly side. The encounter with Christ. Inspirations coming out of the higher worlds for the material world; examples: Wallace, Darwin.

DECEMBER 18, 1913, COLOGNE..196
As soon as we begin an esoteric training the soul changes. A consequences of esoteric training: loosening of the physical, etheric, and astral bodies and the "I" and thereby peculiar experiences appear that were imprinted in the etheric body. We incarnate again and again to achieve truthfulness and morality in the physical world.

DECEMBER 30, 1913, LEIPZIG..197
View of psychologists of the Middle Ages: the entire soul life is intentional. Thinking without an object. Astral body and "I" during sleep are pulled out of the blood and nervous systems; strong penetrating of the sense and glandular systems. Luciferic warmth and the warmth raying out of the spiritual world-warmth that reveals itself as cold in meditation. The Rose Cross and the Rosicrucian mantra.

1914

JANUARY 2, 1914, LEIPZIG 209
The subsidiary exercises as a means for learning to know the different members of the human being. About the pain that appears in connection with meditation. Observation of the physical body through concentration of thinking; knowing the etheric body through the will exercise; becoming conscious of the astral body through equanimity; of the "I" through positivity; of the manas through openness. Harmonization of the various capacities. Necessities for esotericists: practice patience and truthfulness. Development of an ordinary, good memory. Penetrate all actions with attention and reflection.

JANUARY 11, 1914, BREMEN 219
The contracting of the warmth ether during meditation. Being ashamed. The attention toward the inside and toward the outside.

JANUARY 24, 1914, BERLIN 220
The way into the spiritual world: an easier ascent for those feeling-natures with a religious disposition; a harder ascent for will-natures, suffering through the emotions. The path of thinking: longest but safest way. The Rosicrucian mantra.

FEBRUARY 7, 1914, HANNOVER 223
Advice for meditation. Feelings of warmth and coolness during prayer with exotericists or esotericists. Effects of subsidiary exercises. Will exercise, feeling oneself in the etheric body. Equanimity, and expanding of the etheric body. The experience of the first two sentences of the Rosicrucian mantra in the first three subsidiary exercises; of the third sentence in the fourth exercise positivity.

MARCH 5, 1914, STUTTGART 226
Etheric body as originator, physical body as mirror of thoughts. "Sein" [existence] comes from "Sehen" [to see]. Matter as nothingness; the spiritual world as actual reality. Feeling the nothing as resistance. Consciousness of the strengthened soul life for the elemental world. Transformation of good thoughts into eternal imaginations; bad or evil thoughts as waste products. Comparison with the origin of the mineral kingdom -- the earthly dust from which Yahweh created the human being -- through the errors of the elohim on the old moon; the work of Lucifer. The relation of the physical and spiritual worlds. Instructions for mantras.

MARCH 27 AND APRIL 14, 1914, VIENNA 235
Becoming independent of our thought life through the mantra: "I turn to the things..." The living "I" becoming conscious of itself through "spirit light warmed me...". Feeling the sense world as pearls of existence in the real being of the spirit: "Luminous 'I' and Beacon-soul...". The connection with the Rosicrucian mantra.

Progress through the right mood of the soul with meditation. "It thinks me," instead of "I think." Concentrating of the self in the etheric body. The experience of our own goodness and badness. Instructions for the mantras: "I turn to the things..."; "Spirit light warm me..."; "Luminous 'I' and beacon-soul...".

MARCH 31, 1914, MUNICH 253

Hindrances to becoming conscious of progress. Thoughts: reflections of thinking by the physical body. Feeling ourselves spread out or expanded as a sign of weakening. What underlies the good and the bad thoughts. Instructions for the three mantras: "I turn to the things..."; "Spirit light warm me..."; "Luminous 'I' and beacon-soul...". The Rosicrucian mantra.

APRIL 25, 1914, BERLIN 260

The yearning for the physical body as cause of the lack of consciousness in the spiritual world during sleep. The work on the twelve senses by elemental beings serving the spirits of form; these elemental beings will make up the future Jupiter zodiac. The work on the blood system by elemental beings serving the spirits of movement; these elemental beings will build the future Jupiter sun. Lucifer's working: sense experience. Ahriman's working: world experience.

MAY 9, 1914, KASSEL 272

Contact with the spiritual in dream, in memory. Day-consciousness comes about at the boundary between the new soul core and the old spirituality. Nature as the remaining memory of what the hierarchies once thought. Lucifer strives even yet to think the error. Instructions for the three mantras: "I turn to the things..."; "Spirit light warm me..."; "Luminous, 'I' and beacon-soul...".

JUNE 3, 1914, BASEL 281

Lucifer's working: burning through the fire of the passions, drives, desires in the heart of the higher beings' imaginations, inspirations, intuitions that are contained in the perception. Moses and the burning thorn bush. The working of Ahriman in the brain: cooling down Lucifer's fire. Lovelessness is fuel for Lucifer's fire. "I turn to the things...".

JULY 14, 1914, NORRKÖPING 285

Becoming body-free in the proper meditation. The human organs as script signs of the gods. The "small brain" (cerebellum) as the remainder of the old Moon period. Re-forming of lungs and heart of the Moon human being to the pineal gland and mucous glands of the Earth human being. Formation of the Jupiter human's brain from the deeds ("large brain" cerebrum) and thoughts ("small brain"cerebellum) of the Earth human being. Christ as helper and as judge; the "Last Judgment." The results of the incorrect description of Yahweh by H. P. Blavatsky. The connection of spiritual science with Christ-knowledge.

PART II
NOTES OF THE ESOTERIC LESSONS

1920 to the New Founding of the Esoteric School as
the "Independent School for Spiritual Science"
at the Goetheanum 1923/1924

Written from Memory by the Participants
With Facsimiles from Rudolf Steiner's Handwritten Notebook

Foreword 295

FEBRUARY 9, 1920, DORNACH 298
The lack of the earnestness of the members of the Society. Critique and trust in their proper place. The necessary change of one's view of life after seven years of membership. The necessary uniting of the streams from the spiritual world with the living stream from the organism. Karma of the individual and karma of humanity. Humanity at the threshold. The dangers of not using the inner forces given by the Mystery of Golgotha: more and more soulless bodies with automaton-intellect. Meditative provision for the path: "I imagine..."; "I think..."; "I feel..."; "I dream..."; "I will..."; "I sleep...". At the beginning and at the close of the lesson the mantra is spoken: "Human being, know yourself...".

FEBRUARY 17, 1920, DORNACH 304
Life in three realms: 1. in the physical world; 2. at the threshold; 3. on the other side of the threshold. The experience at the threshold. The connection with Christ. "The divine gave me an 'I'...". Secret societies and spiritual science. The Jesuits. At the beginning and at the end of the lesson: "Human being, know yourself...".

APRIL 16, 1922, LONDON 311
"Mirror of the world...".

NOVEMBER 12, 1922, LONDON 324
Nature-knowledge, moral duties, and religious consciousness. The two parts of the world ether: 1. The warmth, light, chemical, and life ethers; 2. The moral being of the world ether is only near the stars and planets.

SEPTEMBER 30, 1923, VIENNA 313
"Human being, know yourself...". The Temple legend.

PART III

The Esoteric Youth Group

Foreword 329

Some Documents of the Origin and History of the Anthroposophical Youth Movement

1. Appeal for the Forming of a Youth Branch 341
2. Undated Circular, March/April 1920 344
3. Circular from Paul Baumann, April 1920 346
4. Circular from Ehrenfried Pfeiffer 348
5. Appeal of the Association for Independent Spiritual Life 352
6. Memorandum for the Committee of the Independent Anthroposophical Society for its Orientation, March 1923 356

Reports from the Founding Members of the Youth Group Concerning Rudolf Steiner's Presentation for the Esoteric Youth Group

Preliminary Remarks 359

1. Rudolf Steiner's Presentation for the Founding of the Esoteric Youth Group 363
2. Notes from Rudolf Steiner's Comments at Two Meetings 386
3. Further Notes from Presentations by Rudolf Steiner 393
4. Notes from Memory by Herbert Hahn 399

Two Esoteric Lessons for the Youth Group

JULY 13, 1923, STUTTGART 406

People are asleep today in relation to the word. The word "I." The physical body is subjected to gravity; opposite is the force of the light. Experiencing lightness in the dream of flying. The force of lightness is connected with the Sun. Lighting up of dammed-up etheric substance in lightning. The mantra "My being is interwoven...". The vertical pulsating of plants in the light. Becoming free from the Earth by breathing. Rosicrucian mantra and the mantra "My being is interwoven...". Experience of gravity (physical): connection with the Father forces. Experience of lightness (etheric): connection with Christ. Experience of the breath (astral): connection with the divine Spirit. Image of the lotus flower. "AOUM Mane padme HUM" — "My 'I' is enclosed...". Explanation of the Sanskrit.

DECEMBER 30, 1923, DORNACH... 414
The three-part mantra: "Human being, know your self..."; "Know first the earnest Guardian..."; "I stepped into this sense world...". Youth: do not know *more*, but know *differently*. Experience the Earth as a star that rays forth; gleams; has density. Love gleams from the star, and truth forms the star. "Yasmajjatam jagat sarvam...". End of Kali Yuga. Beginning of the Light Age. Most people meet the Guardian of the threshold unconsciously between their thirtieth and fortieth year. Making elemental beings noticeable. The warmth-love cloak from human karma and the Earth. Human thinking should shine out into the universe. Necessity for soul courage to connect again with the ancient sacred knowledge. Today's answer to the demand, " Human being, know your self," is no longer "AOUM," but is: *yes, I am there for your world deeds.*

The Youth Group Meditations

Meditation given on October 13, 1922..426
Mantras given on December 30, 1923..430

The Three-part Mantra (Three Tablets)

The mantra of the Esoteric Lessons from 1920 to 1923..............437

Editorial and Reference Notes 447
Rudolf Steiner's Collected Works 479
Significant Events in the Life of Rudolf Steiner 495
Index 511

INTRODUCTION

CHRISTOPHER BAMFORD

The origins of Rudolf Steiner's Esoteric School lie in the Theosophical Society, dating back at least to 1884, when some members of the London lodge "petitioned the Masters" for the formation of an inner group of students for esoteric training. Following the initial request, the number of those seeking to become "disciples" rather than simply students of esoteric content increased until, in 1888, under the direction of Madame Blavatsky, the Esoteric School of the Theosophical Society was founded: "to promote the esoteric interests of the Theosophical Society by the deeper study of esoteric philosophy...." Blavatsky led the School until her death in 1891, when Annie Besant took on the task, sharing it with William Q. Judge until he died in 1895, but then leading it alone. By that time, it was common knowledge that the School was not only the esoteric heart of the Theosophical Movement, but also answered the need for shared experience and insight in those who led and represented it to the public. Not surprisingly then, when the German Section of the Theosophical Society was founded in Besant's presence in Berlin on October 20, 1902—with Rudolf Steiner as General Secretary and Marie von Sivers as Secretary—one of the first things Steiner requested of Besant was that she enroll him as a member (not yet as teacher, but as student) of the "Esoteric School."

It is not difficult to imagine why he did so. Clearly, he understood that if he was to create an authentic esoteric school, he would need to link his teaching and approach with existing traditions and lineages. A few years later, indeed, we see him making a connection with Freemasonry, and attempting to forge bonds with other groups, such as the Order of the Golden Dawn, for instance, in order somehow to bring together all those working broadly out of the Western esoteric and Rosicrucian roots. To begin with, however, for whatever reasons of karma or providence, his own work (which would be anthroposophical from the start) was destined to unfold not within any explicitly Western tradition but within the global—and, in some sense, more Eastern—impulse represented by Theosophy. From this point of view, irrespective of where his own spiritual mission was to lead him, preservation of continuity was essential. As he writes in his *Autobiography*:

> I always wanted to link whatever I did with what already existed and was present historically. I wanted to do this in the Esoteric School just as I had done in relation to the Theosophical Society. Thus my more intimate circle arose in connection with the School. But the connection [to Theosophy and its esoteric school] was limited to external arrangements, not to the suprasensory knowledge I imparted. Thus, in the early years my smaller circle was seen as part of Mrs. Besant's esoteric school, but according to its inner nature it was completely unrelated to that school. And in 1907, when Mrs. Besant attended our theosophical conference in Munich, even that outer connection was severed completely by mutual agreement.

The history of Steiner's involvement with the Esoteric School and the foundational teachings he gave are documented in *From the History and Contents of the Esoteric School 1904-1914* (CW 264). We learn that almost before he assumed any official position in the German Section, Steiner was asked for esoteric instruction—although it was not until he visited Annie Besant in London in May 1904 that she officially named him "Arch Warden," thus officially "authorizing" him to teach. It is also clear that from the beginning Steiner realized the critical importance of a dedicated core of committed students, who were serious "meditators." As he wrote to Marie von Sivers in April 1903: "Without a body of true Theosophists to improve the karma of the present by hard-working meditation, theosophical teachings would be expounded merely to half-deaf ears."

*

The three volumes of the Esoteric Lessons trace in a remarkable way the continuous deepening and unfolding metamorphosis—as it were, the honing or sharpening—of Rudolf Steiner's spiritual path, while at the same time accompanying and illuminating his always-ongoing spiritual research. As such, the lessons provide invaluable sources of insight and inspiration not just for students of Anthroposophy but also for anyone seeking guidance in the practice of a spiritual path that paradoxically is both contemporary *and* profoundly connected to humanity's primordial spiritual nature, and also simultaneously—especially as it develops—deeply and esoterically Christian in nature.

The first volume (1904-1909) parallels the writing of the three foundational anthroposophical works (*Theosophy*, *How to Know Higher Worlds*, and *An Outline of Esoteric Science*). It tracks the development of Steiner's mission and teaching within and out of its framework in Theosophy and continues through the landmark 1907 Whitsun Congress (see: *Rosicrucianism Renewed* CW 284), which marked the completion of the seventh year since providence (and karma) had first brought him into the theosophical orbit in 1900. As a new beginning or "second octave," the Congress inaugurated the turning point after which Steiner's teaching and spiritual research emerged openly in its own authentic, "mystical Christian" (as Besant called it)—or truly Rosicrucian—form. Steiner had already over the past few years not so subtly begun to change the nature of "Theosophy" by covertly including in the lineage of theosophical teachers his own "masters" from Central Europe—figures such as the mystics Meister Eckhart and Angelus Silesius; the alchemists Paracelsus, Basil Valentine, and Jacob Boehme, who led into the Rosicrucians; the Romantics poets Goethe and Novalis; and the philosophers Fichte, Hegel, and Schelling. But the Congress allowed what had heretofore been implicit to become explicit. More generally speaking, the Congress marked a watershed in the emergence of Western esotericism into the outer, public sphere as a vehicle for cultural and social renewal. Thus, in the esoteric lessons that followed, the focus became increasingly more Christian and Rosicrucian and less focused on theosophical-anthroposophical cosmology.

The second volume (1909-1912) continues the deepening Christian emphasis, best exemplified perhaps by the epoch-making lectures on the Gospels, the visionary understanding of the reappearance of Christ in the etheric, and the dawning realization of the Archangel Michael's crucial role in the present stage of human evolution—all this and more occurring against the background of the prolonged, acrimonious political conflict over the pretended Messianic status of the young Krishnamurti, which would lead to the complete break between Adyar (India) and Berlin on December 28, 1912. In retrospect, the breach with Theosophy was inevitable. As early as December 1911, following the foundation of the Order of the Star in the East to promote Krishnamurti as the coming World Savior, some of "those active on the basis of Rudolf Steiner's work" had already presciently formed a new association, one whose statues had "nothing whatever to do with the Theosophical Society either in form or content." Throughout the first half of 1912, the new association continued to hold meetings. Then in August, to prepare for any eventuality, Rudolf Steiner himself proposed that the new society be called the "Anthroposophical Society." Finally, on December 8, it was determined that one could no longer be a member both of the Order of the Star in the East and of the German Section. Members of the former were requested to leave the Theosophical Society. If they did not, they would be expelled. At the same time, on December 11, a telegram was sent to Annie Besant requesting her resignation on the grounds that her campaign, waged from Adyar against the German Section, had betrayed the fundamental theosophical principle "No knowledge higher than the Truth." The die was cast; and on December 28, 1912, in Cologne, without further celebration or formality, the Anthroposophical Society was founded. Over New Year 1912/1913, representatives of different countries gathered to deliberate the nature and form of the new society; and, on January 2 and 3, 1913, quietly and without fanfare the General Meeting for the founding and constituting of the Anthroposophical Society was held.

*

Dramatically enough, in precise parallel with this momentous event, on January 2, 1913, Volume III (1913-1923) begins.

The volume falls into three parts, the first part being separated from the second and third parts by a *nearly six-year hiatus* that begins with World War I and continues for almost two years after the end of hostilities. Such bare facts, however, fail to do justice to the reality that as a consequence of the spiritual and cultural rupture, whose earthly manifestation was the war, nothing could be the same afterward. A new world had to be birthed. Even today, nearly a century later, to follow this reality inwardly and meditatively is truly to hear an earnest summons to action—to "get serious" in a new and radical sense.

The collection begins with thirty-nine lessons, held in various cities throughout Central and Northern Europe (Germany, Holland, Finland, Norway, Sweden, Denmark, and Switzerland) and running from January 2, 1913, to July 14, 1914. Little new esoteric "content" is given. Strangely, sparse mention is made of otherwise significant events, such as the selection of Dornach, near Basel, Switzerland, for the site of the new "John Building," which would later be named the Goetheanum; new books and significant lecture courses are equally sparingly referred to. The emphasis is on meditative practice: inner work. Students are expected to continue their daily verses and meditations, subsidiary exercises, and various individual practices—but with a new, almost exclusive focus on the threefold, Trinitarian Rosicrucian "signature" (corresponding to the Christmas, Easter, and Pentecost experiences):

Ex Deo Nascimur (E.D.N.)— "From God we are born"
In Christo Morimur (I.C.M.) —"In Christ we die"
Per Spiritum Sanctum Reviviscimus (P.S.S.R.)—"Through the
    Holy Spirit we come to life again."

Rosicrucian Meditation was not new. In fact, it is continuous with Rudolf Steiner's teaching and may be found implicitly in his first book of spiritual practice, *How to Know Higher Worlds*. Goethe himself, as well as Novalis, Hegel, and Schelling, all of whom were major formative influences on Steiner, were tacit Rosicrucians. In addition, to understand the transformation they had wrought, Steiner had immersed himself in intense, meditative study of Paracelsus, Boehme, and Basil Valentine, who, if anyone can, may be called "Rosicrucians." Then, too, there was his meeting as a student in Vienna with Felix Balde, the herb gatherer, who in turn (as Steiner puts it) led him to an encounter with "M" (the Master), perhaps Christian Rosenkreutz himself. In this sense, Rudolf Steiner was always a "Rosicrucian." However, over the previous years (approximately 1907-1912), that is, at least since the Whitsun Conference, Rosicrucianism in its various forms had become an increasingly and explicitly central aspect of anthroposophical inner work, as well as anthroposophical work generally. Indeed, with the publication of *An Outline of Esoteric Science* (1910), where the practice of the Rose Cross imagination—a black Cross, with seven radiant red roses arranged in a circle at the intersection of the two beams of the Cross—is described, Rosicrucianism had become part of Anthroposophy's "official" meditative path. The Trinitarian "signature," while always present in the background as the "meaning" of the Rose Cross meditation, however, was never previously so exclusively focused on until the period of the lessons collected here.

Ex Deo nascimur – In Christo morimur – Per Spiritum Sanctum reviviscimus: these three sentences present an almost unfathomably rich sequence of ideas. Deriving from the original "Announcement (*Fama*) of the Rosicrucian Brotherhood," which was first circulated in 1610 and first published in 1614, in a way this threefold mantra may with justification be said to contain "the whole Work"—microcosmic and macrocosmic, divine-spiritual and cosmic-human-earthly. Indeed, only a little thought will reveal that its three sentences unfold the deepest essence and real meaning not only of the Incarnation—the Mystery of Golgotha—but also, and simultaneously, of human and cosmic evolution: that is, of creation itself. As Steiner points out, the meditation or mantra in Latin contains ten words, implying, though he does not say so, that it is a Holy Decad (as are the first ten numbers; Aristotle's ten categories, which, Steiner said, if meditated, would reveal the making of the whole world; and the ten members of the human being as Steiner mentions in these lessons) or what in Pythagorean tradition was known as the Holy Tetraktys:

I	E
I I	D N
I I I	I C M
I I I I	P S S R

In the words of a founding mother of alchemy, Maria the Jewess, also called Maria Prophetessa, the legendary sister of Moses: *"One becomes two, two becomes three, and by means of the third and fourth, realizes unity: thus two are but one."*

But Steiner's aim in these lessons is hardly theoretical: it is practical and meditative. It is to show how these three sayings, if repeatedly and seriously taken into our soul and allowed to permeate our whole being so that not only do they become our own, but we also become theirs—and their being becomes our being—is one of those fundamental meditations that can change us completely. In lesson after lesson he weaves a multidimensional, ever-deepening tapestry of association and instruction. The cumulative experience of reading them—especially if they are well "chewed over" and taken to heart and practiced—is transformative. There is repetition—not only are all the available notes of each lesson given, but then, too, more or less the same lesson is given in different cities to ensure that all (or at least many) members of the Esoteric School are practicing in the same way. Yet the repetition is never exact. No two sets of notes by the different note-takers are ever identical (far from it!), and each lesson is given fresh, to a different set of students. In fact, the stark differences between the different sets of notes for a given lesson are most telling. Note-takers clearly recall what was important to them—what struck them, and especially what struck them as "new." It is only in putting the different notes together that we can have a real sense of what Steiner taught. The effort is worthwhile.

Essentially, we learn how through meditation of these sentences we are led to a participation in the Trinitarian Mystery of the Father, Son, and Holy Spirit, coming to an experience of each in an appropriate way. From the Father, through the previous evolutionary cycles Steiner that calls the Saturn, Sun, and Moon epochs of evolution, we receive the "chalice" of our physical and etheric bodies. As he puts it: "Everything that has led us through Saturn, Sun, and Moon, and further up through the line of heredity right up to our present birth is expressed with the saying *Ex Deo nascimur*." Once we have crossed the threshold into the spiritual world, our body appears no longer single but a great multiplicity, "the work of all the elemental beings, all the hierarchies." What Christ, the "new Adam," brings us through the Mystery of Golgotha is the new spiritual substance—the essentially human soul substance spoken of in the saying, "When two or more are gathered together in my name, I am there"—that allows us to develop consciousness of the spiritual world after death. Therefore, when entering sleep—for sleep is a little death—and obviously not only then, but also when we otherwise aspire to remain conscious in the spiritual world, we should immerse ourselves in the selfless, ego-overcoming feeling *In Christo Morimur*, for the Mystery of Golgotha, the turning point of time, brings us not only the possibility of spiritual consciousness, but also of self-consciousness—conscious awareness—in the spiritual world: *Per Spiritum Sanctum Reviviscimus*.

Steiner shows us further how these three sentences can also be meditated indirectly. A number of lessons work with the threefold meditation: *It thinks me*; *It weaves me*; *It works me*. In the first, we include all the cosmic forces that through evolution have brought us here. In the second, we include all the beings weaving with Christ within our *feeling* to create our higher "I." In the third, we include all the beings working through our *will*. Corresponding to these three meditations, three moods should fill our soul: with the first, *devotion*; with the second, *reverence*; with the third, *gratitude*. In other words: devotion to the Father in our thinking; reverence for the Son in our feeling; and gratitude for the Spirit in our willing. Again *Ex Deo nascimur – In Christo morimur – Per Spiritum Sanctum reviviscimus*: "the primordial prayer of humanity," "the crux of Rosicrucian esotericism."

The full fruit of this teaching is of course available only through meditation. Meditation is extraordinarily important because, finally, it is the only way to transform ourselves. Accordingly, throughout the lessons, we find Steiner interpolating valuable meditation instruction and advice. Anyone who does not know how to meditate will find help here. Basically, it is very simple:

> In meditating, we must first immerse ourselves totally in the content of the exercise. We must empty our soul of all ordinary, everyday thoughts and feelings, and live in the content of the given exercise. Then we must empty our consciousness of all contents—including the content of the meditation—and then listen and watch...

Ordinary life, which is illusory or Maya, depends on understanding that the great illusion is that we understand the world. Ordinarily, we stand before an object, look at it, form a concept of it, and understand it. Ordinary thinking (and perceiving) of this kind is intentional, that is, it assumes all soul-processes have an object, a specific intention or content. Meditation is different: it seeks to be "without intention." It seeks to eliminate intention: to empty consciousness. Practices of concentration have precisely this goal: that the attention meets itself without content. Then imaginations, thoughts, ideas come to us and we unite with them. Thus meditation is experience, not understanding. We experience something—something comes to us, becomes one with us—and we must allow that experience to ripen, to follow its own life within us. We must not rush to conceptualize or understand it intellectually. This whole process takes patience, and, above all, fidelity to practice, repeated effort, calmness, and composure. The experience of the emptiness, of inner silence is critical. Perhaps we hear our blood flow, our nerves crackle: living into those inner sounds we enter and can live in the sphere of experience. A great deal depends on the mood or disposition of soul that we bring to or allow to arise in and through our meditations. Certainly, we can bring to a meditation a given mood—such as, for instance, a mood of devotion, reverence, gratitude, surrender, or love—but at the same time what lives in the words, sounds, and shapes of what we are meditating itself brings about a mood, and we must pay attention to that mood and live into it. Thereby different experiences are given to us. We can rise into the spiritual world, or descend into ourselves—experience expansion and bliss, or contraction and a kind of intense self-examination, a sense of our failures and weaknesses. At the same time, all manner of distractions can disturb our meditation; or we can fall asleep or develop intense physical symptoms like headaches. In all such cases, the advice is the same: return to the theme.

While always returning to meditation and the Rosicrucian signature, this sequence of lessons nevertheless also continues to surprise and instruct us with its esoteric insights. Students are exhorted to feel that they are living within a great communicating "soul-spiritual sea" and to learn to "read" that world. And not only read, but to breathe it in, digest, and become one with it. Frequently, too, secondary topics for meditation are suggested, such as: "as the lungs inhale the air, so too the physical and etheric bodies breathe in the spirit upon awakening." Yet always, one can sense that whatever Steiner is speaking of —whether, for instance, about "matter," the "I," Lucifer, Ahriman, the Guardian of the Threshold, or about our relationship to the planets or to karma—it may be taken as food for meditation.

The overriding purpose of the lessons, however, remains (and continuously turns around) the being and nature of the Christ: "The task of all esotericists must be to grasp more and more the Spiritual Sun, Christ, and to waken him and sense him ever more strongly in themselves." Obstructing and distracting us from this task, as Steiner increasingly details from varied perspectives in the course of these lessons, are Lucifer and Ahriman, whose objective is to draw us away from Christ and into their field of influence. Above all, they obtrude in the form of false concepts—preconceptions. We must learn to identify Lucifer's and Ahriman's influences and return to Christ's "middle path." Here, too, is much good advice both for life and for spiritual practice. To protect ourselves from Ahriman, we must be grateful and satisfied with what we have been given. As for Lucifer's grasp: "the only antidote we have…is the deepest humility and self-modesty."

Thus, as the lessons progress, the subject matter changes—new themes arise, such as the Fall, or children and their development—but always the focus remains the Mystery of Golgotha and the mission of Christ as the central riddle of the Rosicrucian signature (the fifth letter of the ten, as Steiner repeatedly stresses.) New insights are given. For instance:

> E.D.N: disposes the divine human being
> I.C.M. so that the divine can be born
> P.S.S.R the force that carries it upward

On August 14, World War I began, and esoteric lessons were suspended. Neither the spiritual atmosphere surrounding the planet, nor the political atmosphere, which made private meetings illegal, permitted them to continue. Anthroposophical work, on the other hand, continued, even with a renewed vigor, manifested above all perhaps in the ongoing construction of the Goetheanum in Dornach by a large international group. But there were also new emphases: a deep focus on our relationships with the dead; the importance of learning to deal with Lucifer and Ahriman; the need to understand history "symptomatically;" and, increasingly, a growing awareness of the overriding presence of the Archangel Michael, the Regent of the Age, who is, in a sense, the Patron or Guardian of Anthroposophy.

Steiner's own spiritual research continued as much as conditions allowed and, toward the end of the war, flowered in a new understanding of the "threefold human being." Not unrelated, during this same period (1917), Steiner also began to formulate and think through what he would come to call the "Threefold Social Order," which he saw as not only the antidote to the follies that had led up to the bloodbath of the previous years but also as the only solution to the social, economic, financial, legal, and spiritual chaos to come.

Once the war was over, Steiner threw himself wholeheartedly into the tasks of the hour—rebuilding society, including promoting the Threefold Social Order and starting the first Waldorf School. At the same time, he was continually asked to re-open the Esoteric School. Clearly he was hesitant to do so. The Anthroposophical Society was not strong. Bickering, criticism, and irresponsible behavior were rife. Something new was required: one could not just continue with the old work. Yet, whatever the new impulse would be, its nature did not ultimately, so to speak, depend on Steiner alone: the spiritual world would first have to speak. Nevertheless, Steiner did occasionally agree to requests and a few—four—lessons were held. These are contained in Part II. Fragmentary though they are, they express great seriousness, even, we might say, a new earnestness, a new urgency, despite the self-evident continuity of purpose:

> Humanity belongs to the Earth organism and so takes part in the karma of the Earth…Today humanity as such is experiencing the meeting with the Guardian of the Threshold, and the crossing of the threshold has already begun in recent years. That is also the beginning of the split of humanity, and that signifies a critical point in time at which we have arrived. The forces that formerly streamed out of spiritual beings into humanity are used up, exhausted. We are now on our own, and must bring these forces out of our subconscious. The Mystery of Golgotha will have happened for nothing if human beings do not use these inner forces, but reject them instead. That would bring about the destruction of Earth evolution. Souls would indeed still descend into bodies, but they would abandon them again in the thirty-third year…

> Soullessness is the danger that hangs over us, threatening evolution and the very being of the Christ, now united with the Earth. We can with effort find the "I" in ourselves, but the Christ we can find only in humanity, that is, "when two or three are gathered together…" The task is self-knowledge. A new mantra is given—"O Human Being, know yourself"—that, as it develops, will become a central core of anthroposophical inner work, as manifested in both the Foundation Stone Mantra and the First Class, the last incarnation of the Esoteric School.

The rarity of esoteric lessons during the period leading up to the Christmas Conference 1923/24, which was the foundation of the present General Anthroposophical Society, reveals Steiner's reluctance simply to continue as before in the face of what he perceived to be an utterly changed reality. For that moment, he would have to wait. But before that, the opportunity to do something new, to start afresh, would come with the Youth Movement, whose esoteric lessons form Part III.

*

The story of the Youth Movement has been told in the Introductions to *Becoming the Archangel Michael's Companions* (CW 217) and *Youth and the Etheric Heart* (CW 217a), and is explained with fascinating documentary detail by the German editor in her Foreword to Part III.

In brief, out of the general chaos following the war's end, many young people sought a way to contribute meaningfully to the rebuilding of culture and society and were drawn to Anthroposophy, above all by the Movement for the Threefold Social Organism. Rudolf Steiner immediately responded to their heart's call. He had been waiting a long time for a new generation of seekers. Anthroposophical student groups arose, and, in 1920, the Association for Anthroposophical College Studies. College courses were held in Dornach and elsewhere. Thus, out of these meetings, passionate, intelligent, sophisticated, and deeply spiritual young people were able to enter into an intimate relationship with Rudolf Steiner, who welcomed them with open arms. The result was predictable: older members resisted, while the young people in turn found the older members "out of touch." In the end, however, after three years of struggle, an independent Anthroposophical society was founded, *de facto* for the Youth Movement, within which then arose an "Esoteric Youth Group." It is the documents relating to the founding of this Group, as well as the two esoteric lessons given to it, that constitute this section of the book.

There is no question as to the importance of the Esoteric Youth Group. Asked about the "new" esoteric work in relation to the work that came to an end in 1914, Steiner said: "When I began teaching I had to connect my work with the thread of the old tradition. What came into being in this way was broken off due to external circumstances. What has taken place now is a first in the post-Christian age: human beings themselves chose, out of freedom before the spiritual world, to join together esoterically."

The documents relating to the many meetings and circulars surrounding the founding of the Youth Group are deeply interesting, even moving. They show us both the spiritual idealism, perfectly melded with truly pragmatic realism, of the young people and the utter seriousness with which Rudolf Steiner met them and undertook to guide their spiritual work. Reading them, we can sense how much it must have pained him that many older members simply took Anthroposophy for granted, living in it automatically without effort or thought, and how delighted he must have been to meet young people who were truly willing to commit themselves. He stresses that "one can only join such a cause as a completely free human being." "Free" here means without preconceptions or prejudgments—so that everything may be discussed "in a frank, free, and unperturbed manner." Only then can one truly act out of the spiritual world, and only then will the spiritual world—without which any true esotericism is impossible—be able to be present. This means that spiritual or esoteric groups must be *alive*: they must be filled with the life of the spirit. At the same time, to be a group means to take on each other's karma: to accept one another's imperfections. In this way, a living "third" enters in. All this has to do with what Steiner calls the "first requirement," that is, spiritual *loyalty* : loyalty to what one has set as spiritual intention. In addition to these essentials, important topics of interest from many different points of view, both anthroposophical and general, weave in and out of the various accounts of the founding.

The Youth Group was founded on October 16, 1922. Three days before, he had met with the twelve founders. Entering the room, he counted them, pointing a finger at each. Then, with a deep, calm voice, he read some prepared words, after which he gave certain meditations. He spoke of the power of meditating a common meditation and stressed that each person would have different tasks, and that no jealousy or rivalry should enter into their common work. They were about to embark on a great work: "Uniting yourself through a mutual promise to strive toward a common spiritual goal—and leaving one another completely free in actions and judgments—such a community is something completely new in the evolution of humanity…" He then closed with: "We will form your community according to your heart's desire."

At the founding itself, after some conversation and paying homage—linking again—to Madame Blavatsky, Steiner spoke of the importance of the group as a seed and premonition of what was to come. This was followed by an oath, which he "dictated freely by speaking the oath word for word, as if bringing it out of the spiritual world in the moment." Then, after a pause, he said: "And now consider your community as having been founded by the spiritual world itself." Finally, as he was leaving, he went around the group, taking each person's right hand in both of his, and looked into each person's eyes. The solemnities over, he told them: "Get to know each other well."

However fascinating and instructive the documentation leading up to the two Youth Group esoteric lessons may be, it cannot compare with the truly inspirational depth and utter seriousness of the two extant lessons. One senses a rare initiatory quality. Not a word is wasted. Rudolf Steiner speaks with exceptional clarity. There is a total focus on the work at hand. Yet there is continuity, too. The Rosicrucian signature still remains the deep reality: *Ex Deo nascimur; In Christo morimur; Per Spiritum Sanctum reviviscimus.*

The first lesson takes up the signature in relation to the true "I." Powerful meditations are given to aid in the purification of the three "bodies"—the so-called physical, etheric, and astral sheaths—whose egotism must be overcome before one can encounter and "release" the "I," which can then in turn assume its rightful cosmic role. In the East, Steiner tells us, this truth is conveyed by the image of the Lotus Blossom, whose innermost core is surrounded by three circles of petals. Thus, in addition to the three meditations, one for each of the bodies, echoing the three sentences of the Rosicrucian signature, Steiner also gives the ancient Sanskrit mantra, well known from Tibetan Buddhism: *Aoum mani padme aoum,* (more usually, *om mani padme hum*), *Behold the Jewel in the Lotus,* which Steiner translates: *My 'I" is enclosed in the Lotus Flower.*

The second lesson, of equal solemnity with the first, begins with the invocation/mantra/meditation: "O Human Being, know yourself..." Steiner then turns again to the stark reality: "human beings are losing the force of thought." Human beings must therefore relearn how to think; that is, they must learn to know in a different way. To do so is not a matter of changing thinking's content, of knowing something new or different, but of *knowing differently what we already know.* We must change *how* we think, not what we think. One path to this is to experience the Earth as a star—a shining star, raying out our willing, shining with our feeling, and wrapped as in its aureole in our thinking. In other words, all our thinking, feeling, and willing must be at the service of the cosmos—so that, as Steiner puts it elsewhere, the Earth may become a star. In this lesson, too, Steiner gives a Sanskrit mantra, for "it is again time for today's youth to bring the oldest wisdom of humanity back into consciousness." The Kali Yuga has ended. We must pick up again the thread of the previous "Age of Light." For this, we are being led across the threshold of the spiritual world. Hard work will be needed to acknowledge its guardian and pass over. It will not be easy. Courage is need. But such is the human task: we must cross the threshold *consciously*.

Anyone reading and rereading these lessons slowly and meditatively, and entering into them with an open heart, can sense the power of those moments with Rudolf Steiner and take something of the original inspiration into their lives. Indeed, the same is true of this whole volume, which should lead those interested toward the Foundation Stone Meditation of the Christmas Conference and, should such be their call, to the First Class—the last "Esoteric Lessons" Steiner gave. Whatever may be the reader's destiny may he or she read and reread this volume with inspiration and understanding!

Related reading:

From the History and Contents of the First Section of the Esoteric School 1904-1914 (CW 264)

Freemasonry and Ritual Work (CW 265)

Esoteric Lessons I (CW 266/1)

Esoteric Lessons II (forthcoming 2012) (CW 266/2)

Rosicrucianism Renewed (CW 284)

Becoming the Archangel Michael's Companions (CW 217)

Youth and the Etheric Heart (CW 217a)

Preliminary Words from the Editor of the German Edition

Within Rudolf Steiner's Collected Works, which are divided into three areas of writings, lectures, and artistic work, all of the documents having to do with his esoteric teaching activity are to be found in GAs 264–270. Details of the history of Rudolf Steiner's Esoteric School as it existed from 1904 until 1914 can be found in GA 264 and GA 265, as well as the Foreword to the German Edition of 266/1. This first volume encompasses, as completely as possible and in chronological order, all of the available notes from memory written by participants for the Esoteric Lessons from 1904 through 1909. The notes are from memory, as are those of the second and third volumes. The second volume contains all the available records from 1910 through 1912. This, the third volume, begins with the lessons from 1913 to 1914. Of course the lessons in 1914 extend only until summer, because, due to the outbreak of World War I on August 1, 1914, Rudolf Steiner closed the Esoteric School. After the war, he was asked by various [members] to take up the esoteric work again. Because of this, he held several Esoteric Lessons from 1920 on, until, with the new foundation of the Anthroposophical Society at Christmas 1923/24, the Independent School for Spiritual Science at the Goetheanum was to be formed. Due to his untimely death, only a beginning could be made in this effort.

This volume is divided into three parts:
1. Record of [Esoteric] Lessons from 1913 and 1914.
2. Records from 1920 to 1923.
3. Records of the origin of the Esoteric Youth Group; and records of two Esoteric Lessons in 1923 given to the youth.

We are grateful to the Archive at the Goetheanum for printing [the German edition] of this volume, and for making their records available for comparing and expanding our records.

Because this book contains records of the Esoteric Lessons, and students were not permitted to take notes during the lessons, the records were written later from memory. For this reason, they must be considered as fragmentary, garbled, and in some places incorrect. On the other hand, they come, however, from students who are familiar with general spiritual scientific contents. In addition, the deficiencies and possible errors of the records can be corrected and supplemented by bringing Rudolf Steiner's writings and lectures about the path of training to bear upon them. As is seen in many records, Rudolf Steiner himself indicated the difference between the Esoteric Lessons and the rest of his spiritual scientific communications less in the content than in the way they were presented; [less in the *what* and more in the *how*].

Other than correcting clear errors that distort the meaning, the editors have stayed away from any stylistic editing. Insertions made by the note-takers are shown in parentheses; those from the editors are in brackets.

More details about the documents can be found in the Editorial and Reference Notes of this volume.

PART I
NOTES OF THE ESOTERIC LESSONS
1913 AND 1914

Written from Memory by the Participants

Meditation Verses Used Repeatedly in the Esoteric Lessons
from 1913-1914

Die Sprüche an den Tagesgeist

Meditationen, die das Zeitwesen der Hierarchien erfassen

Freitag Abend für Samstag: Saturn

Großer umfassender Geist,
    der Du den endlosen Raum efülltest,
    als von meinen Leibesgliedern
    keines noch vorhanden war:
Du warst.
    Ich erhebe meine Seele zu Dir.
Ich war in Dir.
    Ich war ein Teil Deiner Kraft.
Du sandtest Deine Kräfte aus,
    und in der Erde Urbeginn spiegelte sich
    meiner Leibesform erstes Urbild.
In Deinen ausgesandten Kräften
    war ich selbst.
Du warst.
Mein Urbild schaute Dich an.
    Es schaute mich selbst an,
    der ich war ein Teil von Dir.
Du warst.

Verses Directed to the Spirit of the Day

Meditations for Understanding the Time Nature of the Hierarchies

Friday Evening for Saturday: Saturn

Great encompassing Spirit,
    who filled infinite space
    when of my bodily members
    none was yet present:
You were,
    I lift up my soul to you.
I was in you.
    I was part of your force.
You sent forth your forces,
    and the Earth's primal beginning
    mirrored the first archetype of my bodily form.
In your outflowing forces
    I myself was.
You were.
My archetype beheld you.
    It gazed on me,
    I, who was a part of you.
You were.

Samstagabend für Sonntag: Sonne

Großer umfassender Geist,
    viele Urbilder sproßten aus Deinem Leben,
    damals, als meine Lebenskäfte
    noch nicht vorhanden waren.
Du warst.
    Ich erhebe meine Seele zu Dir.
Ich war in Dir.
    Ich war ein Teil Deiner Kräfte.
Du verbandest Dich
    mit der Erde Urbeginn
    zur Lebenssonne
    und gabest mir die Lebenskraft.
In Deinen strahlenden Lebenskräften
    war ich selbst.
Du warst.
Meine Lebenskraft strahlte in der Deinen
    in den Raum.
    Mein Leib begann sein Werden
    in der Zeit.
Du warst.

Saturday Evening for Sunday: Sun

Great encompassing Spirit,
    many archetypes spring from your life
    when my life forces
    were not yet present.
You were.
    I raise my soul to you.
I was in you.
    I was part of your forces.
You united
    with the Earth's primal beginning
    with the living Sun
    and gave me the force of life.
In your radiating life forces
    I myself was.
You were.
My life force radiated in yours
    in space.
    My body began its becoming
    in time.
You were.

Sonntagabend für Montag: Mond

Großer umfassender Geist,
    in Deinen Lebensform leuchtete Empfindung,
    als meine Empfindung
    noch nict vorhanden war.
Du warst.
    Ich erhebe meine Seele zu Dir.
Ich war in Dir.
    Ich war ein Teil Deiner Empfindungen.
Du verbandest Dich
    mit der Erde Urbeginn,
    und in meinem Leibe began
    das Leuchten der eignen Empfindung.
In Deinen Gefühlen
    fühlte ich mich selbst.
Du warst.
Meine Empfindungen fühlten Dein Wesen in sich.
    Meine Seele begann in sich zu sein,
    weil Du in mir warst.
Du warst.

Sunday Evening for Monday: Moon

Great encompassing Spirit,
    perceptive feeling sensation shone in your life forms,
    when my sensation
    was not yet present.
You were.
    I raise my soul to you.
I was in you.
    I was part of your perceptive feeling sensations.
You united
    with Earth's primal beginning,
    and in my body
    my own perceptive feeling sensations
    began to shine.
In your feelings
    I felt myself.
You were.
My perceptive feeling sensations felt your being in themselves.
    My soul began to be in herself,
    because you were in me.
You were.

Montagabend für Dienstag: Mars

Großer umfassender Geist,
     in Deinen Empfindung lebte Erkenntnis,
      als mir noch nicht Erkenntnis gegeben war.
Du warst.
     Ich erhebe meine Seele zu Dir.
Ich zog ein in meinen Leib.
     In meinen Empfindungen lebte ich mir selbst.
Du warst in der Lebenssonne.
     In meiner Empfindung
     lebte Dein Wesen als mein Wesen.
Meiner Seele Leben
     war außerhalb Deines Lebens.
Du warst.
Meine Seele fühlte ihr eigenes Wesen in sich.
     In ihr entstand Sehnsucht.
     Die Sehnsucht nach Dir,
     aus dem sie geworden.
Du warst.

Monday Evening for Tuesday: Mars

Great encompassing Spirit,
    cognition lived in your perceptive feeling sensations
    when cognition was not yet given to me.
You were.
    I raise my soul to you.
I drew into my body.
    I lived in my perceptive feeling sensations.
You were in the living Sun.
    In my perceptive feeling sensation
    your being lived as my being.
My soul life
    was outside your life.
You were.
My soul felt her being in herself.
    Yearning arose in her.
    The yearning for you
    out of whom she came.
You were.

Dienstagabend für Mitwoch: Merkur

Großer umfassender Geist,
    in Deines Wesens Erkenntnis is Welterkenntnis,
    die mir werden soll.
Du bist.
    Ich will meine Seele einigen mit Dir.
Dein erkennender Führer
    beleuchte meinen Weg.
    Fühlend Deinen Führer
    durchschreite ich die Lebensbahn.
Dein Führer is in der Lebenssonne.
    Er lebte in meiner Sehnsucht.
    Aufnehmen will ich sein Wesen
    in meines.
Du bist.
Meine Kraft nehme auf
    des Führers Kraft in sich.
    Seligkeit zieht in mich.
    Die Seligkeit, in der die Seele
    den Geist findet.
Du bist.

Tuesday Evening for Wednesday: Mercury

Great encompassing Spirit,
    in cognition of your being is world cognition
    which will come to me.
You are.
    I will unite my soul with you.
May your cognizing leader
    light my path.
    Feeling your leader
    I pass through the path of life.
Your leader is in the living Sun.
    He lives in my yearning.
    I will take up his being
    in mine.
You are.
May my force take up
    the leader's force in itself.
    Blessedness draws into me.
    The blessedness in which the soul
    finds the spirit.
You are.

Mitwochabend für Donnerstag: Jupiter

Großer umfassender Geist,
    in Deinem Lichte strahlt der Erde Leben,
    mein Leben ist in dem Deinen.
Du bist.
    Meine Seele wirkt in der Deinen.
Mit Deinem Führer gehe ich meinen Weg.
    Ich lebe mit Ihm.
    Sein Wesen ist Bild
    meines eigenen Wesens.
Du bist.
Des Führers Wesen in meiner Seele
    findet Dich, umfassender Geist.
    Seligkeit is mir
    aus Deines Wesens Hauch.
Du bist.

Wednesday Evening for Thursday: Jupiter

Great encompassing Spirit,
    the Earth's life streams in your light,
    my life is in yours.
You are.
    My soul acts in yours.
With your leader I go my way.
    I live with him.
    He is an image
    of my own being.
You are.
The leader's being within my soul
    finds you, encompassing Spirit.
    Blessedness is mine
    from your being's breath.
You are.

Donnerstagabend für Freitag: Venus

Großer umfassender Geist,
      in Deinem Leben lebe ich mit der Erde Leben.
      In Dir bin ich.
Du bist.
      Ich bin in Dir.
Der Führer hat mich zu Dir gebracht.
      Ich lebe in Dir.
      Dein Geist ist
      meines eigenen Wesens Bild.
Du bist.
Gefunden hat Geist
      den umfassenden Geist.
      Gotteseligkeit schreitet
      zu neuem Weltschaffen.
Du bist. Ich bin. Du bist.

Thursday Evening for Friday: Venus

Great encompassing Spirit,
    I live in your life with the life of the Earth.
    In you I am.
You are.
    I am in you.
The leader has brought me to you.
    I live in you.
    Your spirit is
    my own being's image.
You are.
Spirit has found
    the encompassing spirit.
    Divine blessedness walks onward
    to new world creation.
You are. I am. You are.

[Nach dem vorigen jeden Tag]*

Großer umfassender Geist,
    mein Ich erhebe sich von unten nach oben,
    ahnen mög es Dich im Allumfassen.
Der Geist meines Wesens durchleuchte sich
    mit dem Licht Deiner Boten,
Die Seele meines Wesens entzünde sich
    an den Feuerflammen Deiner Diener,
Der Wille meines Ich erfasse
    Deines Schöpferwortes Kraft.
Du bist.
    Dein *Licht* strahle in meinen Geist,
    Dein *Leben* erwarme meine Seele,
    Dein *Wesen* durchdringe mein Wollen,
    daß Verständnis fasse mein Ich
    für Deines Lichtes Leuchten,
    Deines Lebens Liebewärme,
    Deines Wesens Schöpferworte.
Du bist.

---

*These words, which were lacking in the original, were given by Marie Steiner for the first printing of *Aus den Inhalten der Esoterischen Schule,* Vol. III, Dornach 1951.

Every day after the preceding meditations:

Great encompassing Spirit,
    I raise my "I" up from below,
    may it be capable of intuiting you encompassing all.
May my being's spirit be illuminated
    with your messengers' light,
May my being's soul be kindled
    by the fiery flames of your servants,
May the will of my "I" grasp
    the force of your Creator Word.
You are.
    May your *light* stream into my spirit,
    may your *life* warm my soul,
    may your *being* penetrate my will,
    so that understanding may seize my "I"
    for the burning of your light,
    for the warmth of your life,
    for the Creator-Word of your being.
You are.

Meditationsspruch
"Im Geiste lag der Keim meines Leibes…"

Im Geist lag der Keim meines Leibes.
Und der Geist hat eingegliedert meinem Leibe.
Die sinnlichen Augen,
Auf baß ich durch sie schaue
Das Licht der Körper.
Und der Geist hat eingeprägt meinem leibe
Empfindung und Denken
Und Gefühl und Wille
Auf daß ich durch sie wahrnehme die Körper
Und auf sie wirke.
Im Geiste lag der Keim meines Leibes.

In meinem Leibe liegt das Geistes Keim.
Und ich will eingliedern meinem Geiste
Die übersinnlichen Augen,
Auf daß ich durch sie schaue das Licht der Geister.
Und ich will einprägen meinem Geiste
Weisheit und Kraft und Liebe,
Auf daß durch mich wirken die Geister
Und ich werde das selbstbewußte Werkzeug
Ihrer Taten.
In meinem Leibe liegt des Geistes Keim.

Meditation
"In the spirit lay the germ of my body…"

In the spirit lay the germ of my body.
And the spirit has imprinted in my body
The eyes of sense,
That through them I may see
The light of bodies.
And the spirit has imprinted in my body
Reason and sensation
And feeling and will,
That through them I may perceive bodies
And act upon them.
In the spirit lay the germ of my body.

In my body lies the germ of the spirit.
And I will incorporate into my spirit
The supersensuous eyes,
That through them I may behold the light of spirits.
And I will imprint in my spirit
Wisdom and power and love,
So that through me the spirits may act
And I become the self-conscious organ
Of their deeds.
In my body lies the germ of the spirit.

Meditationsspruch
"Zu den Dingen wend ich mich…"

Zu den Dingen wend ich mich
Wend ich mich mit meinen Sinnen;
Sinnensein, du täuschest mich!
Was als nichts das Dasein flieht:
Dir ist's Sein und Wesenheit;
Was dir nichtig scheinen muß,
Offenbare meinem Innern sich.

Geisteslicht erwarme mich
Lass in dir mich wollend fühlen,
Gutgedachtes, Wahr Erkanntes
Wie erlebt dich leuctend Ich
Irrtumsweben, bös erdachtes
Zeige dich der Leucthe-Seele
Dass ich webend in mir sei.

Leuchtend Ich und Leuchte-Seele
Schwebet über wahrem Werdewesen
Das Erdachte, das Erkannte
Wird jetzt dichtes Geistessein.
Und wie leichte Daseinsperlen
Lebt im Meer des Göttlich-Wahren
Was den Sinnen Dasein täuscht.

Meditation
"I turn to things…"

I turn to things,
I turn with my senses.
Sense being, you deceive me!
What flees existence as nothing
Is being and essence to you.
May what must seem to you worth nothing
Reveal itself within me!

Spirit Light, warm me,
Let me feel myself willing in you.
What is well thought, cognized truth,
How does the luminous "I" experience you!
Weaving error, badly thought out
Show yourself to the beacon of my soul
That I may be weaving in myself.

Luminous "I" and beacon-soul,
Hover above true being of becoming
What is thought out, what cognized
Condenses now to spirit being.
And like pearls of existence
There dwells in the sea of divine truth
What deceives the senses' existence.

Esoteric Lesson
COLOGNE, JANUARY 2, 1913

Record A

Before we begin our actual esoteric contemplations and studies, it must to be said, especially for our friends from other countries, that we have to separate ourselves completely in our esoteric stream from that other stream that passes through the world and is represented by Mrs. Besant.† We can [must], on the basis of truthfulness, separate ourselves from the deeds of another person and yet maintain our love for the person as before; perhaps even because of it we can turn increased sympathy toward her, precisely because we must reject her deeds.

The words of Mrs. Besant from 1906 are read,† wherein she asks of all those who love her that should the day come when she would fall, precisely out of love for her no one should call white, what is black. Esotericism is a dangerous path, and everyone should bear in mind that in the depths of the human soul, forces can slumber that perhaps in ordinary life do not make themselves known; yet when one enters upon the dangerous path, they come to light. For this reason, it is necessary that we keep ourselves constantly awake in our own soul and be mindful of the Word: "Watch and pray."†

Those who want to enter into the spiritual worlds must, above all, practice strict self-knowledge. The Essene Order†—the exalted teachers of which taught the Nathan Jesus† of the Luke Gospel the extract of all the wisdom that precisely this being would need—had two especially important rules that can show us how far we are from the spiritual in our modern time. The first rule was: Before sunrise and after sundown, no Essene shall speak of worldly things. And for those who had achieved a higher level, this rule was further enhanced in that they were also not to occupy themselves with thoughts of worldly things during this time. A second instruction was: Before the Sun rises, every Essene shall ask that the sunrise will indeed take place and that the power of the Sun will shine over humanity everywhere. These rules give us tidings of the importance of our being's connection with the events of the spiritual world, out of which we emerge in the morning and into which we enter when we go to sleep in the evening.

One can see in the way people behave today in relation to such an outer event as the transition from New Year's Eve (Sylvester) into the New Year and what they undertake before going to sleep how little we live with these laws of outer and inner cycles. What people do at those times appears to be oriented toward uniting themselves especially deeply with materiality, instead of using the transition moment as a time of looking back.

This outer cycle corresponds to an inner one: waking and sleeping. In the evening human beings draw their astral body and "I" out of the physical body and etheric body and live, with their astral body and "I," in a purely spiritual world. Let us bring to mind the moment of going to sleep until unconsciousness gradually comes about.

Ordinary human beings have no consciousness during the night in the spiritual world. It can be that a clairvoyant moment occurs and that they see an image of what they left lying down below. What they see will be different from person to person, according to the state of mind, the temperament, and character, of each individual. Those who sense life in the physical and etheric bodies as if they are living in a house, whose orientation is more toward outer life, will see the physical and etheric bodies as a house with a door through which they must enter. Human beings who experience the transience of earthly existence as a disposition of character, rather than as a momentary mood, will see the image of a coffin with a corpse lying in it.

If human beings have already taken in something of the spiritual life, it may happen that the image of an angel appears, a light-form that hands us a chalice. This image shows a symbol for the fact that our physical and etheric bodies were already prepared for us during the old Saturn and old Sun times and represents the ancient, primeval word of humanity: From God we are born: E.D.N.

In place of what the Essenes practiced in the morning before sunrise, which is not possible today because we live in different times, modern esotericists should, when they dip down into their physical and etheric bodies in the morning, fill themselves with the sacred feeling that lofty gods have prepared our god-willed physical and etheric bodies over the long ages of the Saturn and Sun periods of evolution in order that we might develop consciousness within them. In this consciousness, esotericists should ask the spiritual Sun, which the physical Sun represents, to allow them to receive the physical and etheric bodies every morning, when human beings come back from the spiritual world, in order to develop consciousness in the physical world. For what would happen if someone were to take away our physical and etheric bodies in the night? The feeling of unconsciousness would then overwhelm us. If we penetrate ourselves properly with knowledge of the fact that the gods built our physical and etheric bodies for us, then we will have the experience that our brain—and we can have this experience with every part of our body—is not merely bound to our physical body, but rather that it can be expanded to a hollow sphere in which the stars are imbedded. These stars take their course in this sphere; and our thoughts are these stars that take their course. The microcosm thus becomes the macrocosm! Compressed within our brain are the mighty forces of the whole cosmos, and we feel their connection with us. Everything that has led us through Saturn, Sun, and further through the line of heredity right up to our present birth is expressed with the saying: E.D.N.

Just as we would remain unconscious if we could not enter into our physical and etheric bodies in the morning, so also is all conscious life blotted out by going through the portal of death. Before the Mystery of Golgotha, human beings received consciousness through the store of power given by the gods to humanity on its path after death. Out of this god-given reserve of power, human beings could have consciousness in the spiritual world. But gradually this gift of the gods was used up, and the Greeks knew that it was their lot to live in the kingdom of the shades after death. This was the will of the gods. Consciousness was shadowy and dulled-down. For this reason, the greatest spirit among the Greeks said the words: "Rather a beggar in the overworld than a king in the kingdom of shades!"† Through the Mystery of Golgotha a new substance was created that could give human beings consciousness when they were in the spiritual world after death. This substance flowed out of the Mystery of Golgotha. Through immersing ourselves in this Christ substance, it is possible for us to develop consciousness in the spiritual world after death. For this reason, every evening when we go to sleep and enter into the spiritual world, we should remember and fill ourselves with the feeling: In Christ we die! For only the Christ impulse can, through its death-conquering life force, keep us conscious in the spiritual world. Because nothing in the physical world is great enough or sacred enough to understand the sacred mystery that was given to humanity through Christ Jesus, nothing belonging to the world, not even the sound of speech, should be used to indicate this mystery, this unfathomable secret that is contained in what flows out of the Mystery of Golgotha. Therefore, esotericists are silent in word and thought at that moment when the sacred name, the unspeakable, must be spoken. They feel deeply the sacredness of this moment: I. - - - M.

However, even if human beings have consciousness after death, they do not yet have self-consciousness. They do not have the consciousness with which they can recognize themselves as individual beings in the spiritual world, nor can they find themselves with their brothers and sisters with whom they lived in the physical world. The only help for finding our being and for awakening in self-consciousness in the spiritual world is the experience of our higher "I." This higher "I" was bestowed upon us by the Holy Spirit through whom we have the hope: In the Spirit we are resurrected — P.S.S.R.

Thereby you should think of all of those who are not here— perhaps due to suffering and pain. You will send them thoughts of strength if you practice in the correct manner what is prescribed for us by esotericism. It is the case in the spiritual world that we must make ourselves worthy to be allowed to use as a blessing for others or for ourselves what is given to us in esotericism.

You should not conceive of such lessons intellectually or in a brain-bound manner. Rather, you should allow a feeling in your soul that tells you that the meaning and significance of such words as E.D.N, I.C.M, and P.S.S.R, which are given to us by the Masters of Wisdom and the Harmony of Feelings, cannot be completely exhausted by manifold contemplations, and must be gone into ever more deeply.

And thus even today, when you have grasped the primordial human prayer somewhat more deeply, you should still have the expectation that, at a later time, yet deeper revelations of it can and will be given.

In the spirit lay the germ of my body...

* * *

Record B

On the esoteric path, untruthfulness, ambition, and so forth, can cause the downfall of a human being. Larger communities, or a whole esoteric stream, can thus lose their way and get caught up in error. Because we know how easy it is for an individual to fall, we must also understand how larger groups stray from the path. Where this occurs, it would show only egotistical love if we were to follow someone loyally when we know that the person is going astray. Thus, it would show egotistical love in relation to Mrs. Besant if we were to close our eyes to the fact that the direction she represents has to be designated as wrong and that its further propagation would bring harm. Mrs. Besant herself asked, when she wrote about Leadbeater's [†] downfall, that one make her aware of and warn her should there ever be a threat of her own downfall. We are only doing our duty when we draw Mrs. Besant's attention to the threat. However, we must understand clearly that the direction itself which she represents is in error, and that from the moment we recognize this, the portal of our temple must remain closed to the followers of her esoteric direction.[†]

In the Essene community that existed before and during the Mystery of Golgotha in Palestine, there were two definite rules that were given to the pupils of this community at different stages. The first rule, which applied to everyone, was the obligation not to busy oneself with worldly tasks after sundown and before sunrise, and even to refrain from worldly thoughts. This is a rule that cannot be followed today, because we live in a different age. For the Essenes this rule was the expression of the connection of each individual soul with the cosmos. People today have lost the proper sense for the great transitions; one has only to look at the way the transition from the old year into the new year is celebrated. In the time before going to bed, people today have the tendency to busy themselves with the most trivial things that, for the most part, embroil them in matter. What significance does it have for us when the human being is in the spiritual world between going to sleep and waking up?

The ordinary person today is not conscious there. The best possible transition into the spiritual world for esotericists is a recollection of the saying: *Ex Deo nascimur*, etc. This replaces the first regulation of the Essenes. Should it happen that we experience moments of consciousness during sleep, we would each see a different picture, according to our temperament. For instance, those who consider the body to be a house in which the human being lives will behold a picture of a house with a door through which they have to enter. Thus, they see in advance the moment of their awaking. Those who have a melancholic tendency and feel in earthly existence more of the doomed-to-death aspect of the earthly forces will see a coffin with a corpse in it. And those who because of their temperament have a strong feeling that the gods have built their body for them will be able to behold an angel who hands them a chalice. All of these are just beginning, preparatory visions of the life of imagination, and can be expressed in the saying: *Ex Deo nascimur*. The divine beings, whom we summarize with the name "Deus," built up the human physical body during the Saturn and Sun evolutionary conditions. If we did not have this physical body into which we enter in the morning, we would not be able to become conscious on the physical plane. Imagine what would happen if the gods were to take away our physical body during the night. Imagine what would become of us, since we would then be unable to attain consciousness! This thought should bring us a sense of gratitude toward the gods.

The Essene at the higher stage of development was given, in addition, the obligation to pray before sunrise. This prayer was that the Sun would rise and ray out its blessings to the Earth. This is also replaced today by another feeling. Just as we could not become conscious in the morning if our physical body had been taken from us in the night, so it is just as true that we cannot become conscious after death unless we also find a body across the threshold into which we can enter. In the time before Christ, souls were clothed after death with a spiritual substance in which they went through their experience between death and a new birth. This spiritual substance was gradually being exhausted, and humanity felt this tragedy as the Mystery of Golgotha approached. For the human soul had became a shadow in the life after death. Among the Greeks, the lead civilization of that time, the feeling held sway: "Better a beggar in the overworld than a king in the kingdom of shadows." However, from the cross streamed a new substance. The souls could clothe themselves with this new substance in order to develop consciousness after death. We can feel this in the second part of our saying: *In – – – morimur.* When we take this saying with us after death, it can bring about that everything of earthly nature soon falls away and that, out of this Christ-substance, we can develop consciousness.

Because our consciousness is not yet self-consciousness, we may still hope that to the consciousness we can develop in this body will be given complete knowledge, self-consciousness, by the Holy Spirit: *Per Spiritum Sanctum reviviscimus.* Through the self-knowledge that the Holy Spirit gives to us, we prepare ourselves for our life after death.

Love, humility, and self-knowledge can be the result of a real understanding of this saying. Whoever properly meditates this saying will receive the strength to help those who are ill and to send loving thoughts to those who could not be here today because of their illness, or other reasons. This should penetrate our outer life as a sacramental feeling. We thus receive a new view of this saying, and this view may awaken in us the trust that we will be able to penetrate this saying ever more deeply in the future.

* * *

Record C

We find ourselves here at a significant moment, not only in an outer sense, but also in an esoteric sense. When an esoteric movement arises in one place,† something occurs in another place. Wisdom is only in the truth,† and that is what we want to seek. Those esoteric directions that do not go along with ours must loosen and separate themselves from ours.

Mrs. Besant's letter, which she wrote after Charles Leadbeater's downfall, was read. In it she asks, approximately in these words: Judge† has fallen and Leadbeater has fallen. Should it lie in my karma that finally also I fall, I ask all who hold me dear not to support me in it. One should not declare black to be white, but rather confidently declare black to be black. What significance does an opinion have in one life? The Masters will correct us in another life. May this be the rock upon which we build.†

*

Within the Essene school, where Jesus of Nazareth was once instructed, there was a regulation that goes as follows: After the Sun has set and before it rises, the pupil should not speak or think of worldly, material things. That was a demand for that time. We will see later that this rule can no longer be followed by us and has transformed into a different one.

The second rule was: Before sunrise, every Essene should send a prayer to the spirits who send forth the Sun into the world, that they might send the Sun also on that day. No Essene was allowed to neglect this.

Let us consider how few human beings today realize that when they go to sleep they enter into the spiritual world. This moment, which should be something sacred to us, is all too often profaned. Human beings connect themselves in the end mostly with all possible worldly, material things. We modern esotericists, however, should always remain conscious of the sacredness of the time before going to sleep. And when we come back into our physical body, we should do so with the same feelings. We must ask ourselves how it would be if we no longer found our physical and etheric bodies upon awakening. Gratitude should pass through our soul when in the morning we again enter into this work of the gods, our physical body. If we have a moment of consciousness between going to sleep and awakening, we can sense this experience symbolically in various ways. We can see it reflected to us.

Three examples:

1. Some see a house with an opened door. That is our physical body, through which door we are to enter again.

2. Others, especially those who in a melancholic mood—they do not need to have a melancholic temperament—see a coffin with a corpse in it. This is ourselves; it is our physical body.

3. Others see an angel who hands them a chalice. Thus we should sense the deep meaning of our core saying: *Ex Deo nascimur*. This saying should be contemplated from various sides and our understanding of it should be deepened. With this saying, we should express our gratitude to the gods, who have built up our physical body, and whom we summarize with the term "Deus."

Instead of actively turning away from worldly things as the Essenes did, we replace this gesture with complete silence. We do not speak the name of the highest: *In – – – morimur*.

We express our gratitude for being able to find ourselves again—that we proceed from consciousness to self-consciousness—with the saying: *Per Spiritum Sanctum reviviscimus*.

* * *

RECORD D

Watch and Pray!

If we wish to enter into the light-filled halls of the suprasensible worlds, we must learn self-knowledge. For this, we can receive direction from two sayings of the Essene Order. These sayings also influenced the development of one of Jesus boys (the one from Nazareth, of the Luke Gospel). The first saying was: Before the Sun has risen and after it has set, you shall not occupy yourself with worldly thoughts or activities. The second saying was: Before the Sun rises, you should pray and ask that this rising come about, so that the Sun's force of day should unfold over you and over humanity. Through these sayings we should become aware of how significantly our being is connected with the spiritual world, out of which we emerge when we awaken in the morning and into which we enter again when we go to sleep. How little consciousness human beings have today of such outer and inner cycles is shown by their behavior at the turn of the year on New Year's Eve, and also by what they do before going to sleep each night, when it appears that in all they do, they seem determined to fix themselves in the physical body and in the world of physical phenomena. Developing esotericists should, with sacred feeling, be conscious of the fact that their "I" and astral body leave the physical and etheric bodies, and live in the suprasensible world until the time of waking up. To begin with, they bring back no conscious memory of this experience, but gradually certain pictures arise that can fill them with the right feelings in relation to their physical and etheric bodies, which they find upon awakening in the morning. These pictures will vary, according to the individual's temperament and disposition of character.

Thus, some, with their energetic "I" focused more on the outer human being, will have the picture of a house with a door through which they must enter upon awakening. The house is to be seen as the symbol of the physical body. Those who are melancholic—not in the sense of a disposition of character, but rather as a mood of the moment—will perhaps see the picture of a coffin in which they themselves are lying as a corpse. This comes when a human being is often influenced by thoughts of the transitory nature of the physical. Or it shows itself to spiritual sight as a light-form offering a chalice. This is, to a certain extent, a symbol indicating that the higher powers now hand us again, as a gift of grace, our conscious life in the physical body. This thought can greatly deepen the first verse of the ancient wisdom saying, the Rosicrucian saying: *E.D.N.*

When esotericists awaken in the morning and see their physical and etheric bodies before them, they should fill themselves with the sacred feeling: exalted gods have, in the immense cosmic spaces and in the eternal cycles of time, built up the god-willed physical and etheric bodies during the Saturn and Sun stages of evolution. This was done so that these bodies might become a dwelling place for the spirit of the human being. With this sacred feeling, the esotericists will ask the gods to let them have, maintain, and protect this physical body, without which they would not be able to lead a conscious life. And the esotericists can further imagine that their brain is not isolated and bound only to the physical body, but rather that, because the brain's forces originate from out of the cosmos, it extends like a half-globe, or half-sphere, into the cosmos. Thoughts, as cosmic forces, are written like stars onto this half-sphere and thereby illuminate the physical body.

Now, imagine that we do not find the physical body in existence anymore. In this case, we would be overwhelmed by the feeling that if we were to pass through the portal of death, all conscious life would be obliterated. Had there not already been a certain cosmic substance before the Mystery of Golgotha, life after death would have been dull, shadow-like, and unconscious. That is what the writer of the Greek Tragedies meant when he had their greatest hero say, "Better a beggar in the overworld than a king in the realm of the shades."

However, through Christ's sacrifice on Golgotha, a new substance was created into which human beings can immerse themselves, in order also to shape their life after death into a conscious state. For this reason, esotericists should, before going to sleep, fill themselves with this thought and feeling: *I.C.M.* This means that only through the Christ impulse can we receive what streams out from the great Mystery of Golgotha. For this reason, we esotericists do not speak the sacred word that expresses the "name of the inexpressible, unspeakable."

Even if human beings have consciousness after death, they do not yet have self-consciousness, through which they can recognize themselves and again find their brothers and sisters with whom they were connected in the physical world. In this, one can be helped only by the higher "I." The Holy Spirit helps one to come to the higher "I," which carries the individual through the portal of death to self-consciousness.

Esoteric Lesson
COLOGNE, JANUARY 4, 1913

RECORD A

When speaking of the esoteric circumstances in which we live, it is often said that our Western movement or stream has separated from the Eastern one. However, that is, especially at this time, quite incorrect. It has been the case for a long time already that it is not a matter of Western or Eastern, but rather of truth or untruth. As long as it was still a matter of the differences about suprasensible questions, one could absolutely say: "That is something which I cannot judge." One could still speak about two directions. Now, however, the differences have descended to the physical plane; it now has nothing more to do with Eastern or Western esotericism. People today like to have physical documents in order to judge these things. They now have them. Everyone can, through the material documents, be convinced that what Mrs. Besant said in 1909 is a contradiction of what she maintained in 1912.† It is a question, however, as to whether the world will indeed recognize what she otherwise swears by. When it goes so far that a general secretary (the English secretary) writes that Mrs. Besant must have forgotten her letter of 1909,† then things are quite bad. When we designate the other stream—that esoteric stream of Mrs. Besant—as the Eastern, we insult the true Eastern esotericism and philosophy. At the beginning of the Theosophical Movement, when there were still true Eastern impulses in the Theosophical Society, H. P. Blavatsky, for instance, still had the correct idea of what an avatar is.† Mrs. Besant never had the correct idea about it, and so it is no wonder that she understood nothing about the Christ. It was a matter only of enforcing personal wishes and opinions. It would be disastrous for the world if what Leadbeater holds as truth were to spread through the whole world.

It often happens that esotericists, after years of practicing, have the feeling that they have not progressed at all. However, this can only be the result of inattentiveness. Some people may try to meditate in order to let peace enter into the soul, but thoughts buzz around from all sides and do not let anything spiritual announce itself. It is a good sign, however, when we feel these thoughts buzzing around, because then we sense them in their reality. This is progress over the condition of not noticing them. Let us assume that, after having meditated in this manner, we go back to performing our daily activities. It can happen that we sense: I was getting dressed but was not present in my thinking; something was thinking into me. This feeling receives its full power and significance when we transform it into the mantric formulation: *It thinks me.* Concerning this, we may not object that it is always said that we should not ascribe any worth to what goes on unconsciously within the human being, since we are making conscious precisely what goes on within us. We bring it into our consciousness and thereby incorporate it into our "I." Esoterically, *It thinks me* is the same as the exoteric expression: "Within your thinking cosmic thoughts live."† It is an important aid for esoteric life to fill oneself as often as possible with this thought. This thought should always be imbued with the feeling of devotion; only then does it work in the right way. And even if we do not notice that cosmic powers think into us, they do so just the same. For our "I" is of the same nature as the cosmic powers that think into the human being, and the content of our meditation is taken from the cosmic thoughts themselves. We include in this *It thinks me* all the forces and beings that worked upon us during the Saturn, Sun, and Moon stages of evolution.

The feeling expressed in the saying, "It weaves me," summarizes our feeling of how the higher hierarchies work upon us when we strive to develop ourselves through our spiritual exercises. This saying, in turn, corresponds to the saying: "Within your feeling cosmic forces weave." Cosmic forces weave in our higher "I," and gratitude toward the spiritual beings should come with the thought *It weaves me.*

Then human beings can look at themselves and perceive their karmic relationship to their surroundings. We progress in esoteric life only when we regard practically—and not theoretically—everything that happens to us as karmic consequence, even if the circumstances are often hidden, or not so straightforward. To imbue ourselves with this idea gives us the necessary humility that we need in the face of the view expressed in the Mystery Drama *The Soul's Probation*: that the human being is the result of the working together of all the gods.[†] Everything in the world makes its way toward the human being. This is expressed exoterically in the words: "Within your will cosmic beings work."[†] It is expressed esoterically in the mantra: "It works me." Reverence must come over human beings when they deepen themselves in this thought.

These three thoughts with their corresponding feelings (*It thinks me* with devotion; *It weaves me* with gratitude; and *It works me* with reverence) form, together with what we have said about our Rosicrucian saying, a powerful aid for esoteric development. A similar organic connection exists between these mantras and their respective feelings as exists between the air we breathe in and our blood, which is purified by the influx of the air.

We can take into our soul yet another thought: how human beings live together through their karma. In pre-Christian times, the spiritual beings brought those together into the same tribe and family who had to endure or work out something karmically with each other. Through blood relationship, the circumstance was created in which personal karma could play itself out. This process changed after the coming of Christ. The forces that allowed human beings to work out their karma in such a simple way through blood relationships were gradually exhausted. The apostle Paul speaks of the First Adam, from whom human beings have descended physically.[†] For Paul, Christ is the Second Adam, from whom human beings in the future must derive their soul, just as they had received their physical body from the First Adam. At the time of the Mystery of Golgotha, human souls were about to die. The Greeks knew this, and it is tragically expressed also in the book of Job, when Job's wife tells him: "Renounce God and die."[†] Outside of the direct connection with God, there was only death for souls. Paul also knew this, though he could not express it in this way at that time. Had the Christ impulse not come, all human souls would have died. Human bodies would have still wandered around on Earth, but their souls would have lived as automata within them. Human beings would have become like animals, though maintaining physical human form. Those today who have not yet taken the Christ impulse into themselves are drawing on the last remnants of the old soul forces. When human being find a relationship to the Christ, their soul life is saved and permeated with new forces. How can one achieve a relationship to the Christ impulse? We can achieve it only by receiving what has been given in order to lead us into an ever deeper knowledge of the Christ impulse. Christ said: "Where two or three are gathered together in my name, there I am in their midst."† This means that when two people who have a personal karmic relation with one another achieve a relationship into which the Christ can work, Christ will reconcile their personal karma. This requires a trust that lifts everything personal to a higher level.

In this way, Christ will work ever more within our exoteric relationships. Therefore, we again bring to new light the saying:

> *From God we are born*
> *In Christ we die*
> *Through the Holy Spirit we come to life again.*

* * *

Record B

Whenever we think that we do not see any results from our exercises, it is mostly because we are not attentive enough. It can happen, however, that we do not notice anything immediately after doing the exercises, but later that day we notice that we are doing our ordinary tasks automatically and, for a moment, we notice thoughts that we ourselves did not think. In that moment something thinks in us. We then realize that great cosmic thoughts are thinking in us, and that our "I" must be of the same nature as the cosmic thoughts, because our "I" is taken hold of by these cosmic thoughts and thinks, without having any "I"-experience thereby. We can therefore feel ourselves blessed by the spiritual worlds. It is through grace that the high cosmic powers think us in this way, and that we can feel *It thinks me* and can thereby have a strong, heartfelt feeling of devoutness.

And then we can further think how our soul life is gradually woven through and through by the powers that built us up during the Saturn, Sun, and Moon periods of evolution. We feel as if this weaving of the cosmic powers was not just in our thoughts but in our whole being. We can feel *It weaves me*; we are what is woven. The cosmic powers have woven and formed us through long planetary stages, and we then feel immense gratitude.

And then we can think a third thought: "It works me." We sense how all the great spiritual beings work together to bring about the human being and how the goal of evolution is the human ideal of the god-willed, perfected human being. Then let us think about what we have made of ourselves, our personal karma, and look at how small and how far this is from the high cosmic ideal of the human being. Then we must feel respect, deep respect and reverence, toward the high beings in *It works me*.

And just as there is an organic interrelation between the air we inhale and our blood, which is cleaned by the influx of the air, so must there also be an organic interrelation between the sayings (*It thinks me*; *It weaves me*; and *It works me*) and the feelings that belong to them (devotion, gratitude, and respect and reverence).

How is it with regard to personal karma? Our earthly development cannot achieve its fullest aim if personal karma is not reconciled. In the past, karma was balanced out differently from how it is today. Formerly, those who had specific personal karma with each other were born into the same race, tribe, and so on, and the powers that were connected with the blood took care of the working out of karma. The forces that were effective from the time of Adam dried up around the time of the Mystery of Golgotha. After the Mystery of Golgotha, karma had to be reconciled in a different way. At the beginning of evolution, everything came about through one spirit. Afterward, differentiation came about and through this, personality, personal karma, and so on. Now, regarding the soul life, Christ must become our second progenitor, just as, in regard to the flesh and all that concerns the blood, Adam is our progenitor. Had the Christ impulse not come, the soul, which was no longer bound to and maintained by the then-dying forces that were connected with the blood, would have become ever smaller and poorer. Humanity would have become ever more similar to the animal, without an independent, inner soul life. The Mystery of Golgotha saved the human soul life and nourished, strengthened, and built it up anew. Now human beings can find a relationship to Christ. Christ has said: "Where two or three are gathered in my name, there I am in their midst." What does that mean? It means that two people, who have a specific karmic relationship with one another, can achieve a higher relationship into which Christ can work. This relationship is based on the trust that Christ himself is the power that will reconcile the karma. Personal karma does not preside in this case, but the Christ power in the soul working between them. Christ himself guides the working-out of karma. Thus karma, insofar as it is necessary, is reconciled. However, the leading force within this is the Christ himself, so that the relationship has become such that Christ can work within it. This means to be purified in Christ's name. In this way Christ will be able to work more and more in everything that concerns our life.

* * *

Record C

First, we were cautioned about our choice of expressions, especially as it concerns how we speak about Rudolf Steiner. We should avoid the term "master," so that we do not awaken the hatred and jealousy of our opponents. Opinions have not changed, but only the manner and methods of the battle have changed today. Formerly, people were accused of being heretics and were burned at the stake, or other methods were used to destroy them. Now people just use ridicule or make others seem suspect, and so therefore ineffective.

There is not an Eastern esoteric stream and a Western esoteric stream, but only a truthful, real esotericism and something else that merely calls itself true esotericism. The latter would be an insult to true Eastern esotericism. Something that follows personal purposes may not be called esotericism. In our movement, we wish to avoid all that is personal, and for this reason, we want to make a strict separation and settlement between us and what has come out of Adyar, India, and from Mrs. Besant since 1906. We want a strict separation between what Mr. Leadbeater wants the world to believe and what is given here in the strictest truth and with full responsibility.

Esotericists complain often that they do not make any progress, and that when they want to meditate, thoughts buzz around them like bees and prevent them from meditating. Be happy that the thoughts come like that. They want to show you that they are a power and are stronger than you are. It can seem that one meditates diligently for years to let the inner stillness enter in afterward, yet nothing—absolutely nothing—pours itself into the soul from the spiritual world. This only appears to be so, for attentiveness is necessary to notice the fine, subtle steps of the soul, since it has to do with a quite intimate process. Then, you notice something as you go about doing your daily tasks: that you have been doing things mechanically, as if you were spiritually absent, and yet it is not so. For in spiritual life it is not only a matter of remaining conscious during the experience, but of remembering what we experienced. To remember means to bring something up into consciousness. The meditants can now have the feeling that something pours itself into them, and they can sense that it is of the same nature as human thought itself; and yes, as the "I" itself.

Three important mantras are now given. These are to be used in the following way:

It thinks me. It is actually not I who thinks, but rather it thinks in me. The three sentences or mantras are expressed exoterically in *The Soul's Probation*: "Within your thinking cosmic thoughts live; within your feeling cosmic forces weave; within your willing cosmic beings work." They are expressed esoterically with the following: E.D.N – I.C.M. – P.S.S.R. The manta, *It thinks me,* must be imbued with the feeling of devotion.

It weaves me expresses the true nature of the human being. It expresses what the true nature of the human being really is and what we ourselves are in relation to it. This mantra should stimulate self-knowledge. It should give rise to a feeling of being integrated into the whole of the life of the world, and should express itself in gratitude.

It works me. The entire cosmos, everything, is to be seen in light of the human being as the goal. This mantra should give rise to a feeling of reverence, devotion, and dedication. We must learn humility and modesty when we see ourselves in our imperfection and incompleteness in relation to the goal that the gods have set for the human being.

E.D.N. – I.C.M. – P.S.S.R. This is the fourth saying that you will need. It is the primordial prayer of humanity.

Wherever we are—whether we are walking or standing; out on the street, or at home—when we let these words (the three mantras and the primordial prayer of humanity) rise up in our soul, they can help us progress in our esoteric life. However, the soul must silence these words in itself, if it cannot think them in a sacred manner. This means that we must forbid these words from rising up in our soul, if they are not accompanied by the corresponding feeling.

The Mystery of Golgotha changed the dying process of souls. As the physical body stems from Adam, so the soul stems from Christ. The substance of souls had gradually exhausted itself. Had the Mystery of Golgotha not taken place, a time would have come when physical bodies would have existed on Earth only as soulless automatons.

The reconciling or balancing of karma will come about in the future in such a way that Christ's words, "Where two or three are together in my name, there I am in their midst," comes true.

Souls die, but the karma or destiny that humanity has built together remains in existence. Humanity has proceeded out of a kind of group-soul nature and has differentiated and individualized. Because of this, relationships formed between individual human beings. Formerly, karmic reconciliation was brought about through the divine-spiritual beings who made sure that those who had karma to work out together would be born into the same tribe. This is no longer the case. Now Christ's words come true: "Where two or three are gathered together in my name, there I am in their midst." Christ is the Lord of Karma!

All souls stem from Christ. A time will come when this will become known, and it will therefore be understand that reconciliation among human souls can take place only through Christ.

* * *

Record D (Extract)

[…] How is an esoteric stream like ours actually possible? In the primordial beginning there existed a soul substance that divided itself into the manifold differentiated, individual human souls. Through this differentiation, karma arose, which consists in the soul connections from human being to human being. Before the event in Palestine, these karmic relations were bound up within blood relationships. They were bound to the blood. However, by the time of the Mystery of Golgotha this soul substance had gradually dried up. If the Mystery of Golgotha had not occurred, human beings would have come to wandering soullessly upon the Earth at the end of earthly evolution. They would have fallen into an animal nature within human physical bodies that would have been a caricature of animal bodies. The "I" (the "I" does not die; karma is bound to it until the end) would become empty and soulless had the Mystery of Golgotha not taken place. Christ is the soul-spiritual progenitor of modern humanity, just as Adam is the progenitor regarding the physical body. Only by filling ourselves with the Christ substance, the Christ impulse, do we avoid soullessness. We fill ourselves with the Christ substance when we take in the knowledge and findings concerning the Mystery of Golgotha and allow this to live within us. Then our lives and our relationships with one another will become ever more spiritual.

Esoteric Lesson
BERLIN, JANUARY 6, 1913

RECORD A

There are many esotericists who believe that they are not making any progress. This is impossible for those who apply themselves with zeal to their exercises. We must differentiate between progress and the noticing of progress. Those who are not satisfied and wish to say along with Meister Eckhart, "What good is it if I am a king if I do not know it,"† must develop a finer feeling, a listening, to what is happening within their soul.

Above all, esotericists complain that they fall asleep while doing their evening exercises. Assuming that you fall asleep during your backward review, you will wake up again. When you then remember back to the point where you fell asleep, you will become aware that, in spite of your day-consciousness being extinguished in sleep, your meditation continued. This can possibly be of more use than a meditation done with full consciousness. Of importance here is the fact that in the state of being outside your body, your consciousness worked further and a transition was found from ordinary day-consciousness to a higher condition of consciousness. This is already an expanding of consciousness, and in this expansion is the actual progress. [Note: In another lecture, which otherwise is the same, the following was recorded: "It is not thereby a matter of something subconscious, but rather of raising what was experienced into consciousness."]

Our dreaming also shows that we have made progress. We must just observe our soul; we must become attentive to what is happening in our soul. It may happen that in a dream, shortly before awakening, we see a coffin, or a house with a door, or an angel who hands us a chalice. Before we are able to see our body, we see it in pictures that correspond to our own disposition. Those who are melancholic from time to time and who frequently think about death, will behold a coffin with a corpse in it as symbol of their physical body. Those who are more optimistic and of a more joyous disposition, will see a house before them, and a door that they must go through to enter into their physical body. Those with a religious disposition will see an angel who offers them a chalice. This is [a symbol for] the waking day-consciousness that comes back into them.

Of course, such symbols appear only at the beginning of esoteric training. Esotericists who have progressed further will not see these images anymore, but will sense how their etheric body grows ever more out into the cosmos, and how the individual organs of their physical body send out streams into cosmic space. They will feel themselves to be cosmic beings.

We have also said that the feelings of the esotericist change. In the Essene Order, which existed during the time of Jesus and wherein Jesus remained for a time, there were two rules. First, the Essene brothers were not allowed to speak of worldly things between sundown and sunrise. Those who had reached a higher level were to go further and also not think worldly thoughts during that time. As long as the day-star (the Sun) stood in the heavens, they could occupy themselves with worldly thoughts, but they had to shut them out when the Sun went down.

The second rule was that before sunrise they were to ask the Sun to rise, and in the evening they were to thank it for having shone. People today will not be able to follow these rules to the same extent. However, must we not also be just as grateful as the Essene brothers—who were filled with gratitude and reverence in their anticipation of the Sun's appearance—that we return to our physical bodies in the morning? For it was *no more* certain for the Essenes that the Sun would rise again than it is that modern human beings will return to their physical bodies. Materialists know nothing about this, but as esotericists you have heard that our physical body template was built throughout the Saturn, Sun, and Moon periods by all of the spiritual beings that stand above us. They made the human being so artfully by bringing in the cosmic forces of all the ages. The gods have built this temple for the soul; this temple arose out of the spiritual. *Out of God we are born.*

There is yet a second feeling that we must develop. Formerly, there was the remnant of a primordial, divine substance into which human beings poured themselves after death. Through this they kept their consciousness intact. The divine substance became less and less. This differed from epoch to epoch and with individual nations, but in the fourth post-Atlantean epoch it was almost completely lost. Not the "I," but the souls, were affected by this loss. The Greeks were conscious of this and said: "Better a beggar in the overworld than a king in the realm of shades." But this substance was built anew through the Mystery of Golgotha. Now we enter into the Christ substance after death, and again become conscious there. As Adam is the progenitor of our physical body, so is Christ the progenitor of our souls. *In Christ we die*. However, because the name is so sacred to us that we dare not to speak it, we say only: "*In – – – we die.*"

When through the Christ force we attain consciousness after death, we have not yet achieved self-consciousness. We certainly recognize the things around us, but we cannot behold ourselves. We can achieve this only if we prepare ourselves on Earth. Just as we can find a button here in the physical world when we have consciously placed it in a certain place, so is it also [the same with finding ourselves] after death. We cannot expect to remember what we have not done with full consciousness. We are given methods for attaining this through the teachings of Rosicrucian Theosophy. If we seek to understand the spirit of the Theosophical worldview—if we fill ourselves thoroughly with the spiritual—the spirit will awaken in the life after death. *In the Spirit we are reborn.*

Let us sense that this Rosicrucian mantra is not an ordinary saying but was given to us by the Masters of Wisdom and the Harmony of Feelings. They infused cosmic forces into this mantra. The mantra does not exist in order to be just spoken but to be experienced. Through years of practicing it, we will reap ever more knowledge from it. Trained esotericists behold how the etheric body of those who have immersed themselves in this mantra begins to widen ever more, and begins to unite with the forces of the macrocosm. Thereby their organs become force-centers into which the streams from the spiritual world flow. Let us penetrate ourselves with this mantra when we are inwardly still and composed. And when we need to be comforted, when we are depressed, this mantra will bring us courage and strength. However, let us not use it only as a remedy to bring us comfort, but also when our soul is completely peaceful. Then this mantra will become ever more our friend and helper on our esoteric path.

* * *

Record B

Even when beginning esotericists think that they are making no progress, this is absolutely no proof that there has been no progress. Often they simply do not notice it. They often complain that they fall asleep during their evening exercises. It can happen, however, that they notice later when they wake up that they had continued their exercises in a different state of consciousness. The remembering of the continuation of the exercises in another state of consciousness is very important. Precisely such remembering can carry more weight than the simple practice of one's exercises in day-waking consciousness. Esotericists must also pay attention to their dream life. They can then sometimes see their body in a symbolic form just before awakening, either as a house into which they must enter; as a grave (this vision comes to those who think often on death or the transience of earthly life); or as an angel with a chalice in hand (this comes to those with a basic religious mood and who are aware that the body is created by the gods).

Later, esotericists will behold their body more realistically, and they will see how different it is from the maya of the physical world. They will then see the physical and etheric bodies expand extensively. They will see how the heart grows like a tree out to the whole universe, while the head spans half of the cosmos, like the starry heavens. It will take a long time, however, for the esotericist to progress from beholding the symbols at the beginning of this vision.

We can transform for our own esoteric life, our thoughts about the first Essene commandment that they should not occupy themselves with worldly things from sundown to sunrise (and for the higher degrees, they were not even to think about worldly things), so that we enter into sleep with a sacred feeling. And the second Essene commandment, that they ask the Sun to rise every morning, can be transformed by us into a feeling of sacredness and gratitude toward the gods who gave us our body; it is through our gratitude that we find our way back into our body every morning. When we rightly realize that without our physical body it would be impossible for us to develop consciousness upon awakening, we can then feel gratitude for finding our body again. We can then think with reverence upon the mantra: *Out of God we are born*, and bring this into connection with a sacred feeling toward our body, which was bestowed upon us by the gods. When we contemplate the E.D.N. in this way, we can make a wonderful discovery: that shortly before we awaken, we pray that we might find our body again. This discovery, that we pray in this other state of consciousness in which we dwell before awakening, is of great significance. (The E.D.N. with gratitude for our body.)

In contemplating the I.C.M., we can feel the same gratitude for the spiritual substance that we immerse ourselves in upon awakening in our physical body, which does the same thing for us in death that it does for us when we awaken. This spiritual substance, which had exhausted itself before the Mystery of Golgotha, is now the Christ substance.

We must also learn to develop our self-consciousness. We will accomplish this when we take the theosophical teachings into ourselves more and more as a living power. These theosophical concepts are living forces, and depending on how our soul life is formed by them, we will also maintain our consciousness in the life after death if we remember all that we have learned there as truth. This is the Holy Spirit: P.S.S.R.

Thus, by meditating this mantra—which is the crux of Rosicrucian esotericism—we receive more and more strength from it. The more we meditate this mantra—this truly magical saying—the more it brings us into connection with spiritual forces and spiritual beings and this living together with the spiritual worlds will develop. Also when we are sad and weighed down and depressed, this mantra can bring us comfort and strength. It will succeed if we also work with it when we are joyful and composed; when we live with this mantra in such a way that it becomes the path upon which the angels also come to us. Thus can our teachings build us up spiritually and create our soul life anew. And we will become ever more conscious of the sacredness of everything and will, with devout and composed feelings, live into the mantra: E.D.N. – I.C.M. – P.S.S.R.

Esoteric Lesson
BERLIN, FEBRUARY 8, 1913

RECORD A

My dear sisters and brothers!

When we observe all and practice all that has been given in the lectures, the Mystery Dramas, and the esoteric lessons—when we carry all of that out with complete devotion, we can enter very, very far into the high spiritual worlds. Modern humanity does not need more than this to reach the high spiritual worlds. We must give ourselves totally to meditation, concentration, and contemplation; we must leave everything else outside of this. Only through strict adherence to the given instructions can something be attained. The time spent in meditation should be regarded as something beautiful and sublime in our esoteric life. In meditating we must first immerse ourselves totally in the content of the exercise. We must empty our soul of all ordinary, everyday thoughts and feelings and live in the content of the given exercise. Then we must empty our consciousness of all content—also of the content of the meditation—and then listen and watch. This is quite difficult; this is true. Some maintain that they hear their blood pulsing through their body, and that bothers them. May they hear the blood pulsing; may they listen to that. Then they will sense the life in the blood and in the nerves, and thereby perceive a part of the life within.

Exoteric life takes its course in the world of understanding. By our standing before an object, looking at it, and forming a concept of it, we understand it. The process is different in meditation. Through meditation we enter into a different world. There we have our imaginations, our thoughts and our concepts before us; they are outside of us. We know that we are connected with them. We cannot get rid of them; we run after them. Thoughts rise up out of the depths of the soul; and we see a beast of prey as if it would devour them. We bind ourselves completely with the thoughts, and so on. Thus, here [with meditation] we *experience*, whereas in exoteric life we *understand*. We are, here in meditation, in the world of experiencing. We must take care not to immediately form concepts about what approaches us thusly in this world. We should only open ourselves, listen, feel-into what wants to stream into our soul. This builds the Lotus Blossom (the chakra), so that it can become active.

Still further along, we enter the world of bliss, or the world of forms. But only for those who have made themselves ready (mature enough) for this experience is it the world of bliss. For those who are not yet properly developed, it is a world full of horror and dreadful things, and it crushes them. For the unprepared, love turns into hate, and beauty turns into ugliness. Here they will like what they found revolting before, and so on. Everything is warped and distorted. Only those who go through the training of self-knowledge are truly prepared and developed enough to properly experience the world of forms.

What did the gods do to protect us from experiencing this world of forms before we are ready? They gave us pleasure: pleasure in the joy of creating and working here in the physical world. What we find beautiful in a piece of art—for instance, by Raphael or Leonardo da Vinci—is not what is lasting in it; the piece of art itself (such as presented or intimated in the third Mystery Drama with the two paintings by Raphael and Leonardo da Vinci)† is also not the element that is lasting. What is eternal is the spiritual process that went on in the artist's soul while creating the art work: the spiritual process out of which the piece was created.

What is God's presence in the world of maya? What must now be said will sound quite paradoxical. It is not God that we experience in the spring with its building-up forces, with its sprouting and forming of shoots, or in all of its beauty and radiance, but rather God is really working where we see devastating nature forces: in the storms in the fall; in all the smashing, destroying, and crushing. God is there within it. It sounds terrible and distressing, but it is true: God is most effective in everything that is wrecking and smashing. Joy in creating in the physical world is given to us to protect us from entering too soon into the world of forms, the world of bliss. We, in our day-waking consciousness, are separated from it, as though by a thin layer of ice. When we are involved with esoteric training, we should not introduce these esoteric teachings into our exoteric life, nor should we want to arrange our exoteric life according to these teachings. That would lead to distortion, absurdity, and error. Our training in the exoteric life must proceed out of exoteric pedagogical principles. It should become an ideal that the esoteric life proceeds quite independently, on its own.

Just as we should remain calm and composed—and not become "beside ourselves"—in relation to all the events and thoughts in our daily life, so too we must maintain composure, absolute composure, in relation to the world of [spiritual] experiencing. We must be able to remain calm and composed in the face of everything in both worlds. Through correct thinking-into, feeling-into, and living-into the three mantras—*It thinks me; It weaves me; It works me*—we achieve this calmness and composure. We accomplish this by letting these mantras pass through our soul again and again.

Then we will rightly understand our Rosicrucian mantra:

> Out of God we are born,
> In Christ we die,
> In the Spirit we are reborn.

* * *

Record B

Everything that is necessary for us to progress in esoteric development has already been said in our esoteric contemplations and, actually, in everything that has been communicated outside of the esoteric lessons. It depends upon each of us, as to whether we have the necessary patience, attention, and perseverance to attain the goal of reaching into the spiritual world.

No word in these esoteric contemplations is without significance, and every one can receive from them what we need for our own development. We can each sense something personal in them, something for each one in particular, because, in fact, there is something personal for each of us contained within them. When we allow these ideas, together with all that has been given in the individual lectures and lecture cycles, to work further into our soul, it will bring us the greatest spiritual growth possible for us in this incarnation.

What we especially need for our esoteric development is patience. We need the patience to ever again completely empty our soul, so that we can grasp the more intense experiences that take place in the depth of our soul. If we pay close enough attention, we will notice how our soul life gradually changes. For instance, we will notice that we no longer think simply in concepts, but that we actually become what we are thinking. Experiencing replaces understanding.

When we are totally still within ourselves, we will then also sense that it is as if there were beings there, so to speak, like beasts of prey that want to steal or devour our thoughts. At first it is often such that, when we become quite still in our meditation, we sense nothing other than the murmur of our blood; the effects of the blood and nervous system; the flowing of a fine fluid around the nerves. That is also correct. Through the stream of the blood we come into the realm of experiencing, where we actually live our experiencing. It can happen that immediately after meditation we do not find such thoughts that we ourselves have become, but that we find them within us unexpectedly at another time. Such experiencing is of much greater significance than the mere beholding of visions which will come later of its own accord.

We must ascend to a yet higher world, the actual spiritual world. Our ordinary, intellectual comprehension actually casts a veil over everything that lies behind the physical world. And this is a blessing for human beings, for we must be completely prepared in order to come into contact with the spiritual world, without harsh consequences arising for our ordinary life. If we are not prepared enough, what we are and feel as ordinary human beings can change into the exact opposite. If in ordinary life, for instance, we love someone very much, it can happen that—but only when the training was not the correct one—after our ascent into the spiritual world, we begin to hate that person. Or our courage can change into fear, or what was formerly pleasant and agreeable to us becomes highly unpleasant and disagreeable.

In order to understand this, we must become conscious of the fact that in our ordinary life, for our own well-being, the pleasure we find in things veils deeper-lying forces. The manner in which the works by Raphael and Leonardo da Vinci are presented in the third scene of the Mystery Drama, *The Guardian of the Threshold*, expresses much of significance. For, in the artwork there is something eternal, but it is not the artwork itself; rather, it is in the creative forces that worked in the soul of the artist. Everything that appears as beauty on Earth is transitory, and when we are enjoying this beauty, the pleasure veils the eternal for us.

Where do we find the eternal, working forces? Where do we find God most apparent in the physical world? Is it where we see sprouting and blossoming; what is rising to the surface of the Earth? No, we see God most intensively where we see form being destroyed, where the outer beauty disappears. In the sprouting and blossoming, we see the end or result of the path of God. In the physical world, God is most active and affective where we see destruction and death. This appears to be a great paradox when we think about divine love. It is given here as a first remark about something for a meditation content, out of which great conclusions are to be drawn; but about which we may not yet speak. Only this one intimation may be spoken.

Those who have not attained full calmness and composure in the face of all experiences in the physical world cannot sustain and maintain themselves in the spiritual world. For them love changes into hate, courage changes into fear, and so on. Those who have decided to make great strides in their esoteric life must be seriously cautious that they do not change anything regarding their ordinary, daily life. They should first of all remain what they have become through their disposition and karma. Outer life should remain as unchanged as possible; and when changes must be made, they should be caused, not by the esoteric life, but rather by the circumstances of exoteric life. Those who, for instance, notice in their exoteric life that they are unloving or unkind, should find help for this through exertion in their outer life, but should not expect any help in this regard from the esoteric life.

When we can always maintain our calmness and composure and immerse ourselves repeatedly in the given meditation (*It thinks me –*

It weaves me – It works me), we will then bring the right forces with us to be able to sustain ourselves in the spiritual world.

* * *

Record C

For our esoteric development we need, above all, patience. We need the patience to repeatedly empty our soul of content, in order to be able to grasp the finer experiences that appear. If we are quite attentive, we will notice how our soul life has changed. We will notice, for instance, that we no longer think in concepts the way we used to; we notice, rather, that we really are what we think. In the place of *understanding* comes *experiencing*. We will then become aware, when we wish to quietly experience our thoughts within us, that beings—as if they are beasts of prey—want to tear away our thoughts and devour them.

At first it is often the case that when we become quite still after our meditation we notice nothing but the murmur of our blood; the processes in the blood and nerves; the flowing of the fine fluid around the nerves. However, that is good. By way of the stream of the blood we then come into the realm of experiencing, where we truly *live* our experiencing. It can also happen that after meditation we do not immediately find the thoughts that we experienced and which we have completely become; but later at another time, and often unexpectedly. This experiencing is of much greater significance than the clear seeing of visions, which ensues of itself. However, we must enter into a still higher world, the actual spiritual world. Our ordinary, intellectual concepts actually cast a veil over what stands behind the physical world. And this is a grace, because we must be quite prepared, in order to come into contact with the deeper-lying world without it having harsh consequences for our ordinary life. If we are not well prepared, it is possible that everything we are and feel becomes the opposite. For instance, after our entering into the spiritual world it can happen that (but only if the training is not correct) we hate someone whom we loved before entering the spiritual world.

And our courage can turn into fear. We also can develop a preference for something that we otherwise found to be objectionable. In order to understand this, we must grasp the fact that in ordinary life, our experience of pleasure in things veils the deeper-lying forces for our own good. The way the paintings by Raphael and da Vinci are represented in *The Guardian of the Threshold* is very meaningful. The eternal element of the artwork is not within the paintings themselves, but in the creative forces that worked in the artists' souls. Everything that appears on Earth as beauty is transient. And while we enjoy the beauty, the pleasure veils what is eternal.

Where do we find the eternal, spiritual forces most clearly in our physical world? Do we see them where there is sprouting and blossoming on the surface, or where we see form being destroyed, where outer beauty disappears? The spirit is active in the latter. In our physical world, the spirit works in the annihilating, destroying element.

For this reason it is true that those who enter the spiritual world in a wrong way cannot sustain themselves, and this causes them to hate where they formerly loved; to fear where they were formerly courageous, and so on. Because of this it is necessary that complete composure is attained upon entering into the spiritual worlds, and that those who have made the decision: "Now I want to progress quite far in my esoteric striving," must always be absolutely careful not to change anything that has to do with ordinary life, regarding their love, their courage, their inclinations, etc. As far as possible, the outer life should remain the same. When changes must be made in the outer life, they should not be caused by the esoteric life but by exoteric circumstances. When we remain continually calm and composed and immerse ourselves, for instance, in the given mantra (*It thinks me — It weaves me — It works me*), we will also bring with us the necessary strength to protect and preserve ourselves in the spiritual world.

Every word of these esoteric lessons is significance. And everyone can receive from them what is necessary for spiritual development. Everyone can find something personal within these lessons, because within them is something directed to each individual. Letting the ideas and stimuli connected with all that is given in the lecture cycles work further upon our soul can bring us to the greatest spiritual growth that is possible in our current incarnation.

* * *

Record D

The meditation content given in the esoteric lessons and in the lecture cycles is strong enough to lead the meditant into the spiritual world, but the meditant must understand how to transform understanding and recognizing into experiencing. After letting go of the content of the meditation, many feel the pulsing of the blood and the relaying of the nerve impulses. By way of this stream, esotericists must reach the world of effects.

We tread through maya on a thin layer of ice, under which is the pulsating spiritual reality. If human beings now proceed with composure, in this way they can enter into the second world, where they experience their thoughts. They see them, as it were, from outside. The thoughts go out, and it is as if these thoughts were being pulled back and forth and were being devoured by beasts of prey. From here we reach, after further practice, the third world. This world has a confusing and destructive effect upon those who enter it without due maturity, without enough preparation, and without composure. This world can be a blessing to those who live into it with patience and with the proper training. Those who are unprepared experience their feelings change. Perhaps, in their outer life, they have developed a great love for someone; in the spiritual world this love changes into hate. Where they loved, they must hate. Thus, joy can turn into disgust. Pleasure (?)† is a protection in life.

When we consider the building-up and the tearing-down, destructive forces in the world, we see the divine working more in the destructive element. Ever again the divine smashes the maya so that human beings can learn to see through it. The paintings of Raphael and of Leonardo da Vinci are maya as compared to the soul experiences of these artists. Their soul experiences have eternal value.

As esotericists, we must not allow ourselves to feel impatience, but rather we must practice calmness and composure. After the meditation, we must give ourselves over to inner composure for a while. This builds and strengthens the Lotus Flower.

It would be most ideal if esotericists would leave their outer life unchanged, and if powers were to come to them out of their esoteric life, they would spiritualize the duties in their daily life. Changes in the outer life should come only in this way.

Esoteric Lesson
STUTTGART, FEBRUARY 17–20, 1913

RECORD A

Es denkt mich [It thinks me.]: E.D.N.

Out of a mystical mission, a quite specific language is given for central Europe. In this language every individual sound, as well as the sequence of sounds, expresses something esoteric. For instance, in the sentence, *Es denkt mich*, the broad *e* expresses the prevailing, weaving, creating divine in the world order and in the human being. The stretched or lengthened *s* expresses the winding, surging, rising and falling (welling up and down as in a wave) astral element, as it were.

Mich means our "I." Thus the divine thinks us in the "I."† (Empty the soul of content and feel deepest devotion.)

The second mantra is *Es webt mich* [It weaves me.]. Again, the divine forces are in the *e*, and the astral is in the *s*. And there should be a feeling of reverence and devotion or prayerfulness.

Now, there is another exercise, another meditation. The ancient Essenes were given the rules that between sundown and sunrise they were not to speak of material things, and that every morning before sunrise they were to fervently beseech the spiritual world to let the Sun rise, and then to give thanks to the Godhead that it caused the Sun to rise. There was even a specific, formalized prayer for this: "You gods, I thank you...." Modern human beings can no longer practice these wonderful, elevating customs and meditations. Esotericists must be completely truthful—truthful right to the depths of their heart. It would be a falsehood if modern esotericists were to beseech in fervent prayer for the Sun to rise and then to want to give thanks that it did.

At the time of the ancient Essenes, human beings still had the view that in the cosmic system the course of the stars was subject to the will of divine beings; and they had the view that it was possible that one morning the Sun might not rise. This exercise has no meaning for modern human beings. Thus it would be untruthful, if esotericists wanted to do this practice. Even the first practice between sundown and sunrise is no longer possible today. However, today's esotericists know that every night the astral body and "I" leave the physical body and etheric body. Now, the esotericists must first of all bring the imagination before their soul that a demon takes control of the physical body and etheric body, and that in the morning the astral body and "I" can no longer move into their home again. Upon awakening, esotericists should call up the question in their soul: "What did you do or think just before awakening?" (The advanced esotericists do this with full consciousness.) At first, you cannot remember that you thought or did anything. But after giving yourself up to this thought for a longer time, there comes—at first flitting by and then taking on an ever more fixed form—the thought: "You have thanked the Godhead that you were allowed to move back into and enliven again the body they have built."

Out of the divine we are born: E.D.N.

We should repeat this sentence, this triad, every morning, and we should experience therewith the feeling of deepest gratitude. The Godhead has built up the temple of our body: during the Saturn, Sun, and Moon periods of evolution the Godhead built our physical body, etheric body, and astral body. Thus we attain our consciousness again every morning.

When we cross the threshold of death, we enter into a different condition of consciousness. The ancient Atlanteans still had a bright, clairvoyant consciousness. At death these old Atlanteans were fully conscious when they entered the spiritual world. This consciousness was gradually lost, and in the fourth post-Atlantean age everything after death became shadowy. Fear of the unknown, shadowy condition was so strong that in this period the words were coined: "Better a beggar in the overworld than a king in the realm of shades. The Christ event changed this. By taking Christ into ourselves, we can again achieve the ability to consciously enter the spiritual world after death.

Into Christ we die: *In Christo morimur.* We must meditate this triad only while we are having the deepest feeling of devotion in our heart.

And now we must attain consciousness of our divine "I"; Our "I" must, so to speak, be born again: *Per Spiritum Sanctum reviviscimus.*

* * *

Record B (Extract)

We must become conscious of the fact that spiritual mysteries are hidden in the individual sounds of mantric words. Initiates gave, out of a mystical mission, a specific language for Central Europe. In this language every individual sound and the sequence of the individual sounds, express something esoteric, such as in the little word *ich* [I] that contains the initials of Christ.

Let us look at the first sentence: *Es denkt mich* [It thinks me.]. We must sense the *e* as a long, broadened *e*. It expresses the reigning, creating divinity in the cosmic order and in the human being. The *s*, spoken so that it is lengthened, is the astral element that wends and surges through everything, as it were. For *mich* [me] we could also (inwardly) imagine "mein ich," [my "I"], thus: The divine thinks my "I." After that, one empties the soul and has therewith the feeling of deepest devoutness.

Es webt mich. This means the divine weaves my "I." Again we experience the divine forces in the elongated *e*, and the astral in the *s*. With this we sense the feeling of deepest gratitude.

Es wirkt mich. This means that the divine works my "I." Again, sense the divine forces in the *e* and the astral in the *s*. With this we sense the feeling of deepest reverence and devotion.†

* * *

Record C

Out of a mystical mission, a certain language was given for Central Europe. In this language every sound, just as the sequence of sounds, expresses something esoteric. An example is the sentence *Es denkt mich* [It thinks me.]. There the *e* is elongated twice as much as usual.

That is the expression of the reigning, weaving, creating divinity that streams out of the divine cosmic order into the human being. The *s*—elongated in speaking it—is the surging, weaving astral that winds through everything. *Mich*: that means my *ich* ["I"]. Thus, the divine thinks my "I." When we meditate this, we should empty the soul and have only the deepest feeling of devoutness.

The second mantric sentence is *Es webt mich* [It weaves me]. Again, sense the divine forces in the *e* and the astral in the *s*, and have with this the deepest feeling of reverence and devotion. Today's esotericists know that every night the astral body and "I" leave the physical body and the etheric body. Now we must imagine that a demon has taken over the physical and etheric bodies so that the "I" and astral body cannot enter again into their homes. As we awaken, we should ask ourselves inwardly: what have I thought and done shortly before awakening? The advanced esotericists do this with full consciousness.

At first, we cannot remember that we have thought or done anything at all. However, after we have given ourselves over to this thought for quite a while, there comes, at first flitting by, but then taking on more shape, the thought: you have thanked the Godhead that you were allowed to move back into and occupy the temple of the body which they built. From God we are born: *Ex Deo nascimur*.

We should repeat this sentence, this triad, every morning, and should feel therewith the deepest gratitude that we have again sent our "I"-consciousness (Earth) into the temple which the Godhead built for us throughout the Saturn, Sun, and Moon evolutionary periods.

We do not have our earthly "I"-consciousness after death. The ancient Atlanteans entered the spiritual world with a bright, clairvoyant consciousness. In the post-Atlantean epoch, however, this consciousness was lost to the same degree that the earthly "I"-consciousness lit up. In the fourth post-Atlantean age the fear of the shadowy consciousness, the unknown circumstance, was so great that the statement was coined: "Better a beggar [in the over-world than a king in the realm of shades]." Everything became shadow-like after death.

Through the Christ event this changed, and by taking Christ into ourselves we can enter consciously into the spiritual world after death. This is the meaning of I.C.M. We must meditate this triad with the feeling of deepest devoutness. Consciousness of the divine "I" helps us with this. This consciousness must be born in us, so that through this consciousness we can enter into the spiritual world: P.S.S.R.

Ei = Revealing into the human being of the divine, before which timid reverence draws back.

Oe = Expresses the above even more so. Human beings feel themselves enclosed in their form, and feel the active Godhead outside.

Esoteric Lesson
BERLIN, MARCH 12, 1913

RECORD A

It is our task in these esoteric lessons to become clear about our meditation. We must expect and be prepared that things will be different from what we had previously thought. Esotericists must relearn things. Even in our daily life, we must change our concepts and must value things differently and give them a different significance than we have up until now. We will see, for instance, how this can be the case with our exercises. Often people complain about falling asleep with the evening exercise. Esotericists have the tendency to think of this as a shortcoming. In truth, it is different. Falling asleep can even mean progress. Naturally, we must make an effort to stay awake when doing the exercise or meditation. When, however, we are overcome with sleep in spite of this, it is not an error. It can even be that the exercise continues after we have fallen asleep. When we awaken in the night or in the morning, we should try to remember where the exercise broke off. Then we will feel as if the exercise might have continued, as if something had worked further in us. This can then gradually become progress and can eventually bring about entry into the spiritual world. We are always told that those who are trained must be fully conscious in the spiritual world. Yet, it can also happen that human beings are at first only half-conscious in the spiritual world. This is not an error, if the students try afterward in waking life to fully, consciously remember what occurred during their sleep.

Students lose their consciousness and fall asleep so easily because everything we experience in the physical world is maya, and what we would experience—without our being prepared—in the spiritual world would shatter us. For this reason, the higher beings dull down our consciousness, until we have enough strength to face the shattering experiences and are able to bear them. We fall asleep, because we are not yet *allowed* to experience these things. When, through our dreams and experiences, we have become developed enough to bear what is so shattering, then it does not appear to us to be so terrible. We are so surrounded by maya that we are caught up in it in everything we are and do. When we consider, for instance, the four little statements that people always hold to be true, we can see immediately how the words we use daily deceive us. The four sentences are: "I am;" "I think;" "I feel;" and "I will." Of all of these, only the first is really true: "I am." We become thus aware that our thoughts are mostly not thought by us but are imposed upon us from outside through social relationships, through our surroundings, and through other circumstances. Human beings are stimulated from outside to think this or that, to feel, or to do. It is a great illusion when we say, "I think;" "I feel;" or "I will."

If human beings had become what the progressing hierarchies had intended, everything would have been different. Then, during sleep, human beings would have experienced an imaginative world; of course, it would have been different from what it was on the ancient Moon. During the day people would have remembered the pictures that they had seen in this condition. The images would have accompanied them and would have fructified them during their life. However, Lucifer took ownership of our thoughts and thereby dulled our imaginative world. He thinks in everything in us. When we enter the spiritual world and attain spiritual sight, we experience what Lucifer thinks in us, and that is something quite shattering. For this reason, the good divine beings veil Lucifer from us in order to protect us. Thus, it is not Lucifer who darkens our night consciousness.

So, we see how wrong it is to say: I think. Esotericists can also recognize it so clearly when they do their meditation. Thoughts bombard them, and no matter what they do, they cannot get rid of them. They are very sad because it goes so poorly, but yet they experience that they do not think the thoughts, which are so much stronger than they themselves are. They even see that their so often incomprehensible dreams come to them from outside. In reality, most—about two-thirds—of our thoughts come from Lucifer. Lucifer thinks in the human being. Human beings have formed absolutely false ideas about thinking. The value of thinking does not lie in how much we learn, how much we understand, and how much we know, but rather how we progress through thinking, what forces we develop through thinking. We can see this, for instance, with scholars who know quite a lot, and yet from the spiritual standpoint are no further along than they were as students. One says of such people that they are dried-up, and the clairvoyant can see how, in reality, the astral body is shrunken, contracted. We should not say "I think," but "Lucifer thinks in me." If Lucifer had not intervened, when human beings while they were awake had wanted something, they would have had memory pictures that would have led them, rather than outer circumstances. When we become aware that other beings think in us, we can then say: *It thinks me.* This can have a good effect on us, if we connect the correct feeling of devotion with it.

With the second statement, "I feel," it is easier to see that it is totally false. We do not bring about the drives and desires that live in us; for the most part, they rule us. Two-thirds of these feelings—in the best of cases, one-half—come from luciferic and ahrimanic beings, through the maya of the outer sense world. It would have been quite different with human feeling if the progressive, developing hierarchies had been the only ones to work in it. Then human beings would have been in a world of archetypes. For instance, they would have seen the archetype of a flower. When they then would have seen the flower during the day, they would have seen along with it and at the same time, the archetype of the flower as etheric forces that swirl around the plant. Forces also weave through human beings in this way; and when we make this into our feeling and our view, it can have a good effect on us. We can recognize the plant as something related to us in its being and nature. And we can bring the belonging-together of all beings to consciousness in the mantric words: *It weaves me.* However, this must take place with the right feeling: the feeling of gratitude.

The last statement, "I will," is the most obvious that it is an illusion. We need only a little exoteric self-knowledge to see that it is actually absurd to say, "I will." If only the progressing hierarchies had worked on the human being, this illusion would not have come about. This illusion occurred because of the ahrimanic influences. The whole outer world is maya. When we have before us a cut flower, that flower is not the truth. A flower is the truth only when it is connected with its root and is in the soil. It is the same with the human being. The human being is not, in truth, to be thought of as separate from the rest of the world. Just as the plant is connected with the Earth, so is the human being connected with the cosmos and its forces. Only through the ahrimanic forces did the human being enter into the maya, feeling the self as a single, separated being. If human beings had become what the progressing hierarchies had intended, they would have always been aware that cosmic forces stream through them. Esotericists can become conscious of this: they can feel themselves connected with these cosmic forces and can imagine themselves in these weaving cosmic forces that hold sway and take effect through their wave-like, surging power. These words were not selected out of emotion, but they contain the feeling that they should awaken in us. And our will impulses should be influenced by the active, working cosmic beings when we say: *It works me*. Yet, this mantra must be connected with the feeling of reverence.

Esotericists can use these three formulas—*It thinks me* with devoutness; *It weaves me* with gratitude; *It works me* with devoted reverence—in various ways as meditation: either together or singly; at various times of the day; and also in-between other activities. They can have a great effect on meditants. There have been people who have worked with these formulas for their whole life and have progressed quite far through them.

The central meditation for the esotericist, however, should always be the ten words with which we close the studies: the Rosicrucian mantra. We must feel how these words were selected out of wisdom, so that already in the sound we can instinctively grasp the deeper meaning. It is not without reason that the mantra begins with two "*e*"s: *Ex Deo*. For with these words is said that, upon awakening, human beings descend out of a divine-spiritual world and are born in their physical body. And this physical body is not, as is often believed, something low or base. What remains on the bed when we vacate it in sleep is base only because we have made it so through our various incarnations in the stream of heredity. The body, as it was originally given to us, is a temple, a great work of art. And how the human being senses this in returning into the physical body upon awakening is expressed in the two "*e*"s in *Ex Deo*. The vowel *e* always signifies a joyful awe. The *o* in *Deo* signifies the soul embracing the physical body and the etheric body. The sound *o* always means an embracing. However, another feeling connects with this: a kind of shy pulling back with trembling. This lies in the *a* in *nascimur*. The *i* of this word expresses the "I" or self-consciousness, which awakens through the entry into the physical body and etheric body. The *u* of the last syllable signifies the completion of the union.

In the following three words, the middle word always remains unspoken, because we should then fill ourselves with what should not even be intimated with sense-perceptible sounds. In these words we should experience—not just intellectually but in feeling—already in the sound of the letters how the human being, when leaving the body, flows into Christ, flows into the spiritual world. In the *i* in *In* we feel the being of the human being that is lifting out; in the *o* of *morimur*, the receptive spiritual world prepared to embrace the being of the human. Then *i* and *u* follow again, in which we can experience the accomplished envelopment of the "I" by Christ.

In the last four words, the consonants play the main role. The *p* and *r* of *Per* signify something that is placed in a certain relationship to something else: in this case, it is the soul that has entered into a relationship with the spiritual world. Both "*s*"s at the beginning of the following words are the swinging and vibrating of the soul, the wave-like weaving of the spirit in the soul, which is expressed in the physical and shows itself in the form of the spine. In the two "*t*"s is expressed the individual being of the human being living in the spirit. In the *r* of the last word is expressed the purely spiritual, the absolute, the quiet willing out of which springs forth the surging spirit world that speaks again in the two "*s*"s of this last word.

Thus we have in the sounds of these ten words something that should take effect in our feeling, if we comprehend it in the right way. Much in this lesson has already been spoke about; it must simply be looked at from various standpoints.

* * *

Record B

> *Es denkt mich [It thinks me]*
> *Es webt mich [It weaves me]*
> *Es wirkt mich [It works me]*

We should have the feeling as of a warming, light-filled spirit body that is brought into being for us by the power of the mantra.

Lucifer approaches us at the moment of going to sleep.

Ahriman approaches us when the astral body and "I" leave the [physical] body.

Esoteric Lesson

BERLIN, MARCH 16, 1913

RECORD A

First Oda Waller† was spoken of. She became so intimately connected and completely related to our Movement in such a short time because she actually belonged to the future time when our Movement will come into its own. It was said that Doctor Steiner was able to hold her funeral in the mood of the words: "We will remain loyal to her, just as she was loyal to us."

Expressions in ordinary life that are actually maya are, "I think," "I feel," "I will." Only when we say, "I am," do we say something that is true. Regarding our thoughts, we can often notice how they press themselves upon us when we actually want to shut them out. This proves that we ourselves do not think, but that something else thinks in us. If only the progressive, good gods had worked in us, we would never have had the illusion that we think. At night, instead of falling into deep, dreamless sleep, we would have seen around us a great imagination of our thoughts and ideas, but they would have been completely imbued with the life, with the substance of the higher beings. During the day, we would have remembered and always known that actually the life of a higher being is in our thoughts. However, Lucifer worked and wove himself into our thought life. And, in this case, during the day we would have constantly experienced that Lucifer thinks in us as something terrible. To protect the human being from this, unconscious sleep overcomes us at night, and we live in the maya-idea that we ourselves think. But we must, as esotericists, learn to look the truth in the eye. And we receive the strength to bear the thought that Lucifer thinks in us when we, with constant devoutness, completely imbued with devoutness, meditate the mantric sentence: *It thinks me.*

It is simpler in our feeling life than it is in our thought life to recognize that we are not the ruler. Feelings rush up in us and we often cannot control them much. If also here our development had remained connected only with the progressive powers, then in the night we would have had seen in imaginations how our feelings are of the same substance as the life that weaves through nature's life realm. We would see the etheric archetypes of the plants (totally different than the physical plants), and we would know that what pulses through the etheric life realm is also in our feelings. We would remember this during the day when looking at outer nature. However, Ahriman intervened in all of this. And so we can say that Ahriman lives, in a best case scenario in two-thirds, but most of the time in three-fourths of our feelings, with the benevolent gods living in only a quite small part. We would have seen this in imagination during the night because we would have remained conscious, and during the day, when looking at outer nature, we would have known that Ahriman lives in our feelings, which are related to the weaving of the life realm. And we would feel in a terrible way that Ahriman feels in us. Again, in order to develop the strength to bear this truth, we must meditate the sentence, "*It weaves me*," with intense gratitude toward the good gods, who have not totally abandoned us.

Regarding our will impulses, it is more than clear that our will is almost always determined by causes *outside* of ourselves; the attractions and stimuli of the outer world drive us to our actions. Also here, if Lucifer and Ahriman had not intervened, we would have seen in the night the working of spiritual beings, and we would have felt ourselves to be united, or one, with that activity. During the day we would have known nothing else than to work in harmony and unison with what the spiritual beings, the goods gods, are wanting. Our will would have been the same as the will of the gods. However, Ahriman also influenced this, and we should see this fact and know it during the day. We receive the strength to bear it by meditating, with deep reverence and adoration, the statement, "*It works me*."

Thus we see that the expressions mentioned above, "I think;" "I feel;" "I will;" are given to us as maya in our ordinary life because we are not able to bear the truth. And the meditation of the mantra—*It thinks me, It weaves me, It works me*—can of its own accord, without other meditations, give the human being a mighty thrust forward into the spiritual world.

The following, concerning the letters in this mantra [in the German] is of importance. *Es denkt mich [It thinks me]* = *e e i* is the drawing near, with awe and reverence, to another being. The *i* means becoming one with this being that we are approaching. The *d* (Tau), however, indicates a feeling of still being secluded, with reverence, from this being.

In *Es webt mich* [It weaves me] we have the vowels, *e e i*, but instead of the *d* there is the *w*, an approaching that is of a more intimate nature. We weave and undulate over into the other being; the wave-like nature of the *w* itself carries us over.

In *Es wirkt mich* [It works me], everything is just the opposite: *e i i*. We are completely in the other being, we work upon ourselves from there. We have become completely one with this working and this being.

The ten words of the Rosicrucian mantra are also ordered so that the letters are significant. *In Ex Deo nascimur*, there is the mood that we can feel with regard to our body upon our awakening: *e e o a i u*. In the *e* we have shyness and awe toward approaching our physical body and etheric body, which the gods built up over the course of great, long cosmic periods. The *o* is the wanting to encompass; the *a* is a pulling back with a mighty reverence, as if these bodies were too great and holy to approach. The *i* signifies the wish to become one with the bodies. The *u* unites everything.

In (Christo) morimur is the sentence in which the one word is unspeakable. We could call this the *post-mortem* mood, the dying in Christ: *i i o o i u*. Being one; encompassing; becoming completely one; all of it being united.

Per Spiritum Sanctum reviviscimus. This is the expression of the attaining of self-consciousness in the realm we enter after death. Here the consonants are of more importance. The *p r* signifies feeling placed within. The *i* stands for the "I"-feeling; for the realizing of oneself as "I"; for self-consciousness in the *post-mortem* condition. The *s* is the form of the spine. Thus the Masters have laid the Mysteries of the Creative Word into this mantra. And still more mysteries are to be found within it (the tenfold nature of the human being).

* * *

Record B

First the death of Oda Waller was mentioned. It was said that she was one of those spirits who descended to Earth earlier than is usually the case. For this reason, she actually belonged to a later time and—like our whole Movement—never felt completely at home on the Earth. Therefore she immersed herself deeply in our Movement and also in such a very short time in the Christ impulse. She immersed herself so intimately with the Christ impulse that she could not live beyond the age at which Christ abandoned the physical body. It was her inmost wish to be surrounded by only Theosophists when her body was to be buried, and this also happened. And so the main motif of the funeral could be: we will remain loyal to her as she was loyal to us.

Much holds true for ordinary life that becomes quite different in the spiritual world. Thus, here on Earth, we should always try to preserve and maintain life, even if it is our own. Nevertheless, it can happen that when someone who is connected with us in a sacred sense is called by higher powers to abandon the body, such a person can also become, outside of the body, our greatest helper.

It is also not correct for us to think that it is always wrong to fall asleep in meditation. This can even mean the continuation of the meditation in another condition of consciousness.

One of the things that has value only for ordinary life, but which is basically totally maya, is our habit of saying: "I think; I feel; I will." Only when we say, "I am," are we saying something that is correct. When we notice how thoughts work through us, we can bring to mind that the great cosmic spirits think in us and on through us. If only the regular, progressing spirits—and not Lucifer and Ahriman—had worked upon us, instead of falling into a deep, unconscious sleep in the night, we would see our thoughts and ideas as a great imagination before us; we would, however, see these thoughts and ideas thoroughly imbued with the substance of the higher spirits. We would then retain the memory of this during the day and would know that the spiritual beings think in us. Lucifer, however, intervened, and now it is almost exclusively Lucifer who thinks in us. And because we would otherwise see this at night, it is covered up so that we do not need to go around during the day with the memory that Lucifer thinks in us. We are protected by the maya: "I think."

As esotericists we must contemplate all of this; and we achieve the strength to do this when we meditate, always with devotion: *It thinks me.*

Still more difficult to differentiate is the maya of "I feel." We know that, in the best of cases, we are the ruler over our feelings about two-thirds of the time; mostly, however, it is about one-fourth. If Ahriman had not intervened, we would see our feelings at night in the form of the life that weaves in the great realm of plant life outside in nature. We would see the etheric archetypes of the plants—totally different from the physical plants—and our feelings weaving in them. We would remember this during the day when we look at outer nature. However, because Ahriman has had an effect, all of this is covered up for us. Otherwise we would have the terrible experience in the night of seeing how Ahriman works in us; and see, during the day, Ahriman weaving in nature.

In order to receive the strength to bear this, we must meditate the following with gratitude for the good gods which also live in us: *It weaves me.*

And also with regard to our will impulses, we know that it is maya when we say, "I will." It would have to be said in connection with our will to action: "Ahriman wills in me." And the strength to bear this is given to us through the meditation: *It works me.*

Each of these three mantras can bring us a great way forward in the spiritual world when they are always entirely imbued with the corresponding feelings.

Also the sequence of the letters [in the German] is of significance here. *Es denkt mich* [It thinks me]: *e e i*. The *e* refers to "awe" and "reverence" for everything that approaches us. The *i* refers to becoming one with the being we are approaching. Through the *d*—in "*denkt*"—however, there is to be felt a separation still in the first two words.

Es webt mich [It weaves me]. Again the *e e i*, but *a w* in the place of the *d* already shows less separation. One already weaves and undulates over into the other being.

Es wirkt mich [It works me]: *e i i*. Now it is just the opposite. One is in the other being and works from out of that being.

Also the ten words of our Rosicrucian mantra are ordered in this way:

The letters *e e o a i u*: *Ex Deo nascimur* [Out of God we are born].

- *e*: To approach the body with awe, as it was given to us by the gods.
- *o*: To encompass, to want, to embrace.
- *a*: To retreat in great reverence, as if the experience were great and sacred.
- *i*: To want to become one with.
- *u*: Uniting all of the foregoing vowels.

i i o o i u: *In Christo morimur* [In Christ we die]. A *post-mortem* mood.

p s s r: *Per Spiritum Sanctum reviviscimus* [Through the Spirit we are reborn]. Here the consonants are of more significance than the vowels.
- *p r*: The feeling of being placed within.
- *s*: To realize oneself as an "I"; the "I"-feeling; the self-consciousness *post-mortem*.

Thus the Masters of Wisdom and the Harmony of Feelings have laid the Mystery of the Creative Word into this mantra. We cannot realize this in us enough, for there are still deeper mysteries in this mantra.

Ten words, the tenfold nature of the human being, of which the fifth word is the unspeakable name.

* * *

Record C

The Vowels of the Rosicrucian Mantra

E.D.N. We come out of the spiritual world. We enter a sacred temple that the gods have built for us out of divine-spiritual forces: the temple of the body. Sacred awe and admiration before the glory and magnificence is expressed in the *e d*; and in the *e o* lies the feeling of becoming encompassed by the temple of this body. The *n a* expresses a certain fear in the feeling of one's own unworthiness; it is a pulling back in the face of the glory of the divine gift of this temple. In the *i* is expressed trusting surrender and devotion; and in the *u* is again the full uniting with the physical body and, along with it at the same time, with the Earth consciousness.

I.C.M. The *i*, sounding three times and strengthened ever anew, means the taking hold of our own inwardness; the immersing of ourselves, the wanting to become one, with Christ. In the *o* and *u* lies the complete merging, the uniting of oneself with Christ. Through this mantra the post-mortem consciousness should be created. As the life in the physical body helps us to develop earthly consciousness, so does the dying into the Christ substance in the I.C.M. help us to have post-mortem consciousness.

P.S.S.R. should produce self-consciousness; this means the consciousness of being able to live in the higher self which lifts itself out of the lower. Here it is not the vowels but the consonants that predominant. The *s* expresses the going forth of the human being out of the bosom of the gods. When the *s* resounded at one time through cosmic space, the human spine was created. However, the wave-like, surging of the *s* is also the sign of Lucifer, the serpent. We must overcome the serpent, in order to attain the reality of P.S.S.R.

* * *

Record D

a:	Surrendering and willing, wanting
i:	Full surrendering – Becoming one
e:	Prayerful, rapt (Reverence toward the high divine beings)
o:	Encompassing lovingly
u:	Uniting (of all of the preceding vowels above)
d (*t*):	Standing on one's own
p:	Confronting
w:	Interweaving with the divine working
s:	Knowing or consciousness (connected with the spine)
E.D.N.	Earthly consciousness
I.C.M.	Post-mortem consciousness
P.S.S.R.	Self-consciousness from one incarnation to another

* * *

Record E

e:	Commanding awe-filled reverence
b:	Something individually defined by boundaries, self-contained
w:	Something wave-like, going without boundaries or limitations into the far distances
i:	Giving impulse
a:	Something insufficient or inadequate, connected with yearning
o:	Something encompassing
u:	Encompassing what is drawn more into the depths
Per:	Giving a connection
s:	Seeking the spiritual (also represented in the spine)

Esoteric Lesson

THE HAGUE, MARCH 21 (GOOD FRIDAY), 1913

Our contemplation today shall be dedicated to how the soul can rise into the spiritual worlds. Those who do their exercises and meditations regularly with patience and enthusiasm will make progress. What matters is that we notice our progress.

After the meditation, it is good to let a quiet period take place, make the soul completely empty, and wait to see which imaginations come to us out of the higher worlds. Much depends on the mood, the attitude of our soul; we should approach our exercises only out of devoutness and joy and with great devotion. The experiences that take place are quite different according to each individuality and the karma of the meditant. Out of the multitude of possibilities, I would like to take up two today.

One experience is being lifted out into space, into infinity. We feel ourselves as if expanded, as if lifted up; naturally, an abandoning of the body is connected with this. At this lifting up, we see a reddening; yellow-red clouds come toward us. Gradually, figures crystallize out of these clouds. This experience creates a feeling of delight and blissfulness.

Another experience that occurs is the diving and immersing ourselves into the depths. With this we have the feeling of contraction, of being tied up. The spiritual beings that we sense in this immersion appear in a blue-violet color-gleam. They trigger in us a feeling of reverent shuddering and cause us to do a kind of self-examination. They show us what we really are with our failures and errors, all of our moral weaknesses in their total magnitude and reprehensible nature.

Indeed we are already led to this every evening in our backward review of the day; however, with our physical consciousness, we are not able to know it so clearly. These beings that surface out of the depths bring us also to see clearly what habitual errors and false thinking bring forth in us. The beings that appear in blue-violet light, and that make our errors visible, belong to the hierarchy of the angels;

whereas the higher, red-yellow light-forms belong to the hierarchy of the archangels. These experiences can also approach us through other means, such as through sounds and tones, which is still more dreadful to bear, as our judgment is pronounced with the thunderous voice of the archangel. But when this hour [of judgment] comes—and that is after the meeting with the Guardian of the Threshold—we must have overcome our fear.

Another example will be given to make sure this is understood; the imaginations can also show something different. We can see that the figures ascending in blue-violet colors out of the depths have worried, pain-filled countenances. These high beings feel sadness and distress because of our errors; this awakens in us a feeling of boundless shame. When human beings truly grasp their errors and regret them, they will see the faces of these beings radiating joyfully. Human beings must feel this connection between the microcosm and macrocosm.

The beings that descend in red-yellow light-clouds upon human beings and surround them in a circle release upon the human beings the feeling of fear as a punitive justice. In addition to this fear, a feeling of joy can come when these beings show us what developmental possibilities lie within us, and how it depends on us to carry out this development.

Always, however, something like a conflict arises in us when we experience the red clouds of concentrated figures trying to unite with the blue-violet figures that strive upward out of the depths. We hear clearly a voice that speaks: "Do not believe these beings; believe what comes out of your own soul." That is Lucifer's voice, and that is the greatest temptation that human beings can have, because Lucifer outshines all other beings in beauty, cunning, and seduction. Lucifer climbs also, like the blue-violet beings, out of the depths.

We must also be clear that in these realms, form is no longer of significance. The spirits of form—the elohim, as they are called in the Bible—have their significance on Earth. Within the spiritual worlds we find that we rise above the spirits of form, and that the spirits of motion can approach us.

We must never forget one thing: the feeling of deepest gratitude toward the higher beings and the spiritual worlds. Just as the Essenes, full of gratitude, looked toward the approach of the Sun and prayed that it might rise, so also should we, with reverent thanks toward the spiritual beings, return to the temple of our physical body, which was built for us through the Saturn, Sun, Moon, and Earth periods, and in which alone we can attain Earth consciousness: *Ex Deo nascimur*.

And then, with this attained feeling of reverence and gratitude, we live into the divine-spiritual which releases us from the bonds of the bodily nature and brings us into the spiritual, suprasensible realm, helping us to attain the greatest bliss. It is so great and powerful that esotericists do not dare to speak the name of the highest being: *In – – – morimur*.

And finally, in the last part of our ten-word Rosicrucian mantra, self-consciousness, which brings human beings over into a new incarnation, is expressed: *Per Spiritum Sanctum reviviscimus*. Living in the consonants and vowels of this mantra will bring us much further than meditation in the three parts of the mantra, which consists of 2 x 3 words and 1 x 4 words.[†]

Esoteric Lesson

THE HAGUE, MARCH 21 (GOOD FRIDAY) & MARCH 25, 1913

When we manage to have complete quietness of soul after our meditation, a feeling can come over us as if we go upward out of ourselves and come into contact with the spiritual beings around us. This experience is accompanied by the feeling of expanding ourselves, of being spread out, in a sphere above us. However, we can also come out of ourselves by going down into our being, and can then come into contact with other spiritual beings. Along with this, there is a feeling of becoming narrower. We climb deep into ourselves and feel ourselves becoming tight or cramped, and then come out of ourselves on the path down, just as we come out of ourselves on the path upward. This going-out-of-ourselves, and the accompanying feeling of becoming wider, bring a feeling of bliss. It is as if we are climbing up toward spiritual beings that are approaching us there. If we climb downward, we meet spiritual beings who let us know deeply our shortcomings; and we become one with these beings. Yet, we then also notice that the sphere in which we find ourselves adjoins the sphere above us and that now, in the knowledge of our faults, we feel the spiritual beings who approach us as avengers of those that judge and penalize—the archangel with the fiery sword. In contrast we feel the beings of the sphere below to be mourning over our errors, and we feel deeply that our errors effect not only, us, but that spiritual beings—the messengers, the angels—mourn over our errors and faults. We can either experience this only inwardly or also see it outwardly as a colored imagination. In the latter case, the sphere in which the spiritual beings reveal themselves will spread itself in red and red-yellow colors above us, and under us the sphere will show itself as blue and blue-violet colors. Then both spheres meet together, and we feel ourselves moving in them and looking back upon our body as if looking upon something we had left behind. We can have this experience if we correctly meditate: *Es denkt mich* [It thinks me]; and we can see this imagination if in the night we become conscious of the working of the good gods.

In the March 25th repetition of the Esoteric Lesson that was held in Berlin:

The *s* as the sign of Lucifer. Feelings (expressed there): Ahriman and Lucifer. Ten words: tenfold being of the human being, of which the fifth is unspeakable.

Esoteric Lesson

THE HAGUE, MARCH 25, 1913

In the previous lesson, we saw what is in our consciousness above and below. We saw how, from below, messengers in blue-violet color, the angels, come up; and in contrast how from above, as if dipped in fire, the archangels [come down]. And we saw that all these beings join together to a certain extent to form a sphere into which human beings can see.

Today I want to give you another meditation, which is so significant that spiritually striving people have prepared the way into the higher worlds through it alone. We must be clear that our whole earthly thinking is actually totally false. Of the expressions: "I am," "I think," "I feel," and "I will," actually only one is correct. The correct one is: "I am." All the others are from two-thirds to three-fourths wrong.

It has often been pointed out that if we had only developed ourselves according to the intentions of the good gods, there would be no unconscious sleep. If only the good spirits had worked on us, we would have had in sleep, even though not quite the picture-consciousness of the old Moon period, a lively imagination of the surging effects of the cosmic spirit that weaves us. However, Lucifer entered our earthly development.† And the good gods took our consciousness away during our sleep so that we would not bring back with us the terrible knowledge that Lucifer thinks in us. So, modern human beings say: *I* think. All esotericists can see how wrong this is, when they have the experience that every time they begin their meditation, thoughts [of events] that often lie quite far back in time buzz around them, without their being able to do much about it. Only later, through practicing over a long period of time, do they manage to become master of their thoughts and at the same time feel the truth of the mantra: *Es denkt mich* [It thinks me]. Modern human beings who think materialistically are quite far from accomplishing this. Even in day-waking consciousness, unwanted thoughts and ideas almost always occupy them; these thoughts and ideas come from outside and are of a luciferic nature.

What is materialism actually? The reasons for materialism are not those that people usually give, but rather the reason is fear—fear of the nothingness that human beings find before entering the spiritual worlds. This fear slumbers unconsciously in the depths of the soul, and it drives human beings to see things only outwardly, only materially. When we live into the great cosmic thinking—of which human beings are actually only a thought—when we, in reverent awe, sense the spiritual around us, we will increasingly learn to sense the maya of luciferic thinking, the lie of the phrase, "I think." Yes, we will increasingly have the feeling that this "I think" is sucked away, as if burned, when we manage ever better to feel our way into and give ourselves totally to the divine-spiritual: *Es denkt mich* [It thinks me]. We should always, however, approach this divine-spiritual with the feeling of deepest piety.

Let us take the second phrase, "I feel." If we were conscious during sleep, we would have to say that Lucifer-Ahriman feels in us. Just as countless unwanted thoughts swarm around us, so, too, do feelings rise up in us without our knowing where they come from. Think of all the drives and desires that want to be fulfilled. But the good gods have dampened down our consciousness during sleep, and so we feel we are correct to say, "*I* feel." With the greatest gratitude toward the high beings who form us, we should devote ourselves to the second mantra: *Es webt mich* [It weaves me].

It is no different with our will impulses as it is with our thinking and feeling. In truth, we would have to say not "I will," but "Ahriman wills in me." For most of our will impulses are ruled by Ahriman. Esotericists should, with a feeling of deepest reverence, imagine that higher beings work in them and have an effect. This is expressed in the third mantra: *Es wirkt mich* [It works me].

These three mantras—*Es denkt mich*; *Es webt mich*; *Es wirkt mich* [It thinks me; It weaves me; It works me]—have high esoteric value. They can be meditated singly or together. The Masters of Wisdom and the Harmony of Feelings themselves gave these mantras and placed something quite specific into their vowel system [in the German].

Es denkt mich: two *e*'s and one *i*; *e* is always the sign of sacred awe and admiration with which we draw near to the Godhead. In contrast, the *i* means the giving of oneself, the feeling of oneself within the Godhead.

With *Es webt mich*, we have the same vowels and organization of the vowels: two *e*'s and one *i*. However, the *d*—in *denkt*—becomes a *w*—in *webt*. We must feel the difference here. There lies in the *d* a putting or placing of something, a placing or standing on one's own; the *w* points to the surging, wave-like working of the divine which we should live into entirely.

In the third mantra, *Es wirkt mich*, there is one *e* and two *i*'s. Again, the *e* means the pious awe and admiration; in contrast, the two *i*'s is the inward grasping, the feeling of oneself being within the Godhead, of being one with it.

However, we should never meditate these mantras without the specific sacred feelings being aroused: with *Es denkt mich*, the feeling of devotion; with *Es webt mich*, the feeling of gratitude; with *Es wirkt mich*, the feeling of reverence.

Let us scrutinize our Rosicrucian mantra according to its vowels. This mantra was given out of the mysteries of ancient times.

Both regulations that were strictly followed by the Essenes—not to think worldly thoughts after sundown and, before sunrise, to ask that the Sun may rise—are difficult to bring into harmony with modern scientific thinking. However, something else can take its place. Think about the first part of our Rosicrucian mantra, *Ex Deo nascimur*. Upon awakening, we come out of the spiritual worlds to enter again into the temple of the physical body, which the good gods so artfully prepared for us through the Saturn, Sun, and Moon periods. We should feel astonishment and admiration—sacred awe—about this. This is expressed in the two *e*'s —*Ex Deo*. In the *o* lies the encompassing. In the *a* in *nascimur* there is a certain fear, a pulling back. In the *i* there is again the complete devotion or the giving of oneself; and in the *u*—which is to a certain extent a repetition of the *o*—is the full joining together with the physical body and the earthly consciousness.

In the second part of the Rosicrucian mantra—of which the second word is unspeakable—let us think of the substantiality with which we unite ourselves after death. We die into Christ and receive through this death full consciousness in the spiritual worlds, the post-mortem consciousness: *In Christo morimur.* Here we have the three-times-intensified *i.* That signifies the grasping of our own inwardness and the immersing of ourselves in, and becoming one with, Christ. Then the *o u* signifies the complete encompassing and joining together with Christ.

Even if life in the physical body helps us to have earthly consciousness, and dying into the Christ substance brings post-mortem consciousness, we still do not yet have knowledge of ourselves—self-consciousness. For this the messenger of Christ, the Holy Spirit, must help us: *Per Spiritum Sanctum reviviscimus.* Here the consonants are the most important. The *p* means to place something, to place something over against something. The *s* is the going forth out of the bosom of the gods. As the *s*-sound resounded through cosmic space, the spine of the human being was created. The wave-like surging of the *s* is also the sign of Lucifer, in whose serpentine slithering the *s* is mirrored. If we manage to overcome Lucifer, we gain the spiritual force that gives us the proper self-consciousness: *Per Spiritum Sanctum reviviscimus.*[†]

Esoteric Lesson
BERLIN, APRIL 11, 1913

RECORD A

Again and again, beginning esotericists complain that they are disturbed by all kinds of thoughts invading their meditations and exercises. That should not surprise us, because thoughts are the only spiritual element of the physical plane. And when we attempt to meditate, the thoughts announce themselves. We should also not want to fight all too hard against these thoughts, as it will not do any good. The only thing we can do is to persist in exerting our will in order to return ever again to the content of our meditation. The exertion of the will is much more important than how well a meditation goes. When we return repeatedly to the content of the meditation, we push the thoughts back, and at the same time create a sphere around ourselves in which there are no thoughts that would disturb us. Precisely this sphere is the most suitable for being able to have suprasensible experiences.

Esotericists also experience that they begin to notice certain characteristics in themselves that they had never recognized before. Here again here, it is not a matter of fighting against these characteristics; there would be no method or remedy for doing so. The only thing one can do is to continue with strength to do the given exercises. These exercises are what have brought out the characteristics and have made them noticeable, and by continuing these exercises, the characteristics will disappear of their own accord.

Now perhaps you will, through your practice of the exercises, come so far as to have this or that suprasensible experience, for instance, seeing imaginations. Then, the beginners always ask whether what they saw was just imaginary or whether it was a reality in the spiritual realm. You can ask this question when you are judging according to the manner of the physical plane; this can hardly be otherwise at the beginning of the esoteric path. This question has meaning only on the physical plane. In the spiritual world, what is of importance is totally different.

Let us assume, for example, that a man—it need not be a meditant—has seen his double.† It could be that he had planned to go to a gathering or a meeting at which someone intended to poison him. Now, he enters a half-dark room and sees himself standing there. Because of the impression of this experience, he does not go into the gathering and, as a result he does not get poisoned. The form in which the experience clothed itself is not what is important. The most significant thing is that the spiritual being that accompanies the human being from incarnation to incarnation wanted to make an impression on him. Just such a being exists, which belongs to the hierarchy of the angels and is called, by various religions, the guardian angel of the human being. This being could not influence the man's thinking in such a way that he would have known through thinking: "I should not go to the meeting tonight." The angel cannot influence our thinking, because our thoughts—all except for those that arise through spiritual science—belong to the physical plane. And, for this reason, they cannot be influenced by the suprasensible.

After death—and already during sleep—we must lay aside our thoughts, with the exception of the spiritual-scientific thoughts. However, our feelings and will impulses reach far beyond, into the suprasensible realms, and therefore, an impression can be made upon them. That happens, for instance, in the seeing of the double. It can also happen, however, that people see their double, not because their angel shows it to them, but because the etheric body becomes free—even if only for a moment—and they see their physical body standing before them. It is also possible that they see their double simply because they have upset their stomach, and because of that the etheric body—perhaps only that part which serves the stomach—is freed for a moment. We must carefully differentiate between these ways of viewing the double.

It can also occur that an impression that must be made—as in the case of the attempted poisoning—is made in a different way. In one instance, a person might see the double, and in another, the person might enter a room and at the same moment, with a loud noise, a painting inexplicable falls from the wall. This corresponds approximately to the writing of a message in German one time, and in Latin another time.

Therefore, it does not make much sense to ask whether what you have seen is real or not. And a teacher of esotericism would never give an explanation for an imagination that you have had merely once, but only for one that has often repeated itself or is important for some other reason. It is just as if someone were to write BIN on the blackboard and someone else were to say: I see a vertical straight line with two little curved arches, a vertical line, and then three lines connected to each other. However, another person who had learned to read would immediately say: that is the word "bin." There is no immediate definite explanation of the imaginations; rather, you must first learn how to read them.

Or it can happen that esotericists, at the very beginning of their path, see some kinds of figures in the air [see the illustration below]. Then they would perhaps go to an eye doctor who would tell them that it was an illness of the eyes. From the standpoint of the eye doctor, that is correct; for the eye doctor, the whole belief in Theosophy is an illness. But [the figures in the air] all stem only from the fact that the etheric body is beginning to make new movements, and that these carry over once in a while to the physical body. That is why the esotericist sees these figures.

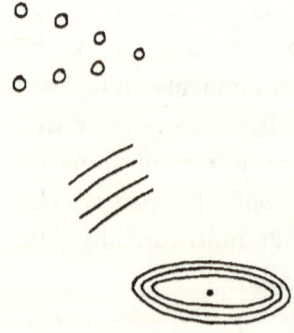

Some esotericists might say that their physical body is then damaged by the exercises, if the etheric body affects it in this way; and then esotericists are overcome by a terrible fear of every little pain and complaint. Yet there is absolutely no danger with these things; with time the etheric body itself will remove them. Also, for this, the only remedy is to calmly persevere!

Occasionally, people complain that they get a terrible headache right above the bridge of the nose and ask what to do about it. It would be best to do nothing about it, but to calmly continue with the meditations. At first the pain will get worse to the point that they feel as if their head would split open. However, first of all, their head will not split open; and secondly, it will be possible that, precisely because of this pain, they will break through the wall that separates them from the suprasensible. Only through pain and suffering can we further develop ourselves.

Often also, with the illnesses that arise, these are the karmic results of certain evolutionary conditions that you have already gone through in an earlier life and which you cannot eliminate or remove in any other way than through illness and suffering. Many times, people notice that after an illness is over they have progressed in their development. One should feel that everything that comes is karma.

* * *

RECORD B[†]

It happens again and again, that beginning esotericists come to me with an overwhelming experience of their meditation. They complain especially, as happens often, that the moment they begin their meditation, thoughts buzz around them like a swarm of bees. Memories arise that are often of a sorrowful nature, and they often lie quite far back in time.

We must be clear that all esotericists, under all circumstances, make progress. When their thoughts buzz around them, that is a sign of progress. For they must become aware of the fact that when they do their exercises and meditations, they receive more spiritual forces. Thoughts and memories are the only spiritual elements on Earth; when they press themselves upon the human being, that is a good sign.

The *what* is not the main thing in meditating, but the *how*. For this reason, we should persevere and ever again make our will active. The steadfast will is the main thing; and even when the meditation absolutely does not go well, the will is still strengthened. Precisely in such a space or sphere, out of which the swarming thoughts have been driven, is the best possibility for a manifestation or phenomenon to come out of the spiritual world.

Others come and tell me that they have experienced this or that, and ask if it is a reality or an illusion. That is difficult to answer. Naturally, it is a truth, a reality; however, one must be careful not to credit it with too much significance. This question has meaning only on the physical plane; in the spiritual world, it means nothing.

Others have complained about a strong pain just above the bridge of the nose (at the root of the nose), between the eyes, and ask what they can do for it. You see, you must simply bear it; just keep on meditating. The pain will get worse. It will feel as if your head is going to split open; but firstly, your head will not split apart, and secondly, through this you can break through the wall that separates us from the suprasensible.

Only through pain and suffering can we further develop ourselves. Often illnesses that arise are the karmic results of developmental circumstances we have gone through in an earlier life and which our soul can reject or get rid of only through illness and suffering. We often notice after such an illness is over, that we have progressed in our development. We should think of everything that comes as karma.

Even when specific characteristics appear, such as egotism, vanity, etc., we should not fight against them but simply continue meditating. We should not apply any method or remedy against them, but rather continue to exert ourselves with our exercises, because they will indeed drive such traits out of us.

Beginning esotericists often see their double. For instance, a man enters a room and suddenly finds himself standing in front of himself. Let us also imagine that he wanted on that particular evening to go to a social gathering, where he was to be poisoned. (That could, of course, be karmic.) Now, he encounters the appearance of his double, which would most likely keep him from going into the gathering.

How did that happen? Yes, you see, each of us has an angel that leads our life from one incarnation to the next; in religions, orders, or spiritual movements, it is called the guardian angel. The angel wanted to protect the man, to warn him. How was the angel to do this? The angel could not speak to the man, especially since he was not yet an esotericist his thinking was completely earthly. Only spiritual thinking is suprasensible; physical thinking is of a purely earthly nature. Feeling and willing, however, are connected with the spiritual worlds. The angel seeks therefore to make an impression on feeling and willing, and sends the man an imagination.

The double can be karmically contingent on yet something else. For instance, through a sudden shock the etheric body can be loosened, and one finds oneself facing one's own physical body. Or, a quite trivial thing can cause it. One may have upset one's stomach. The etheric body leaves that particular place, and one sees one's self.

The form in which the occurrence clothes itself is not the main thing. It can just as easily happen that someone enters a room and that at that moment, with thunder-like, deafening noise, a picture falls from the wall. It is the same situation as if one were to write a communication one time in German, and another time in Latin.

An imagination is of value only when it appears often. One person will understand it, and another will not. It is precisely as if someone would use all kinds of straight and curved lines to write the word BIN on the blackboard. For some it would be just lines; others would read the word "bin." There is no definite reading of imaginations, however.

Or, people may see small circles (as below) and not know what to make of them.

A medical doctor will think it is due to an illness of the eyes. For the doctor, belief in Theosophy is already an illness. In reality, the circles are just proof that the etheric body has begun to move and carries this movement over to the physical body. Because of this the person sees these things (the small circles).

Many people think that the physical body suffers damage through spiritual development, and therefore they fear it. Yet there is no danger present; after a period of time the etheric body itself eliminates these effects.

* * *

Record C

It is not a bad sign when all kinds of thoughts storm us during meditation, because in meditation everything becomes intensified, and, so this is quite natural. However, precisely this is of greatest importance: that we hold them at a distance. In the empty space we create around ourselves through meditation we have, through holding back what wants to storm us, the best chance to see esoteric phenomenon. Also, our strength increases because of it. The fact that our will succeeds in getting through this—no matter what happens—is of greater value than the meditation itself. It is important not to expect some other blessing or well-being, but we should continue our meditations strictly and with the deepest earnestness. This will to proceed ever further is of the greatest significance.

Many meditants asked if this or that imagination that they have had is real or not. The question should not be put in that way, because an imagination can indeed be real but that is not what matters. What is important is to grasp the meaning of what stands behind this meditation (imagination). For example, we could see our double. This imagination can come about either through our guardian angel—for instance, to keep us from going out for the evening—or it can come about because, through the exercises, the etheric body separates from the physical body for a moment. Or it can occur because the stomach is overburdened, and so the etheric stomach leaves the physical body for a moment. Thus, it is important here to develop further to the point of a sensing or feeling which is at the same time a knowing of what the imagination signifies. It can also happen that meditants see all kinds of figures, and a doctor would say that something is wrong with their eyes.

The seeing of these figures can occur because, through the exercises, the etheric body takes on other forms and therefore works differently upon the physical body.

Some meditants complain that they get a terrible headache. However, it would be best if they would not complain at all but simply persevere, even when their head appears to be about to burst. Precisely the strength and the exertion you have to apply to get through this brings you forward. After a while, such phenomena—it can also be disagreeable warmth, sound, or aromatic impressions—cease on their own. Through persevering and going through this, something is overcome, and the real experiencing of the etheric world begins. But esotericists are sometimes fearful of facing this, even though they know that fear is something that wants to come to us when we go through our training, and is precisely what we must conquer in order to become ever stronger. We know that our path upward leads through suffering and difficulties. Also, we should not forget the reality of karma. Consciousness of karma must help us to bear everything. We can, for example, become ill as a result of a development in a previous life and, through wrestling with the forces of the illness, we can reach a further stage of strength than we had attained in a previous life. The powerful force that leads us upward is perseverance, always going forward, and seeing all difficulties in the right light. Also, meditating our mantra (E.D.N. — I.C.M. — P.S.S.R.) with the right feelings will lead us onward.

* * *

Record D

Through the esoteric exercises, we will more and more come to do certain daily tasks automatically. We must, however, not lose control over them. During meditation, we must, through strength of will, attempt to push aside all the thoughts rushing in. The space freed up through this effort will afford spiritual facts the best opportunity to enter in. The experience of the double can occur early on. It can happen that we enter a dimly lit room and see a picture of our own physical body facing us. Then we must distinguish the three possible meanings of this. First, it can be a warning given to us by our guide from the hierarchy of the angels. For example, our angel might be warning us not to go to a social gathering where we would be poisoned. The experience then keeps us from going. The guide cannot send us thoughts, for thoughts belong only to the physical world. Feelings and will impulses belong to the spiritual world. Second, we may have, through our concentration exercises, loosened the etheric body so that it lifts—even if only for a moment—out of the physical body. Then we can experience our double. Third, we may have a stomachache. The etheric body departs from this part of the body, and we can see the double then also.

We must learn to know what the experiences signify; then we will not be able to say that we do not know if something is a reality or an illusion.

Esoteric Lesson

STRASSBURG, MAY 14, 1913

RECORD A

Our meditations gradually have the effect that we, in a body-free state, enter into the higher worlds and learn to know and to see there. It does not matter only *that* we enter into the higher worlds, but also *how* we enter is important. The soul attitude we have when entering the higher worlds must be a good, moral one. Now, it is so that human beings, as sense-physical beings, have first of all been abandoned by the good. They no longer sense the morality and goodness that could and should speak to them out of the All of creation. In order to give human beings freedom, Lucifer drew out the moral, so to speak. Human beings must now find it and awaken it at first in themselves, and then bring it back again to the spiritual-divine worlds.

Today, when we observe the Sun rise and set, we do not feel any moral impulse streaming to us from there. If it were not for Lucifer, we would feel streaming from the Sun forces that pulse through us in such a way that we would know and feel ourselves to be an "I." When we observe the Moon with the methods of astronomy, we know that in the time from the new Moon to the full Moon, and from the full Moon to the new Moon, constellations bringing balance hold sway. These constellations bring it about that we see at first a quarter, then a half, and then the whole surface of the Moon illuminated. We no longer feel that if the constellations were totally different ones, and if the Moon changed its position only a tiny bit, then living beings such as human beings in their physical bodies could no longer exist at all. For the forces of reproduction flow from the Moon. When we look at Mercury, our staring no longer gives us the ability to recognize that without Mercury no connection between the Sun forces and the Moon forces would take place—between the "I" forces and the forces of reproduction. In the same way, with Venus we do not feel that without its mild light all of those love relationships between people that make them so happy would not exist.

Lucifer permeated the human astral body with egotism. This was necessary for the sake of the development of the freedom and independence of the individual. However, it must not go so far that human beings become insensitive to the moral element. This has happened, however, in relation to nature; it has happened, for example, in our relationship to the elements. We should have been able to sense from air, fire, water, and earth that they exist in order to create a punitive compensation for our human sins; that in them live the elemental forces, the ill-making forces. We must and should allow these forces of illness to work themselves out in us so that they can purify us.

The same words can be both true and false, depending on who speaks them. When Lucifer says, "Nature is sin—spirit is the devil," these words are a mockery. In the sense just developed, that material nature should punish us for the sake of our sins, and that we should sense the spirit in nature as something that brings us illness and suffering, these words are true. For pain and suffering are the god-given remedies to recognize and overcome egotism. When Lucifer says, "You will be like God," it is a lie; but understood correctly, it is true. Christ says: "You are gods"—the sons of the Godhead. The human being is called to become a god.

What does modern materialism that breaks the world up into atoms—into physical matter—want, and what is it doing? It wants to make the forces of sin eternal. For matter is condensed error. Through spiritual development, matter must turn into spirit. We must wrest from nature the moral element that was laid into it by the divine cosmic wisdom. Rosicrucian wisdom foresaw this whole materialistic development. For that reason, it gave methods and showed paths to an elevated morality, without which we shall not enter into the higher worlds for salvation and blessing. We would perhaps indeed enter therein, but we would not find that Lucifer approaches us there as the guide into the knowledge of the higher worlds as he should be. He would be there as tempter who feigns all kinds of divine spirituality and shows us what is not real.

Ex Deo nascimur. Thus we should speak; and at the same time, with elevated soul, look up to the Moon as the giver of the opportunity to incarnate ever again, and to perfect ourselves in the physical body on the Earth.

In Christo morimur. Here we look up to the Sun in order to sense from there ourselves as "I"-beings, as divine-spiritual beings, through Christ, the lofty Spirit connected with the Sun.

Per Spiritum Sanctum reviviscimus. We look up to Mercury and Venus, neither of which manifest in physical representations, but reveal themselves purely spiritually. This is because the power of the spirit that trains the human being to spiritual love is distributed on these (Mercury and Venus) and the other planets (Mars, Jupiter, and Saturn).

Plato felt—like an echo—that human beings had been abandoned by the good. He felt that the good lived withdrawn, deep in the bosom of the Godhead, in controlled silence. Plato said: "God is the good."† Christ Jesus also said that the good had withdrawn from human beings: "No one is good, but God alone!"†

Thus, we want to strive unceasingly for higher morality, so that we will become able to sense the moral impulses in nature, the Sun, the Moon, and the stars, and to bring back to the spiritual world again the moral element that Lucifer had taken away for the sake of our freedom.

* * *

Record B

Two things are necessary for esotericists. First, they should devote themselves faithfully to doing their exercises; and second, they need to develop a specific fundamental attitude that I will describe. In ordinary life, no one asks upon awakening why the Sun rises again; nor does it move people when they see the progression of the phases of the Moon from full Moon to new Moon and back again, or when they see the individual planets shining in the starry heavens. People do not think they have to connect any moral significance to all of this. The moral world and the natural world are thought to be separate from one another. This brings it about that human beings really do live in a world that is abandoned by the good. For esotericists, the moral world and the natural world must be united again.

When esotericists observe the sunrise, they can never describe it as the astronomer does. They know that without the sunlight, an "I" could never live within them. The influence of the sunlight always works upon human beings; even when they are sleeping in the night, a spiritual influence goes forth from the Sun. When esotericists see the Moon, they know that if the Moon did not pass through its phases, humanity would not be able to exist; it would cease to be. If the Moon were shifted even just a little out of its path in relation to the Sun, the existing human race would wither. It would not be able to bring forth any descendents, because the Moon brings the power of reproduction. When esotericists look at Mercury they know that it unites the forces of the Moon with those of the Sun. The "I"-forces of the Sun could eternally descend, and the reproductive forces of the Moon could continue to build people, but without the uniting force of Mercury these forces would always remain separated. And from Venus streams the force of love through which the possibility for this uniting comes about.

The fact that we can no longer sense these relationships as being moral comes from the luciferic influence. We are set in a world abandoned by the good because Lucifer pulled the moral element out and separated it from the natural world. Through this, forces that make us ill came into matter—illness-bringing forces. People today have so little knowledge of things that they know the word "Kränkung" [to make or become ill] only in connection with the soul; that is, as it is used today [in the sense of one's feelings being hurt, or as in hurting someone's feelings].

The good is not to be found in this world, but only outside of it. Plato said, "God is the good." Also, Christ pointed to it when he said, "No one is good but God alone." The good gods laid evil into matter so that human beings will learn, out of freedom, to turn away from it. This may be expressed only out of a specific mood; for the meaning or significance of what was said depends on the mood out of which it was spoken. Thus, Lucifer maintained, "You will be like the gods;"[†] and Christ Jesus spoke as the highest truth, "You are gods!"[†]

Only in a special state of mind and soul may it be said that matter is nothing other than concentrated wrongfulness. Concentrated sin is matter!

Materialists think of matter as being divided into atoms, and that these atoms have an eternal existence. However, these atomic theories of the nineteenth century are based on nothing other than the wish to pull sin together into little atoms and then to make them eternal. There is also the wish not to recognize anything else besides this in the world. Goethe spoke out of deep esoteric knowledge when he said, "Nature is sin, spirit is devil."† However, he said this as a mockery, because he knew that one may not express such truths in a conventional manner.

Through the influence of Lucifer, egotism came into the astral body. As a remedy for egotism, the gods gave something that is itself also egotistical; that means, it is experienced in the "I." This remedy is pain. The gods chose this remedy in order to help human beings overcome this sin, and yet leave them free. For this reason, it is necessary that human beings develop morality before they ascend into the higher worlds. Our movement is reproached for stressing the necessity of moral development so much. You can indeed enter into the spiritual world without morality, but if you do not know Lucifer, you will see a spiritual world populated with the most beautiful figures, but which are false.

Modern science considers the human being to be made up only of matter, which is actually sin. Rosicrucianism foresaw that this would come about and therefore caused a different thought to flow into the world through the mantra: *Ex Deo nascimur*. When we consider the Moon, we can think that we are born out of the forces that are connected with the Moon. The Sun reminds us of the Sun-Spirit, of Christ, who was connected with the Sun and who gave us the force of the "I": *In Christo morimur*. And when we speak the mantra, *Per Spiritum Sanctum reviviscimus*, let us think of those beings who are connected with the five other planets, and whom we address in their totality as the Holy Spirit.

Esoteric Lesson
STUTTGART, MAY 18, 1913

RECORD A

Esotericists can progress only when they make themselves increasingly conscious of certain things. They must deeply and earnestly imbue themselves with what was discussed yesterday in the public lecture.† It must become a real experience that just as the air we inhale and have in our lungs is a part of our surrounding atmosphere, so too does the soul-spiritual in us belong to the whole soul-spiritual surroundings. Esotericists must be quite clear that waking up and going to sleep are nothing other than an inhaling and exhaling of the soul-spiritual. They must understand ever more clearly their surrounding world.

Let us assume that some people in exoteric life have no consciousness of the air surrounding them; they can perceive only the minerals, plants, solid and liquid elements, the mountains, and so forth. They might see the clouds and perceive thunder and lightning or something similar, yet are not conscious of the air between these things. This person would be like the exotericists who have the spiritual world surrounding them, but know nothing of it. First of all, in the current epoch, it is appropriate and in correspondence with this point in earthly evolution that exotericists hold the surrounding physical world to be the reality in which they should consciously work. Esotericists, however, should understand the physical world quite differently. What is this difference?

It is correct that exotericists assess physical things everywhere according to cause and effect. And today natural science is quite proud to prove cause and effect in all outer processes. For the esotericists, it should be different. When they, for example, contemplate history, it should not be thought that facts and events occur as the result or effect of something else, but rather that these physical events are only signs of spiritual occurrences. They must learn to connect these signs with each other and, through this, read them correctly. People cannot read properly when they know only the individual letters of the alphabet. Just as those who can read, combine letters in a sensible manner, and do not ask, for example, when they look at the word "but," if the letter *u* is the result of the letter *b*. So too must the individual signs of outer history, of outer events, be read in the right way. Therein lies the true nature of the esotericist: that he or she learns to do this more and more. We will consider an example of this from human life that is itself quite difficult to understand.

We know that the most essential thing in human life between birth and death is the consciousness that connects individual experiences. We are conscious of our past back as far into our childhood as memory reaches. This memory is important in our life. In abnormal cases human beings lose this consciousness. For example, a man—let us say in a city in central Europe—went to the train station and bought a ticket to another city. Upon arriving in this city, he bought a ticket to another city, and so on. He also traveled by ship, and after a time, he arrived in North Africa. But he had forgotten everything that happened from his original station of departure onward. In fact, he had forgotten his whole life from birth on. Yet, he had acted in a totally reasonable and intelligent manner all the way from buying the tickets, traveling, and arriving in Morocco—perhaps more reasonably than other people. This shows that reason and consciousness are not one and the same thing. Students in school, for example, can learn much and grasp it with their reason, and yet if their consciousness is not there, they cannot use what they have learned; it is like having a tool that they leave unused. How is it then with people—such as the man described above—who, in abnormal instances, lose the consciousness that connects everything and brings continuity?

When these cases are examined, it shows that such people already had earlier in life the characteristic of not observing outer things exactly. For modern human beings, it seems reasonable to look at things according to whether those things call forth sympathy or antipathy. Many people—like the one described above—could travel through many countries and notice everywhere only what aroused their sympathy or antipathy. That is a deficiency, for we should strengthen our "I"-consciousness precisely through observing all things and events exactly and with interest. It is quite necessary to hold this up, especially for Theosophists, because precisely Theosophists are easily inclined, through their Theosophical interests, to become one-sided and to lose interest in many physical things. Yet, they should observe all occurrences and things with interest, love, and sympathy. For the soul-spiritual in us—the soul-spiritual is inhaled out of the spiritual world into our body upon awakening—attains full self-consciousness through observing, with interest and love, outer events and beings. Esotericists should become ever more conscious of this. They should become aware that this is one important side of life: this soul-spiritual which goes out from the soul-spiritual world, enters into the physical world and ignites its self-consciousness in the physical world. Esotericists learn to know this part of their life like a letter [of the alphabet] in world events. The "I"-consciousness is like a sign or letter for the soul-spiritual core of the human being, but there is still more to it.

Today, there are a certain number of human beings on the Earth; with time, the sons and daughters of these people will come; before that, others—the parents of today's adults—were here. We know that, through this lineage, heredity takes place: heredity of the body, the abilities, and characteristics. It becomes an evermore conscious reality that the forces streaming through the hereditary lineage make up the other important side of life. At birth or conception, the soul coming out of the spiritual worlds unites with the forces of physical heredity. These [two sides of life] form two letters, and esotericists will become increasingly able not only to see the nature of these letters as single letters, but to read them together correctly.

Esotericism also gives an outer symbol—which can be drawn—for the connection between the two letters or signs. When we want to indicate, with this [symbol], the "I" entering in from out of the spiritual world, it is thus, the consciousness that forms by drawing—as if magnetically—the forces of heredity to it, and surrounding itself with them. This is represented by a circle with a point in the center.

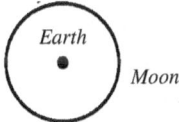

Now, this sign also really already exists in the world. The gods drew it, and we find it in the sky. If we regard the • point [in the drawing] as the Earth, the ○ circle is the path of the Moon. And thus we can see in these celestial bodies a sign written by the gods. It is a sign that the Earth is the place of the developing "I"-consciousness, while the physical orbit of the Moon and the physical Moon, which turns through all of its phases—from new Moon to first-quarter to half Moon to full Moon—is the outer sign for the forces working in heredity. Through the physical Sun directing its light onto the Earth, and through objects on the Earth raying this light back to the Sun, self-consciousness can be kindled in the human soul. Were the Sun to stop shining even for only a moment, the possibility for a self-conscious human life would cease. And without the forces of the Moon, physical heredity could not continue. If the Moon were to be pushed out of its orbit even only by a little bit, the forces that are necessary for the continuity of the physical heredity of the human being would cease to work. Human beings would still live a while longer with the forces inherent in them, but then physical reproduction would come to an end. Indeed, a time will come in the future when the forces of the Earth become so strong that the Earth will again take the Moon into itself. Then the forces that now work from the Moon and bring forth heredity will no longer exist. The human being will cease to be a propagator [of offspring], and the human race will come to an end.

All of this must become ever more a reality for esotericists. They must learn to understand correctly the •[point] within the ○ [circle] in the manner described.

Just as when people—when they can read—write the word "up," they do not write the *p* and the *u* in just any manner, but the *u* and then the *p*; so is it also with the signs of the point and the circle. Esotericists put them together correctly, and they can then read the symbol for their nature, in which the soul-spiritual becomes conscious through union with the forces of heredity.

Yet there are still other forces acting in order to bring about the life of the human being the way it is. If we go back in the history of humanity to the ancient time of the Egyptians and Persians, we see how human beings everywhere progress through their thinking. Human beings have had to contribute to the process of development through their thinking by living on Earth as beings with reasoning ability. But these other forces do not come from human beings themselves. Such a thought can be believed only by a science that would so gladly talk people into its fantasies. These forces do not come from the Moon either. They come from regions that reach beyond the orbit of the Moon, and so we must represent this with the second circle in our drawing. And we find this also placed in the cosmos by the gods. This second circle is the apparent orbit of Mercury (the Venus of today).† In the spiritual forces that have Mercury as their physical expression, we can see what bestows reason upon the human being.

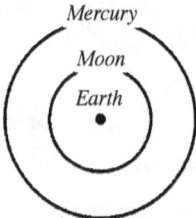

Esotericists must learn to understand this. While in ordinary life, they look only outwardly at the Moon and Mercury, they should not merely try to grasp this Mercury with their intellects, but should see in it the outer sign for spiritual forces through which human beings are given the power of reason. They should look up to the planet with feelings of awe and gratitude. Were the forces of Mercury to cease, human beings would have consciousness on Earth, but they would have no reasoning power. Yet, even this is not all of it. Still other forces must be added to bring about the life and development of the human being. If only reason or intellect had worked in previous epochs of humanity, no progress would have occurred. Human beings would have indeed thought, but no new thoughts would have entered into evolution. In truth, we see that new ideas are always flowing into humanity. Today, children in school learn things that were unknown to the human being at the time of Pythagoras. Without such new thoughts, all the inventions and progress would not have been possible. From where do these thoughts come? They come from a yet higher sphere, which we represent with a further circle: the apparent orbit of Venus (today's Mercury). Venus is the physical expression for the spiritual forces that fructify the human reasoning or intellect with new ideas that go beyond the ordinary brain-thinking.

There are still further forces which, although they do not directly work upon the Earth and human beings, work indirectly by raying upon Venus. These are the Mars forces. In order that these Mars forces do not work in a war-like manner when they radiate onto Venus, and through Venus indirectly onto Earth, there streams onto Mars a lofty divine force out of the surroundings of Jupiter. This force is not easy to describe in words. It can be described as a spiritual light that cannot be physically perceived. Human beings can, however, experience this light inwardly as the force of love when they look up in awe and gratitude to this cosmic being [Jupiter], and become conscious of the grace that streams down upon them from there. The love-light-forces working upon Mars prevent the Mars forces from working in a war-like, combative fashion upon Venus and the Earth.

And finally, from the yet higher sphere of Saturn come forces of which we can form a concept if we think of the warmth of enthusiasm. These warmth forces stream onto Jupiter and unite with its light. Now, we must draw here between Venus and Mars the path or sphere of the Sun (see drawing on following page). We then have the three orbits of Moon, Mercury, and Venus between the Sun and the Earth; they are the forces that work directly [upon the Earth]. The three on the outside—Mars, Jupiter, and Saturn—work only indirectly through Venus upon the Earth.

From the spiritual Sun forces, human beings receive the "I"-force—the consciousness of self that unites with the Moon forces, and so on—in order to bring about the whole being of the human being.

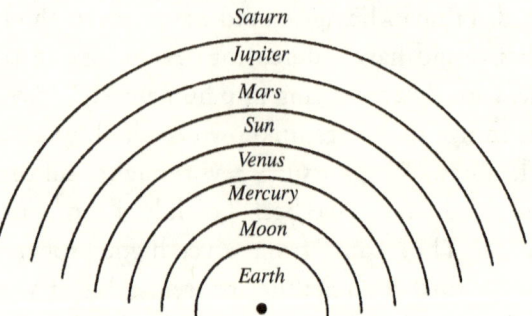

First of all, there are two Suns: the spiritual Sun that gives us the "I," and the physical Sun that enlivens the physical Earth through its rays of light and warmth. Then we must grasp a third Sun,† namely the mediator of the highest spiritual forces, which unites the outer Sun forces with the inner Sun forces, and which sends its forces of grace onto the Earth, and has ever since the Mystery of Golgotha took place. This spiritual Sun is the Christ principle: it is what human beings can experience within themselves when they truly comprehend the statement of Paul: "Not I, but Christ in me."†

This third Sun was always revealed to the candidate for initiation in the centers of Christian initiation. It was a great tragedy that Julian the Apostate,† who knew about this third Sun, could not inwardly experience it completely.

Thus, we have this sphere of the threefold Sun, and outside of it are the three circles that represent the forces which work indirectly upon the Earth. Inside of the Sun circle are the three circles of the forces that work directly upon the Earth. In each of these seven circles, there stands one of the seven heavenly bodies, or planets. Thus, we can also see our Rose Cross with its seven roses as a symbol of this sevenfold heavenly rose.†

The being of humankind is born from out of what streams onto Earth from the three inside spheres: *Ex Deo nascimur*. The three outside circles denote the high, spiritual forces through which our higher nature is founded: *Per Spiritum Sanctum reviviscimus*. The connection between the two is formed by the middle half-circle, this sphere of the Sun—the physical, spiritual, and Christ-Sun: *In – – – morimur*.

* * *

Record B

When esotericists want to make progress, it is good to work with a statement such as: "As the lungs inhale the air, so too the physical and the etheric bodies breathe in the spirit upon awakening." They should make its full meaning clear and contemplate it meditatively. In our materialistic age only what can be perceived with the outer senses is counted as real. However, just as this age can deny the spirit, so too could someone deny the existence of air because it is sensed with the finer senses. Esotericists should accustom themselves to look at outer occurrences only as letters, as signs of a cosmic word. Esotericists would not ask, concerning the word "but," whether or not the *u* is the result of *b*; rather, they know that these letters have to be put together in this way to form the word. Thus, esotericists should not concern themselves so much about cause and effect, but should tell themselves that the things and events are necessary to form cosmic words.

Exotericists (those who occupy themselves only with outer things) are inclined to consider everything only according to sympathy and antipathy. They are prepared to very quickly pay attention only to what they like and, when possible, to ignore the other. A special kind of mental illness that can be observed: A totally normal-acting man begins to travel from place to place, but finally upon arrival at some distant place, it is as if he suddenly awakens. Upon reflection, he finds that he cannot remember anything that has happened since he departed on the trip. When we examine the past of such a person, we can find that already earlier he passed by many things of this world without having any interest in them. Through this, he weakened his "I" to a great degree. It is a weakness, almost like a temporary loss of the "I."

Theosophists are also often inclined to turn themselves away from the outer world. However, if we want to make progress, a loving interest in our surroundings is absolutely necessary. We do not have to neglect what we are striving for theosophically in order to have this [interest in the outer world].

Thus, the "I" takes hold of and grasps itself in our memory. High beings have given us the "I" and memory. The "I" grasping itself in the memory is like a letter that esotericists must learn, and which the gods have written in cosmic space. The high beings who bring the "I" have their dwelling on the Sun; they give us what goes from incarnation to incarnation. We received our physical bodies from forces that work down through the generations, and these forces work upon us from a circle inscribed by the Moon orbit. What goes thus from generation to generation is like a second letter. We can draw this schematically. We will draw the "I," which becomes conscious in the memory as a point. Around this we draw a circle as the orbit of the Moon. What would happen to the Earth if the Moon were pushed, through some force, to another place? The forces of reproduction working through the generations would dry up. Humanity would not be able to reproduce, and would thus die out. True esotericists must therefore look up, full of reverent gratitude, to the beings who influence them through the Moon forces. They must tell themselves that they have these beings to thank for their development through the generations. When, as is supposed to happen in the future, the force of attraction of the Earth becomes so great that the Moon is pulled into it, humanity will arrive at the end of its physical evolution.

From the Sun, we receive the forces that strengthen our "I." We should not just passively observe the Sun, but allow the thought to arise: Oh, you magnificent cosmic body! Through you—through your Sun forces of grace—I received my "I" and all the forces that are connected with it. In all-filled reverence, I thank you!

We can draw the Sun forces as a second circle.

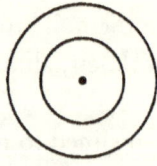

In order for both what comes out of generations and what comes out of the sequence of incarnations to come together, forces that live above the Sun sphere must work: the Mercury forces. Through them we received our intellect, which is bound to the brain. When we look in the direction of Mercury, and in general, when we use our power of reasoning, we should feel gratitude toward these beings who have given the intellect to us.

Yet there is something still higher than the mere intellect. Evolution would not have been able to progress, but would have remained at the same point, if ever new, creative thoughts had not flowed into it. Children in school today learn things that the Pythagoreans, in all their wisdom, did not know. And these new thoughts flow in continually from a sphere above Mercury: from Venus. Through Venus creative thoughts flow into evolution that manifest, for example, in inventions. Only through this is progress possible. This kind of thinking does not go through the intellect, as it is not bound to the brain; rather, it is lighter and more related to feeling.

Above the sphere of Venus are lofty forces that do not work directly upon humanity. They work through and fructify the Venus forces. These are the Mars forces. In order that these Mars forces, in their collaboration with Venus, do not have a war-like effect, there streams in from a still further surrounding—the sphere of Jupiter—a lofty, divine light-force, which is imperceptible and is seen as darkness by ordinary human beings. Esotericists, however, can attain a sense for it when they look up in gratitude to the elevated cosmic beings who let their grace stream down upon us. We then sense this inner, spiritual light, which we can grasp only inwardly. When we concentrate on yet further heights, we can sense the warmth of the beings of the Saturn sphere, which allow their warmth to stream down through the other spheres.

Between the collaboration of Mars and Venus is the Sun circle of the third Sun. All of the Mysteries have talked about this third Sun. The first [Sun] is the creative physical one that sends us its warming rays. The second stands behind the physical Sun and is the spiritual Sun which bestows the "I" upon us. The third Sun is the high bearer of the Christ principle: the Christ who grants us, with his Sun forces of grace, the higher "I." Since the time of the Mystery of Golgotha, a connection goes from this third Sun to the Earth. It is the Sun of which Paul spoke: "Not I, but Christ in me." It is the

Christ, whom every human being can receive since [the Mystery of Golgotha]. This third Sun became manifest to the candidate during the Christian initiation. The tragic fate of Julian the Apostate is that he knew of the third Sun and could not identify it with Christ.

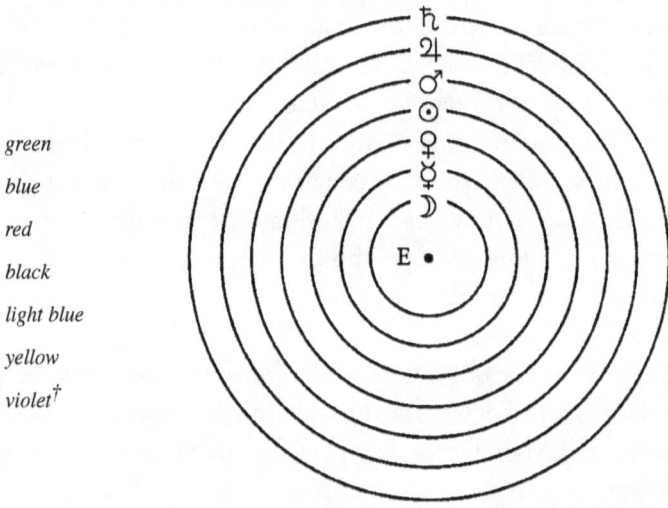

We should remember these seven spheres when we contemplate the seven roses of our Rose Cross; they are the symbol for these seven spheres. Through the Christ-circle, the effects of the spheres are divided into two parts: a part underneath consisting of four circles of forces that work from below, and a spiritual part above, made up of three circles of forces that work indirectly. For the spiritual upper part, the mantra is valid: *Per Spiritum Sanctum reviviscimus*—In the spirit we will be reborn. For the part underneath: *Ex Deo nascimur*—. Christ is the connection between the two: *In – – – morimur*.

* * *

Record C

Esotericists are able to attain something in their spiritual development only if they earnestly, truthfully, and constantly attempt to sense themselves in the physical world as soul-spiritual beings from a soul-spiritual world. It was already explained yesterday in the public lecture how we should sense the condition of going to sleep as the exhaling and the condition of awakening as the inhaling of spiritual nature, just as we inhale and exhale the air that surrounds us. Esotericists must be able to sense such things. They must differentiate themselves from the exotericists in their feelings.

Modern people look at animals, plants, minerals, the Sun and stars, seeking to discover the cause of all the manifestations in their surroundings. This is in a certain sense justified and necessary for our age. However, esotericists must manage not only to recognize the outer lawfulness of all things, but when they look around at the animals, plants, minerals, and the Sun and stars, they must see in all these manifestations the expression of the spirit standing behind them. They must come to be able to read the words that are put together out of individual letters and written in the heavenly space, the same way that we create a word by putting letters together and thereby give the word its meaning. Esoteric script signs are to be found everywhere in cosmic space; they have only to be deciphered.

Let us consider such an esoteric script sign. We must first of all regard the human being as a conscious "I," established in a "self." All human beings possess the ability to remember back to a certain point. This occurs because they are conscious of their "I." There is, however, a state of illness in which the "I"-consciousness is lost. It has happened that, for instance, a man buys a train ticket to a station of his choice while he is still in a quite normal condition. Then he travels from station to station, and suddenly only comes to himself again, finds himself again, at some place in Africa. Such a person has actually lost his "I" for a time. Through spiritual-scientific methods, this can be seen very clearly. The activity of the intellect is not turned off or lost, but the "I"-consciousness, the essential part of the "I," is lost. Such people are traveling from city to city, often in a more practical manner than other people.

We strengthen "I"-consciousness when we bring interest to all things that confront us in the outer world. Many Theosophists, for instance, become one-sided in their striving. But that is not correct. We may not become indifferent toward the things and facts around us; we should take everything in. Many people feel sympathy or antipathy immediately with everything they see. They say immediately: I like this, but not that. And what they don't like, they don't pay attention to. When this happens with only the intellect, it is less dangerous. Then it remains objective. Through feelings, however, things becomes subjectively colored. We should look at and pay attention to everything—which includes what we don't like or find interesting. Through this the "I"-consciousness is increasingly strengthened.

Let us imagine that this "I" established itself as this point in cosmic space: ●. In order for such an "I" to experience itself and become active in the physical body, forces must be involved. These forces can be imagined as the ○ circle around the point ⊙. The great cosmic spirit had already placed this script sign in cosmic space many long ages ago. This sign is the Earth with the Moon. From the Moon rays forth to human beings the forces of reproduction and the heredity that goes from generation to generation. The Moon moves in a quite specific path around the Earth; its phases are first quarter, second quarter, third-quarter, full Moon, and new Moon. If this sequence were interrupted even once with the Moon torn from its orbit, the human race would soon perish. When the Earth comes to the end of its evolutionary course and exerts too strong a force of attraction, it will pull the Moon into itself again, and human beings [as physical beings] will perish. Thus we look, full of gratitude, at the Moon which sends its forces of generation into the evolution of humanity. We must see in the way the Moon moves around the Earth a sign from the esoteric script that was placed in cosmic space by lofty beings, as the lowest expression of their high working.

The Moon and Earth are shone upon by the Sun that rays into our inner being, in which the human "I" is reflected. And when we look up to the Sun, we must say: Oh, you heavenly star in the firmament that sends your rays into the inner being of the human being and rays back the innermost being, the "I," of the human being.

And still other forces stream to us from the heavenly bodies. The forces of the intellect flow into the development of humanity from Mercury. When we search further, we must ask where the forces come from that give the intellect what we call the progress of the human race. How many thoughts have flowed, as inventions, into the various epochs right up to ours! Children in school are taught now what could not be taught before the Greek-Latin epoch: the Pythagorean theorem.† These forces, which weave and work slowly into the human intellect and which come to expression in the inventions of all the epochs, come from Venus. They flow, bestowing strength and creativity, into the forces of Mars. In order to guide these Mars forces into the right paths, as it were, so that not just the creative intellect would reign, Jupiter sends loving streams down to us out of yet higher worlds. And when love intensifies more and more in the human soul, this love becomes warmth that flows down to us from Saturn. Between Mars and Venus is the Sun, yet not just one Sun but a threefold Sun: a physical Sun; a spiritual Sun behind the physical; and a still more spiritual Sun that we call the Christ.

Thus we see seven heavenly bodies in space. They are the seven roses of celestial space such as we see in our symbol of the Rose Cross; and as an eighth, so to speak, the threefold Sun.

The mantras that were given in the last lessons here (February 17-20, 1913) can be meditated in the sense of what was said here today, and with the feelings connected with them. The task of all esotericists must be to grasp more and more this spiritual Sun, Christ, and to awaken him and sense him ever more strongly within themselves. There was an initiate in the time after Christ who could not raise himself up to this Christ or grasp him, which laid the basis of his tragic end. This was Julian the Apostate. Thus, through meditative contemplation of what was given in this lesson, we must come more and more to understand the words of our Rosicrucian mantras: *Ex Deo nascimur—In Christo morimur—Per Spiritum Sanctum reviviscimus*. And we must also come to an ever-increasing understanding of the mantra that was given to us by the Masters of Wisdom and the Harmony of Feelings, and which we hear at the end of every esoteric lesson:

> *In the spirit lay the germ of my body.*
> *And the spirit has imprinted in my body. . . .*

Lead   — Beech   — Saturn
Gold   — Ash — Sun
Silver — Cherry   — Moon
Iron   — Oak — Mars
Mercury — Elm — Mercury
(Quicksilver)
Tin   — Maple   — Jupiter
Copper — Birch   — Venus

Moon   — Wisdom
Mercury — Receptivity for the divine
Venus   — Religiosity; Morality
Sun   — Love
Mars   — Willingness to fight; Resistance capability
Jupiter — [Indication missing]
Saturn — Willingness to sacrifice

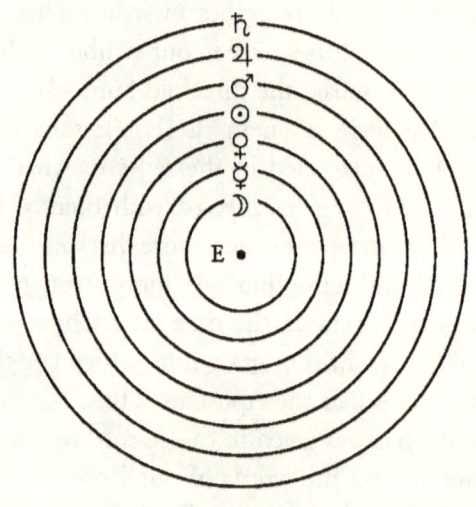

* * *

RECORD D

Esotericists should take into themselves with deep earnestness everything that is said. Also, what was said yesterday in the public lecture ["Life Questions and the Riddles of Death"] has deep meaning and significance. The example given there should be thought through deeply by esotericists. This was the example that just as people inhale the air that surrounds the whole Earth, so too they inhale the soul-spiritual—which surrounds us in exactly the same way as the air—upon awakening, and exhale it when going to sleep. The people who are connected only with the exoteric part of life ask about cause and effect for everything. All of modern science is based on this. Our age is proud of being as exoteric as possible and of relating everything to cause and effect. Esotericists, however, should act differently. They should not ask about the cause or the effect of manifestations, but about their meaning and what they represent in the entire cosmos. For esotericists, everything becomes a sign, letters, words. Just as we would not ask, upon seeing or hearing the word "but," whether the *u* is the effect of *b*, so too we would actually not be able to do that with other manifestations. Esotericists are esotericists because they regard things as letters of a script that they must seek to combine into a whole.

Thus, esotericists can have two experiences that are signs for them of something else. One [experience] is that we are aware that we experience ourselves as soul because from a certain point in our life we can recall or have memories; we can sense ourselves as "I." If this memory were to be blotted out, as can occur, we would be obliterated as an "I," as soul. It can happen that a man, for instance, buys a ticket to a city in central Europe. While on the trip his memory of himself is wiped out. In spite of this, such a person can keep traveling, and perhaps can even act in a much more sensible manner than in normal life. He travels farther and farther, until he finds himself again, for example, in a place in North Africa. A letter in the cosmic word that this soul represents has been lost, as it were. And when we investigate such people to see what else is lacking in this [cosmic] word, we usually find that they already had, in their normal life, a lack of interest. Esotericists should develop interest in everything in their surroundings and in everything that happens around them. They should not remain just at the point of what they like and don't like; that is, with only sympathy and antipathy. This standpoint is not so dangerous when we are judging only with the intellect, but it becomes dangerous when the feelings are involved.

The other experience is that we feel ourselves as human beings in a line of generations. Before our generation were those of our parents, our grandparents, etc., and after us come those of our children, grandchildren, and so on. We have this stream of generations to thank for our bodies. If we take these two thoughts together, we can draw the symbol below. The point in the center is our "I," and the ring around the point symbolizes that from which the effect of the generation proceeds and gives us our bodies.

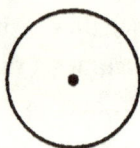

The gods have written this sign for us, and we can see it when we contemplate the Earth with its Moon circling it. For the "I," we look up to the Sun and know that, without the Sun there could never be an "I" in the human being, just as without the Moon or with a displacement of the Moon, the human race would have to waste away.

And when we lift ourselves to Mercury—in the sense of the spiritual hierarchies; that means, taken esoterically—we see in it what made the earthly development possible by giving human beings thinking. Without this, human beings, though having a body and an "I," could not do anything. Yet, through thinking alone, nothing new could come about in evolution; there could be no progress. In order for progress to occur, discoveries, new thoughts, are necessary. We have Venus to thank that new thoughts and discoveries exist. Today's school children already learn what was earlier the only deepest wisdom, for example, the theorem of Pythagoras. Therein lies progress.

Let us go beyond the effect of the Sun to what comes from Mars. The Mars forces combining with Venus make new, creative thoughts possible. Mars gives us inspirations for the progress of humanity. That these Mars forces in their connection with Venus do not lead to war-like consequences is due to Jupiter. Those who live into the Jupiter forces feel themselves in a sphere of light that bestows wisdom upon them. And when they steep themselves in this light, they can distinguish cold rays and warm rays within it. That is what proceeds from Saturn.

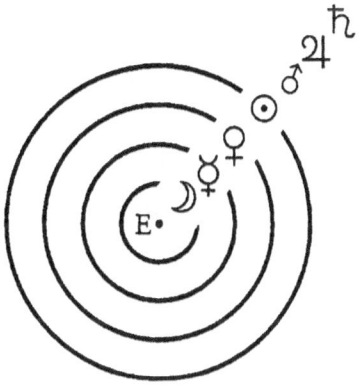

Between the series of Moon, Mercury, Venus and the series of Mars, Jupiter, and Saturn stands the Sun and its working. The planets underneath work directly upon the human being and Earth conditions. Those above work indirectly. Mars works by uniting with Venus and through this gives the inspiration that makes it possible for humanity to proceed further. Jupiter works like a grace, influencing the Mars forces in such a way that they do not become combative. And Saturn gives enthusiasm.

The Sun stands in the middle between these two series of planets and has a double, indeed a triple, nature. It is a secret of esotericism that there are three Suns. The first is the Sun that brings the light that makes visible the physical objects on Earth. And in this light is something spiritual that comes from the second Sun, which bestows upon us the "I," through which we have memory, so that we can have a self-contained soul life. Behind this lies something still more spiritual. This is the third Sun. The third Sun is the Sun Spirit, Christ. He gives the possibility for the "I"—which merely exists through the memory—to go from incarnation to incarnation and to attain eternal life. This third Sun has been united with the Earth ever since the Mystery of Golgotha took place. Rosicrucianism has preserved the knowledge of this. Julian the Apostate had a presentiment of the three Suns. That he could not find the spiritual Sun—the third Sun—the Christ, became his undoing.

Let us take—as is right—the Moon and Earth together as a unit; or let us not count the Earth. Then we have in the seven planets the seven light-roses which Rosicrucianism places before us. And with the Moon, Sun, and the other planets is connected the three-part Rosicrucian mantra:

Ex Deo nascimur
In Christo morimur
Per Spiritum Sanctum reviviscimus

From God we are born
In Christ we die
In the Holy Spirit we come to life again

* * *

RECORD E

Esoteric sign: ☉ Fore-boundary with lotus flower.

Everything around us is the outer expression of the spiritual, which stands behind it. Esotericists must come to be able to read the word that is made up of individual letters and written into the celestial space. They must learn to read this spiritual script. Esoteric script-signs are everywhere to be found in space, and esotericists have the task to decipher them. Such an esoteric script-sowing that has the most manifold and greatest meaning is 0. If we want to decipher its meaning, we must contemplate the human being as a self-contained being, inwardly conscious of his or her own self as "I." All human beings have the capability of remembering back to a certain point in their life. This occurs because they are conscious of their "I" in the normal way. There is, however, a condition of illness in which the human being loses this "I"-consciousness. Such people act apparently quite reasonably. They can take a trip in a practical manner, for instance, but without purpose or goal, and they know nothing concerning themselves—often not even their name. The activity of the intellect is not wiped out, but the consciousness of the "I" is. It comes to them again suddenly. We can strengthen our "I"-consciousness if we bring a loving interest to all things that confront us in the outer world. Never may we become one-sided or indifferent toward the things, facts, and people all around us. We should take things in without immediately feeling sympathy or antipathy toward them. We should not immediately say that we like this and dislike that, and so, not pay attention to the latter. We should seek to understand everything without our subjective feelings, even everything we do not like. Through this, the "I" will be strengthened more and more.

Let us imagine this "I," established in itself, as a point • in space. The "I" is such a point. So that the "I" can experience itself in a body, forces must enter in. Let us imagine this as a circle ○ around the point ⊙. Already long ages ago, the great cosmic Spirit placed this script-sign in space representing the Earth with the Moon. From the Moon the forces of reproduction, heredity—everything that goes from generation to generation—radiate to human beings. The Moon moves in a quite definite path around the Earth. This path shows itself as a first-quarter, second-quarter, third-quarter, full Moon, etc. If this course were interrupted, the Moon torn from its path just once, the human race would have to go under. At the end of Earth's course, when the Earth will exert too great a force of attraction, it will again take the Moon into itself, and the human beings, as physical beings, must go under.

Thus we look, filled with gratitude, upon the Moon that sends its forces as forces of gravity into the evolution of humanity. We see in it a sign from the esoteric script that the lofty beings have placed into space. This script is the lowest expression of their high working.

The Moon and Earth, however, must be shone upon by the Sun. The Sun radiates into the depths of the human being, and in these depths it reflects the human "I." When we look up to the Sun, we must say: You magnificent heavenly body in the firmament, we thank you that you send your rays into the inner being of the human and that you reflect back this inner being—the "I" of the human being.

And still other forces stream to us from the celestial bodies. From Mercury the forces of the intellect and reason flow into the evolution of humanity. When we seek further, we must ask where the forces come from that give the intellect what we call the progress of the human race. How many thoughts have flowed, as inventions, into all the various epochs right up to our own! School children now learn what could not be taught during the Greek-Latin epoch: the Pythagorean theorem. These forces, which slowly work into the human intellect and drive human beings to discoveries, come from Venus. And these forces are intensified in creative inspiration by forces from Mars. In order to direct these Mars forces in the right way so that not just the creative intellect operates, Jupiter sends loving streams down, out of still higher worlds. And when the love intensifies more and more within the human soul, this love will become warmth which then flows down to us from Saturn.

There we see the seven roses of celestial space, and in their midst the eighth rose: the threefold Sun. For there is not just the one Sun that we perceive physically. Behind that Sun stands the spiritual Sun of which the physical Sun is only the outer garment. And behind this spiritual Sun is a Sun that is yet more spiritual, and which we call Christ. The task of the esotericists of the Rose Cross must be to understand ever more deeply this spiritual Sun, the Christ, and to awaken him ever more strongly within themselves.

There was an initiate in the Christian era who could not reach up to the most spiritual Sun, the third Sun, to Christ. He could not grasp the Christ being, and this led to his tragic end. That was Julian the Apostate.

☉ human-"I"   ☉ Moon   ☉ Sun
and its sheaths   and Earth   and "I"

☉ the seven celestial roses with the eighth.

Moon: Wisdom — Silver — Cherry tree
Mercury: Receptivity for the divine — Quicksilver — Elm
Sun: Love — Gold — Ash
Venus: Religiosity; Morality — Copper — Birch
Mars: Willingness to fight; Resistance capability — Iron — Oak
Jupiter: .... — Tin — Maple
Saturn: Willingness to sacrifice — Lead — Beech

RECORD F

Introduction concerning inhaling and exhaling:
Awakening: inhaling the soul-spiritual.
Going to sleep: exhaling the soul-spiritual.

Exotericists recognize everything as cause and effect. For the esotericists, it is like reading in a script of the divine-spiritual. Thus, esotericists must learn to differentiate between the inner core of the human being and what is in this core as the spiritual. This is the twofold inheritance: The one is what develops itself from generation to generation and reproduces; the other is the spiritual which moves through it. The germ or core of the human being that is clothed in, or surrounded by, what is inherited from the fathers, can be expressed in "letters" in this script. The germ: a point with a circle around it. [...]

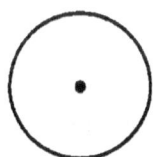

Esoteric Lesson
HELSINGFORS (HELSINKI), JUNE 1, 1913

In our esoteric lessons we must raise ourselves up to the divine beings around us. Because we esotericists know that many levels separate us from the divine beings who are spoken about in the outer life in such a thoughtless manner, let us turn to the gods who stand between us and the highest spiritual regions. These are the gods of the days. Thus, let us consciously experience time; let us experience the reign of the various gods over their respective days. [Here apparently the prayer to the spirit of the day—Sunday—was spoken.]

Much of what is in ordinary life must become different for us as esotericists. We must begin to feel ourselves as living in the great sea of the soul-spiritual around us. We must know that, just as we are one physically with the surrounding world through the common air that we inhale, so too are we embedded soul-spiritually in the spiritual world all around us. Upon awakening in the morning we inhale, in a long pull of the breath, the spirit that we ourselves are. Upon going to sleep we exhale [our spirit] again into the spiritual world. Everything around us becomes different. As esotericists, when we see the sunlight we no longer see just the physical Sun. We know that without the sunlight, we could not feel ourselves as an "I." We know that the sunlight also contains the force which brings about the "I." And when we look at the Moon with its changing form (in the phases), we know that connected with it is the force that enables us to have offspring. The life that goes through the generations is connected with the Moon. We can see this everywhere in symbols. We see the Sun rise and set. We see the four phases of the Moon, and the symbol with the four roses, which can be a symbol for us of the Sun "I"-force and the Moon reproduction force (regeneration force).

However, in addition, we must learn to read and not just stare blankly at things. Then we see in Mercury the messenger, and we know that through its force, our "I" is brought into connection with the force of reproduction—that the messenger, the esoteric Mercury, produces the union. Thus, thinking about the sphere out of which we come every morning, but also at every birth, we can feel with reverence the following mantra sounding in us: E.D.N. And then we know that, behind the physical Sun, and the "I"-engendering Sun, there is yet a third Sun. This is the Christ-force with which we unite ourselves: I.C.M. We may then allow to follow, full of hope, the mantra: P.S.S.R.

Esoteric Lesson

HELSINGFORS (HELSINKI), JUNE 5, 1913

One of the complaints of esotericists is that they are bombarded by thoughts during meditation, but that is natural. Those are luciferic and ahrimanic beings whom we did not notice before, but who become noticeable precisely through meditation. It does not help to not see Lucifer and Ahriman. To say that the thoughts which inundate us are not there would be just as foolish as to say that someone we feel in a dark room is not there because we cannot see him or her.

We must not fight against such thoughts. That would be like trying to fight against a swarm of bees. Precisely through calm, still continuation of our meditation, they will have to leave us of their own accord. With many things we must learn to think differently. Our meditation does not actually depend on the amount of time involved, but rather on the intensity, on the complete interest in the content of the meditation.

The events in Adyar† caused us much pointless, useless thinking, and many of our Theosophical friends were obliged—because they had to give time [to the situation]—to think useless thoughts, instead of being able to dedicate themselves to spiritual progress. There are forces at work that want to harm us, but because they do not have many possibilities to attack us in the realm of pure esotericism—where truth and purity are strongly maintained—they try now to hinder us and harm us by causing us to use our forces on useless writings, when we could make better use of our time in other ways.

Esoteric Lesson
STOCKHOLM, JUNE 8, 1913

It is not comfortable to become an esotericist, and as strange as it may sound, it would not be possible to become an esotericist if it were comfortable.

One of the things esotericists need the most is to follow the ancient Greek word of wisdom: "Know yourself!" It sounds odd, but it is true; human beings basically know everything else on the physical plane better than they know themselves. Self-knowledge is so difficult because those who begin to practice it soon make discoveries that are unpleasant to them. Then they would rather leave it alone and not go into it.

We should, however, also practice a self-knowledge of the human being in general. When we do this, we soon make three discoveries. These consist of the facts that human beings, as they are in their physical incarnation, first, do not want to acknowledge the spirit but deny it; second, they want to run away from the spirit, in fact, they fear it; and third, in the depths of their soul they do not even love the spirit.

People do not want to acknowledge the spirit when it approaches them on the physical plane in its true form. For example, when people see a rose, they will say that they have formed an idea of the rose, but they will believe that this idea comes from the outer world. That is a non-knowing, a not-recognizing the spirit; for in reality, our ideas and thoughts do not come from the outer world but are bestowed upon us directly from the spiritual world. When people hear this, they say: no, I will not accept the spirit in this form! Actually, however, they basically do not want the spirit at all, but would rather run as far away from it as possible.

Let us assume that an advertisement is posted to announce two lectures. One lecture is announced as a Theosophical topic in which people know up front that they will have to think along with what is said, that they will have to work with their mind. The other lecture is one with slides. Where will the most people tend to go?

With the lecture with slides, they do not have to direct their attention themselves; rather, it is compelled by the slides to stay with the objects. However, it is precisely this compelling element that brings it about that we ourselves are not the ones who think, but rather it is Ahriman who thinks. With the Theosophical lecture, everyone is invited to be "present." With a lecture with slides, Ahriman is invited to think for human beings.

The greatest conjurers of the spirits are the materialists. Every materialistic gathering is nothing other than a conjuring of Ahriman, because people, in the depths of their souls, fear the spirit. People run from the spirit because they cannot love it. It is still fortunate today that there are individuals who feel instinctively that they should get involved with what Theosophy has to give and who thus come to the spirit. Out of the usual tendencies of people in physical existence, no one would reach the spirit. And also, human beings do not love the spirit.

What is love actually? When clairvoyants research this, they can come to bitter experiences, as long as they do not contemplate or consider these experiences in the light of the yet greater whole. Let us assume that two people are born who, through their karma, are required to love one another in this life. Then, a clairvoyant can often observe that, before birth these two people hated one another in the spiritual world. Or, a mother has a child that she, according to the wise arrangement of the world order, rears with love. Yet, before the mother was born, she had perhaps hated the child. Here we come to an area where the wise cosmic guidance has acted with special wisdom.

What unites people in "love" is, namely, by far in most cases, egotism. We love the other person because we feel it to be pleasant to be near the loved one. The good gods had to use egotism in order to train human beings in love. Without using the means of egotism—which is often where luciferic influence occurs—no one could be brought to work out karmic connections through love relationships. A mother would not even want to bring the child who is connected with her karmically into the world. Thus, in this world, everything is really reversed. Love is given by Lucifer and

Ahriman, and egotism is given by the progressive gods so that, through the ennoblement of egotism, human beings can achieve true love.

This is said in order to point out the following. Beginning esotericists often complain about the thoughts that inundate them during their meditations. It is actually a sign of progress that they sense these thoughts. It proves that they no longer have Lucifer and Ahriman within themselves, but that they are beginning to perceive Lucifer and Ahriman as powers outside of themselves; for such thoughts that are rising up come totally from Lucifer and Ahriman. If everything had remained as originally intended, then human beings would never have been able, after the luciferic temptation, to forget their thoughts. They would always have had access to the akashic chronicle, but it would have been Lucifer and Ahriman who would have written this chronicle for them. For this reason, the good gods had to arrange that human beings can forget their thoughts.

Everything that sinks into unconsciousness is dead, however, Lucifer and Ahriman consume it all. They make it into a part of their being, and then as luciferic and ahrimanic nature, it comes out again during our meditations. The moment we set about to meditate, there arises in Lucifer the hope: perhaps I will conquer the world yet! Then Lucifer storms us with our discarded thoughts. People actually love going from thought to thought. What they don't like is contemplation, remaining inwardly filled with a thought content.

Observe how long non-esotericists will carry out an intention when they have made this resolution in freedom (with esotericists there is a certain self-imposed compulsion—for instance, like the Essene pupils who thank the Sun every morning for rising). How few will manage to do it for more than a few days!

In reality, human beings do not love the spirit at all. They must force themselves to hold definite thoughts in their soul for a longer time. In truth, it is actually Lucifer and Ahriman that human beings love. As protection against this, we have our Rosicrucian mantra:

Ex Deo nascimur
In Christo morimur
Per Spiritum Sanctum reviviscimus.

From God we are born
In Christ we die
Through the Holy Spirit we come to life again.

Esoteric Lesson
MUNICH, SEPTEMBER 3, 1913

RECORD A

The mantra for Wednesday was spoken.

Going forward, our task will be to bring out all the esoteric elements that are between the lines of all of the outer things that we experienced during our time together.† All esotericism consists of taking in and grasping with our mind and soul what we can understand outwardly.

Mainly, what we have spoken about during this whole time are the Guardian of the Threshold, Lucifer, and Ahriman. We must learn to know and recognize Lucifer and Ahriman, in order to protect ourselves from attacks from them. Above all, we must avoid taking concepts that we have formed and accepted on the physical plane, and which are correct for the physical plane, into the spiritual realm when we cross the threshold.

Philosophy is not something that many of you here think about, but you know that it attempts to give views of life and of the world. Philosophers speak chiefly about two things. The first is multiplicity or plurality, in which everything is reduced to its smallest particles, atoms, and monads. For example, Leibniz's philosophy† is a monadic-spiritual worldview; Haeckel's materialism† is one of atomism. The second is unity [or indivisibility]. An example of this is Spinoza's philosophy,† and also Hegel's worldview† can be counted here.

Multiplicity and unity, however, are concepts that have meaning only for the physical plane and not for the spiritual world, at any rate not for the elemental world. From among earlier friends who were philosophers and were working along with us, one day, one of them came to me† to tell me that since unity alone is true and because we did not believe this, it would be impossible to work with us any longer. This person left us.

Those who worship unity and take this concept with them into the spiritual realm, succumb to Lucifer. Those who regard only multiplicity to be correct, succumb to Ahriman. Those who become conscious in the spiritual realm—and that is the main requirement for advanced esotericists—so that during meditation they are conscious outside of their body, will first of all see themselves. As the main impression, they have themselves before them: their physical body and their own relationship to their physical being. Here in the physical plane, we feel ourselves to be a unity in relation to the environment, which we regard as a multiplicity. We see the clouds, mountains, and trees; in short, we see the various kingdoms of nature around us. Were we to believe that the cloud up there is a part of ourselves, like a finger is a part of us, we would give ourselves over to a great error.

In the spiritual realms we perceive our own self as a multiplicity. In the elemental world, we see all the forces and beings at work upon our physical body as multiplicity. It is as if we were seeing a hundred thousand revelers there, like a legion. However, we would fall victim to Ahriman if we were to regard this multitude of revelers only as a multiplicity and not say: all of you together are simply myself; you all, in your multiplicity, make up my unity! We must say this with all our strength, energy, and thoughtfulness and not just in a theoretical, intellectual manner. We must really experience the conviction that multiplicity is unity in the spiritual realms.

If we were not to strengthen our soul to feel this, but rather regard the hundred thousand revelers as a hundred thousand revelers, pieces of us would fly off; we would be torn apart into the multiplicity. Ahrimanic beings would take pieces of our being, and these beings would veil themselves in the pieces and reflect error and lies to us.

Certain primitive tribes know lions only as multiplicity. They cannot think of them as a unity, as a species. We must really accurately grasp the concepts of unity and multiplicity, and those concepts that are suited only for the physical plane we must leave behind when we cross the threshold. *The Soul's Awakening*,[†] Fourth

Scene, Romanus: "but when I left their doors, my reason swept aside the temple's mood, for daily life."

Through meditation we must strengthen our soul so much that when beings in the spiritual world draw near to our soul, we feel strongly that we can immediately recognize whether or not these beings want to lead us into error. Our soul must be able to recognize: you are builders of my physical body.

In Theosophical literature, we often find diagrams that are useful as far as they go. They start from a unity, and then divide and go more and more into multiplicity. Or they begin with multiplicity and go until they reach unity. Even if these presentations are perhaps not quite correct, no great harm is done. It does some harm, but not so much as long as it remains on the physical plane. If we wanted to take this concept along when crossing the threshold, it could be terrible. A scheme can serve as a teaching tool when it is serving only as a symbol, and when we remain conscious of the fact that we can also represent the same thing through this or in hundreds of other ways. If we are not aware of this, we succumb to Ahriman.

Feelings and emotions play into all presentations. One must present something to one person in a lively manner and to another in a totally different way, which could perhaps have affected the first person antipathetically. It must be that way.

No one should ever through eloquent means force a spiritual truth, so to speak, upon an esotericist. That would mean that Lucifer is involved. Students of esotericism must be free in their willingness to be receptive.

Thus, you must keep life on the physical plane properly separated from life in the spiritual worlds. When you cross the threshold, you must not take with you the concepts that are valid in the physical. It is the same when coming back [from the spiritual world into the physical—the spiritual concepts and moods must be left behind] (as said by Romanus in *The Soul's Awakening*).

The working of the ahrimanic and luciferic beings is necessary for the world order, as long as they remain within their appropriate bounds. Esotericists must so strengthen their soul that they can recognize and protect themselves from the attacks of these beings. Only when human beings have managed in physical life to maintain the balance between Ahriman and Lucifer—when they know the origin of everything that meets them—only then will they have self-assurance in the spiritual world.

From what is given in the esoteric lessons and through their meditative life, esotericists should accustom themselves to feel differently from the exotericists. The esotericists should let their whole life and all their actions be shone through by the spiritual so that there is no possibility for trouble and strife to reign in their ranks. It works—really, it works! In exoteric life, the esotericists must behave as exotericists. It is only that they must feel themselves like an adult in relation to children. However, they must be purely objective and not be arrogant or presumptuous.

It would be as if a forty-year-old man went bowling with children and, when the bowling ball hurts his finger or hits and blackens his eye, he would want to beat the ball. It would be natural for a child to vent anger this way. Adults can play the game better than the children, but they have different feelings about it. The adult can stand above the game, whereas the child is wrapped up within the game.

Many of our dear friends have told me that my book *Theosophy*† is so difficult to understand and have asked if it could not be presented in a simpler way. Once in a while, I have started to write it again. Yet one should not think that it would be easier and less strenuous to have *Theosophy* written in popular form. I have always put my pen away again. If people wanted to take in *Theosophy* without challenging their thinking, they would be offering Lucifer points of attack. It is quite proper to suffer somewhat thereby.

There are also many false concepts in the physical realm. For instance, the assumption that light is based only on waves is wrong. It is quite wrong with regard to spiritual things to speak of waves, oscillations, and vibrations. Some people say of an esoteric lesson that sympathetic vibrations reigned there. People like to say this; they should not do this!

During these days there has been much talk about all the dangers that await students of the spiritual along their path into the spiritual world. When people say: No, I do not want to go with this path; I do not want to raise myself up to be a bearer of the spirit, because there are too many dangers connected with it—this is the same as when someone would say: I would love to live in the house that will soon cave in, but I just don't want to hear about the cave-in.

Everyone must go on this path sometime, and so therefore it is necessary that we become acquainted with the dangers that we will face on this path. Humanity must undertake this path into the spiritual, if it is not to become sclerotic and withered. And it is the task of the esotericists to strengthen their souls in order to recognize all the difficulties: Lucifer, Ahriman, and the Guardian of the Threshold.

Esotericists are to look these beings in the face so that they do not fall victim to these hindering powers, but they will conquer them in order to show humanity the way.

*

Im Geist lag der Keim meines Leibes.
Und der Geist hat eingegliedert meinem Leibe.
Die sinnlichen Augen,
Auf baß ich durch sie schaue
Das Licht der Körper.
Und der Geist hat eingeprägt meinem leibe
Empfindung und Denken
Und Gefühl und Wille
Auf daß ich durch sie wahrnehme die Körper
Und auf sie wirke.
Im Geiste lag der Keim meines Leibes.

In meinem Leibe liegt das Geistes Keim.
Und ich will eingliedern meinem Geiste
Die übersinnlichen Augen,
Auf daß ich durch sie schaue das Licht der Geister.

Und ich will einprägen meinem Geiste
Weisheit und Kraft und Liebe,
Auf daß durch mich wirken die Geister
Und ich werde das selbstbewußte Werkzeug
Ihrer Taten.
In meinem Leibe liegt des Geistes Keim.

*

In the spirit lay the germ of my body.
And the spirit has imprinted in my body
The eyes of sense,
That through them I may see
The light of bodies.
And the spirit has imprinted in my body
Reason and sensation
And feeling and will,
That through them I may perceive bodies
And act upon them.
In the spirit lay the germ of my body.

In my body lies the germ of the spirit.
And I will incorporate into my spirit
The supersensuous eyes,
That through them I may behold the light of spirits.
And I will imprint in my spirit
Wisdom and power and love,
So that through me the spirits may act
And I become the self-conscious organ
Of their deeds.
In my body lies the germ of the spirit.

* * *

Record B

Many hear the lectures, and many have heard the esoteric lessons over the years. In spite of this, one sometimes hears that one or another person finds it difficult to differentiate between the exoteric lectures and the esoteric ones. In fact, it is difficult to differentiate and to determine what should be designated as esoteric. We can have a simple measure for it by being clear that the communications, which are also given exoterically, actually come from the spiritual world and should be understood in that way. Only the nature and manner of the understanding is what makes a person an esotericist. When we manage to make inward, to spiritualize, what was brought to us outwardly, then we are esotericists. This spiritualizing or making inward of the exoteric is esotericism. We are esotericists when we really experience in our inner self what was communicated to us outwardly; when we experience not just with the intellect, but with all the senses and all the soul forces.

In everything that surrounds us in the physical, sense-perceptible world, the ahrimanic and luciferic are to be found. These two forces flow together in the physical, sense-perceptible world. This should not occur, however, in the esoteric life; there the ahrimanic and luciferic should be kept apart. How should this be done, since we do not have a measure for determining what is exoteric or esoteric, or what is ahrimanic or luciferic? Also in science and in art—in short, in the whole outer life—these forces are working without the human being knowing it.

When we look at the various philosophies and worldviews, we can differentiate two main groups. There are philosophers who think that everything in the world is based on a unity-thought, on a unity. To this group belong all the modernistic and standardizing philosophers; whether they are philosophies related to the physical, the spiritual, or to the soul. On the other hand, there are those philosophers who think that everything must lead back to a multiplicity. Those who want to base everything on a unity are permeated with luciferic impulses. Those who want to have everything lead back to a multiplicity are imbued with ahrimanic impulses.

Now, since both streams [luciferic and ahrimanic] are justified in the physical, sense-perceptible world, it is necessary to know how far this justification goes. And so the question is how far is the one and how far is the other justified; [what their respective justified areas of working are]. The ahrimanic, a multiplicity, is justified in the physical world, and to a limited extent in the elemental world. But it is not justified in the spiritual world. There are no atoms in the spiritual world. There are no vibrations of light in the physical.

Even a concept itself exists only in the physical, sense-perceptible world. We cannot ever bring a concept into the spiritual world. Even the mathematical is not valid on the spiritual plane. We cannot base anything there or build on the fact that three-times-three equals nine. If someone comes into the spiritual world with such a dogma, it is almost a certainty that an ahrimanic being will interfere with the first "three," and because of that a totally different result will come about. Thus, even mathematical concepts and arithmetical axioms have no validity or worth in the spiritual realm. The whole of atomism has validity only on the physical plane, and to a limited extent, in the elemental world, but none in the spiritual world.

People who have the tendency to bring everything together in a unity are working with luciferic impulses. Those, however, who have a tendency to regard everything as broken into atoms or monads work under Ahriman's influence. Leibniz and Haeckel break everything down into atoms, and so are influenced by Ahriman. Those who ascend into the higher worlds with such views hide from themselves the things as they really are. The things of the spiritual world are shown to them in a false light. Just as when children playing nine-pin (a bowling game) beat the ball when something goes wrong, so it is approximately the same when people put the blame for what happens to themselves onto other people. What happens to them is karmic. The fault for it is not that of the one person alone, but also that of the other. We must also come to grasp the fact that what happens to someone else is our fault.

In this way, we find how the multiplicity becomes unity again.

* * *

Record C

Our esoteric work is to spiritualize, make inward, what we receive in the exoteric lectures. In the last two weeks,† much has been given to us that we must take into our soul and work on esoterically, so that it has a true value for us. Much has been said about the threshold [to the spiritual world], at which we must leave quite a lot behind. What must be left behind is what is valid and right for the physical plane. Some of the concepts of this plane that we carry over the threshold are innocent (without severe consequence). Much, however, becomes serious because the ahrimanic and luciferic forces seize hold of it. Thus, for instance, we must completely change our concepts of unity and multiplicity on the other side of the threshold. Philosophers occupied themselves a lot with precisely these concepts, and they have created systems and worldviews through which they regard the world as a unity (monism) or as a multiplicity (the worldviews of Spinoza, Hegel, Leibnitz, Haeckel). Such philosophies are justified on the physical plane, and these philosophers are like innocent children compared to esotericists who would do this kind of thing. In general and without falling into arrogance or conceit, but with humility, esotericists should have the feeling in relation to other people that adults have when playing with children. From their standpoint, children are right to take their game seriously and to engage in it that way, whereas adults always stand above the game. The esotericists should stand above much in which the others, justifiably, are embroiled. Esotericists who have once crossed the threshold into a place where they receive esoteric teachings, and then proceed in their outer life exactly as before—still giving reign to their antipathies, jealousies, anger, and other drives—have not yet penetrated into the spirit of what is meant. They have not yet comprehended and taken on the earnestness of the matter.

When we cross the threshold into the spiritual world and are outside of our body, our body will appear like a great multiplicity. We will recognize this body to be the result of the work of all the elemental beings, of all the hierarchies. We must, in spite of this, recognize [the multiplicity of the body] as our unity, that we are a unity with it. Then the elemental beings show us their true countenance. If we hold the body to be a multiplicity as such, then Ahriman seizes our error, and all of these elemental beings will tear a piece from us and will approach us as false-figures, like a hundred thousand jesters or revelers. Every error related to a multiplicity falls victim to Ahriman, and every error related to a unity falls to Lucifer. If we want to reduce ourselves to being a unity, we succumb to Lucifer. The various philosophies of the multiplicity or of monism are ruled by Ahriman and Lucifer respectively. If we are awake, the influences of these two beings are not so easily able to damage us. Indeed, it is dangerous to enter unprepared into the spiritual world, but we should not let fear keep us from crossing the threshold because sooner or later every soul must take this step. The best way into the spiritual worlds is to immerse ourselves deeply in the truths given to us; to take them up with our whole soul and with boundless *Gemüt* [mind and soul or heart] and to let it penetrate us. People who mean well have often asked if I could not give an easier, more popular book than *Theosophy* as a beginning, and so I have often started to write such a book. But there are dangers in making this easier for many minds and souls, for whom this would be poison. Thus, I have always left it undone.

* * *

Record D

The esoteric life is the spiritualizing, making inward, of the exoteric knowledge that we acquire about the evolution of the world. In this lecture cycle† much that is esoteric flowed into what is, so to speak, behind what is spoken, and it will be our task sometime soon to find it and bring it out. Much has been said about the threshold to the spiritual world, across which we all must go at some point. At this threshold, the ahrimanic and luciferic beings can be dangerous for us. It cannot be stressed too often that we should not take with us into the spiritual world the concepts that have proper validity for the sense world. These concepts could become dangerous for us there. Multiplicity and unity are just such concepts. Philosophers, who are esoterically intellectuals but have naïve, childlike souls, develop systems in order to explain world phenomena. They lead everything back to multiplicity, monadism, or to atomism—Haeckel's philosophy. In these systems or philosophies, ahrimanic impulses are at work. Or the philosophers move back to unity, monism, Spinozism, or Hegelianism in which the luciferic impulses hold sway. These concepts [of multiplicity and unity] are foolish in the sense world and dangerous in the suprasensible world. They would lead us, when we are outside of our body, to see a hundred thousand jesters or revelers. In the suprasensible world, we must learn to recognize multiplicity as the unity of our body which is outside of us there. We must recognize and realize that countless elemental spirits are working there and yearning to build the human being. We must tear the mask of lies off of these beings and recognize them as subordinate helpers of the higher hierarchies.

The desire is often expressed for an easier, more popular version of Theosophy than is present in the book *Theosophy*. The theosophical concepts must be worked for. If as students we wanted to work through the content of the teaching in some other way, for example through beautifully elegant speech, we would let Lucifer flow into Theosophy. To speak of "vibrations" in Theosophy, as is often done, opens the door to Ahriman. We must return to the sense world from out of the esoteric life in the same way as adults taking part in children's games. If we return to our old strife, emotions, and passions, we are like those adults who, like children, beat the ball that hits them in the eye.

Esoteric Lesson

MUNICH, SEPTEMBER 4, 1913

RECORD A

The verse for Thursday was spoken.

My dear sisters and brothers!

We have spoken again and again during our time here of Lucifer and Ahriman and the fact that these are powers which must be in world evolution and which, when they remain in their rightful place, are good. We must, however, argue against and protect ourselves from attacks by these powers. For that purpose, we must learn to know them and to differentiate them.

Lucifer is in mystical esotericism, such as we see with Meister Eckhart, Ruysbroek, Tauler, Suso,† and so on. In their pure devotion to the divine, in this pure and noble striving toward the spiritual, Lucifer is present in a good way. We can say that he was "pious" in the souls of these mystics.

However, just as soon as a personal element flows into this pure striving and devotion—that is, the minute mystics devote themselves simply out of their own joy of devoting themselves—this would signify an encroachment or attack by Lucifer. We must be wakeful that nothing of this kind enters into our striving. With mystical meditation and contemplation, it is relatively easy to be awake; it is already more difficult with the beholding of visions. Lucifer is also in this, leading the mystics to believe all kinds of things that are difficult to differentiate from true visions. Something subjective mixes into all beholding; thus searching manifestations, illusionary figures, or similar phenomena are repeated for the individual. We must direct our attention to these things. Here we must also be awake.

If we see eyes or faces or conceive of such things imaginatively, we are not so easily exposed to error; we receive through this the strength to reject Lucifer.

It is not a reproach when it is said that bad characteristics and traits live in the human subconsciousness. These must be; they are a part of earthly life. Human beings can have attained a certain degree of holiness and yet, have slumbering in their subconsciousness such desires and inclinations that would shock and disgust them if they were to perceive them. It is necessary to bring the greatest carefulness and wakefulness here also. In everything of an emotional nature, in mystical meditation and contemplation, in all visions, Lucifer is working. He is also active in all enthusiasm, and also in artistic activity—both in what the artist creates and in what the artist is doing in the act of creating.

There can be materialists who unfold themselves totally in the material or physical; they can express themselves only through physical matter. When we have the good fortune to look into their souls, we find a deeply religious striving, a yearning for the divine. Lucifer is the instigator of this also.

In everything of a will-nature Ahriman is working. He approaches us in everything that shows itself to be a gesture in word or writing. He shows himself in everything that a medium writes—whether it is from a trained medium or from a natural medium—and also where someone feels compelled to write something automatically. Whereas manifestations of figures, heads of light, etc., produced by a medium are caused by Lucifer. People can work against this urge, when they feel compelled, for instance, to write. They can stop and not give in to these impulses or inspirations that they think they feel or perceive. They can bring a firm will against these promptings and can decide not to follow them. Through this exertion of the will they can gain undreamed-of spiritual forces.

Ahriman is in what we say in words that we form and send to others. As soon as the ear hears the sound, the larynx gives forth sound, and words are written, Ahriman comes and hardens the tone or sound, the words, and the writing. For this reason, it is important to strengthen the soul and to test our thoughts most subtly.

Swedenborg's worldview,[†] his visions of the future, and his experiences (prophetic dreams), are imbued with Ahriman. Ahriman also permeates what Kant was interested in, and what he took from Swedenborg's writings.[†]

Quite often—almost daily—the question is asked whether or not one should set any store in what one sees, hears, or perceives. Is it the truth? Certainly, you should set some store in it; certainly it is the truth. Every small thing in esoteric life is important and is true. It is just a matter of knowing what stands behind it. We must be tremendously careful and pay attention—be awake!

But we must acquire a certain delicate feeling of tact not to talk about and spread these experiences around. Entirely within our innermost depths, we must seek to find out and sort out for ourselves whether Lucifer or Ahriman is involved. Naturally, we can speak about such experiences with our closest friends and get advice from those we trust. But we should be less willing to build teachings based on these experiences or pass them along as doctrine. Something that can happen to us daily, or even on an hourly basis, is that when we are walking along the street, we have a vision of a person and then actually meet that person after a few minutes. Now, it can be that we have something to say to the person in question; we have this presentment of his coming and hurry our steps to assure that we meet—precisely as a result of this presentment, this spiritual faculty. However, we must not do that. We may not use spiritual capabilities to our advantage in physical life. On the physical plane, we must act in accordance with the laws that have validity there, as if we knew nothing of esotericism. Such an occurrence may serve only as an indication to help us notice such things.

In the exoteric lectures, we have spoken repeatedly about how Maeterlinck wanted proof of the spiritual life.[†] If people were to experience Goethe's soul standing before them and had true proof that it was Goethe's soul, and if they spoke with this soul of Goethe, they would quite certainly say that this is an irrefutable proof of the immortality of the soul.[†] [Compare this with Record D.] According to the laws of the physical plane, this conclusion would be the only right one. And yet it is not correct; it is not right to say: that is Goethe's soul. Lucifer is hidden in [this] soul of Goethe and leads us to believe that it is Goethe's soul from such and such a year. Only when we are conscious that Lucifer is hidden in [this] soul of Goethe, do we have the possibility to penetrate to Goethe's real soul (which develops further in the spiritual world). Only then can we approach his true soul, and thus have a real proof of the immortality of the soul.

People approach esoteric exercises quite thoughtlessly. Many begin to do them but don't continue out of laziness, half-heartedness, etc. But the meditations are for the soul what breathing is for the physical body. If we gave up breathing, Ahriman, as Lord of Death, would intervene immediately. The soul must come to the point of not having to struggle or force itself to do the meditations; to the point where it does not want to live without them anymore. The meditations must become for the soul what breathing is for the body.

Over against this half-heartedness and laziness is the impetuous wish and yearning to penetrate the spiritual worlds. We must not wish to enter the spiritual worlds before the soul is properly strengthened. The main condition is quiet and peacefulness in the soul (*The Soul's Awakening*, Scene Three†). Only thus can we gain the proper strength for the soul that it must have in order to find a middle path—not right and not left; not to fall victim to Lucifer and not to Ahriman, but to keep to the middle path.

[Holding to the middle way] is hard—very hard and difficult, my dear sisters and brothers! But then we must remember the words of the prologue of the John Gospel (John 1:1-18) and of the verses in John 8:12-14. When we are standing in the middle of the tumult and chaos of the spiritual world, visions and figures come from all sides, and we do not know the way and are torn from here to there, then we should place before our souls the words: "In the beginning was the Word...," and so on, or "I am the light of the world. Whoever follows me will not walk in the darkness but will have the light of life." Then everything will scatter, and we will be able to behold the right and the true. In this sense, we should ever again place before us the Rosicrucian mantra: E.D.N. — I.C.M. —P.S.S.R.

And further, we will find more and more what is right along this difficult path when we are mindful of the simple but deep mantra with which we close our esoteric lessons:

In the spirit lay the germ of my body.
And the spirit has imprinted in my body
The eyes of sense,
That through them I may see
The light of bodies.
And the spirit has imprinted in my body
Reason and sensation
And feeling and will,
That through them I may perceive bodies
And act upon them.
In the spirit lay the germ of my body.

In my body lies the germ of the spirit.
And I will incorporate into my spirit
The supersensuous eyes,
That through them I may behold the light of spirits.
And I will imprint in my spirit
Wisdom and power and love,
So that through me the spirits may act
And I become the self-conscious organ
Of their deeds.
In my body lies the germ of the spirit.

* * *

Record B

We want now to attempt to point out the subtle effects that the luciferic and ahrimanic beings exert upon the most intimate stirrings of our soul. For it is the duty of all who seek the way to the esoteric life to know these [effects]. There are especially two kinds of people who seek in totally different ways the path of spiritual knowledge. This seeking for the spirit is within the disposition of all human beings, even though not everyone wants to admit it. Even in the worst materialist there lies quite deep in the subconscious the yearning for the spirit. They cannot attain this knowledge because they seek physical proofs for spiritual matters. Maeterlinck can be cited as an example. He, who comes so close to the spiritual, also desires physical proofs.

Now, there is another type of human being. There are human beings who, out of their most inward consciousness—out of their deepest soul-feeling—feel themselves drawn to the spiritual. And they have an intimate knowing that does not manifest in visions. They do not need, either through physical proofs or through sense-physical theories, to have the existence of the spiritual world explained. They have this knowledge out of their own feelings, out of the deepest sensing of their hearts. Such people were the mystics, Johannes Tauler, Ruysbroek, and others. The mysticism such as these people had was often under the influence of Lucifer, but in a good sense. It was in the sense that Lucifer himself—who led these highly developed souls upward into beautiful, divine rapture—progressed, through them, in his development. One could say that in mysticism, Lucifer had the inclination to become pious. In this mysticism, only the pious devotion—the pure, religious feeling—confronts us.

In contrast, there is yet another mysticism, namely, that of the prophetic seer; mediumistic mysticism that can either be a natural, innate disposition or that is also often attained through specific training. From time to time, such people also turn into mediumistic writers, and that sort of thing. Here we see only the impulses of Ahriman holding sway. He wants, for his part, to turn everything into a multiplicity or to make things fixed in writings or symbols. We find the ahrimanic principle also in writing that is momentarily impulsive and arises out of inspiration, without being mediumistic in nature.

We must bring the right harmony between the state of entering into rapture and that of immediate, direct writing under the influence of Ahriman. For this, we must suppress the impulsive writing down of things as soon as it begins to appear. It can be pushed back, as it were, until it becomes clear in us. Only then will we be able to connect the two forces with each other in harmony. It was essentially ahrimanic impulses, for instance, that mixed in with Swedenborg's great gift as a seer (his foreseeing on the physical plane, his prophesying physical events).

Thus, the luciferic and ahrimanic principles exert themselves in many visionary manifestations that esoteric students often have in the beginning as experiences of the spiritual worlds. The visionary objects that students see—figures, heads, eyes—are real facts that are seen. They come up from the depths of the subconscious of the human being. Hidden away lie furtive, secret inclinations, drives, and desires of which human beings know nothing in their upper consciousness. They do not always need to feel ashamed of these inclinations and desires because they belong, in a certain sense, to human nature, and without these things, earthly evolution would not be conceivable.

Such feelings of the most hidden drives and desires surface, through our esoteric training, as visionary forms. They can even appear as the figures of the most exalted personalities, and yet they are human desires slumbering deeply hidden in our subconscious that Lucifer holds up to us symbolically. It would be good to let such visions pass on by us in peace and to not speak much about them—or, at most, only to those people who are called to explain these things to us. Even more important, we should not use [these visions] as teaching material.

Esoteric students could now despair and ask themselves how they are to find their way when Lucifer and Ahriman are lurking there. Concerning this we can always give the comfort and the indication that, when we hold onto what is offered in the John Gospel: "In the beginning was the Word...," and so on; and also in the thirteenth chapter of the John Gospel,† or when we let the Sermon on the Mount or the Beatitudes† work upon us, then we have a certain guidance that brings a differentiating between truth and error.

* * *

RECORD C

Yesterday we learned that luciferic and ahrimanic beings and forces work into humanity. The forces mix and flow together in the human being.

Ahrimanic forces express themselves in human gestures, writing, and movements. All writing media operate under the influence of Ahriman. The luciferic influences and forces express themselves to the human being as visions, images, and in general, through the perceptions of feelings. All of the mystics of the Middle Ages were influenced by Lucifer. Lucifer wanted to redeem himself in Cusanus,† Suso, Tauler, and Miester Eckhart. The redemption of Lucifer happens through love—through the higher love that is free of egotism. The redemption of Ahriman happens through thinking. As a remedy for the ahrimanic attacks that are too strong, thinking through the first chapter of the John Gospel is greatly recommended; "In the beginning was the Word...," and also the eighth chapter. The worst and most seductive images and visions are those that appear in beautiful, glorious color phenomena. There we must be particularly awake. Flattering the teacher is a great danger for the teacher. We should not bring such great admiration toward the teacher. Also, those who teach should endeavor not to let too great an admiration be brought toward them. Those are precisely instances where the ones teaching can take damage upon themselves.

The ahrimanic belongs to the future; it is what flows out of the thinking and is then realized through the will.

* * *

Record D

We have spoken a great deal about luciferic and ahrimanic powers and must, according to the most important regulation in the old Mysteries, learn to recognize their nature and their effects—especially their working in the spiritual world, at the threshold of which we are all standing. People can approach the spiritual world through their feelings; this is feeling-mysticism. All the mysticism of the Middle Ages—Master Eckhart, Suso, Tauler, etc.—was feeling-mysticism. Lucifer was in this mysticism; he attempted to become pious in it. In prophetic seeing—all the mysticism of Swedenborg—we have the ahrimanic impulses; this includes what is of the will-nature, what presses into our gestures, into deeds, into the impulses to write something down. Thus, Lucifer works from outside, separated from the human being, and Ahriman works through the human being. Ahriman works in the natural medium; Lucifer works in the trained medium. When we have visions or inspirations, we must push them back and not let them become active. We must seek to recognize them according to their worth. We should indeed pay attention to them but not let them influence our actions in outer, exoteric life.

People who begin on their own to do exercises in meditations, and then after a time drop them, fall victim to Lucifer. Meditation should never be dropped out of laziness. It must become as necessary to us as breathing is for our body—then it is right. When [mediumistic] spiritualists let the spirit of Goethe appear and want to prove the immortality of the soul thereby, they think it is the soul [of Goethe] as it lives now. That is an error. It can be that it is Goethe's soul as it lived in his body in 1828 and is, through Lucifer, made to appear as if it would be like that now. In order to find our way in the chaos that surrounds us upon entering the spiritual world—in order to have the correct helm for our soul ship—we must call awake in our soul the first chapter of the John Gospel or John 8:2. With those we will not succumb to error.

* * *

Record E

Behind everything that is of a feeling-nature, Lucifer hides himself and intervenes constantly. Behind everything of a will-nature, Ahriman is hidden.

Clairvoyants observe that in most souls, human beings strive toward the highest in their inner feelings. Even with the strongest materialists, one finds this.

There, where quite deep religious feeling is strengthened and intensified through meditation, visions and experiences often come about. Here true esotericists should engage their powers of observation. Naturally, the visions are all true, but we must first learn to read them. We must distinguish what rises subjectively out of our soul and mixes in with the objective soul images. We must know how much is from Lucifer and how much is from our own being. All of the emotions, desires, and passions that slumber in the depths of the human soul strive to surface precisely along with the visions, to mingle with the spiritual images and lead us to error. It is also especially important to observe how what is subjective always repeats itself, for example, in animal forms, and so on. There we can learn to be especially careful and can take our self-education in hand. Wakefulness. Everything that manifests through the word, writing, sound, and gestures is of an ahrimanic nature; also all visions and dreams of the future, and so on.

Everything that is produced from outside [of the human being] in visions, and so on, is luciferic. Everything that goes through the human being such as hearing, writing, and so on, is ahrimanic.

Everything in the physical world that wants physical proof in the spiritual world is ahrimanic. All attempts to convince another about spiritual science through eloquent speech or through suggestion is luciferic.

The main thing is to remain conscientious and honest in our meditation. Bear in mind the content of the John Gospel, and let spirit-peacefulness reign in our soul.

Esoteric Lesson
CHRISTIANIA (OSLO), OCTOBER 5, 1913

RECORD A

When we, as esotericists, climb ever higher from level to level, a number of changes take place in our soul life. Today I will speak about a weakness of esotericists that becomes noticeable to exotericists. From the standpoint of exotericists, it is a weakness; from that of the esotericists, it is much more a strength. It is what I would call the robustness of thought-formation. I will give an example. William Crookes[†] thought and reflected a lot in his life. His most significant accomplishment was perhaps in the realm of spiritualism. Not only had he experimented, but he also thought about the things that come to light in the suprasensible life. One of his most interesting problems was the microscopic human being. He imagined the human being becoming ever smaller and smaller, into a kind of homunculus. Finally, the human being became only as big as a beetle that crawls around on leaf of cabbage. The leaf of cabbage is, for this tiny human being, it's whole world, and the edges of the leaf are like the high mountains. They appear to this *human being* as the Himalayas would appear to an ordinary human being. This little human being is imagined to live rapidly, with a lifespan of only two months in comparison to the eighty years (a high estimation) of the human being today. Obviously, the worldview of such a human being must be totally different, since everything the ordinary human being experiences over a whole lifetime is compressed into two months. The little human would not get to know the transition of the seasons. The growth of the flowers would be experienced in the way a person today researches the whole geological development of the Earth. The Sun would hardly seem to move.

Also, a human being was imagined who lives very slowly, with a lifespan of eighty years. The movement of the Sun, which we can follow exactly, would appear to such a human being as a fiery circle, approximately as if one were to swing a glowing ember in a circle so that one sees a closed circle [of light]. The flowers would sprout and immediately fade away again; a mushroom would shoot through the surface of the ground and immediately disappear.

For esotericists, such pictures are of interest in so far as they see from them to what extent modern exoteric thinking can get carried away. Of the three souls forces, it is the thinking that can digress the most. Esotericists cannot go along with that; they do not have such robustness in relation to thinking.

Why is that? It is because such pictures as those of the microscopic, fast-living human being do not lie in the necessity and lawfulness of world existence. Quite certainly, the good gods were more concerned about human life than the human being was. They created the human being, not as a microscopic human, but as a macrocosmic human being, because the macrocosmic human being alone is suited to world existence as the gods set it up. Now, if William Crookes had been able to become a god, it is possible that he would have created a microscopic human being. The good gods did not do that; they were too weak. But the modern exotericists are strong. They paint such thought-pictures for themselves like that of the microscopic human being. They are stronger in their thinking than the next higher hierarchy is—the angels. Regarding the angels, an ancient document states: "And they hid their face!"†

Why did the angels hide their face? What from? From the error of the human being! The gods created the human being as a thinking being and arranged the whole universe accordingly—because the human being should be a thinking being. When people believe, however, that thinking can exist on its own, when they allow it to digress [from the lawfulness of the world], they must fall into error. They must then lose the connection with the universal thinking, with the source of thinking. Then the angels hide their face. So deep were these religious documents! We must just understand them.

When modern theology speaks about the Bible, it has as much meaning in relation to reality as would be the case if European scholars who do not understand Chinese were to judge the handwritten sacred Chinese writings based on what they could see outwardly. As little value as that has, just so little value does modern Biblical research have for humanity.

Therefore, the exercises that you, my dear sisters and brothers, have been given, contain such thought-pictures that exist in the great cosmic plan. And esotericists will reject imaginations such as that of the microscopic, fast-living, or the slow-living, human being. Such imaginations cause them pain, and they sense them as being unhealthy and unnecessary in world existence. In relation to the microscopic human being, they will feel something like a burning; it becomes hot for them, and then everything flows together into a point. In contrast, everything spreads far out into the universe, for instance, when they imagine a human being who is eighty years old. A feeling of coldness overcomes them; they freeze.

We can also have such a feeling of coldness with various philosophers. With Anaxagoras,† and to a lesser extent with Empedocles,† one has an icy feeling. In relation to Leibniz,† one senses a feeling of beneficial warmth; he is—if the expression is correctly understood—an agreeable philosopher.

One has a feeling of burning, of being hot, also when one meditates on a point. That is, at the same time, a good measure of esoteric development. If I have no trouble imagining a point—if it costs me no effort, such as is the case with how it is taught to the school children today—it is not right. When esotericists have to exert themselves and when they have a hot, burning feeling, it is proof that they are advanced in their training.

Such a picture taken from world processes is: a bowl filled with oil in which a flame is burning and shining.† The bowl stands still, and the oil is consumed. Whoever imagines themselves in this picture receives through it a true image of the nature of the human being. The bowl is the solid, the physical body; the oil that is consumed is the etheric body; the flame is the astral body; and the light is the "I" of the human being. This human essence or being is very different according to each climate and place. And more than we usually realize, human beings grow together with their surroundings. There is a difference if a person travels from Berlin to Sicily, or to here (Oslo). People experience something different when they travel to the North. The etheric body becomes ever larger, especially in the Northeast, for instance, in Finland. When someone travels from here—Oslo—to the south, the etheric body must contract. Through this, strong healing forces can be set free. Of course, it depends on whether the one who is to be healed gives resistance or not, and it depends on karma.

* * *

RECORD B

There are many things that esotericists cannot do; things in which they are weak when compared to the exotericists. Tomorrow we will discuss things that esotericists must acquire for themselves. Esotericists can no longer let their thinking buzz around such as the exotericists do. An example is given of what is meant. Exotericists imagine a little human being, like that imagined by Crookes, which is as small as a little beetle. It is a human being that lives only two months and is in this time span child, adult, and elderly person. In comparison to such thought-out things, the thinking of the gods is weak; they can think the human being only in the size and makeup actually existing now. It must cause esotericists burning pain to think of the microcosmic instead of the macrocosmic human being. The little, compressed one must cause the esotericists pain; the large, macrocosmic human being must create fire for them.

All of this vague thinking about the universe—such as questioning and brooding about what was before Saturn; what was there before God was there, etc.—must create a tremendous coldness for the esotericists. To think or imagine a point and a circle, or a point, or a circle, is difficult for esotericists, but not for the exotericists. The esotericists also train their soul.

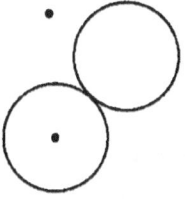

In this way we can get an idea of from where error and evil came into the world. Getting to know the etheric body happens through attention and concentration. Getting to know the astral body comes about through the devotion of the soul, through meditation—through going into our soul—and the result is an expansion of the memory.

A good means of meditation is to imagine a bowl of oil and a flame that shines and consumes the oil. That is a symbol for an imagination that corresponds to a natural possibility. The bowl is the physical body; the oil is the etheric body; the flame that burns and consumes the oil is the astral body; and the shining of the flame is the "I."

Esoteric Lesson
CHRISTIANIA (OSLO), OCTOBER 6, 1913

RECORD A

We all want to attain entrance into the spiritual world. We all see before us—or at least have an inkling of it—a portal with a threshold; and in order to reach it, we are given certain exercises. In spite of that, the way is difficult and full of obstacles. The path leads through a sea of sorrows, and a great deal of patience is necessary so that we do not become exhausted along the way.

Who creates these obstacles? First, our own nature creates them; and second, Lucifer and Ahriman seek to lay obstacles in the path. Both of these beings have their effectiveness on Earth. It is an effectiveness that could be good, if they limited themselves to what they should: to living in the effects of the sense world. However, they are not content to remain in the spiritual realm where they belong and only to send their effects down into the physical plane. They want to reign on Earth also with their "I"-consciousness. We know that human beings attain their "I"-consciousness on Earth; the angels achieve it in the elemental world; and the archangels in the astral world. Thus, Lucifer and Ahriman wish to penetrate into the "I"-consciousness of the human being.

Ahriman is the Lord of Death, as determined through the nature of the human being. There is no life in the stone; that is its nature. Now, Ahriman wants to extend his power to what crosses the portal of death—what belongs to the spiritual world. For this reason, he brings to modern human beings—the materialists and monists—the lie that there is no eternity; that the soul is contained in the physical and ceases to exist when the body dies. Ahriman can draw near human beings, because they have fear. If it is normal fear of which people can easily attain knowledge, it is not so bad; but it becomes bad when this fear slumbers in the depths of the subconscious. Such people fall victim to Ahriman. This fear is present with all the followers of materialistic science, even though they would not believe it if one told them so. But this is so with all the people who have no relationship to the spiritual world.

Goethe quite correctly has Mephistopheles say:

> "People never feel the devil,
> even when he has them by the collar."†

You need only to go into a laboratory where many people are working, and you will see how strongly their etheric bodies are impregnated or fructified by Ahriman. Clairvoyants see in them exactly the same forms that they see in the etheric bodies of people who are filled with fear. When people walk through a room where there is a mirror, they see their image, but that can be only because they are actually there. Thus, what exists on Earth is only their mirror-image; but Ahriman seeks to convince them that that is the reality.

How can we protect ourselves from Ahriman? We can protect ourselves from him by being satisfied with what is given to us:

> "Be pleased with what is given to you;
> Do gladly without what is not granted to you."†

Then Ahriman cannot reach us. People should not be without wishes; they should not be an ascetic who flees from the world, but also should not be full of joy [only]. They should seek to hold the balance between the two; this gives the correct mood for esotericists.

Also, Lucifer could work much good if he would limit himself to his area of endeavor: to lead the human being to "I"-consciousness. Lucifer stands behind all art and all truly independent science. However, he tempts the human being to exaggerated self-consciousness and conceit.

As an example, imagine an artist who creates a statue. As long as it is a copy, everything is in order. However, when he wants to keep his creation for himself—wants to be God—and demands that the statue walk; breaks it, and really imagines that it walks, then Lucifer stands behind this.

Lucifer is effective in the naturalistic-realistic dramas that are written today. Lucifer goes on stage. A hundred years ago Schiller let his "Wilhelm Tell" say things that no human being had spoken before.† For him, as was often expressed, art was a gift from heaven. Today Gerhard Hauptmann† manages to strike everything down in "Wilhelm Tell" that is not consistent with his realistic view (realism).

The only antidote that we have in relation to Lucifer is the deepest humility and self-modesty.

How many tell themselves in the evening, when they do a review of their day's work, that the gods were the ones who guided their deeds and actions? Most people believe they may be proud of what they themselves have accomplished. If we nourish and increase the spirit of humility and modesty in us, we protect ourselves from Lucifer. If we develop satisfaction within our inner being, Ahriman cannot get to us.

* * *

RECORD B

Those will keep Ahriman away who follow the saying: "Be pleased with what is given you; do not desire what is not given to you."

To have the right attitude toward Lucifer, esotericists say: "Practice self-knowledge by looking at your deeds and not ascribing them to the god in you." Human beings see only a mirror-image of themselves on Earth. Human beings are spiritual beings; because they see their mirror-image on Earth, they come to their "I"-consciousness. Human beings must get to know their" I" on Earth. Lucifer and Ahriman commit the mistake of carrying their "I" into the physical plane, instead of carrying its *effect* into the physical plane. We must not stop with just having the imagination, but must learn to read it.

Ahriman has influence in the physical world when only the physical, sense world is acknowledged. And this condition of the physical body and etheric body is revealed exactly to clairvoyants; this is the condition that they otherwise find in human beings who are feeling fear. Ahriman deceives us in the beholding, and so the reading must become beholding, seeing. Lucifer seduces us to seek God in ourselves—to regard ourselves as the Lord God. We can protect ourselves from this through humility and modesty.

Esotericist must learn two things:

1. To be devoted and loyal to doing the meditation.
2. To have patience.

Ahriman is also the tempter in the elemental world. For this reason, we should not say of what we see in the elemental world: I feel myself in a world of warmth; nothing solid, is there, or streams, etc. No, we should not say this. We should learn to read what we see there, and then we can say that it is the old Saturn evolution period. Every being has its world where it must experience its "I."

The angel hides its face before the becoming of the human being. The angels experience their "I" in the elemental world. The archangels experience their "I" in the astral world, but their effects reach down into the physical world. The blood symbolizes the "I" of the human being. Those people who cannot stand to see blood—either their own or someone else's—cannot bear their own "I." These people cannot tolerate even the symbol for the expression of their own "I." Those in question faint when they see blood. Do human beings know their "I"? No, human beings absolutely cannot yet bear their "I." They deaden themselves to it, and do not want to go through the experience of it. They do not want to acquaint themselves with their "I."

When we experience the Rose Cross as an imagination, we must learn to read it. We should not stop with the black wood of the cross; an esoteric word belongs to it, is a part of it. When we see the color blue filling space, we must tell ourselves that there is something behind this blue. Perhaps we penetrate through it, and an angel appears to us. We could also say that behind the blue is hidden red, and behind that is passion. We must penetrate through that, and then there appears the devil (reference to Lucifer in "The Soul's Awakening," the devachan scene, cosmic midnight scene; only clad as a red band [?]). The human etheric body is not the same size in every country. It becomes ever larger the farther to the north, away from Berlin, one goes. It becomes smaller the farther south, one goes, and the farther east.

Esoteric Lesson
BERGEN, OCTOBER 11, 1913

RECORD A

It is always again necessary to provide anew a picture of what must happen in the meditation and how the meditant should act with it.

When you start to meditate, you should be careful that your surroundings are not too warm or too cold, so that you feel as few hindrances from the physical body as possible.† The first thing to appear will be a kind of inner restlessness, as if something in our blood were to prickle and crawl, such that you feel distracted by it. It can even go so far as a murmuring of the blood. Those who have not experienced this could think that this is so because they meditate better. That is, however, not the case, because everyone must finally experience this prickling in the blood. It is even a proof that you are on the right path, for through this something comes into your consciousness that you would like to overlook in ordinary life. Through the prickling of the blood we become conscious of the egotism with which we are encumbered and which hinders us from gaining entrance into the spiritual world. It prevents us first of all from attaining the necessary stillness. Yet with a firm continuation of the meditation, you will come to the point where the prickling can no longer bother you when it is present.

A second obstacle in meditation is a kind of difficulty in breathing. Whereas beforehand, you felt your breathing taking place with regularity, there comes a moment when you feel as if your breathing would falter, as if you have a swelling or constriction in your throat that prevents you from breathing. This is also something that everyone who tries to meditate must experience. This experience shall point out to us a deficiency or lack of the sense for truth; it points to the mendaciousness that is still in you.

A third hindrance is that during meditation, you can suddenly feel weak and break out in a sweat. This is the obstacle which the physical body lays in the way of the etheric body, so that the etheric body cannot progress as it should in the meditation. This occurs especially to those who want to develop themselves esoterically, but who eat too much. And when the etheric body really succeeds in loosening from the physical body, then those people have before them, as it were, a thick wall through which they cannot see, and further attempts to see something of the spiritual light or spiritual beings are fruitless.

A fourth thing that can happen is that everything feels very pleasant and easy to you, and you find yourself in a kind of dream state. When this happens, it indicates that we are lacking in the tendency to be social with other people and that, on the physical plane, we tend to lead a dream life.

A remedy that is recommended against the egotism—which can occur so strongly that one experiences a great disquiet because of it—is to read and let work in us the Lord's Prayer, the Sermon on the Mount, or the beginning of the John Gospel. That will provide quietness at times. Also, what was given recently as *The Fifth Gospel*[†] is meant to prevent a further increase of egotism.

The more earnestly we develop ourselves as esotericists, the more we should nurture within us an offering, a devotion, that we should bring from our soul to the higher beings, for example, the angels. The angels need our esoteric striving and our study of Theosophy as food for themselves. And to the degree Theosophy penetrates us and we make it a part of our being, in the same degree can the archangels use it for the further development of individual peoples and for their own development.

* * *

Record B

What does the soul do when it meditates? It becomes completely one with the meditation content. The hindrances that appear are the thoughts and cares of life that the soul cannot ward off. Then further obstacles arise:

1. A prickling, sticking, or buzzing in the blood during meditation. This reveals the egotism that we have in us, and we should thereby test where the impulses of egotism lie within us. Those who say they are glad that in their meditation no sticking, prickling, and also no buzzing arises, have absolutely not yet meditated deeply.

2. The appearance of a choking in the throat during meditation. That is our untruthfulness, this angel of death. The breathing is felt, and it goes to the point of constriction.

3. We experience during meditation, outside of our body, woven out of dreams or dream-substance, a form of our physical body. It is the phantom:† the form that takes in what will then become the physical body, and which is not buried with us.

When both the blood and the breathing are overcome, and when we meditate further, it can then happen that during meditation the etheric body wants to leave; and because of the impure forces in us, the etheric body is as if pressed out of us in strong sweating. And then we see the physical body like a form woven out of fine material.

Esoteric Lesson
COPENHAGEN, OCTOBER 15, 1913

RECORD A

Through our exercises, we gradually enter into the spiritual world, but this is not possible without, at the same time, coming into contact with Lucifer and Ahriman. In the Bible we find the story of the Fall of humanity† through which Lucifer, and then later also Ahriman, achieve influence over human beings. They work into human beings in such a way that when human beings enter into the spiritual world, it is difficult for them to endure their "I." Certain people, even in the physical world, cannot bear the outer symbol of the "I"; they faint at the sight of blood.

The Fall gave self-knowledge, but with a limitation. Every time we take a step forward in self-knowledge, new temptations attack us, and indeed to the degree that we can just manage to endure them. Just as we are limited in our physical body with respect to the degree of pain we can endure, so too are our forces limited for enduring the higher worlds.

Because Lucifer and Ahriman drove us out of paradise at the Fall, they are again the ones we meet when we want to enter the spiritual world. And these beings bring it about that we feel our limitations.

Ahriman is in everything that comprises the spiritual sounds, words, etc., that we can hear. We should always be distrustful toward these, for in human speech, which is differentiated into the various national languages, there lives untruth. Of course, it is not total untruth, otherwise we all would have to be lying every time we opened our mouths to speak. As much truth as is in the language, just so much truth lies in the "voices." If the voice always spoke the truth, then in the temptation at the Fall, Lucifer could not have said: "You will become like the gods,"†—but would have had to say: "I lie."

Lucifer gives visions. We must break through these visions; otherwise, we do not break the shell that is around every human being and covers up the true spiritual world. The visions and the voices are around us like the shell is around the chick in the egg. In a vision we can perhaps behold an angel; and when we penetrate the vision, the angel turns into a serpent, the symbol of Lucifer; for Lucifer was in the form of a serpent in the temptation at the Fall.† Or, perhaps in our meditation we see the color blue. If we break through the blue, the blue can disappear and become red. This shows that we have seen our own passions.

After the temptation, the human being did not receive through Lucifer everything that the gods have. The human being did indeed receive premature knowledge, but not life. Because of this, everything we know and perceive is imbued with Lucifer and Ahriman. Thus is it basically also this way with the content of our exercises. When we examine our exercises, we will find that they are so formed that they never call on human egotism. Many people find this unpleasant. We do not meditate on "love" or "truth," because that would only foster egotism. However, in spite of that, such concepts like "light," "warmth"—which are found in our exercises†—are things of the physical world which we know at first only through the physical senses. All of this is a gift from Lucifer. For this reason, after the meditation we should drop the content—empty the soul completely of these impressions. By doing this we refuse everything that comes from Lucifer and Ahriman, and we prepare ourselves for the purely spiritual world. Then the world of the senses disappears, and the spiritual world opens up before us. This spiritual world has nothing in common with the physical world.

Ordinary human beings are like the chick that would regard its eggshell as the real world. If the chick could see within its eggshell, this eggshell would not look small to the chick, but quite enlarged; it would look as large as our world looks to us. The content within the shell would look like the whole world. This is the way we see our eggshell: our aura that is spread out around us as the blue vault of the heavens. If we break through our shell, then the Sun and Moon become dark, the stars fall to the Earth, and in their place the spiritual world spreads itself out.

Human beings live in their eggshell—their aura. The elohim gave us our aura, and through the Fall this aura became like a shell around us. We are within it, just like the chick is in the egg. The sky and the stars are our boundary, and we must use our soul strength to break through the boundary, just as the chick has to use its own strength to break through its shell. Then we achieve entrance into a new world, just as the chick has a new world before it when it has crawled out of the egg. And because human beings all actually have the same eggshell around them, and because astronomy could arise such as it now has, this lets the celestial bodies move around on the celestial vault.

The eggshell is: *Ex Deo nascimur*. In order to break through this shell and also take something with us into the spiritual world, we must bring with us what penetrates into our shell from the outer world—that is, from the spiritual world—and what is common to us all. This is Christ. Thus, we speak: *In Christo morimur* and hope that, when we have broken through the shell with Christ's help, we will be resurrected again: *Per Spiritum Sanctum reviviscimus*.

* * *

Record B

We should feel the suppressing of [the content of] the meditation as the fight against Lucifer.[†] We must achieve an understanding for the so-called Fall of the human being. We experience something similar [to the Fall] when we become an esotericist. For what do people do when they become esotericists? They take on, ahead of time, something that humanity must go through only later. And always, when human beings actually do not want to progress in the regular manner, the temptations of Lucifer begin to approach them. Lucifer tempts us when we hear voices within ourselves that speak to us in our language. On the other side of the threshold our language is not spoken; a different language is spoken there. For this reason, we must say to these voices: You all lie! Ahriman tempts us by showing us pictures.

We must penetrate through the voices and the pictures in order to come to the truth. The following was given as an example: imagine a chick before it comes out of the egg. It has the eggshell around it, and this is what the chick knows and sees from inside; it sees the inside of the eggshell in the same way we look at, as our eggshell, the sky and everything that our eyes see. All of this [that we see] is a beholding of the egg from the inside. We see our own aura from inside. We must break through this eggshell, just as the chick punches through its eggshell with its beak, throws it off, and enters into a new world. Only when we also do this, do we then enter the world of the divine-spiritual beings, the hierarchies.

In order to achieve this [breaking through our eggshell], we must let everything in the meditation fall away. We must shut out everything—other thoughts and feelings that want to come over us—except the content of the meditation. Then, however we must also let this [content] fall away; we must shut it out, and yet remain conscious—that is the most important thing. We must feel that.

Lucifer lives in our thinking—also in our thinking during the meditation. We therefore enter into an association with Lucifer in our thinking of the meditation. Now, we must drop our thinking in the meditation; this means we have to make ourselves empty by dropping the content of the meditation and letting go of the thought-force. Through voluntary, conscious suppression [of the content and thought force], we voluntarily and consciously kill what comes from Lucifer.

It is a matter in the meditation of generating a concentrated attention without having an object [of our attention]. To be attentive to an object is the beginning of the meditation, but then we must turn our attention away and give the thinking back to the gods—that is the most important thing. And only then do we enter the true spiritual world.

After the human being succumbed to the temptation of Lucifer, who said: "You will be like the gods!"—then the Godhead said: "No!" And the gods took away the life from what Lucifer gave; the gods inserted death into it.

When we enter the spiritual world, we experience the force that molds and builds the human bodily nature; we come to the truth of ourselves. Through Lucifer, the human beings learn the difference between good and evil; they receive the ability to judge.

The [physical] body has a limit to how much pain it can endure. When this limit has been surpassed, the person faints. The soul too has limits, beyond which unconsciousness enters in.

Through letting go of brain-thinking, we experience ourselves outside of our brain. We feel as if we are circling around our brain in streams. We really slip around our brain afterward [after letting go of the thinking]. If we continue the otherwise ordinary thinking and feel ourselves connected with processes which are otherwise always in effect—and with that [force] through which the thought process arises—then we come to know a feeling that we can express in this way: we have a real fear to let it (what we experience outside the brain) come into our thoughts. A certain willpower and overcoming of ourselves must be brought in relation to the communication of such truths and facts—these spiritual imaginations, which we have experienced outside the brain—because we have now learned what actually works on the human being. We behold the destruction process of ordinary thinking.

Spiritual researchers manage, for a while, not to involve themselves in the destruction process. They place themselves beside their brain. Devoting oneself or giving oneself up to the universe without exerting inner activity is a part of spiritual research. Then spiritual researchers learn to do voluntarily what is otherwise done involuntarily during sleep. Spiritual researchers learn to feel all of the functions of the body (breathing, processes of the glands, etc.), and they face and experience the whole human being from outside. Through devotion and deepening of the soul forces of thinking, and especially of feeling, spiritual researchers accomplish all of this. We must put our hearts into such a meditation, into such an idea. We must engage our feelings in meditating; then we will not only be outside of our brain, but we will circle the whole human being. Then it begins to dawn on us: you were there before conception; you descended down into this incarnation! We look out over earthly life, and we have a typical spiritual experience. It is as if a lightning bolt split this body! This experience shows us in a picture that it is as if a lightning bolt shot through the house—through your body—and carried it away.

That is a distressing experience! It is the experience of coming close to death! Now we see and know what the soul-spiritual core of the human being is!

We must then also learn to concentrate our will selflessly in regard to the outer, daily act of speech. Just as we can release the power of thought from the brain, and the whole human being through the feeling, so too can we release the power of speech from language itself. The speech movements must be silent; we may not come outwardly to speaking. We must practice inwardly, soul-spiritually; we execute the same activity that we would otherwise do in speaking. It must go so far that we do not let the sound even enter the nerves. What is normally used to speak must remain in the gestures.

In the mantric, in meditation, it is not a concept that is involved; it is only inwardly experiencing the sound. We listen to ourselves, but do not let anything come into speaking. Through this we will come to know our earlier earthly lives. That is true memory. The forces of our mind and heart (Gemüt) allow us to look into our life beyond birth and conception; the forces of our will show us earlier earthly lives.

* * *

RECORD C

What is the Fall of humanity? With it something happened that formed the development of humanity differently than it was supposed to be according to the gods, especially according to Yahweh. Human beings were supposed to be a creation that should have followed the instincts of the gods—just the way the animal follows its instincts. But, human beings were given their own ability to distinguish between good and evil: earth-knowledge. They were taught to make their own judgments; but the knowledge of heaven, of the spirit, was taken away from them for the time being. Now esotericists undertake the task to achieve knowledge of the spiritual world and bring it to the earth-knowledge. The esotericists no longer have it easy, like the rest of the people who merely live their lives. There arise for the esotericists earnest duties and responsibilities, for instance, in relation to the truth. They know that when in an incarnation they have told someone an untruth, they must rectify this by telling that person the truth. This is not always easy—it can be terribly difficult—but it must happen, because karma must be fulfilled. For example, if an esotericist suddenly feels about to be sick; that is the spirit of truth that wants untruth eradicated. Esotericists must take this as a warning to speak the truth. Or, in another instance, they feel a prickling in the blood. That is the egotism concealed in the "I." As long as people hide themselves from the egotism and do not want to see it, it is expressed in the fact that they cannot bear to see the expression of the egotistical "I": the blood. They faint at the sight of blood; they hide from the egotism that prickles in the blood.

The luciferic and ahrimanic forces work everywhere, and esotericists become quite explicitly acquainted with these forces. They must fight these forces and must not shy away from the fight. Human beings received earth-knowledge through the serpent, through Lucifer. Earth-knowledge must be led to the point of death, because death is the result of earth-knowledge. Human beings must learn to feel the earth... [handwritten note illegible here], inwardly dead. They must be able to let their thinking die and yet remain awake and conscious. The meditation content is given in words of the human language, but the language is Lucifer's work (Tower of Babel).† The words have covered the actual human language: the proto-language. Thus, we would have to receive a luciferic content right into our meditation. When we believe, at a certain stage of soul development, that we hear voices, and when these voices speak to us in any language, we must absolutely know that it is Lucifer speaking. What the voices speak are lies, and with strong inner force we must break through the shell of these lies in order to come to the truth; that is, to the true spiritual world which is covered up by this shell [of lies]. And when people believe they see pictures or images, this is, first of all, Ahriman at work. We human beings are like a chick in the egg; like a chick that believes that the shell of the egg is like a mirror from which it can see what it itself is. Human beings must have the inner strength—when, for instance, an angel appears—to penetrate with knowledge-force through this picture and discover that the angel changes into a devil. The chick could believe that its shell is the universe. Human beings believe the same thing. People are stuck in their own eggshell and believe that this blue shell, on which they see the stars, Sun, and Moon, is the world. It is not. People are doing the same thing that the chick does, and when the chick uses its strength and bursts through the shell, it is like the human beings who use their inner strength and burst the shell of the world-egg that they regard as the world. Then [when they have burst through the shell] people see that what the astronomers say about the Sun, Moon, and the stars is not entirely true. They see the world of the hierarchies and their working. The stars fall down for them, and the Sun and Moon lose their physical light. They go out into the world of the Father God, of the creator of the world-egg, which before was their whole world. Human beings enter into this world [of the Father God] through death, but also through initiation. Christ belongs to both worlds—their primordial world, but also the world of the egg—because he made the sacrifice to give himself into it (the world of the egg) and to work in it. He did this so that human beings could find the inner strength to burst the shell and so come into the world of the hierarchies: the world of the Holy Spirit. The mantra, *In Christo morimur*, means to let our earth-knowledge die so that the heavenly knowledge can light up again.

Just as the [physical] body comes to its limit of how much pain it can bear and passes out when the limit is surpassed, so too does the soul have limits of its ability to endure. Then it (the soul) cannot manage anymore and must do what the spirit of truth demands of it—it must break through the knot.

The soul feels itself in its own force, which surrounds it like a shell. The soul must break through this shell, and then Lucifer and Ahriman are there immediately.

* * *

Record D

The Fall can be experienced again on the esoteric path because with every advance by the human being, temptation stands in the way.

Those who become esotericists must be aware that they must take life differently than the exotericists. We can numb bodily pain, but we can no longer numb soul pain. We must know that when we speak untruth, we must sometime in a later life rectify this by speaking the truth, but then with the feeling of shame. The [physical] body can endure only a certain amount of pain, and then we faint; we lose the power of our "I." Weak souls can also faint through fear or shock. When immature souls with a psychic nature enter the spiritual world rapidly through the exercises, they fall victim there to a numbing through voices that speak to them in their language. Lucifer places these voices before the spiritual world. We must then awaken a great soul-strength in order to call to these voices: "You lie." Then the voices stop. In our imagination, Ahriman opposes us. Some people see an angel. When they examine it closely, it disappears in mist, and in its place is a devil. If a manifestation has a blue color that, when looked at sharply, turns to red, this shows that there is still desire in us. Human beings sit in the aura of their illusions—also in regard to their physical surroundings—like a chick in the eggshell. We must break through this [shell], in order to enter the spiritual world. We must first learn to understand the speech of the spiritual world. For this, we must imbue ourselves with something that has come from the spiritual world to us in the eggshell. This is the Christ impulse, and we must take it with us [out of the eggshell]. Behind the maya of the celestial vault, we then find the hierarchies. In our meditations, we have something (a part) that belongs to Lucifer's realm—we thus connect ourselves with Lucifer. When we shut out the meditation [content] and shut out all thinking, we call upon our soul to do battle with Lucifer.

Esoteric Lesson

NUREMBERG, NOVEMBER 9, 1913

It is so difficult for esotericists to make progress, because they imagine the experiences they are supposed to have as much too tumultuous. Above all, it is important to pay attention to the subtlest processes.

Imagine that you walk on a quiet evening through an isolated forest. Every smallest sound is perceptible: the falling leaves, an approaching sleigh, and so on. And now imagine, in contrast, the big city. In the noise of the streets, you will perceive nothing of that kind, and yet these still, fine sounds are present here also.

In meditation, there surfaces everything possible that did not reach the threshold of consciousness before. I hear the complaint so often that so many thoughts and pictures surface in people's meditations. They cannot control the thoughts and pictures, nor can they free themselves from them. You can absolutely take this as progress in meditation. Because the astral body and etheric body loosened their connection to the physical body during meditation, the esotericists objectify their *other human being*. In these processes, they should examine their soul-spiritual element that weaves and works without their assistance.

Lucifer's temptation approaches esotericists from within; Ahriman's comes from outside.

An example: let us assume that you live in a well-behaved, quiet family. However, your family lives wall-on-wall with people who often tell or read aloud stories about robbers. Even if you have not heard them with your physical ears at all, their stories imprint themselves on your etheric body and emerge during meditation.

Another example: you experience a dog being run over. In your own body a whimpering and barking can arise, can result after experiencing such an accident. Out of other connections a whole pandemonium sets in during meditation. Meditants should not despair about this, but should be happy because they can get an idea of the connection and learn to examine ever more objectively everything that has worked upon them beforehand.

It is like a feeling or touching of your whole body during meditation. Here and there feelings of pain appear as the result of egotism and other things. With this feeling or touching, you begin above your head and go bit-by-bit down the whole body.

You will also learn, starting with the phenomena of an illness, to draw conclusions about earlier experiences. For example, an inner ear infection can suggest the most peculiar impressions that were imprinted on the etheric body because the person had, as a youth, heard without full consciousness stories about robbers. These stories then had the liveliest effect.

If people fall asleep during Theosophical or similar lectures, what they heard works on in their etheric body—especially when they later have pangs of conscience about having fallen asleep. When they reproach themselves, it often works very strongly in the subconscious.

Regarding the self-recrimination that we are still bad because ugly pictures keep arising during meditation and inner concentration, the word of the Gospel should comfort us: "He took our guilt upon himself."

Esoteric Lesson

NUREMBERG, NOVEMBER 10, 1913

We want to discuss something that can be of value for our whole esoteric life. The goal of this esoteric life is to give us something that, as ordinary human beings, we do not yet have. We act like children in relation to spiritual worlds. Reasonable teachers or educators do not let children do simply whatever they want to do. That is, parents and teachers do not educate children by letting the children have their way with everything. We must consider and examine not what is, but what is becoming in the children, and must arrange everything in their education accordingly. Also in play, for example, one gives a child a gun that shoots blanks [or a cap pistol], because a regular gun would cause damage.

Thus is it also when human beings seek the spiritual worlds. If they were given too early the means to enter the spiritual worlds, they would cause only damage and disaster upon using these means before they were really developed enough to enter the spiritual worlds.

We must treat children as emergent, becoming persons. They express their nature in their playing. A boy plays war; a girl plays mother-and-child with dolls. Likewise, esotericists must be treated as developing, becoming beings by the spiritual teachers and guides, and they must be given what they will need later. Our earthly development progresses. When we enter into new incarnations, it will be evident how important and necessary it was to have occupied ourselves with Theosophy in this life. People will want to recall—they do not do this yet—their spiritual experiences. Those who have not taken in any Theosophy will find nothing. They will brood over it; they will crave and starve for something that they cannot find in their memory. It is important, immensely important, to devote ourselves to the esoteric life, even though we do not enter the spiritual worlds consciously. We must see the spiritual work as a necessary preparation. We should banish everything else from our thoughts and feelings. What absolutely matters is the prevailing mood of the soul.

Imagine a chick breaking the eggshell and hatching. What is the difference between the time before it hatched, and afterward? Beforehand, the chick was completely enclosed in the eggshell, and that was its world. Everything the chick experienced, it experienced as pictures within the eggshell. Where is the chick when it breaks through the shell? Then it stands on the outside of the shell. Then the chick's experience and perception expand around as far as its senses reach. Thus, it is a much larger space than before, and the life in the eggshell seems tiny in comparison.

Human beings in the ordinary sense-life are in the same situation as the chick in the shell. Everything around us projects itself as a picture, and appears to be the size it does because we are enclosed within [this sense-life] and do not have a measure for comparison other than this.

We look up to the blue sky and see the stars. Astronomers calculate their orbits and what they call their [astronomical] laws. And in truth, they see no further than the eggshell. In our astral body, we all carry such an eggshell around with us—an aura-eggshell, a hull. It is only that with the chick, the shell is condensed to the point of being physical, and with us it is not. For this reason, we do not notice it. Materialistic science, for instance, sees the Sun as only a hollow sphere, or suppose it to be imbued with matter similar to what is thought to be in our Earth, but just in other states of being. In truth, however, the Sun is the center of our "I." And when we see the evening star or the morning star, then we know, as Theosophists, that there outside, the forces are working which correspond to our etheric body.

Esoteric Lesson

BERLIN, NOVEMBER 17, 1913

RECORD A

Starting from the often-stated fact that the Mystery of Golgotha is the most important event in the evolution of humanity, and that since this event Christ is connected with the aura of the Earth, Dr. Steiner said that many of us have had, during our striving, the question imposed upon us: where is Christ actually now? (In the lecture before the last one in the Lodge,† Rudolf Steiner already said that people seek Christ where he is not, just as the women at the grave sought him and found that the grave was empty.† And also, like these women, the Crusaders of the Middle Ages sought him where he is not. Only the disciples sought him where he is: in the spirit.)

Then Dr. Steiner spoke about the point in time back to which people can remember. This time lies between birth and the seventh year of life, and it is the time when the self-consciousness of the human being awakens. This point lies between birth and the change of teeth, and in this time the individual form of the physical body is essentially molded. In the first years [of life] human beings live in a dull, dream-like condition of consciousness. The whole soul life of humanity today takes the course it does because human beings awaken to their self-consciousness in the first seven years of life.

Let us assume for a moment that this were different. Hypothetically, we will assume that human beings do not awaken to self-consciousness until they are in their tenth year of life. Then their whole soul life would be different. Let us imagine that such people, who have awakened to self-consciousness in their tenth year, have the intention to wake up at a particular time the next morning. They would upon waking up have the impression that they themselves came to the door, knocked, and awakened themselves. Or they might see themselves coming into the room as a light-form walking up to them, opening their eyes, and thus awakening them. They would then know that Christ is in the same realm, out of which their own light-form comes.

In spite of human self-consciousness entering already during the first seven years, many people will at sometime soon have this experience. We are standing at a significant turning point, and we must point it out. People will then experience how the light-form of their astral body sails up to them, and they will recognize that this light-form consumes or saps the physical body; when the astral body leaves the physical body, it takes a piece with it. And when in the morning the light-form again takes possession of the physical body, we know that the cost of our living is dying. This knowledge can lead people to the deepest sorrow and melancholy. They will no longer value their physical body. Whereas, through outer culture and the accomplishments of technology—airplanes and other things—human courage is immensely intensified and increased, at the same time little value is placed on life. People will fall into a deep earnestness, a sorrow and melancholy, and the number of suicides will increase tremendously. While outer courage grows in the outer sense-life, inner courage, on the other hand, will necessarily decrease and give way to a cowardice, a hidden cowardice. Human beings are becoming ever more materialists and want to know nothing of the soul-spiritual. There is a kind of cowardice behind this. The angels foresaw this in the evolution of humanity and inspired Kant[†] to develop his doctrine of the boundaries of human knowledge. This was necessary in the development of humanity.

Those people who do not find their way to Christ fall victim to boundless sorrow and deepest earnestness when they experience, "I lived at the expense of dying," and they actually see the figure of death walking beside them. But we know that Christ lives in the aura of the Earth. We are always connected with him. And when we know this and keep this knowledge alive in us, the image of death takes on the characteristics of Christ, who walks beside us, even though we do not behold him clairvoyantly. Seeing Christ clairvoyantly does not yet make him alive; we must know it, and because of this the following must now be said.

We cannot withdraw from the spirit of the time. He works everywhere, and we are standing in our time. However, knowing that Christ lives and that we can reach him will preserve our souls from desolation, deep melancholy, and the contempt for life. Through this we will understand the meaning of our Rosicrucian mantra: *In Christo morimur.*

When we can let all of this become quite living in our soul in our moments of stillness, it can become a great help.

* * *

RECORD B

We want to examine something important today. You must inwardly work on all the communications and information that have been given to you in the esoteric lessons. They must fill you completely and be the object of your inner contemplation and reflection in your leisure time. During meditation, or as a result of it, it can happen that we ask ourselves: where then actually is Christ? Where must I seek him?

We know the following: Before the Mystery of Golgotha, Christ was a cosmic being who lived outside of the Earth sphere. In the event that is designated as the John-baptism, Christ descended into the already-prepared bodily nature of Jesus of Nazareth and was active within it for three years. And finally, we know that through the Mystery of Golgotha, the Christ being flowed together with the aura of the Earth, and that since then Christ is to be found in the surroundings of the Earth. Those who were initiated before the Mystery of Golgotha did not yet find him in the surroundings of the Earth. They had to be transported to the Sun to find him. However, since the Mystery of Golgotha, Christ flowed into the aura of the Earth, and everyone can now experience him there. For we know that yet in this century, many people will come to behold the etheric Christ. Naturally, to have a knowledge of Christ is yet something different.

It has already been pointed out often that the forms of the physical body develop by the seventh year of life. The physical body keeps growing, but the actual forms are there. We know further that modern human beings develop in such a way that sometime between birth and the seventh year of life is the first moment that we can recall.[†] Many believe that we can think back only to the seventh year, but that is not correct; it only appears that way, because today memory is frequently covered up by other imaginations. This moment between birth and the seventh year back to which we can remember is the moment when our "I"-consciousness awakens.

Now the following question can emerge and be given as a thorough, detailed meditation to the meditant by the Master: How would evolution proceed, if human beings continued in dream-like life without the "I"-consciousness that modern beings have? How would it be if people's "I"-consciousness awakened only in the second period of their life, perhaps in the ninth or tenth year of life? A part of the question is immediately answered.

Let us assume hypothetically that a man who has developed his "I" only in the second period of his life, gave the order to awaken him in the morning at a particular time. Then in a kind of dream, which begins as the appointed time for being awakened approaches, he has the feeling that he himself—his "I"—knocks on the door, approaches his bed, and wakes up his physical body. He will be as one with this action. Or in the case that he waits until he awakens of his own accord—which usually occurs at the beginning of daylight—he sees a light-form that comes to him and wakes him up. Then he will know that it was not the daylight that awakened him, but that his soul, which was in a sea of light, came back as a light-form into his body.

Also, the whole soul life would be different. There would be no sharp, exact separation between day-consciousness and the dream-filled sleep-consciousness—as is the case with other people—but they would merge into one another. The day-waking consciousness would be permeated by dreams that lead over almost unnoticeably into the night dreams. Because people experience themselves more as a spirit being and feel that this spirit being consumes the physical body and must gradually bring death, they would always experience this death in their dreams. They would always have the image of death before them. Thus, a melancholic mood would spread itself over the whole of life and, in the end, lame the creative forces. But Christ is to be found in this world of death. He is there!

Modern human beings often lack the courage to seek Christ and to penetrate into the spiritual world. In this connection people have become cowardly. We realize that when a characteristic develops on the one side, it weakens so much the more on the other side. Those who have courage in the field of technology—for example in travel by airplane—can be cowardly when it comes to entering the spiritual world. An angel inspired Kant to maintain in his works that reason has boundaries and that our powers of knowledge are limited to the physical, material realm. Thus the striving for the spiritual is quite dampened down today, and people do not even think about or realize how cowardly they are in relation to the spiritual worlds, and how their soul must become more and more desolate because of it. We are all dependent on the nuances of our modern culture—on the commercial, industrial times in which we live—and we must never forget that this is the time when materialism has reached its zenith. However, just as a rubber ball can be compressed only to a certain point and then springs back to its original size, so too will the souls that have been constricted by materialism unfold their wings again. The greater the soul-desolation was, the stronger will be the reaction.

It is always said that all of evolution proceeds in an even, steady fashion. But everywhere in nature there are jumps forward. And the development of the soul is preparing precisely now to make a leap forward into the future. The divine cosmic leadership foresaw materialism. Human beings were as good as cut-off from the spiritual worlds, so the forces of the soul could then move all the more strongly in response; this is because the soul forces allow themselves to be pressed together only to a certain degree. The physical constitution of human beings will remain the same in the future, but their soul life will develop as if their self-consciousness would awaken only in later years.

We must realize that the forces of death and life are in us, and that it is up to us to take hold of the life forces. If human beings do not achieve knowledge of Christ, if they reject the Christ impulse, they will face a boundless soul desolation and hardening and will feel only death beside themselves. They will feel only death forces walking beside them and will always have the feeling: I die into the death. A deep melancholy will take hold of such human souls; it will generate revulsion and weariness of life and lead to epidemics of suicide.

When we, however, imbue ourselves with the Christ impulse, we will know clearly that all life proceeds at the cost of death, but in such a way that death is the seed or germ of a new life in the spiritual world. Death itself will approach us in the form of Christ. And we will grasp correctly the meaning of the words: *In Christo morimur*. Contained in the three parts of our ten-word Rosicrucian mantra we have all the wisdom that can lead us up into the spiritual worlds.

* * *

Record C

What is given to us esoterically we should bring again to consciousness in our leisure hours and meditate on it in such a way that it does not become merely conceptual content, but becomes life with which we can unite ourselves completely. Also now something will be given to us which can be important for us to make into a meditation.

We have already heard much about the Mystery of Golgotha, and some of us have that feeling-experience that Christ is all around us, even though it is not yet a clairvoyant experience. However, even though we will come to this higher experience only later, we can still feel ourselves permeated by Christ. Because we meditate thus about Christ, the question can arise: where do we find Christ who, as we know, was a cosmic divinity at first outside of the Earth and then united himself with our Earth through the Mystery of Golgotha? We know that Christ will not appear again on Earth in a physical body, but we can ask ourselves: where is Christ to be found in the atmosphere of the Earth?

We can, when we are deep in meditation, feel for moments how our teacher poses for us questions out of the spiritual world and that, because we try to answer these questions, we are led further forward in our meditative contemplation. One question that could be posed is as follows. If we were so disposed that we would not receive between the third and seventh years—thus, in the time when the physical body receives its specific form and from then on only grows larger—our "I"-consciousness, but instead in the tenth year, in the second seven-year period of life, how would our consciousness develop?

If our consciousness were such that, until our tenth year we led a kind of dream-life and then our "I"-consciousness awakened, we would have a totally different soul life [from what we have now]. If, for example, we would want to be awakened in the morning, we would see ourselves outside of our body. We would see how we knock on the door, and we would know that we ourselves were within the sound that awakened us. Or, also, we would not wake up the way we otherwise would and see that it has become light, but rather we would see ourselves as a light-form. We would behold ourselves as a light-form and sense, in opening our eyes, how we sail as a light into ourselves and pervade our body with consciousness.

However, the consciousness would not have a sharp boundary between the day-waking life and the dream-life of night; these two would flow into one another. The entire day-life would have a kind of dream-condition passing through it. Yet we would know at the same time that we are, in the form in which we are free of the body, a spirit being that consumes and wears on the body and brings death. We would carry around in our dreams the consciousness of death. We would always behold the image of death beside us. And this would spread a great melancholy and sorrow over life and would steal from us all strength of life.

If all of this were so, the modern materialistic culture would flourish more and more, and human soul life would become desolate. We could not develop courage for life anymore. Courage is indeed decreasing among people. There is a kind of physical courage developing—for instance, in traveling by airplane—but it is at the expense of courage for the spiritual, the courage to lift ourselves above the ordinary, materialistic consciousness.

As strange as it may sound, the good angels inspired Kant to develop his "boundaries of knowledge," because with the materialistic culture that had to come, human beings lacked the courage to enter into the spiritual worlds and so remained stuck in the physical world. Yet, just as a rubber ball that has been compressed to its extreme then springs back, so too will this [pressing of the materialism] call forth in the soul life a reaction, and then human courage will again want to turn to the conquest of the spiritual worlds.

It is not regularly the case that human beings attain self-consciousness only at ten years of age, nor will it be so in the future. It will, however, be such that in the future the consciousness will go through the transformation that has been described, and this time is rapidly approaching. Esotericists must take up many of these things ahead of time. It is precisely for this reason that we have our Theosophy and our esoteric development: so that we learn to understand the future.

In the future, all human beings will constantly behold death beside them and experience death within themselves. Melancholy will be the basic mood of the soul, and suicide will increase in a frightening manner. Yet precisely there, in that world of death, is where we must seek Christ! When we can fill ourselves with an understanding of the Mystery of Golgotha, the image of death will transform itself into the image of Christ, and then we will know where to find Christ.

Without Christ, human beings would have to always go around with the feeling: I am dying; I am dying into the death. Yet this feeling can give way to the knowledge: I die into Christ! This should be a quite special meditation: *In – – – morimur*. Out of this [mantra] the strength can grow in order that human beings can maintain, in spite of the new consciousness of humanity, strength of life and soul-courage, and feel themselves always united with that world in which Christ is present and in which he is always with us and is all around us. "Watch and pray," should be the guide in order to attain that kind of consciousness [of the Christ].

All of this can be given real life for us, if we again and again earnestly meditate our mantra:

> *Ex Deo nascimur*
> *In (Christo) morimur*
> *Per Spiritum Sanctum reviviscimus.*

> *From God we are born*
> *In Christ we die*
> *Through the Holy Spirit we come to life again.*

Record D

Today we will take up something that you must let live further in yourself meditatively, in order that it may help you to progress. It has often been spoken of that Christ, before the baptism in the Jordan, was in the cosmos and could be seen there by clairvoyants. Through the baptism Christ moved into the sheaths of Jesus of Nazareth, and with the Mystery of Golgotha flowed into the atmosphere of the Earth and remained there. For some the question has arisen: where is Christ now—where is he to be sought?

The memory of human beings goes back to the seventh year, which was the beginning of the "I"-consciousness. Also, the form of the physical body is complete and only grows from then on. The "I"-consciousness comes about in this first [seven-year] period. Question: how would it be if the memory went back only to the tenth year, falling thus in the second period?

Let us assume that it would be so. Then everything would be different. Those people who let themselves be awakened in the morning would have a dream-like experience, as if they themselves were the ones who came up to their door and knocked, in order to awaken their physical body. Or if they awakened, as they usually do, when it was light, they would have the experience that they themselves, as a light-form, came up to their physical body, opened their eyes, and let the light ray into them. They would return to their physical body in the morning knowing that they destroy the body through this, and that they bring the physical body toward death. Upon awakening, they would see death standing beside them, and melancholy would spread over their soul. Sleep would be a conscious dream-life. There consciousness would not cease. This is how they would experience the current condition of human evolution.

Now, the "I"-consciousness will never wait until the tenth year to awaken, but humanity is progressing, soul life is changing, and human beings will soon experience what has just been described. Had the Mystery of Golgotha not occurred, they would be, with the progressing of materialistic culture, wrapped in deep melancholy because the figure of death would be a constant companion. Through the Mystery of Golgotha the form of death will transform, for those who have taken into themselves the Christ impulse, the form of Christ. What was just described is the place where Christ is to be sought. And it is our task to prepare the time when the human being will thus experience awakening. Knowing these esoteric secrets, we should wait and look toward the morning star that will rise for humanity. The materialistic culture of technology creates courage for the physical life, but cowardice for the spiritual, for the strengthening of the soul-forces. This is the reason the spiritual is denied. Therefore, the angels inspired Kant to deny human beings the possibility of knowledge of the spiritual, so that the human soul-forces, like a rubber ball, once pressed together and compressed, would spring up and with all the more strength and power grasp spiritual knowledge.

* * *

Esoteric Lesson
STUTTGART, NOVEMBER 23, 1913

RECORD A

Why is it that esotericists who have practiced concentration and meditation for year may still have not attained sight into the spiritual worlds? In order to answer this question clearly we need to look at what meditation actually is. When we want to meditate, we must have the will to turn away from outer things; we do not want them to exert any influence on our thoughts anymore. Outer things should not disturb us in our devotion to the spiritual. Yet outer occurrences and thoughts constantly push their way before our meditating soul. They want to turn us away from our meditation and hinder our devotion, and so we must exert our greatest willpower to fight against them. If we want to examine who exactly fights against our better will, the following example can perhaps give some clarification. Let us assume that a stranger approaches us and says: "You are a fickle person." Ninety-nine percent of the time we would be disturbed by this because until now we had thought we were quite good esotericists who have each searched our own inner being regarding our faults, and now a stranger comes and maintains the opposite. In exactly the same way that the stranger stands in front of us, so too something in all the thoughts that shoved themselves into our meditation appears before us. We believe we do not to know what this is, and yet it is our own self that reveals itself in all of these thoughts, and shows us how fickle we really are and how little we can free ourselves from our daily cares and desires. What always presses into us during our meditation—though we wish to separate ourselves from outer things and to unite with the spiritual—is our streaming life of desires. In the pictures of our daily life, this life of desires streams ceaselessly into our thinking and resists our efforts when we try to connect with the spiritual realm.

That this happens can be of benefit to us, because we therefore come to know ourselves in our desire-life, which is constantly flowing into these pictures and thoughts. It must lead to the self-knowledge: that we have, until now, practiced superficially. Yet, usually we will reach for all kinds of excuses, because we do not want to condemn ourselves or hold ourselves accountable for anything. This is the reason that vision into the spiritual world remains closed to us. Our life of desires draws a veil in front of it. If we would turn our attention away from the occurrences and experiences of our desire-life, if we would turn our "I" and our devotion to the spiritual, we would have already had success long ago. To use a trivial example, even if we were to bring only so much attention to our meditation as we do for all kinds of social conversation, or also for new information about friends, we would rapidly progress in our knowledge of the higher worlds. We would then push back our "I" that is defending itself.

Our thoughts are nothing but memories of earlier occurrences, and these occurrences are nothing other than desires that we have felt. If they had not been pleasurable to us, we would not have stored them in our memory. If we examine our memory, we will find that everything we have enjoyed the most is buried within us. Everything toward which we were indifferent—for which we did not have special interests or have not had pleasure in—disappeared from our memory. It is exactly like the school children who cannot remember in later years the small, specific details of their studies because during the school years they were not so interested in the content, and therefore these details did not leave so deep an impression on their memory.

It is also necessary that we bring devotion and dedication to our esoteric development. It is not the method we use to meditate that should influence us; nor should the wish to meditate often, in order to have many experiences in the spiritual world, guide us. All of that should not move us, as we would thereby see only our own wishes because Lucifer would reign over us then. We will not free ourselves so easily from the world of Lucifer and Ahriman. When we believe to have practiced thorough self-knowledge and yet seek excuses for ourselves, it is Ahriman who stands beside us. It is just as much Ahriman when we seek excuses after someone says that we have done this or that badly. We love Ahriman and Lucifer too much. They accompany us through our whole life, precisely because we love them so much. And why do we love them?

We will give an example to try to make this clear. How does a mother calm her crying children? She does so by caressing them and stroking their face, which calls forth a pleasant bodily awareness. Now, we must know how Ahriman and Lucifer reveal themselves and endear themselves to us. They do this by bringing us into contact with the things of the world in which we seek pleasure, and where the satisfaction [of our desires] is so pleasant. Through the light rays that Lucifer and Ahriman let fall upon the objects and which ray forth from the objects to us, we feel a pleasant stimulus, just as the crying children feel at the caressing touch of the mother. Lucifer and Ahriman stroke us through the magic of the light rays that they spread over the things of the world, and our eyes become aware of these things through contact with the rays.

Above all, these powers show their influence also in modern science and philosophy; for example, in a conversation that a student of Schopenhauer's had with Nietzsche.† Deussen maintained, in relation to Nietzsche,† that denial of the will determines life; whereas Nietzsche said the ennobling of life leads to life. If we look closely and Deussen's statement and think about it, we would have to say that the denial of the will does not lead to life, but to death. Drinkers and vagabonds, who live in the state of will-denial in relation to their desires, and do not keep them in check but allow themselves every pleasure offered, will not attain life, but will find a premature death. On the other hand, people who strive for the ennoblement of their will radiate the forces of a healing seed or germ with which their rays have connected. Scholars believed themselves, with the statements of Deussen, to have looked through crystal-clear glasses, whereas their glasses actually had wooden lenses. We also see here that Ahriman stands before us because we ourselves do not let go of him in all our affairs in life; that is how much we love him. It is necessary to become clear about this, because we must quite consciously recognize Lucifer and Ahriman in what we do or do not do, and especially there where these powers want to stand between us and our meditation in order to deny sight into the spiritual world. The time has come when we must strive to develop ourselves for spiritual knowledge by forming in ourselves the spiritual organs of clairvoyance, so that these organs do not dry up and languish. Slowly and gradually, we must grow in the spiritual realm out of which we are born: *Ex Deo nascimur*.

In the beginning of our life, which has its source in the Godhead, we were still imbued by the divine-spiritual forces; they work on children until the change of teeth—they still work in the milk teeth. The change of teeth is completed in the seventh year, and the new teeth intended for this life appear. Thus, everything with human beings is renewed. The old is pushed away by the new: the hair falls out and is replaced by new hair, and the fingernails are cut and grow again. With the falling out of the first teeth, the milk teeth, the spiritual forces that have worked on the building-up and growth of the child have reached their end. Now other forces or beings begin to work on the building-up process for the current incarnation. With this building-up, however, the decline and dying of the organs begins immediately. They gradually approach death, for even every thought we think causes destruction in the brain cells. Matter is ordained to a slow dying: *In Christo morimur*.

We grow slowly toward the spiritual. Our hair becomes white, and all of our organs pass over into the spiritual. Our whole body strives toward spiritualization. It will be resurrected again in the spirit: *Per Spiritum Sanctum reviviscimus*.

* * *

Record B

Esotericists must become more and more aware that the world is complicated. When we human beings come into the physical plane, something takes place during the first year of life that we can compare with the fight that spiritual beings fought before the creation of old Saturn, in order for Saturn to be able to come into being. This is the fight of the spirits of personality, who worked from within, with the spirits of will, who worked from without. In the first year of our life on the physical plane, we must fight and overcome what we have within us that is inherited. We must thus struggle with the spirits of will and with our personality.

This fight takes place around us in our first year of life. If we examine children, they become similar to their ancestors only later in life, and this is so to the extent that heredity—which comes from the spirits of will—prevails over what is individual, over what the spirits of personality represent.

We love being caressed; we love to enjoy ourselves. Ahriman strokes and caresses us, just like we caress a child. It makes the child feel good. It is Ahriman who whispers the excuse to us for what we do. He says: you could not have done it any differently. You cannot help it, etc.

Lucifer strengthens (and increases) our egotism. There is also a third being that comes to us—the *unknown*—and says: you are a superficial human being. This irritates us. What we experience in meditation as disturbing thoughts is the *unknown* who says this to us; and indeed we are ourselves this being. It is uncomfortable to discover how and what we are! People go to church and pray to beings whom they love. Often we have the name of Christ upon our lips, but we really mean Ahriman.

Concerning the first and second teeth, it is only with the first teeth that we are immortal. The pushing from the spiritual human being brings forth the second teeth. All memory is egotism that has become fluid. We remember what once stimulated desire in us. The stronger the desire was, the better the memory. In meditation, nothing stimulates our desires; for this reason, the desire-nature revolts. The desire-nature wants to be stroked, and this does not happen in meditation. School children learn a lot that does not stimulate their desires. Therefore, they soon forget what they have learned.

Everything concerning the secrets of our existence lies in the Rosicrucian mantra:

> *Aus dem Gottlichen sind wir geboren*
> *In dem Christus sterben wir*
> *In dem Heiligen Geiste werden wir auferstehen.*

Out of the divine we are born
In Christ we die
In the Holy Spirit we resurrect.

E.D.N.: disposes the divine human being
I.C.M.: so that within the divine can be born
P.S.S.R.: the force, that carries it upward.

Esoteric Lesson
MUNICH, DECEMBER 9, 1913

RECORD A

In order to progress in our esoteric life, we must become more attentive to the observation of things that tend to go mostly unnoticed in our daily life. Also, first we must form other ideas about what we will experience. For instance, we complain that thoughts storm into our meditation and disturb and irritate us. Were we really to think about this, we would have to recognize that this is progress. We have become more sensitive, and therefore notice that these thoughts are stronger than we ourselves are. They cause us to exert more strength in our meditation, because luciferic beings bring up into us our own thoughts. These luciferic beings are always in us; it is only that they are drowned out in the surging of daily life. When we walk at night through a quiet woods, we hear quite clearly the soft falling of leaves, the scurrying of animals on the ground, and the coming of footsteps from a distance. However, such quiet sounds would be totally imperceptible in the noise of a large city. It is just the same with our meditations. The stillness that we create allows us to notice what goes unnoticed in the noise of everyday life. All kinds of things can enter our consciousness; for instance, a pain in our physical body that we do not otherwise feel. We can concentrate on our body to look for the pain—this is, however, good to do only in quite special cases. With this process, we start somewhat above our head and, shutting out all other thoughts, concentrate our attention only on this one point. Then we go further down and concentrate on a part of our brain, and so on. We will notice how we can have pain in the various parts of our body. And the more egotistical we are, the more pain we feel and the more clearly we feel the pain. Yet we must not become hypochondriacs and become afraid of this. We must keep our head held high.

However, we must do this also with many other things, because strange things can happen to us: things that can baffle us and that we must examine thoroughly. Our whole constitution—the relationship of our bodies (our members) to one another—changes during meditation. Even when we do the meditation poorly and clumsily, we still pull the "I," astral body, and a part of the etheric body out of the physical body. Through this, in the minutes after the meditation, we can have peculiar experiences in our etheric body. This etheric body is a true preserver of all that we have consciously or unconsciously met in life. We could, in our childhood, for example, have experienced a dog being run over by a train. Over the years, we have overcome the whole terrible scene. Yet the etheric body has preserved it, and after 30 or 40 years we can, through our development, suddenly sense a barking and whining coming from ourselves; it can even be that we really bring forth sounds like barking, and then are shocked at ourselves. This happens because the etheric body is loosened during development, and emerges quite strongly and works upon the physical body.

A second example: after a middle-ear infection, esotericists can have a pain that leads to visions of a horrible scene, the cause of which they cannot explain. The connection is the following. Pains do not dwell in the physical body, but in the astral body. We know this as Theosophists and understand, therefore, how completely wrong it is that Maeterlinck maintained in his last book[†] that a soul that no longer had a body could not feel pain. We know that disembodied souls—in kamaloca, for instance—can suffer great pain. The pain in the astral body is reflected in the etheric body. Esotericists experience the vibrations thus generated in the etheric body, but at the same time they experience similar vibrations that were generated in their childhood by soul-pain they felt when they experienced the terrible scene. They had long forgotten the event, but through esoteric development and the outer cause of pain, the experience emerges from out of the etheric body.

Something even more peculiar is possible. We need only to have lived wall-to-wall with a family who read aloud and told robber stories. Our physical ears did not hear them, but our etheric body took them in. And it can happen, with spiritual development, that we experience these stories in our etheric body. Such things can frighten us if we do not understand them.

Let us assume that people in an esoteric lesson, or let us say in a public lecture, fall asleep due to lack of interest. Their "I" and astral body, however, are still present. When they then awaken, it can happen that the physical body does not want to adapt to what this returning astral body and "I" have taken in. This then leads to the people in question being at odds with themselves. They reproach themselves severely or even feel physical pain. Or, it can happen that people who take in the esoteric teachings with great attention and also do their exercises well, are among those who silently reject Theosophy and esotericism, and they might even express it. This then works on in esotericists, and it can happen that, after the meditation, voices speak out of themselves saying: "That is all nonsense!"—or much more terrible things that torment them. These are, however, the thoughts in their surroundings, which they perhaps did not hear with the physical ear. They are, as it were, possessed by them. Through lifting out the "I," we take everything that is good in us, our good behavior, with us and refine it more and more. We push our bad behavior down, and it takes on a kind of independent life. It can thus happen that we begin mechanically to scold, or to say things that we were reared not to say. This can astonish us and fill us with horror, and perhaps we say: I am not like this; I am too respectable for this. However, we must admit in relation to such things that we are like this, because such things disappear only when we have removed them from us once and for all.

And yet all of these experiences are progress, and the important thing is to recognize their meaning and significance. Above all, it is necessary that we understand that it is our own fault that we have difficulty entering into the spiritual worlds. However, when we ascend [to the spiritual worlds], we will meet him who took our guilt upon himself through the Mystery of Golgotha. He took our weakness upon himself. That is a true word of the Bible, just as everything in the Bible is true. And those who reject having their guilt wiped out by Christ, have not penetrated into the depths of this truth—just as little as the "good Christian" who believes but finds the matter to be quite simple. The development of the world is very complicated and hides a riddle in every atom; and every atom can become a world. The example of the middle-ear infection can teach us that. What is experienced in the etheric body is like a world that comes into being out of something small.

Inspirations for the material world can also come to us from out of the higher worlds. There is something that people pay too little attention to and read right past when they read about the life of Wallace,[†] the friend of the famous nature-researcher Darwin. Wallace himself tells us that the thought that led to one of the most important discoveries in relation to physical heredity came to him in a fever-dream. The fact that this thought came to him in a circumstance in which his physical brain was unfit for thinking should give the materialists who regard thinking as a function of the brain much to think about. Darwin also traveled extensively in the tropics, and it is quite possible that he made some discoveries with regard to physical conditions while he had a fever. In our materialistic age, people will pay attention to such things only when, in such extraordinary circumstances like through inspiration, things are found that can be valued materially; for example, when they invent something in this way that can make them rich. Until then, people consider all such things to be monster products of a sick fantasy.

If we continue our meditation with industriousness, perseverance, and energy, then help will always come to us from the one who brought his impulse into Earth evolution. This help[†] is always present![†]

* * *

Record B

Disturbances during meditation are actually signs of progress. They can have various causes, and are often complicated. For example, an earlier middle-ear infection can later awaken images of painful processes in the etheric body. Or, the neighbors read robber stories in their house. We did not physically hear the stories at all, but yet we took them in through the etheric body. This can then have the effect that, within the meditative state, it is as if we experience such robber stories within ourselves.

Forgotten experiences emerge out of the subconsciousness. For example, a dog that had been run over by a train suddenly barks from within us, because the shock [of this event] is stuck in our etheric body and then surfaces subconsciously during our meditation. We might fall asleep during a lecture. Yet, what we hear penetrates into the physical and etheric bodies, and perhaps comes up later as an unclear imagination or image during meditation. Also, ugly conversations, or conversations that are at enmity with Theosophy, have an effect. What is ugly presses down into the loosened physical and etheric bodies, and works there often quite automatically; whereas the finer soul-stirrings live more in the higher soul-spiritual realms. For this reason, Theosophy often has an unpleasant effect in other surroundings.

Esoteric Lesson
COLOGNE, DECEMBER 18, 1913

Those who take the esoteric path must always have an eye on the goal of entering into the spiritual world through death or through initiation. Things are just the opposite there to what they are in the physical world. Just as soon as we begin an esoteric training, the soul changes—progress begins. The astral body and the "I" separate, and the connection between the two lowest parts (physical body and etheric body) is only a loose one. That thoughts of an exoteric and often abominable nature storm us during meditation is a sign of progress. The high powers place our lower nature before us. These are reminiscences that we sometimes have as voices and whispers around us. It is the lower nature permeated with Lucifer and Ahriman—the nature that so loved Lucifer and Ahriman. For this reason, they are within us.

Also, a high degree of sensitivity to our surroundings is a sign of the loose connection of the four members [of our being]. The etheric body takes in the thoughts and feelings of the surroundings and then reproduces them. (Example: As a child before the seventh year of life, we experience a dog or cat getting run over. We could then, in esoteric training, experience the anguished cries of the animal coming from within us, as memory from the etheric body. Example: a middle-ear infection, a pain nuance in connection with some kind of immortality; in the reminiscence, this can emerge as voices that often call out terrible things.) We must face all of these things with courage and acquire the forces to overcome them, even if only in the next incarnation. The main thing is to always practice truthfulness. Precisely in our time, truthfulness has been lost in the making of judgments. We incarnate again and again in order to achieve truthfulness and morality in the physical world, and to take them with us into the spiritual world. Ahriman has taken possession of the world, and we must hold the counterbalance to him through our esoteric life. We must be conscious of the Biblical saying: "Christ is come to take our weakness upon himself."[†]

Esoteric Lesson

LEIPZIG, DECEMBER 30, 1913

RECORD A

If the view were right, which the soul-investigator of the Middle Ages had and which is shared by modern psychologists, then there would be no esotericism.

During the Middle Ages, the sentence was coined: everything that occurs in the soul is intentional; all soul-processes are based on a specific intention. When I think, my thinking has a specific content; I must think something. When I feel, hope, imagine, and will, I must feel "something"; hope "something"; imagine and will "something." The soul-investigator of the Middle Ages expressed this clearly, much more clearly and exactly than the modern psychologists, because our age is the time of the blurred concept. If this view represented in the Middle Ages were correct, an esoteric thinking would not be possible, as esotericists want to eliminate precisely this "something" from their soul and make it completely empty, so that the divine thinking can flow into their soul. In a certain sense, this is not brought about by our exercises, because in our exercises we concentrate on specific words, images, etc., which are given to us by the spiritual teacher. Thus, [we meditate] indeed on "something"—but not something taken from the sense world. And our soul is prepared through these exercises, when it has matured sufficiently, to receive the divine existence.

What is the purpose, then, of concentrated thinking? Its purpose is to lead us away from the materialistic thoughts around us and, to bring us to rest in a specific thought content. Gradually, we must reach the point in the meditation of disregarding a particular object of our thinking, of making ourselves completely free of it, and of developing the forces themselves that are necessary for thinking.

The soul-investigators of the Middle Ages knew this quite well, but they followed a rule that is still followed by many today. It is a fundamental rule for all theories of knowledge. They said: it is very difficult to achieve thinking, feeling, and willing without having intention;

and what is difficult is impossible for the human being. Therefore, all of those ideas about the limit of knowledge came into philosophy.

Naturally, it is not so easy in meditation for esotericists to remove the content of their thinking, feeling, and willing and to develop only the forces themselves. Only through constant, strenuous meditation will we achieve this. Basically, meditants find themselves in the same situation as the sleeping human being, only they remain conscious.

What takes place in sleep? The astral body and the "I" leave the body, and the physical body and etheric body remain lying on the bed. This is, as I have often mentioned, correct only to a certain degree. Just as the Sun goes down only for part of the Earth's globe in order to rise for the other half, so too only a part of the physical body rests. In the other part, the sun of the astral body and "I" begin to develop their activity. During sleep, the astral body and "I" are indeed pulled out of the nervous system and blood system, but they begin to work with their forces into the rest of the physical system: into the sense organs and gland organs. This will be clear through a comparison. Who has not at some time fallen asleep in an underheated room, and has in addition been not well-prepared for sleep, and then upon awakening has had the unpleasant feeling that their body has grown cool. The reason is that, during sleep, the astral body and "I" are not in the body, at least not in the blood system or nervous system. In contrast, they move, also during sleep, through the gland organs and sense organs. Let us consider those who have a sweet tooth. Naturally, their glands are differently formed, because they have not yet overcome the desire for sweet food. We must bear in mind that during meditation, the organs are left on their own; the astral body and "I" leave once they make themselves independent.

It is no different with the sense organs. It seems paradoxical that the senses are most awake when we sleep. Yet, it is true. Let us take, for example, the eye. While our eyes are closed during sleep, the forces of the "I" and astral body work into them. In contrast, when we are awake, our eyes actually sleep. If they did not do this, we could not use them. It is also true that the sun of the astral body and "I" rises for that half-globe comprised of the sense and gland systems. Those who become conscious while asleep can experience the light that works on the eyes, that build up the senses, and that must stop during the day so that we can see.

Such people can, if they can extend their sight and contract it again, have in their field of vision an image of an angel floating toward them. If they could expand their vision they would see, projected out of themselves, and angel in battle with a demon. This imagination arises because, during sleep, the blood is occupied with taking care of the eyes. The gods, the archangels, have worked upon the human eye throughout the ages. When we become clear about this, we will also sense how disastrous it is that modern physiology sends a probe into what was created over millions of years by the hierarchies of divine beings.

When meditants look at themselves from outside, they can get the feeling of a space filled with only warmth, like a kind of oven. What lives within it is what lives and weaves in our soul life as our own. We know that there are four kinds of ether: warmth ether, light ether, chemical ether, and life ether. Warmth is not merely the movement of molecules, as physicists believe, but it is the first of the four ethers. The warmth we have as our own warmth does not come from physical or chemical processes, but from—at least with human beings; with animals it is different—the fact that an "I" and an astral body are active. During meditation, it is possible to feel our own warmth inside and far outside of our body as a warmth sphere that fills the place where we would otherwise feel our body, and further outwards. We must feel this warmth ether that surrounds us. Much attention is necessary for this. Naturally, if someone would come near us and want to stab us, we would notice something only when the skin is touched. We cannot imagine that we are being stabbed only when the ether around us is struck. Beginning esotericists sense nothing of this ether. They sense something quite different: thoughts that storm them; often long-forgotten pictures, feelings, and cares penetrate into them. They then come and complain. Then the more experienced esotericists can say: congratulations for the progress that you are now noticing!

Appropriate for this is the word of the John Gospel: "and the light shines into the darkness, but the darkness has not comprehended it!"

For this warmth that is in us is darkness. The light wants to penetrate from outside, but it cannot, because in the warmth itself a battle is taking place between two kinds of warmth. It will be difficult for people to recognize that these two kinds of warmth exist.

In order to understand this somewhat more clearly, we must go to the farmers, to the farmer-philosophy or wisdom, at least as it once was. In the last decades, the farmers have fallen away from this wisdom, because they have come more into contact with cities. The old farmers were not dumb; they knew much in their farmer-philosophy.

One time an old shepherd said, as a thunderstorm was approaching, that there were two weathers moving toward one another. Modern physics would speak of positive and negative electricity, but with these abstract concepts its understanding ends. The old shepherd felt and still knew out of the depths of his soul that when a thunderstorm forms, two powers fight against each other. A battle takes place there.

Modern people are no longer conscious of the two kinds of warmth. They can more easily imagine that there are two kinds of light: the inner light, luciferic, and the outer, the divine light that they see approaching them in meditation. Yet besides our own warmth, which is luciferic, there is also the warmth that can radiate toward us from outside, a warmth that we at first sense as a coldness during meditation. It is a good sign during meditation to feel ourselves breathed upon by this coldness, which is the warmth of the spiritual world. Having given ourselves up to this coldness, we feel our own warmth like a sphere around us and within us. We have passed as if through a fiery furnace in which everything luciferic within us is burned, and yet this fire of the divine wrath—which is actually love—is felt as coldness being breathed upon us. When we have gained the knowledge of this process, we come to say: thank God I am being tormented and punished to experience the divine wrath that burns away what should no longer exist in me!

Then the warmth from outside comes to us—which at first is felt as coldness—and with it comes light that, though it is from Lucifer, comes from the good side of Lucifer. (Light that streams into human beings gives them knowledge—Lucifer. The source of this light is Yahweh, who lives in the cosmic wisdom-water.) The spirits of the good hierarchies use Lucifer in order to shine this light into us. (Lucifer = light-knowledge. Warmth—Christ, love. First we must recognize Christ as the highest; then experience him as he himself shines in to us as love—life. It is Christ versus Lucifer.).

In this way, we can come to a soul life that does not have intent, to a spiritual world that is not merely a continuation of the physical, but is a totally different world. The Rose Cross can be a symbol of all of this for us. Often people say that the Rose Cross remains only a symbol for them. This is, however, their own fault. In *Outline of Esoteric Science*† it is already indicated with what feelings we should imbue ourselves so that the Rose Cross will not be just a symbol, but will become a living force. We could also transform what was said today into a feeling: *From God we are born* (*Ex Deo nascimur*). Because Lucifer mixed into creation, the wood of the cross must burn, must become charred and become black: *In – – – morimur.* When we have thus died in Christ, then can there come to us from outside, from the seven planets, the cosmic forces—the forces of the seven red heavenly roses, which shine into us as light and warmth.

* * *

Record B

If the view of the psychologists of the Middle Ages—shared by most of the modern psychologist too—were correct, no esotericism would be possible. The psychologists of the Middle Ages expressed it more exactly and clearly than those today, as ours is a time of blurred, unclear concepts. They said that the entire human soul life is filled with intent. They meant by this that it would always have to have a content. People could not merely think, but they would have to think a "something." Thus, they could also not merely feel, will, hope, expect, or imagine without directing themselves to a specific content. It must be just the opposite in esotericism. All of our exercises have the goal of teaching us to think without thinking something [a content], and so on. What we practice is not the essential thing, but is only a preparation for what we want to achieve through it: thinking, and so on, without an object—objectless thinking.

What purpose does concentrated thinking serve? The purpose is to lead us away from the outer, material thoughts that buzz around us and to direct our thinking to a specific thought. Gradually, we should then also succeed in disregarding or setting aside the object upon which we concentrate in meditation, and make ourselves totally free of it, and develop only the forces themselves that are necessary for thinking.

The psychologists of the Middle Ages knew this quite well, but they used a rule that is also used by a majority of people today. It has become a fundamental rule of all theories of knowledge. They said: It is very difficult to achieve thinking, feeling, and so on, without intent; and what is so difficult becomes also impossible for human beings. From this came, later, all the ideas about the boundary and limits of our capacity for knowledge, and so on.

For esotericists it should, however, become possible to develop a totally different thought life than the ordinary one. Through meditation, we should be able to enter into the same condition as that of the sleeping human being, and yet be conscious. Let us take a concrete example.

When people sleep in a room that has not been properly heated, and upon waking up feel cold, it is more difficult for them to warm themselves than it is when they are involved in their usual activities in their daily life. Why is this? It is said that in sleep, the physical body and etheric body remain on the bed and the astral body and "I" depart. That is approximately correct; just as correct as when we say that, during the night, the Sun has disappeared from the Earth. That is true for one-half of the Earth, but not for the other half. So, in sleep, the astral body and "I" are indeed out of the blood and nervous systems, but then they permeate the sense and the gland systems all the more. It will perhaps seem strange that the sense organs are most awake precisely when we human beings are asleep. Yet, this is the case. When we are awake during the day, our eyes, and so on, are sleeping. If our eyes were not sleeping, we could not see. Thus, for the "half of the Earth" of the sense organs and glandular system, the sun of the astral body and the "I" rises at night.

When we manage to become conscious in sleep, we can experience the light that works on the eyes and builds up the sense organs, and which must stop during the day so that we can "see." We experience this in imaginative pictures. We can perhaps have in our field of vision the image of an angel—projected out of ourselves—that floats toward us. If we could extend our vision yet further, we would behold an archangel fighting with a demon. This would be the image. It would be the image of the blood taking care of the eyes, and through this, the lens of the eye becomes smaller and larger. This is expressed then in the image described.

Ordinary human beings could come and say: then what I perceive would only be something that I create out of myself. Esotericists speak differently, however. They will know that light would not be possible if the archangel were not constantly fighting and overcoming the darkness, and that this is what is expressed in the image. The archangels have worked through the ages on the eye. When we become clear about this, we will then sense in how disastrous a manner modern physiology probes the organ that was built up by the hierarchies of divine spiritual beings over millions of years.

When meditants observe themselves from outside, they can get the feeling of a room or space that is filled only with warmth, like a kind of baking oven. What lives in this is what lives and weaves in us, in our human soul life, as our own nature. This warmth that we have as our own warmth is not a movement, as physics believes, but the first of four kinds of ether. It does not come from physical and chemical processes—at least not with the human being; with the animals it is different—but comes about because an "I" and an astral body live in the human being. In meditation, it is possible to feel our own warmth within, and even outside of our bodies, like a warmth sphere that fills the place where we would otherwise feel our body, and somewhat beyond.

It is not easy to sense this, and much attention is necessary for it. Beginning esotericists will at first experience something quite different than this warmth sphere. They will experience the storming-in of thoughts; these are sometimes long-forgotten thoughts, cares, feelings, etc. To this, the more experienced esotericist can say: I congratulate you on your progress that you are now noticing. The words of the John Gospel apply here: "And the light shines in the darkness, and the darkness has not comprehended it." This warmth that is in us is darkness. From outside the light wants to enter, but it cannot because, in the warmth itself, a battle is taking place between two kinds of warmth.

It will be difficult for modern people to see that there could be two different kinds of warmth. In order to see this, we must go to the farmers who still have the "farmer-philosophy"—at least as it once was, anyway. For in the last decades, farmers have become more and more "dumb," but only because they have come more and more into contact with the cities. The earlier farmers were not "dumb," and they had a farmer-philosophy. An old shepherd once said, as a thunderstorm approached, that it is actually two conditions of weather that are moving toward one another. Modern natural scientists will speak of positive and negative electricity and will have many things to tell, but their understanding ceases the moment they say the word "electricity." The old shepherd felt that, when a thunderstorm comes, there are two powers that fight each other, that a battle takes place there. Modern people no longer have a consciousness of the two kinds of warmth.

We could more easily imagine that there are two kinds of light: the inner light that comes from Lucifer and the outer light that we see coming toward us in meditation. Besides our own warmth, which is luciferic, there is also a warmth that can ray forth to us from outside, which we feel at first as coldness in meditation. It is a good sign to feel ourselves breathed upon in meditation by the coldness that radiates out of the spiritual worlds. Surrendering ourselves to this coldness, we feel our own warmth as a sphere within and around us. We go through a fiery oven in which everything that is luciferic in us is burned. In spite of that, it is felt as cold. Then we come to say: Thank God that I am being tormented, that I would be found mature enough to experience the divine warmth that burns away what should not exist in me. Then the warmth from outside—which at first is felt as coldness—moves into us and comes together with the light that comes from the good side of Lucifer. The spirits of the good hierarchies use Lucifer to shine the light into us.

In this way we can attain a soul life that is not causal, and a spiritual world that is not merely a continuation of the physical world, but is a totally different world. The Rose Cross can become a symbol for all of this.

Often esoteric students say: The Rose Cross continues to be only a symbol for me. Then they must be given as an answer: That is your own fault! Already noted in *Outline of Esoteric Science* are the feelings with which we should imbue ourselves so that the Rose Cross does not remain just a symbol.

What was said today, we can change into a feeling: Out of God we are born (*Ex Deo nascimur*). Because Lucifer mixed into creation, the wood of the cross must burn, become charred, must become black: *In Christo morimur* [In Christ we die]. If we have died in such a way in Christ, then there can come to us from outside the seven cosmic forces, the forces of the seven red roses, which can shine into us as light and warmth: *Per Spiritum Sanctum reviviscimus* [Through the spirit we are reborn].

* * *

RECORD C

In the view of the soul held from the Middle Ages, all thinking, feeling, and willing is intentional, has content. If that were true, there could be no esotericism, as the goal of esotericism is precisely to free the soul life from the content that comes from the physical world. If we meditate really well, all content must disappear from our soul-life. Only then do we become mature enough to feel something stream into us from the other side, from out of the spiritual world. We can make this clear with an example.

When we sleep, we actually do something similar to what happens during proper meditation: we draw, with our astral body and "I," out of the body. Because of this, it can happen that we—when we don't take care that the room is well-heated—feel chilled or cool upon awakening because the "I" and astral body do not, as is otherwise the case, work in our blood system and nervous system and warm us. When we sleep, they do not withdraw totally, but work in the sense organs and in the glandular system. They work on the eyes and the other sense organs at this time much more than during the day when we are using our eyes, etc.; and above all, they work in the glandular system. Because the work is taking place more in the glandular and sense organs, the first visions often manifest in a bodily fashion: an angel that conquers a devil, forces that work in the eyes.

When we make progress in esotericism, we can feel around us the aura of warmth that our "I" and astral body draw to themselves out of the circling warmth ether. We normally do not feel this because thoughts, memories, cares, etc., arise and want to disturb our meditation. When we conquer these disturbances, however, we feel around us the aura of our warmth. We can then feel deeply the truth of the words: "And the light shines into the darkness, and the darkness has not comprehended it." For what we ray out of ourselves is darkness that prevents the divine light from shining into us. It is our luciferic soul-life that presses outward as darkness (warmth) and hinders the divine-luciferic (wisdom) light from raying into us from out of the spiritual worlds (Spirit of Truth—Holy Spirit)—(farmer-philosophy of two storms that collide with each other). Also, with the warmth, something similar occurs. Also, there comes toward the warmth that we radiate from us the warmth of God. This warmth out of the spiritual world is felt by us as the opposite, as a breath of cold upon us. It is not comfortable to feel the divine warmth washing around us—warmth that we feel as cold—but this is precisely the spiritual burning process. We must go through the fiery oven of our own luciferic soul-life that we have set outside of ourselves. And then we feel ourselves washed with the divine warmth that is like the cold, so that the burning process is like a freezing process. Thus must all of our darkness and egotistical warmth be burned before the divine light can ray in upon us. We can think of the Rose Cross: the charred wood, the body, and then the pure light-roses, the divine forces newly radiating into us. Then we will become deeply conscious of the

Mystery of Golgotha. Our passions must be as if burned, so that we can receive the pure light of the spiritual world. E.D.N. — I.C.M. — P.S.S.R.

Concentration on a sentence formulation or on an imaginative picture.

Meditation—soul quiet. [Streaming into us]† of the divine, be it in our cosmic thoughts, or in images, or inspiration and intuition.

* * *

Record D

If we wanted to believe the doctrines of the Middle Ages, we would have to assume that an esoteric life would absolutely not be possible. At that time, people were followers of what we can call intentional (content), thinking, feeling, and willing. People had to think *something*, feel *something*, and will *something*. Esotericists should, however, free themselves precisely from this.

In meditation, a pulling-together of the soul forces must take place in stillness and tranquility. Beginning esotericists almost always complain that they fail at this and that. Pictures and thoughts rise up that they cannot ward off; these cloud their meditation. Experienced esotericists should answer them: Congratulations—you have taken the first steps!

Said in approximate terms, during sleep the astral body and "I" are out of the physical body and etheric body. Yet, this does not fully correspond to the reality. It corresponds fully just as little as when we say that the Sun goes under, and so forth. For the one side of the Earth the Sun does indeed go under, but at the same time it rises for the other half. It is the same for the astral body and the "I" with their forces. During sleep, the senses and glands are actually awake because they are being worked on. During day-waking consciousness, for instance, the eye is not awake at all. Otherwise, it would not be able to perceive things in space; it would not be able to see. Only in the night does the spiritual of the eye awaken. Take the following for example: Someone sees an angel and how it conquers a devil.

The pupils of the eyes contract and expand. The picture does not, however, remain only within, but is projected outward. The archangels have worked on the eyes for millions of years.

We should consciously imitate the condition of sleep in meditation.

We differentiate four kinds of ether: warmth ether, light ether, chemical or tone ether, and life ether. We are at first embedded in the warmth ether. The feeling of being chilled, of not being able to warm ourselves on our own, such as we notice upon awakening in a room that is not sufficiently heated, occurs in meditation. There is an effect on the warmth forces, the nervous system, the sense system, and the glandular system. Especially the glandular system is worked on. It is for this reason that often in meditation something comes up that lies hidden in our depths. An example was given of a person with a sweet tooth having in the glandular system secret desires that announce themselves as pictures, as visions of all kinds.

In the warmth ether, we must not feel ourselves limited by our skin, but must extend beyond it, just as esotericists learn to feel themselves to be far greater than the limits of the skin. We feel ourselves full of inner warmth, like an oven. Into this substance pour the unpurified feelings, desires, and so on, and cloud the meditation by darkening the light (light ether) that wants to enter. Meditate: "The light shines in the darkness, but the darkness does not accept it."

There is a means to make progress: meditating on the imagination of the Rose Cross. Our desires and passions must burn in the smelting furnace of the warmth ether. Because in the spiritual all concepts must be transformed and become their opposite, we must say that the [desires and passions] stiffen; they freeze. It is not comfortable for any esotericist to be surrounded by the region of cold. Because the parts that comprise the Rose Cross are taken from the physical world, we say: burn. This is the reason for the charred wood of the cross. Out of the spiritual the luminous roses blossom forth. The threefold human being offers thinking, feeling, and willing.

In the light ether, Lucifer. When he works from within outward, he becomes an evil force. If he works from outside inward, then he is a good force, because the good gods can thereby make use of him.

Ex Deo—we were subjected to the luciferic influences.

Esoteric Lesson
LEIPZIG, JANUARY 2, 1914

RECORD A

What matters deeply to all esotericists is the success of their meditative efforts. All of them have success, even if they do not notice it. Beginning esotericists complain often about pain. These painful afflictions are disorders that arise in the body because the physical and etheric bodies are not in proper contact with each other. The pain was there earlier, too, but human beings simply did not feel it, because then they were coarser and more robust. Esotericists must learn to endure such pain. Naturally, they must learn to differentiate between this pain and an illness process, in which case they must intervene.

Why is it that we know our physical body so little? It is because we live within it and perceive it only through feelings. We see with our eyes, and so therefore cannot observe them. Esotericists must learn to pull back with their soul-spiritual nature and free themselves from the physical. Then they will manage to observe their physical body. It helps for this if we gather our thoughts together, as much as possible, to a point, concentrate on this point, immerse ourselves in it, and dwell within it for a time. Through such concentration, a strengthening of the force of thinking takes place, and through this we can gradually succeed in observing our physical body. [First subsidiary exercise: control of thought.]

Further, we must learn to know our etheric body. This is still more difficult, because the etheric body is not enclosed in skin as is the physical body. The etheric body is a fine web that sends its streams out everywhere into the outer world, and also receives impressions from everything in the outer world. Often human beings are totally unaware of this.

We learn to sense the etheric body through a proper practicing of the second subsidiary exercise: the exercise of the will. Ordinarily, we are driven to our actions by outer impressions. We see a flower in the meadow, and because we like it, we reach our hand out to pick it. Now, as esotericists, we must attain the ability to act only out of the inner impulses that we can consciously give ourselves, and therefore without a stimulus from outside. Then we come to know that it is the etheric body which causes the hand to move. Thus, we feel our etheric body awaken.

Through this awakening etheric body, we gradually learn to experience ourselves in an etheric world. In reality, there occurs with every movement we make—for instance, in taking hold of an object or bumping into it—an assault on the outer world. Non-esotericists have no inkling of this. They are protected from this knowledge by the Guardian of the Threshold. Esotericists, however, gradually attain the independence of their etheric body that experiences itself in the etheric world. Their organs become finer. They acquire a sense for the fact that every space is filled not only with physical objects, but with countless elemental beings that make themselves noticeable through sticking, hitting, and burning. Everywhere in this elemental, etheric world we must create space for ourselves through will impulses such as reaching out, pulling back (expansion and contraction), hitting, walking forward, etc. Such movements must occur with full consciousness so that we will them out of our own being. That is the second exercise: initiative of the actions. Those who cannot create space for themselves in the etheric world without their initiative-will, can do just as little in this etheric world as people in the physical world could if they wanted to dance on a stage filled with chairs. The chairs must be cleared away first. We learn this in the spiritual realm through the second exercise.

In order to become conscious of our astral body, we must do the opposite. We must hold back the desires surging in the astral body. We must develop tranquility and equanimity in relation to them. We must produce absolute calm and quiet within ourselves. Only then do we feel the outer astral world clash against our inner astral world. Just as we bump up against the etheric world by taking action in it from out of ourselves, in our willing, so do we feel the outer astral world by remaining quiet in ourselves, by stilling all desires and wishes.

Before the astral body is far enough along, it deadens itself through a cry. We know that pain arises when the contact between the physical body and the etheric body is not right. The astral body feels this [lack of proper contact] as pain. When small children feel pain, they cry. They seek to drown out the pain in the crying. Adults will perhaps call out: *ow!* If we have attained the ability to let our pain stream completely into the vibration of the tone, such changes would arise in the formation of the etheric body through the vibrations that we would not feel the pain. It would sink into our subconsciousness.

However, the good gods gave human beings a weaker disposition, and that is good, because otherwise there would be no suffering and also no articulate speech. Esotericists must come to bear quietly, calmly, and with equanimity all pain—absolutely everything that is stimulated in them from outside, and everything that happens within them. Then they will not assault (through their astral body) the outer world, but rather, the assaults turn toward them from the outside. Yet, because they have developed full composure and tranquility, the assaults will touch only their physical and etheric bodies. The astral body remains untouched. The astral body becomes free, so to speak, and hence they can observe it. Thus, through the exercises for equanimity, we learn to know our astral body. Finally, we must also come to know our "I." We cannot feel our "I," because we live within it. Therefore we must pour it out into the world. We learn to know our "I" through what we designate as positivity.

(The Legend of the Dog is told.)†

When we act as Jesus Christ does, we do not see what is ugly, but enter into everything so that we can come to the good in it. In this way, we free ourselves from our "I" and can observe it. "I" is love and will. Through the developed will, we learn to know if the essence of all things that originate in the divine. Through love, we learn to experience the being or essence of the things. Thus, through will and love, we advance to knowledge that is free of the personal "I." We learn, as a spiritual "I," to immerse ourselves in the being and substance of all things that proceed from out of the spiritual Father-ground—such as our own "I." Our "I" is beholding us from out of all created things

("Swan"†). Esoteric students achieve this stage of the "Swan" when they can experience this.

On the fifth stage, we develop *manas* or spirit self. We must not take as our foundation what we have up until now seen, heard, and learned. We must learn to meet everything that approaches us in such a manner that we are as if empty of everything that was experienced before now. We can develop manas only when we learn to consider all that we have attained through our own thinking as being of less worth in relation to what we can attain by opening ourselves to the thinking that streams in from the god-woven cosmos. Everything that surrounds us has come into being from out of these divine thoughts. We have not been able to discover this through the thinking we have had up until now. There, things are hidden from us. Now we learn to sense behind everything the divinity, like a hidden riddle. More and more, we learn in modesty to see how little of this riddle we have been able to solve up to this point. And we learn that we must actually remove everything from our soul that we have learned before. We must approach everything in an unbiased, free manner, like a child, because the divine riddles that surround us present themselves only to the unbiased soul. The soul must become child-like in order to be able to enter into the kingdom of heaven. The hidden wisdom—manas—then streams like a gift of grace out of the spiritual world toward the child-like soul.

It is not necessary for us to go any further because, through these five stages, we will have established contact with the spiritual world. We must then still establish the harmonious working-together of the capacities obtained through the five exercises. This harmony of cooperation is built through the constant repetition of these five exercises. This then builds the sixth exercise [of the subsidiary exercises].†

These exercises are of the greatest importance. The soul can find its way into the spiritual worlds through these exercises. You find in all the writings, lecture cycles, and other lectures indications and instructions for these five exercises. And there would be no need for an esoteric lesson to take place if everyone would read these instructions attentively, and awaken and bring to life in their soul the forces in these exercises. They serve as a support to the special exercises given.

Esotericists must be attentive to the smallest details. As soon as we approach the spiritual worlds, we must observe everything conscientiously, but in a totally different way than in the physical. It is for this reason that esotericists must make these exercises a constant part of their inner life, and must kindle themselves ever again to renewed striving and renewed observations. Otherwise it is not possible for them to achieve insights into the spiritual world. Above all, esotericists must practice patience. Most think that, after they have practiced for a brief time, they can gain entrance into the spiritual world—that all the portals would then be open for them.

Bear in mind that an important impulse or idea needs nineteen years to be grasped and understood well. When esotericists believe that after some practice they are now, without anything further, ripe for entrance into the spiritual worlds, it is like when a child that has just learned to speak would say: It would take too long to wait for years to become an adult. I want to be an adult now.

The second thing that we must learn in the esoteric life is truthfulness. Those who have not learned it in physical life will have great trouble upon their ascent into the spiritual world, because upon entering the spiritual world they must leave behind their logical thinking and everything bound to the intellect, and they will not be corrected by the facts like they are in the physical world. The good gods set human beings in the physical world precisely to learn truthfulness, because every untruth—those things that do not correspond to the facts—is corrected by the facts. The tendency for truthfulness can be gained only in the physical world, not first in the spiritual world.

Finally, esotericists must strive to train themselves to have, as a matter of habit, a good memory. The keeper of the memory is the etheric body, but without the physical body, it would not be able to preserve it well. Impressions are made upon the nerves, and these impressions must be written into the physical body. The body is the recording apparatus, so to speak, of what we wish to retain. When we want to recall something, we penetrate with the etheric body to that place in the physical body where it is written. The memory picture then becomes alive, and we read it from the physical body. Students who must learn something by heart keep repeating it over and over until they have written it into themselves. However, then it can happen, for instance, that when they are learning, "Es stand in alten Zeiten..." [There stood in ancient times...],† that they impress it mightily into the physical body by using the sounds of the words. Such a writing into and reading out of ourselves must take place automatically by our making it an inner habit to penetrate all actions with our attention and thinking.

For spiritual experiences, we cannot use the physical body as an organ of memory; what is habitual or automatic must replace it. We must call before our soul the nuances of impressions that belong to the memory.

The content of what flows to the meditants when, after a meditation, they empty their soul—even of the influence of the meditation—is, in a certain sense, a wage or earnings. A meditation will never again be exactly the same as it was before. What flows to us depends on our morality, and on our love of truth, on how we have lived since the last meditation. If we in some way did not remain truthful or if we have let wrath and anger arise in us, nothing can stream into us from the spiritual world. With this situation, it is as we deserve. Through attentive examination or searching, we will always find that the reason we are not blessed with the spiritual lies in some untruth, in some welling up of wrath, or in something similar.

* * *

RECORD B (Extract)

[...] A second thing that we must practice in the esoteric life is truthfulness. Those who have not practiced truthfulness in physical life will have great difficulty with their ascent into the spiritual worlds, because they must leave behind their logical thinking and everything that is bound to the intellect, and they will not be corrected by the physical world. The good gods wanted to train human beings to truthfulness by setting them into the physical world. The inclination toward truthfulness can be acquired only in the physical world, not first in the spiritual world.

Finally, esotericists must strive to train themselves automatically to have a good memory (this can be accomplished by doing everything with a strong consciousness; by always being totally conscious with everything). We all know the story of the man who did not have much of a sense of spatial relationships and never knew where he had laid things. In order to deal with this, he set up various tables in his room and laid everything on them. There are scholars who can work only if they have around themselves twelve tables upon which their reference books lie open, in order to have the quotes easily at hand; and they must move from one table to the next.

We smile at this, but in reality, this is the way it is in the subconscious of all of us. The preserver of the memory is the etheric body, but it would not preserve the memory well without the physical body. The nerves receive impressions, and they must be written into the physical body. The physical body is, so to say, the recording device for what we wish to retain. When we wish to recall something, we penetrate the physical body with the etheric body to that point where we have written the memory. Then the memory picture becomes alive, and we read it from the physical body.

Students who have to learn something by heart continue to repeat the content aloud, until it is written into themselves. However, it can happen, for example, that when they learn: "Es stand in alten Zeiten ein Schloß so hoch und hehr..." [There stood in olden times, a castle so high and lofty],† they press it powerfully into the physical body with the help of the sound of the words.

Such writing into and reading must become automatic by making it our inner habit to penetrate all actions with our attention and thinking.

For spiritual experiences, we cannot use the physical body as an organ of memory; what is habit must take its place. We must call before our mind's eye the nuances of feeling that belong with it.

* * *

Record C

Much changes through our meditative life, and we must pay attention subtly to everything in order to become aware of the transformation. In ordinary life, we are usually not conscious of our physical body as being part of the outer world, although it belongs to the outer world.

I. Through concentrated thinking—through our concentration exercises—we become gradually conscious of our physical body as something outside [of us]. We feel it as something that is there and that belongs to us to a certain extent.

II. Through the initiative of actions (control of the will impulses), we become conscious of our etheric body. As long as we simply will or want something because of the stimuli of the outer world, we do not feel in the etheric body the streams and currents that come into movement when we act. We must create space around us when we want to do something out of ourselves, just as someone who wants to dance has to first move tables and chairs out of the way. As soon as we do something out of ourselves—without being stimulated from outside—we strengthen ourselves from within; we send our will from within outward, and then feel the streams and movements that must occur in the etheric body with every deed. Every movement is an assault on the outer world. We become more and more conscious that every space is filled with many elemental beings. When we act from within outward, we bump into these elemental beings and, through this, become conscious of our etheric body.

III. In order to become conscious of our astral body, we must do just the opposite. We must hold back the desires surging in our astral body. Instead of letting everything go out from us, we must develop calmness and equanimity. Then, being quiet within ourselves, we feel the outer astral world bump into us. Thus, as we bump into the etheric world by intervening in it from within ourselves (action from the will center), we feel the astral world bump into us because we remain quiet within ourselves and still all desires, wishes, and the welling up of pleasure and pain. Before people have developed equanimity in themselves, they deaden themselves to the desires working within them by crying; they let them go out in sounds. However, because our astral body is weakened by the gods, this [letting things out through sounds] becomes articulate speech and song.

IV. We become conscious of our "I" when we develop positivity in ourselves; when we develop out of ourselves judgments that enable us to see the beauty in everything—even in the ugliest [manifestations].

V. And through impartiality or trust, through going out of ourselves over into the other in order to take him or her into ourselves, we learn to know and feel the spirit self.

Under the influence of these exercises, our soul life changes. Our memory no longer becomes something that is written into the physical body; this must be replaced through the inner habit of independently reflecting upon and thinking about everything. For this we must overcome all laziness. (We must have patience. An important impulse, an important idea, needs nineteen years in order to be properly taken up inwardly and to be understood.).

Our truthfulness must also become an inner habit. It then gives us the sense for the correct and the true.

Thus, we see again that everything for the esoteric life is already given in our literature. Esotericists must be attentive to even the smallest things. We must conscientiously observe everything and must enkindle within ourselves the drive to new striving and to renewed observation and patience.

E.D.N. — I.C.M. — P.S.S.R.

* * *

Record D

Esotericists often notice that feelings of pain appear that they had not known before. These pains were already there before, but did not make themselves noticeable as disturbances. Now we notice them. It is not a matter here of having self-pity, even though we may not neglect anything to do with our health.

How do we come to a feeling of the physical body? We do not feel the physical body when everything relating to it is in order, which means when also the etheric parts correspond to it properly. If the two do not correspond properly to one another, pain arises.

Through concentration of the thinking, we must come to exert an influence on the physical body, or to develop a more aware consciousness of the physical body.

Calling out, "ow," at the sensing of pain is a method of deadening it.

Through initiative of action	etheric body
Through the equanimity exercise	astral body
Through positivity	"I"
Through impartiality, lack of prejudice	spirit self

That is the highest stage to which we raise ourselves at first. Other exercises then reach further upward.

Esoteric Lesson
BREMEN, JANUARY 11, 1914

As soon as we begin to meditate, the etheric body contracts. Through this an inner warmth arises because the warmth ether, the lowest ether, is what contracts. (Above the warmth ether are the light ether, tone ether, and life ether.) When we pay attention to what is outside of us, we will perceive that there is something that is as if flowing—like a kind of religious devotion, a moral warmth—in the cosmic ether. And we become aware that what we have within us is something different. It is like a feeling that we must be ashamed of ourselves before this moral cosmic warmth. Human beings do not like to do this. They do not like to be ashamed of themselves, and so they avoid it. For this reason, they say they are not making any progress. They hide from themselves.

Only through the development of our will-nature can we progress. When we say that we cannot, it really means we will not! We do not want to develop our will.

We should often look and listen into our physical body and seek to perceive, in sacred stillness, the whispers and murmurs there. We must direct all attention away from the outside; that means to be attentive in spite of [what is going on outside]. However, we must conscientiously direct the power of attention inward, because to be merely inattentive to, unconscious of, what is going on outside of us is damaging to us, even right into the physical body.

With the non-attention in question here, we indeed perceive everything—everything makes an impression—through our consciousness should not be directed toward it, but rather toward the meditation. In the physical body, our consciousness must be directed to what is going on outside; otherwise it is not as it should be.

Esoteric Lesson
BERLIN, JANUARY 24, 1914

RECORD A

We differentiate three parts of our soul life: consciousness soul, intellectual soul, and sentient soul. These three parts should not be completely equated separately with either thinking or feeling or willing, because each of the three soul-members possesses thinking, feeling, and willing.

The people who come to esotericism are of a more feeling nature, and indeed, especially those such as have a religious nature. Not all feeling-people are, at the same time, religious, yet those feeling-types that tend toward esoteric development are for the most part of a religious disposition. Such natures, more often than not, quite easily acquire general ideas about the spiritual world and also easily attain imaginations. These people are largely spared what makes the ascent into the spiritual world so difficult for others. Their cares are taken away by an angel being; they are carried across the threshold by their angel. Such people can experience much that is beautiful in the spiritual world; and when they have something to say about it, we should listen well to what they have to say.

Then there are people who act out of the will-like nature, who come out of the emotions and the emotional life to esoteric development. (This does not need to preclude the possibility that they could express critical comments or ridicule.) Such people have infinitely more difficulty than others. Precisely when they stand before the threshold, they are so greatly tormented by their emotions that it can become physical agony. In their meditation, they are tormented and hindered by devils. These people want to enter into the spiritual world, but have the feeling that they cannot.

We ourselves cannot choose how we want to be—whether we belong to one or the other path. Yet, we can to a great extent choose the third path: the path of thinking. In spite of that, this path is taken by very few. One hears people say: I cannot imagine, for example, how the Moon evolution was. Yet, that is our fault! A farmer, at any rate, would easily comprehend the Saturn, Sun, and Moon periods of evolution. When people say that they cannot grasp it, it means only that they do not want to acknowledge it because they have never seen it. When we see people who are 30 years old, we know that they must have been children at one time, not because we have always seen that adults were once children, but because they could not be the way they are now without having had other developmental stages behind them. Even if we had never seen a child, we would still know that an adult must have been a child.

Our mantra, *Ex Deo nascimur; In Christo morimur*, speaks of the Father God who has Christ as his son. It was a deep thought of Christianity to express this relationship with the help of the father-and-son relationship. The father can remain without the son. It is a gift of the father that he allows the son to proceed out of himself. In addition to various explanations that have been given for our Rosicrucian mantra, we can also meditate on this as one of the deepest possible.

* * *

Record B

People who become esotericists more out of their feeling nature have it easier than the others. They can be led through their religious feeling-life to strive esoterically, because only those with a religious feeling-nature become real esotericists. They can then relatively quickly see visions and enter the imaginative world. It is as if they would be carried over the threshold by their angel, and it is their karma to have it easier than the others. These [feeling] natures can often help the other much by giving pictures of what they behold. These pictures must not then awaken a kind of jealousy or envy; rather, we must recognize that they can be of great help.

Others strive esoterically more out of the will nature, which is connected in our time more with the emotions. They too can come into the spiritual world—some even easily—but they have more difficulty than those of a feeling nature. In their meditation, they are often driven as if by devils, and when they come to the threshold they are tormented in the physical body by their emotions, and by the consciousness of their passions and their emotional nature.

The third path is through thinking. It is the surest path, and in the future will more and more become the path for all human beings. However, this path is now actually taken by relatively few, because there are still many people who would rather enter the spiritual world quickly without going through the effort of thoroughly working through everything that can be taken up by thinking. This path [of thinking] takes longer than the other ways. However, when we then come to the threshold—even though it is after a long time—we have gained, through grasping the spiritual lawfulness of things, such a great and broad interest that we can peacefully take our karma upon ourselves, because we have learned to feel at one with humanity to such a high degree. And we then know that our personal shortcomings will be reconciled and compensated for in future lives. We can then come to a deeper concept of the relationship between Father [God] and Son. The Father must be there before the Son can be there, yet it is the free will of the Father to allow the Son to be there. Feeling ourselves one with the Son who is in the God in the human soul, we can then come to a deeper knowledge of the mantra, E.D.N. — I.C.M., and then later we will come to a realization of the P.S.S.R.

Esoteric Lesson
HANNOVER, FEBRUARY 7, 1914

Mantra of the Day: Saturday.

All esotericists will make progress if they simply do their exercises with the proper perseverance and intensity. If they do not progress, it is because they have not given enough attention to what comes from the spiritual world. What comes is totally intimate and subtle. We must live completely in the words given for the meditation. Everything else must not be there for the meditants; they must be as if transported out of the physical body. They must be conscious only of their "I." At the end of the meditation, even its content is to be wiped away, and only the awakened "I," empty of content, is to be there. Those are the most fruitful moments, during which the spiritual world can flow into the meditant. Or also, during the day we may suddenly have the feeling of something flitting by, so that we know: that was something out of the spiritual world. A feeling of deep devoutness overcomes us then.

The content of what flows to the meditants when they have made their soul empty after meditation—also empty of the aftereffects and reverberations of the meditation—is according to what each has earned. It will be the same as it was before. This content depends on our morality; on our love for the truth; on how we have lived and been since the last meditation.

If we have in any way not kept completely to the truth, or if we have let anger arise in us, nothing can stream into us out of the spiritual world. It is as we deserve. Through attentive searching, we will always find the reason for our not being blessed by the spiritual world in some untruth, in an outburst of wrath, or something similar.

When exotericists who know nothing about Theosophy say a prayer, for instance the Lord's Prayer, they easily have with the first words a feeling of warmth, of devoutness. That comes out of a personal feeling, however. Esotericists will at first sense a feeling of coldness with their prayer. They may not carry anything personal into their prayer; they must let only the spiritual content of the prayer work. The inner, real warmth comes then out of the spiritual itself and not out of the personal.

When with the practice of concentration, the first subsidiary exercise, we occupy ourselves with one object—the more unusual the better—that we have chosen, making each thought follow and connect with the one before, and then if at the end of the exercise we do not immediately engage in hustle and bustle but remain still for at least fifteen minutes, we will experience something. Not immediately, or after a week, or after a month, but after a while of continued, earnest exercise we will feel as if something wave-like would come into the head, into the brain. It is as if the etheric body, in wave-lines, came back into the head.

With the second subsidiary exercise, the initiative exercise, in which at a specific time we exert the will to perform some activity, we feel with time as if we had been active in our etheric body. We have the feeling: I have felt myself in my etheric body. A feeling of deep reverence and piety penetrates the soul of the meditant.

With the third subsidiary exercise, the balance (equanimity) between joy and suffering, we should find our way into and accept all happenings. Then our etheric body will gradually expand into the widths of heaven. We will no longer feel ourselves to be within our body with the whole world around us, but we will feel our body spread out into the whole surroundings. We will feel ourselves expanded and poured into the spiritual worlds. We feel ourselves, we know ourselves to be in the spiritual world.

In these three subsidiary exercises, we experience the first two sentences of our Rosicrucian mantra. We experience how we were completely embedded in the divine-spiritual forces and have descended out of them, and how, in the third exercise, we pour ourselves into the spiritual world, into Christ. For Christ is in the aura of the Earth, within the Earth's atmosphere. We must let him work in us, so to speak, beside us.

With the fourth subsidiary exercise, the exercise for positivity ... [at this point a gap occurs in the text]. *Per Spiritum Sanctum reviviscimus.*

Just as we walk through a meadow and see red and blue flowers and know that these flowers are red and blue, we will also come to really experience the truth of our Rosicrucian mantra:

Ex Deo nascimur
In Christo morimur
Per Spiritum Sanctum reviviscimus.

*

In the spirit lay the germ of my body.
And the spirit has imprinted in my body
The eyes of sense,
That through them I may see
The light of bodies.
And the spirit has imprinted in my body
Reason and sensation
And feeling and will,
That through them I may perceive bodies
And act upon them.
In the spirit lay the germ of my body.

In my body lies the germ of the spirit.
And I will incorporate into my spirit
The supersensuous eyes,
That through them I may behold the light of spirits.
And I will imprint in my spirit
Wisdom and power and love,
So that through me the spirits may act
And I become the self-conscious organ
Of their deeds.
In my body lies the germ of the spirit.

Esoteric Lesson
STUTTGART, MARCH 5, 1914

RECORD A

We know that all who strive for esoteric development must gradually transform their whole thinking from what it is in ordinary sense life, in order to find their way into the spiritual world. We must, so to speak, change our ideas and views, and our entire perceptual life and feeling life must change and become different from what they have been up until now. What is our thinking actually in ordinary life? We are accustomed to think that thinking takes place in the physical body, but this is not so. The etheric body is the originator of our thoughts. The only thing our physical body has to do with this is that it serves as a mirror for our thoughts, reflecting the picture back to us so we can attain consciousness. We can make this clear with an example.

When we look into a mirror, we have a reflection or mirror-image before us. The mirror gives us the outer impression of our physical form; thus, a shadow of our outer person. Likewise, when we think the thoughts that have their living seat in the etheric body, they are reflected shadow-images from our physical brain. What purpose then do the concentration exercises given to us serve? They free us gradually from a thought-shadows, because we concentrate and contract ourselves in the etheric body, so that we can penetrate to the true source of our thoughts, which have their life in the etheric body.

It should become ever clearer to us that not only are our thoughts shadows, but that all of our perceptions are really a nothingness, and that only the spiritual world exists as a reality. In the philosophical sense, naïve people say that what they perceive with the outer senses has existence, is reality. Philosophers have tried in all kinds of ways to fathom existence. Spiritual researchers know that the word "Sein" [existence] comes from "sehen" [to see]. "Sein" means what one has seen; the word is actually a participle of "sehen." Yet, no one can see "Sein" [existence] in the physical world, because it rests in the spiritual world. However, we behold the spirit only when we do not see matter. Matter is actually *nothing*; it is surrounded by spirit, which is the real. We can clarify this with the following example.

When we have before us a bottle of soda water and look through the clear water, we do not actually see the water, but rather, we see the gleaning globules of carbon dioxide that rise like shining pearls. And what are these sparkling, shining pearls other than empty air bubbles, only filled with a substance that is much thinner than that of the water—in comparison with the water, it is a *nothingness*! Thus, what we see here is nothingness; in contrast, we do not see the true water in which this rests.

Thus, we must come to realize that all of the space around us is filled with spiritual realities, beings, and facts; and that there where we perceive the things of the physical world is a nothingness, a mere hole. When we stretch out our arm, we are pushing it through the spiritual world. We do not feel this. Only when we hit our hand against the nothingness, against the matter, do we feel a resistance. In reality, we do not see the objects in space, but the contours of the spiritual world that form the boundaries of these objects.

When we have come to the point that we let fall away all the shadow-nature of both our thoughts and our outer surroundings, we grow into the spiritual world. In order to be able to stand in the right manner in the new world, and be able to understand and judge the things and facts of the spiritual world, we must already have changed our entire thinking in the physical world through esoteric development. This is a new world for us, but it is a world of greater reality than the one we have known so far.

There we enter a world of real things and beings, and we connect with them; we grow into this world. This world penetrates us, and we lose our earthly thoughts to it. We could say that we lose our head to this world, while the beings and things of this world move into us; it is as if we were to stick our head into an ant hill. Then the consciousness of the elemental world arises for us. When our soul life is strengthened ever more through the concentration of our thoughts, so that our inner self can separate more and more from the physical body, then the things of that world step before our soul's eye in ever clearer imaginations and visions. We will see that all of our thoughts that we have had on Earth of the good, the benevolent, the noble, have transformed into eternal imaginations that, in their living further, lend worth to the universe. And we will see that all the bad, the evil, and all the lower egotistical thoughts remain behind as waste products. It becomes something that is unfruitful, but that then becomes nourishment for what should develop into the seed of the good. Just as here on the physical plane, the mineral soil provides the nutrients for the plant world, so will all that is badly thought become the precipitate for the thoughts of the good, the true, and the beautiful that are sprouting in the elemental world. For this reason, esotericists can ever so quickly think something bad or false and imagine it in their thoughts, but they do not let it go further. They know that they may go only to the point at which it remains a thought. They do not let it go over into deed, into a reality. They only let it prepare and make up the soil out of which the seed of the good can grow.

And thus it has actually happened in the world order; this is how the mineral kingdom of the Earth has come into being. On the old Moon the elohim thought the error—this was appropriate to do there—and out of this matter, the mineral kingdom arose. Out of this earthly material, earthly dust, Yahweh-Elohim was able to create the human being and provide the physical sheath.

However, Lucifer, who now stands at a similar level upon which the elohim stood on old Moon, wants to carry out this same thing. He can use only human beings for this. He can think the error only within human beings.

We wish to develop ourselves to become an organ of the spiritual world, just as we also developed our physical organs into organs for the sunlight. The germ or seed for that process was within us; likewise, the seed for this spiritual development is present in us. We can develop it only through strict, earnest self-training, self-education. In the book *How to Know Higher Worlds*,† various means are given through concentration, and so on, that will allow us to become really free of the physical body, so that through this split in our being, we can cross the threshold of the spiritual world and can behold the true spiritual reality.

How we are to relate to the physical world and to this new spiritual world is expressed in the lines of the following verses.† Those people who have already received a mantra for their meditation may meditate the following in any way they like. For those who have not already received a verse, meditate the first verse in the morning and the second in the evening. The third verse shall be done only from time to time. It is to a certain extent a testing of how far we have come toward achieving what is striven for in the first two verses.

I. Verse

Zu den Dingen wend ich mich
Wend ich mich mit meinen Sinnen;
Sinnensein, du täuschest mich!
Was als nichts das Dasein flieht:
Dir ist's Sein und Wesenheit;
Was dir nichtig scheinen muß,
Offenbare meinem Innern sich.

I turn to things,
I turn with my senses.
Sense being, you deceive me!
What flees existence as nothing
Is being and essence to you.
May what must seem to you worth nothing
Reveal itself within me!

"I must achieve this": it is the taking of a stance in relation to the new outer world.

II. Verse

Geisteslicht erwarme mich
Lass in dir mich wollend fühlen.
Gutgedachtes, Wahr Erkanntes
Wie erlebt dich leuctend Ich
Irrtumsweben, bös erdachtes
Zeige dich der Leucthe-Seele
Dass ich webend in mir sei.

> Spirit Light, warm me,
> Let me feel myself willing in you.
> What is well-thought, cognized truth,
> How does the luminous "I" experience you!
> Weaving error, badly thought out
> Show yourself to the beacon of my soul
> That I may be weaving in myself.

That is a question within, experiencing in the new existence.

> ### III. Verse
> Leuchtend Ich und Leuchte-Seele — man selbt —
> Schwebet über wahrem Werdewesen
> Das Erdachte, das Erkannte
> Wird jetzt dichtes Geistessein.
> Und wie leichte Daseinsperlen
> Lebt im Meer des Göttlich-Wahren
> Was den Sinnen Dasein täuscht.
>
> Luminous "I" and beacon-soul, — oneself —
> Hover above true being of becoming
> What is thought out, what cognized
> Condenses now to spirit being.
> And like pearls of existence
> There dwells in the sea of divine truth
> What deceives the senses' existence.

In expectation of truth. It is a guess, a feeling of the new self. It is the experiencing of truth, the experiencing in the spiritual world.

Each of these verses in turn contains an elaboration of what is given in sequence and compressed into ten words in our Rosicrucian mantra:

> *Ex Deo nascimur*
> *In Christo morimur*
> *Per Spiritum Sanctum reviviscimus.*

* * *

Record B

I want to add the following verses and meditations for those who have not been able to receive a mantra for meditation. The first verse is to be done in the evening after the review of the day. The second verse is to be done in the morning, and the third is to be done every now and then. [Translator's note: the order is reversed in Record A.]

I. (E.D.N.)

I turn to the things,
I turn with my senses.
Sense being, you deceive me!
What flees existence as nothing
Is being and essence to you.
May what must seem to you worth nothing
Reveal itself within me!

II. (I.C.M.)

Spirit Light, warm me,
Let me feel myself willing in you.
What is well-thought, cognized truth,
How does the luminous "I" experience you!
Weaving error, badly thought out
Show yourself to the beacon of my soul
That I may be weaving in myself.

III. (P.S.S.R.)

Luminous "I" and beacon-soul, — oneself —
Hover above true being of becoming
What is thought out, what cognized
Condenses now to spirit being.
And like pearls of existence
There dwells in the sea of divine truth
What deceives the senses' existence.

The last verse should be thought through only now and then as a test of what has been experienced in the other two verses. These will then become clear to us.

In these meditations is elaborated what is compressed into the ten words of the Rosicrucian-prayer: E.D.N. — I.C.M. — P.S.S.R.

The etheric body is the author or creator of our thoughts. Our physical body has only so much to do with it as to be the mirror of our thoughts. It reflects the image of the thoughts, and through this the thoughts become perceptible to us. Through our concentration, we should come to free ourselves from the shadow-thoughts. Through the contraction of our soul, of ourselves in the etheric body, we should attain pure thinking, which has its seat in the etheric body. It must become evident to us that all of our perceptions are a nothingness, and that only the spiritual world exists as a reality. The spiritual world is the true existence. When we understand the word *Sein* [existence] properly, we realize that all of the space around us is filled with spiritual things and beings that are realities. And we realize that when we see physical things and beings, there is a hole, a nothingness. When we stretch out our arm, we penetrate through this filled spiritual world. It is only when our hand bumps against the nothingness, against the matter, that we feel resistance. In reality, we do not see the physical objects in space, but rather the outlines or contours of the spiritual world.

No one can see being-ness, existence, because it rests in the spiritual, and we see the spiritual only when we do not see matter. If we have trained ourselves so that we let the shadow-nature of our thoughts and surroundings fall away, we then grow into the spiritual world. In order for us to be able to get used to the spiritual world, we have to transform our entire thinking here in the physical world. This esoteric development helps us to grasp properly the things of the spiritual world.

* * *

Record C

I turn to things,
I turn with my senses.
Sense being, you deceive me!
What flees existence as nothing
Is being and essence to you.
May what must seem to you worth nothing
Reveal itself within me!

Spirit Light, warm me,
Let me feel myself willing in you.
What is well-thought, cognized truth,
How does the luminous "I" experience you!
Weaving error, badly thought out
Show yourself to the beacon of my soul
That I may be weaving in myself.

Luminous "I" and beacon-soul,
Hover above true being of becoming
What is thought out, what cognized
Condenses now to spirit being.
And like pearls of existence
There dwells in the sea of divine truth
What deceives the senses' existence.

[For verse I:.]

Sense being, you deceive me— feeling of being banished to the physical body; to harmonize.
Reveal itself within me— E.D.N. Attainment of this belief.

[For verse II:]

First line: petition to the spiritual light.

Second line: *a* force of the soul: the willing feeling and the feeling willing in the spiritual world.
Fourth line: petitioning question, questioning petition!
Sixth line: again a petition!
Seventh line: only a petition to experience in a distant future the good and the evil separated out. Between death and birth our deeds distance themselves.

[For verse III:]

Feel yourself more and more at home in the world that is to be known through clairvoyance. Self-examination! To what extent can you experience concretely what is there?
What deceives the sense's existence— the adept experiences as cosmic life.
The last three lines are a calm, quiet statement of spiritual happenings.

When we meditate these three formulations or verses with feeling, the higher hierarchies promise us their help. We may then say: we are coming closer to you. Then they reach out their hand in help to us; they keep their promise. Feel P.S.S.R. as truth. *Sein* [existence] comes from *Sehen* [to see].

Esoteric Lesson
BERLIN, MARCH 27, 1914

RECORD A

It was discussed how difficult it was going to be that he (Rudolf Steiner) could not be with us anymore this winter,† and that we must feel all the more intensively that we are united in the spirit. Then we went into the fact that if we just do our exercises earnestly and intensively enough, we do make progress on the esoteric path, whether we notice it or not. We must only pay more attention to ourselves and ever more have the feeling: it is not I who thinks, but it thinks me; thus, it is not the physical body that thinks but the etheric body. The physical body is just the mirror or an echo. Just as we, looking into a mirror, pay attention only to a mirror image and forget the real figure, so too with an echo, we do not pay attention to what we call out but only to the call bouncing back. Thus, we do not notice that thinking takes place in the etheric body and is only mirrored by the physical body. The more we make our etheric body independent, we experience two things. These experiences are, that at one time our "I" expands into the widths of space, and at another time we experience our inner being in solitude and find our other self in the depths. Human beings, in their skin, are only as if in hulls in which spiritual forces surge up and down. It is as if our thoughts emerge as figures out of us and place themselves around us. We will then experience our good and our evil. We experience them as follows: of the good, that it points into the future and leads there to a sprouting, plant-like life; and of the evil, that may not come to be a deed but remain only purely in thought, such that in the future it might serve as nourishment for the good. The nourishment for our three kingdoms came about only because the beings that went through their human stage on the old Moon experienced their evil meditatively and consciously, without letting the evil come to be a deed. Evil arose on Earth because the Moon beings that remained behind, luciferic beings, did not meditate their evil on the Moon, but do so now on the Earth and implant it in the human beings. On the other hand, we must feel our "I" expanding more and more into space, and not within our physical body. We must experience the surroundings of this sense world, in comparison to the spiritual world, as an air bubble in water, as a spherical nothingness. We should experience these things often, and ever again, in thought. For this we are given, as a help, three formulations that we meditate mornings, evenings, and Sundays. They will help us in the near future to make the etheric body independent.

The first formulation (verse) expresses what is said in *Ex Deo nascimur*; the second, in *In Christo morimur*; and the third, in *Per Spiritum Sanctum reviviscimus*.

> I turn to things,
> I turn with my senses.
> Sense being, you deceive me!
> What flees existence as nothing
> Is being and essence to you.
> May what must seem to you worth nothing
> Reveal itself within me!

> Spirit Light, warm me,
> Let me feel myself willing in you.
> What is well-thought, cognized truth,
> How does the luminous "I" experience you!
> Weaving error, badly thought out
> Show yourself to the beacon of my soul
> That I may be weaving in myself.

> Luminous "I" and beacon-soul,
> Hover above true being of becoming
> What is thought out, what cognized
> Condenses now to spirit being.
> And like pearls of existence
> There dwells in the sea of divine truth
> What deceives the senses' existence.

Record B

Even when we cannot be together much physically, we can still be conscious of being together spiritually. We are not separated. In the etheric world, where our thoughts touch each other, the separation does not exist as it does in the material world. And more and more we will become aware that our "I," as it were, expands itself in our thoughts and becomes all-encompassing. That is an instance of progress to which esotericists must pay attention, because the thought-life becoming independent is proof that we are making progress through our exercises and meditations. We feel as if the thoughts are being thought within us, independent of us; and not as we had formerly, when we felt as if we ourselves brought forth the thoughts. We feel as if the thoughts within us are surrounded by an ever further expanding spiritual atmosphere. It is as if we send out a part of our "I" into the thoughts, and are thereby united with what we are separated from in the physical. We expand and stretch ourselves into our whole surroundings. And in this feeling of being spiritually united with the things, we can gradually become aware that the true being of the things lies in this invisible, though sensed as real, spiritual atmosphere; whereas the material things will more and more divulge their characteristic of unreality.

In order to inwardly realize this more and more, we can meditate the following:

> I turn to things,
> I turn with my senses.
> Sense being, you deceive me!
> What flees existence as nothing
> Is being and essence to you.
> May what must seem to you worth nothing
> Reveal itself within me!

Yet there are other times when we must do the opposite, to a certain extent. We must then feel ourselves totally within ourselves, as if the second self were to arise out of ourselves. This self is our true "I" and must become ever more powerful. (These two situations must alternate with each other.) And then, feeling ourselves in solitude and gaining strength in ourselves, we will gradually feel more powerfully than ever before the good and the evil within us. The good in us will reveal itself such that we sense it as a growing; it is growing into the future, where it will bear fruit. We sense how the evil, which is still in us and which we can place clearly before the spirit in ideas, must become nourishment for the growing good. We feel how the evil is something withering and dying, whereas the good is something growing. However, we also sense that the strong growth of the good depends on the nourishment it can receive through the dying evil. We must be able to feel both the good and the evil in us at the same time. And we must know at the same time that the evil that we can think must never become a deed. It is important that we know it, but never do it.

From this, we see again how earnest the esoteric training is. For when we become clearly conscious of the possibilities of the evil in us, we are at the same time tempted also to do it. And we should know that just as certainly as we must recognize the possibilities of the evil in us and let them become an idea for the strong growth of the good, so must we never, even in the smallest way, allow the evil to become a deed.

What is around us in the kingdoms of nature and what serves us as nourishment exists, because the gods on the old Moon thought the evil, as well as the good, in the way that we must now also do it. Just as the mineral soil provides the nourishment for the plant world, so will our ideas of the evil become the soil or ground out of which the good will nourish itself. The mineral kingdom of the Earth arose because the elohim on the Moon thought the evil, the error. Out of this, the matter, the mineral kingdom of the Earth arose, and out of this matter Yahweh was able to make the human being, the material sheath.

The fact that we also have in our Earth evolution the evil in this form, as evil actions and everything that is bad, is due to the luciferic gods who did not think the evil on the old Moon (where its rightful place would have been and would have them become nourishment), but who now think it on Earth. Thus, the luciferic gods thinking the evil on Earth is the cause of the evil actions and errors of human beings.

The second verse expresses the living "I" becoming strongly conscious of itself. The "I" begins to feel itself within itself weaving, shining, living; and it has clear insight into everything that it bears within itself as the future blossom of the good. It also grasps in clear ideas its possibilities of evil that should never pass over into actions. This second verse is as follows:

> Spirit Light, warm me,
> Let me feel myself willing in you.
> What is well-thought, cognized truth,
> How does the luminous "I" experience you!
> Weaving error, badly thought out
> Show yourself to the beacon of my soul
> That I may be weaving in myself.

And then the "I" that has become self-conscious can turn itself toward the outside again. Then, however, it rises again out of itself and recognizes the spiritual meaning and significance of the things. It realizes that where the senses see objects, there is really nothing; there are openings or gaps and a much more real and more condensed existence around them. [The "I"] experiences the sense world like round holes, like existence-bubbles. It feels itself living and weaving in the dense spirit world, which became real life there where the sense organs cannot perceive anything. Thus, with the third verse that we meditate for this, we can put ourselves to the test. If the other two verses, for instance, are meditated daily in the morning and evening—the first verse in the morning and the second in the evening—then on Sundays we can, in addition to these two, take up the third verse at a time that lies between them. This is in order to test to what extent it has all become reality. This then is, in turn, a strengthening of another formulation that is actually contained in these three verses: E.D.N. — I.C.M. — P.S.S.R. In the first verse, we can feel the true creative power that lies at the foundation of sense existence: E.D.N. In the second verse we enter into solitude, as if we were withering or dying, in order to find in us what knows itself to be united with Christ: I.C.M. In the third verse, we resurrect out of ourselves; we are really born into the spirit and know the spirit existence: P.S.S.R. We must develop ourselves, as "I"-being, to be an organ of the spiritual world.

> Luminous "I" and beacon-soul,
> Hover above true being of becoming
> What is thought out, what cognized
> Condenses now to spirit being.
> And like pearls of existence
> There dwells in the sea of divine truth
> What deceives the senses' existence.

These verses must, however, be meditated; then they will bring much progress. It is not enough to know the content. Even the most highly developed esotericists, who have already known [the content] for a long time, must meditate them ever again, alternating them.

* * *

RECORD C†

My dear sisters and brothers

Everyone is concerned about progress in esoteric development and may ask themselves if they are really progressing in their development toward the spiritual. Yes, all students, who really conscientiously use the exercises given by the teacher, progress further than they think. It is just that they may not think that something tumultuous will occur during their exercises; or as a result of them; this is because the spiritual world approaches us intimately and quietly. Of course, one thing is certain: all who want to find their way into the spiritual world must change their thinking; their whole perceptual life and feeling life must become different. It is just that this "becoming different" is so often misunderstood. People like to think that they can carry over into the spiritual world what they have amassed in knowledge on the physical plane. Using the same means with which they have made themselves clever within the physical world, they believe that they can knowledgeably enter the spiritual world. Esotericists must learn to see that the means through which we progress on the physical plane are totally different from those we must use to enter the spiritual world. [Esoteric] students must more and more learn to feel their way into the spiritual world through their devoted feelings. They must learn to tell themselves that it is not so much the content of the thoughts that matters in meditating, as it is the whole attitude and mood of soul with which the meditation is done. These [attitude and mood] are what transform the soul and gradually form the organs of the soul. Such a devoted, reverent mood of soul does not work only into the astral body; rather, esotericists will come more and more to feel their etheric body. And when this happens, it is a very important moment for the process of esoteric development.

Become clear about the following, my dear sisters and brothers: I stretch out my hand and bump the blackboard. In the physical-sense realm, we would say that here is an object upon which my hand met resistance. In the spiritual, however, there were I bumped the blackboard is a nothingness. In the spiritual world, there is a hole there—a gap. Emptiness, holes, are there in the spiritual world where, in the physical world, objects exist. However, before my hand arrives at this "nothingness," I reach my hand through a spiritual world that is, in turn, empty—a nothingness—for physical vision. It is spiritually, however, completely filled with realities—with spiritual beings. When we, as students of spiritual science, think through what has just been indicated, we must learn to say to ourselves: thus, when I look at something physical, I see in reality the outlines or contours of the spiritual world. Students must wrestle through to such knowledge. They must see the spirit behind everything; only then will they see the physical correctly.

What do we see when we look at an autumn landscape? We see a withering and dying in the physical, but behind it we sense already the new, living seeds that wrest themselves free from what is dying. It is the new life that wrenches itself from the death, which is still spiritual and will, however, clothe itself with matter in the spring.

A quite simple example can show us that where objects exist in the physical-sense realm, only nothingness or emptiness exists in the spiritual. Take a bottle of club soda. You do not see the water. You see only the sparkling bubbles of carbon dioxide. These are merely air—nothing. You do not see the water, the physical, outside of these bubbles of carbon dioxide. Thus, we also do not see the spiritual in the midst of the physical. These shimmering things of the perceptual world are covering it up for us.

When esotericists have lived into and become accustomed to this fundamental truth, that they are surrounded in the physical-sense world by a mere nothingness, them a second truth will open up to them, and this truth is: *it thinks me*, and not *I* think. Until now, they believed that *their* thoughts had value in the world. Now they gradually learn that in the spiritual realm there is a cosmic power which, when it thinks, also creates. And they learn that all human thinking is only a shadow-like reflection of this cosmic thinking. The cosmic thinking is produced by a lofty spirit-being, for whom thinking is characteristic to the same degree that sense perception is for the human being. The students learn that human thoughts are only shadows that are mirrored by the physical body. These human thoughts have the value of shadows only, and yet they are necessary for the physical world. Esoteric students must transform these thoughts through their meditation, so that realities come into being out of the shadow structures.

Esoteric students learn to look upon their proud thinking with ever-increasing modesty. They ask themselves: how can I change my thinking so that, through the transformation of the shadow-thoughts, I can create an instrument through which, with time, to enter into the spiritual world.

The students, by striving to free themselves from the shadow-thoughts, will gradually be able to concentrate themselves within their etheric body. No longer will they feel themselves as a human being within only their physical body. They will sense the physical body more and more as a shadow when they have to experience themselves on the physical plane. When they step before a mirror, it gives the outer impression of their physical form; it is not the human being himself or herself, however, but only a reflection of the human being. When they step away from the mirror, the image is gone—seemingly they are gone. Yet, in spite of that, they are there, even without the mirror. The mirror produces only a shadow-picture of their outer form.

When esoteric students have trained themselves to recognize the shadow-nature of the thoughts in themselves and have this as a basic mood of their soul, they then grow into a spiritual world. This mood of soul consists of recognizing that the thought-shadows are in the outer physical world in science and in social life, and that we ourselves as physical human beings are only shadows of our own inner being.

The students look back into the past, out of which they have become what they feel in themselves at this moment of their soul development. And they look into the future that lies before humanity. And then they know the following.

Everything has come into being out of the thoughts of the lofty spirit being. [How can we free ourselves from all the shadow-thinking around us?] How can we learn to think in such a way that, when we as human beings draw near in reverence to this being, we will be accepted? We recognize that all of the thoughts we think on Earth of the good, of good will, of the noble, of love, become enduring, everlasting assets of existence, which do not pass away like shadows that disappear. We see them before us—perhaps still a long way off in the future. They are living there and working for the welfare of humanity. And we see that also all the evil, the wrong and the deceitful, live on! They do not pass away! We see the lower, egotistical elements of human beings in the future, but we know those are waste products of human evolution. They are, in themselves, unfruitful. Yet they still have their task. These waste products serve as nourishment for what will develop as the good. All of the evil, the bad, becomes what shall later develop into nourishment for the seeds of the good.

Just as here on the physical plane, the mineral soil yields the nourishment for the plant world—as the fertilizer made of stone makes the growth of plants possible, the one nourishing itself from the other—so will all the evil thoughts, and all that is falsely known, be the basis or fundament for the sprouting thoughts of the good, the noble, and the true in the elemental world.

Through such knowledge, esotericists can better interpret the bad, the error, and the evil they see around them in the world. They see it around them and should imagine it in thought, but they know that they may not go further than the point where it is thought. They do not let it pass over into deed, which is always luciferic-ahrimanic. They look calmly upon all the bad and the evil, knowing that it will all at some time provide the ground upon which the seed of the good will someday grow.

It has also actually taken place thus in the evolution of the Earth. For how did the mineral kingdom of the Earth arise? On the old Moon—the Earth was not yet there—the hierarchies of beings, from those going through their human stage at that time on up to the spirits of form, gradually worked their way up to what surrounds us here in the Earth condition as wisdom. They thought error upon error. That was appropriate there. However, all of those errors became waste products out of which the material, mineral kingdom on Earth came into being.

And out of this Earth material, Yahweh-Elohim was able to form the human being, to give the physical sheath. Lucifer, however, who is now at a similar stage as the elohim [were on the old Moon], still wants to carry this on. Yet, he can make use only of human beings for his work, by letting the error and the lie be thought within the inner being of human beings.

My dear sisters and brothers, today I wish to give you three meditational formulas for your further work on your path into the spiritual world. You can meditate them in any way you like; for instance, the first in the morning, the second in the evening, and the third on Sundays. Or you can also do the first and second verses on Thursdays and Mondays and the third one now and then, as a test of what was experienced in the first two verses. With time, the whole depth of these meditations will become clear.

Verse I

I turn to things,
I turn with my senses.
Sense being, you deceive me!
What flees existence as nothing
Is being and essence to you.
May what must seem to you worth nothing
Reveal itself within me!

[First line:] *I turn to things*—actually the soul should turn, as with an inner gesture, to the things of the outer world. The second line: *I turn with my senses*. This should strengthen the first line. We should inwardly really feel how we turn ourselves to the things of the outer world with a swing, and not just glancing fleetingly, but wanting to know them in their essence or being. The third line: *Sense being, you deceive me*. In the third line, the semblance of the senses is addressed. The soul should learn to free itself intensively for moments from the nothingness of the sense world. By knowing ever more clearly the character of the nothingness of the sense world, they will completely change their inner stance to the physical-material realm. They will learn to see the material, the matter, as necessary for life in the sense world, but at the same time, to raise themselves above it to what is creative cosmic existence behind the nothingness. They will gradually learn to free themselves from the nothingness in such a manner that they spread themselves, as with a swing of the soul, out into space. There they will behold and feel: Everything material is perishable. However, the good and the true in me are not perishable. They are eternal! I may co-create the eternal, co-build the seed for the future, through my soul living in the flood of the divine truth and the good—in what is the divine-creative that creates and works in the world. *E.D.N.*

Verse II

Spirit Light, warm me,
Let me feel myself willing in you.
What is well-thought, cognized truth,
How does the luminous "I" experience you!
Weaving error, badly thought out
Show yourself to the beacon of my soul
That I may be weaving in myself.

If in the first verse we have lifted ourselves, as with a swinging of the soul, above the merely earthly, the second verse lets us find the way into our own self. We immerse ourselves deeply into the solitude of the soul. The soul draws itself together more and more tightly! It (the "I") knows ever more what our soul bears within it of good and noble thoughts, and of evil and foolish thoughts. And the "I" acknowledges that both are necessary in the course of development of the earthly human being. The task of the evil shows its self to be the future nourishment for the good. The good will nourish itself, like a sprouting seed, from the soil of the evil. It will consume all the evil and corruption, and will itself found an eternal existence.

And the soul knows that both the good and the evil will be taken up by Christ. *He* will separate them! We must bring to Christ our whole soul existence, so that it may one day bring fruits of eternity. We must learn to carry it (our soul existence) into Christ, to let it die into him. *I.* — — — *M.*

Verse III

Luminous "I" and beacon-soul,
Hover above true being of becoming
What is thought out, what cognized
Condenses now to spirit being.
And like pearls of existence
There dwells in the sea of divine truth
What deceives the senses' existence.

One could consider it to be an error that in the first line there are two subjects and, in spite of that, the verb in line two is in the singular.† I must admit that I did not notice this at first when the meditation was given to me out of the spiritual world. One merely takes it up at first and becomes clear about it only later. In the spiritual world, there is nothing, however, that could be assessed theoretically. There, everything is experienced and felt.†

There is just as little personal intention involved in each of these three verses consisting of seven lines.

This last, third verse should be a test for the first two. When we meditate it, this verse shall show us if the first two have proven themselves fruitful. If they have borne fruit, we can experience how our whole being forms itself as if into a chalice. And we experience that our soul-chalice takes into itself, and unites itself with, the cosmic spirit weaving and flowing through the universe—the Holy Spirit. The soul takes the awakener into itself; in the Holy Spirit the soul awakens to a new existence. P.S.S.R.

When we learn really to live in these three mantras, we thus experience at the same time, in ever new form, the inexhaustible content of our ten-word Rosicrucian mantra, which is of such an infinitely deep, manifold significance.

* * *

Record D†

Progress in esoteric development is important to us all. All who practice conscientiously come forward [in their development]. Many who do their exercises punctually and conscientiously make perhaps more progress than they believe. We must only observe with exactitude, as the spiritual world approaches us quietly and intimately.

Of course, one thing is certain: all who want to enter into the spiritual worlds must change their thinking. Their whole perceptual life and feeling life must become different. This "becoming different" is so often misunderstood. People think that they can carry over into the spiritual world what they have amassed in knowledge on the physical plane. Esotericists must learn to understand that other means are necessary to enter into the spiritual worlds than those necessary for making progress on the physical plane. They must more and more feel their way into the spiritual world. They must tell themselves that the important thing in meditating is not so much the content, the thoughts, but the attitude, the mood of soul, with which they execute the meditation. That is what transforms the soul and builds the organs of the soul. When esotericists find themselves in such a proper soul state, they will also come more and more to feel their etheric body.

When I reach out with my hand and bump against the blackboard, we would say on the physical-sense plane: there is an object against which my hand found resistance. On the spiritual plane, there is precisely a nothingness there; there are holes there. There are gaps there in the spiritual world where sense-perceptible objects are in the physical. However, before I come up against this resistance I penetrate through the spiritual world that is completely filled with realities, with spiritual beings. In truth, it is not the object we see in space, but the outlines of the spiritual world.

Esotericists must penetrate through to such knowledge. They must see the spirit behind everything. When they stand before an autumn landscape, they must already sense, in the wilting and dying, the new, living seeds and see them wrest themselves free—these seeds that will offer themselves up in the spring by clothing themselves with matter.

A quite simple example can show us that where a sense-perceptible object is present in the physical, mere nothingness exists in the spiritual. Take, for instance, a bottle of club soda. Although the water is denser, we do not see it because of the shining bubbles of effervescent carbon dioxide that are actually only air—a nothingness. Thus, we also do not see the spiritual because of the shimmering things of the sense-perceptible world.

When the esotericists have accustomed themselves to this truth, that they are surrounded in the physical, sense world by pure nothingness, a second truth will soon dawn on them. That truth is: *it thinks me*, and not *I* think; namely, that all of our thoughts are only shadow-like. We are accustomed to believe that thinking takes place in the physical body, but that is not so. In reality, the etheric body is the originator of our thoughts. The physical body is involved only in that it serves as a mirror, reflecting back the thoughts produced in the etheric body.

When we look into a mirror, we see a reflected image. The mirror reflects the outer impression of our physical form; without our physical form there would be no reflected image. This mirrored image is only a shadow-picture of our outer form. In the same way, the thoughts that have their living origin and domicile in the etheric body are only reflected picture-shadows when we think them in our physical brain. Through meditation and concentration, we should come to free ourselves from the shadow-thoughts. This will occur through the concentration of our soul, of our self in the etheric body, so that we penetrate to the true, actual source of our thoughts that live in the etheric body.

When we have trained ourselves to recognize and know the shadow-nature of our thoughts and our outer surroundings, we then grow into the spiritual world. We will then also know that all the thoughts we engender on Earth of the good, of goodwill, and of the noble will transform into eternal existential value and will remain in existence. We see them at a distance, in the future. There they live for the well-being of humanity.

And we also see all that is evil, bad, untruthful, and all lower egotistical thoughts as if in the distance, but they remain behind as waste products, which become nourishment for the good. All that is evil and bad becomes what is in itself unfruitful, but becomes nourishment for what will develop out of the seed of the good.

Just as here on the physical plane, the mineral soil provides the nourishment for the plants, and the one always feeds the other, so too will all bad thoughts and what is poorly known become the basis or soil for the thoughts of the good, the noble, and the true that are sprouting in the elemental world. For this reason, esotericists can interpret the bad and the error so well. They should imagine it in thought. Yet they know that they must not let it go further than thought; they must not let it pass over into deed, into reality, which is always luciferic and ahrimanic. They know that it (the bad and the error) provides the soil from which the seed of the good shall grow one day.

It has actually also taken place thus in the evolution of the Earth. In this way, the mineral kingdom of the Earth arose.

On the old Moon, hierarchies from [those at the stage of] the human being on up to the spirits of form thought error. This was appropriate there, and out of this the material, the mineral, came into being on Earth. And out of this earthly material, Yahweh-Elohim was able to build the human being and give the physical sheath. However, Lucifer, who is now at a similar stage as the elohim were on the old Moon, still wants to perform the same thing. He can make use only of human beings for this. He can allow the error to be thought only within the human being.

Because it is not possible at the moment for me to speak with each of you individually, I wish to give three formulations that can be meditated in which ever way you wish. For instance, you could meditate the first one in the morning, the second in the evening, and the third on Sunday. Or you could do the first and second on Mondays and Thursdays and the third only now and then as a test of what was experienced in the other two meditations. They will then become quite clear to us.

Verse I

> I turn to things,
> I turn with my senses.
> Sense being, you deceive me!
> What flees existence as nothing
> Is being and essence to you.
> May what must seem to you worth nothing
> Reveal itself within me!

First line: *I turn to things*—the soul should, as if with an inner gesture, turn to the things. Second line: *I turn with my senses*—strengthens the first line. I should really feel it inwardly. In the third line, I speak to sense existence. The soul should free itself from the physical, from the nothingness of the sense world. It should raise itself from the physical-material to what is behind the things. This soul should spread itself far out into the space, and sense: the good in me is eternal; it is the seed of something in the future—*Ex Deo nascimur*.

Verse II

Spirit Light, warm me,
Let me feel myself willing in you.
What is well-thought, cognized truth,
How does the luminous "I" experience you!
Weaving error, badly thought out
Show yourself to the beacon of my soul
That I may be weaving in myself.

With this verse we should immerse ourselves in ourselves, into the solitude of the soul. The "I" contracts, pulls itself together, as tightly as possible. It recognizes what it bears of the good and noble and of the evil and foolish thoughts in its soul. Yet, the "I" senses that both the evil and the good are necessary. The evil is the future nourishment for the good; the good will feed itself like a sprouting seed that consumes the evil and the depravity. And the good remains eternally. Both [the good and the evil] are taken up by Christ and carried into the future. If the good that we have engendered is to bring forth fruit there, we must carry it into Christ—*In — — — morimur*!

Verse III

Luminous "I" and beacon-soul,
Hover above true being of becoming
What is thought out, what cognized
Condenses now to spirit being.
And like pearls of existence
There dwells in the sea of divine truth
What deceives the senses' existence.

One could consider it an error that there are two subjects and that, in spite of this, the verb is in the singular. I must admit that I did not notice this at first, as the mantras were given to me out of the spiritual world. One just accepts them and becomes clear about them only later. In the spiritual world, there is so little that is theoretical; everything is experienced. Just as little was there any [personal] intention behind every verse consisting of seven lines.

The third verse should be a test for the other two. We should examine how much the meditating of the other two has worked in a fruitful way. Then we will behold a chalice. As in a spiritual communion, our soul will unite with the cosmic spirit weaving and flowing through the universe. We shall be resurrected through the Holy Spirit—*Per Spiritum Sanctum reviviscimus*.

When we really live in these three mantras, we experience, at the same time, what is said in the three parts of our ten-word Rosicrucian mantra that is of such infinitely deep and manifold significance and meaning.

Esoteric Lesson
MUNICH, MARCH 31, 1914

It has already often been stressed that we must differentiate between our progress in esoteric development on the one hand, and the noticing of this progress on the other. All esotericists make progress if they do their esoteric exercises loyally and regularly, even when they are dissatisfied with the results. The sincere striving is what matters.

We actually become a different human being through these exercises. This happens in any case, even though we do not notice it. For in all of these exercises—whether given in books or orally—lie the forces that loosen the etheric body and draw it out of the physical body. It is quite something else, now, to become aware of these changes. This soul can actually already have [spiritual] organs, but the difference is whether the soul is asleep or awake in its spiritual surroundings. The soul needs great strength and preparation in order to awaken and become conscious. For this reason, in these lectures, descriptions will be given of what the soul experiences upon awakening in the spiritual world. Many make the becoming-conscious difficult for themselves, because they still always imagine the spiritual world to be like a second physical world, only finer. That is a great hindrance, because they do not notice the fine, subtle symptoms of awakening. Such prejudices must be eliminated. Those who still have them are like people who go up in a hot air balloon and think they can disembark at any moment up there and rest on a mountain peak. Those who take in the esoteric explanations correctly, however, can first of all grasp how the spiritual world is experienced upon the awakening of the soul.

In order to achieve this, we must ask ourselves: What is thinking actually? What thinks in me? Materialists who deny the suprasensible would say: the [physical] body, the brain, thinks. One should ask them if they have ever perceived thinking with the senses. Naturally, they have not. Never has thinking been heard, seen, or felt—not as warmth or anything similar—by anyone. It follows that it is not physical or corporeal, because what belongs to the body is sense-perceptible.

Thus, thinking is suprasensible. The materialists would either have to admit that the suprasensible world exists, or should renounce thinking as nonsense—which would perhaps be good.

Thus, with our thinking we are always within the suprasensible world, but in such a way that we do not experience it ourselves. Just as if we were to go out on the sea but would not see ourselves or our boat, so it is approximately with human thinking. We do not experience the thinking itself directly; what we experience of it, the thoughts, are reflections of the thinking and of our body. Just as when we stand in front of a mirror we see our reflected image, so the thinking soul sees the reflected image of its thinking. The brain is the mirror. Through the esoteric training we should now come to experience the thinking itself and not just the thoughts. Just as we see the surface of the mirror when we step in front of it, so too must the soul come to see the body from outside as a mirroring apparatus. Then we will know how the thoughts come into being, and we will experience ourselves in the world out of which the thinking reaches, as thought, into the sense world.

All of this can be grasped by every healthy intellect. And it is important for Theosophists to become quite clear about all of this in order to be armed against the objection that Theosophy is based on belief and faith, that one would have to believe in the existence of the suprasensible world. This is not true. Everyone can grasp this existence if they apply their thinking correctly. Those who cannot understand it are foolish, even if they are philosophers. It is yet a long way from grasping the possibility of experiencing the suprasensible world through thinking to the actual knowledge itself. Only through long work of the soul upon itself can this [knowledge] be attained; but it will be achieved.

The first sign of awakening in the spiritual world is a feeling of becoming larger, as if we spread ourselves out, as if we float out. In the sense world I am here, and the object is there; from the object an impression comes to me. Consciousness arises because we bump against the objects with our organs of touch, hearing, seeing. In the spiritual world we cease to be closed up within ourselves. We feel ourselves as if spread out into other beings. In the physical world we experience everything from within our skin; for instance, a prick of a needle. It is different in the spiritual world. There, thinking and feeling flow out. We feel pleasure and pain in others. For instance, if we meet someone who died and who is in pain, we must experience the pain together with this person, as long as we are spiritually connected with each other.

Through this change, our relationship to the sense world also becomes quite different. The way we usually experience the physical world depends on the fact that our body, through which we experience, is also material. If we bump our head against a hard object, we feel it because our head does not give way; that is, because it is hard and of the same nature as the object. However, if we view this sense world with our suprasensible perception and experience, no impression comes toward us from the object. The spiritual organs are, as it were, too soft, and give way. For this reason, all of the physical things appear like empty spaces. A comparison can give an idea of this. Water in the glass is itself invisible. In soda water, the bubbles are visible, and yet the bubbles are much thinner than the water. They are, in comparison to the heavier fluid, a nothingness. Thus, here a nothingness is visible, and a something is invisible. Truly, this is how it is for the spiritual sight in the physical world. All of the atoms—which for science until recently formed the basis of all materiality—are, like the bubbles in the water, merely holes or empty bubbles in the spiritual. All physical things are composed of an enormous sum of such holes. We bump against these holes, this nothingness, when we touch. It is this way also with the human form. For instance, the brain is, spiritually seen, a spiritual form. Within this form are countless holes or empty bubbles; these make up what the scientists examine with their instruments.

And there ensues that we feel all the good, the correct, and the true streaming out of us. We feel it as if growing into the future, as building seeds for the future. However, also the incorrect, bad, and ugly that we think and feel grow outward. We feel it as something quite real that streams out from us, and we know that the bad thoughts flowing from us will serve as nourishment for the good in the future. Therefore, we learn to understand why so many bad, incorrect, ugly thoughts and feelings assault us during meditation. When we know that they are necessary forces, nourishment for the future, we will also judge them correctly. We will not need to complain about them, if we are strong enough not to let them flow into our will and our actions. And therein lies a great secret. The same forces that form the basis of our evil thoughts were rayed forth on the old Moon from hierarchical beings from the angels up to the spirits of form. But Lucifer and Ahriman remained behind and ray forth these forces only now. Now, however, these forces work into the physical nature, which has condensed further in the meantime; they work right into the blood of the human being. Through this, the evil comes into being. In themselves, they are not evil. Esotericists must let these forces work upon themselves, but must not allow them to condense into the physical. Then they remain of value for the good thoughts of the future.

In order to further advance and support the experience of these first steps in the spiritual world, the following formulations (verses) are given. Beginning esotericists should use them so that the first verse is done in the morning; the second is done in the evening after the review of the day; and the third is done every few days. More experienced esotericists should not disturb their exercises with these, but should take them up occasionally, doing the first and the second directly after each other. The third verse can be taken up once a week, for instance on Sundays.

That each of these verses has seven lines was not intentional or made up. Such a thing emerges quite naturally on its own. The spiritual content reveals itself in such a way that it presses itself into this seven-line form.

I.

Zu den Dingen wend ich mich
Wend ich mich mit meinen Sinnen;
Sinnensein, du täuschest mich!
Was als nichts das Dasein flieht:
Dir ist's Sein und Wesenheit;
Was dir nichtig scheinen muß,
Offenbare meinem Innern sich.

II.

Geisteslicht erwarme mich
Lass in dir mich wollend fühlen,
Gutgedachtes, Wahr Erkanntes
Wie erlebt dich leuctend Ich
Irrtumsweben, bös erdachtes
Zeige dich der Leucthe-Seele
Dass ich webend in mir sei.

III.

Leuchtend Ich und Leuchte-Seele
Schwebet über wahrem Werdewesen
Das Erdachte, das Erkannte
Wird jetzt dichtes Geistessein.
Und wie leichte Daseinsperlen
Lebt im Meer des Göttlich-Wahren
Was den Sinnen Dasein täuscht.

I.

I turn to things,
I turn with my senses.
Sense being, you deceive me!
What flees existence as nothing
Is being and essence to you.
May what must seem to you worth nothing
Reveal itself within me!

II.

Spirit Light, warm me,
Let me feel myself willing in you.
What is well-thought, cognized truth,
How does the luminous "I" experience you!
Weaving error, badly thought out
Show yourself to the beacon of my soul
That I may be weaving in myself.

III.

Luminous "I" and beacon-soul,
Hover above true being of becoming
What is thought out, what cognized
Condenses now to spirit being.
And like pearls of existence
There dwells in the sea of divine truth
What deceives the senses' existence.

Lines one and three of the third verse gave much to think about. The verse was revealed—but it seemed to be grammatically incorrect—that it says [in the German] *schwebet* [hovers, floats] instead of *schweben* [hover, float]. Later it became clear that this was intended. *Leuchtend Ich und Leuchte-Seele* [Luminous "I" and beacon-soul] are to be thought of as one entity. In the same way, in the following line, *Das Erdachte, das Erkannte* [What is thought out, what cognized] should be handled as one. In the physical world, to think and to know are not one and the same; in the spiritual, they flow together. Something that has been thought out is either false, in which case it destroys itself; or it is correct, and then it is also a revelation—knowledge.

Such formulations—also all that, for instance, are given in *Outline of Esoteric Science*[†]—are not thought up or invented. The intellect plays at first absolutely no part in it; the things are revealed to the seers. Revelations stand there on their own. Only then must the seers go to work on them with the intellect—just as do those to whom the seers communicate the revelations.

The first verse indicates the experience that the physical things appear, like bubbles in the water, to consist of nothingness. The soul recognizes the usual sense existence as illusion and strives for knowledge of the truly real.

The second verse describes the experience of the raying forth of the good and the evil thoughts.

The third formulation or verse is to be used, as it were, as a test for the progress made. When we meditate it, we must speak the words inwardly in such a way that they all make sense. We should try, through these lines, to discover how far we are: whether, for instance, we already experience something with the words: *Das Erdachte, das Erkannte / Wird jetzt dichtes Geistessein* [What is thought out, what cognized / condense now to spirit being]. Naturally, the work with this verse must be continued each week with perseverance and patience.

We can also see these verses as a paraphrasing of the mantras that always form the close of these lessons. The first verse indicates how sense-materiality becomes insubstantial upon our growing into the spiritual world, and how the spiritual reality is recognized as that out of which we come into being: *Ex Deo nascimur*. The second verse describes the experience of the good and evil thoughts as forces working in the future. However, that is possible only when the soul is surrounded and illumined by the spiritual light—Christ—after it has lifted itself out of the physical: *In Christo morimur*. And the third verse represents how knowledge reveals itself to the soul that is awakening in the spirit: *Per Spiritum Sanctum reviviscimus*.

Esoteric Lesson
BERLIN, APRIL 25, 1914

RECORD A

We spoke in our last esoteric study of how the soul should more and more spread itself out and pour itself into space; and of how it then should contract into itself to see what weaves and works within itself. For this, dear sisters and brothers, formulations, meditations, are given that you can use in the way you wish, and that can be given to others who are not here with us to hear the esoteric lesson.

Today you will receive a different contemplation placed before your soul—something concrete, a mood that can help you enter into the spiritual world.

Let us call to mind what takes place during sleep. The etheric body and physical body remain in bed, while the astral body and "I" are outside in the spiritual world. Why is it then that human beings do not experience consciously the world they find themselves in during sleep as they do the physical world during day-consciousness? They do not have conscious experience during sleep because, while they are outside of their body, they have a yearning, a strong impulse, to return to their physical body. This yearning works as a darkening in relation to the brightness of the spiritual world, such that the human beings do not perceive anything of it. The astral forces active in them work so strongly that they would not leave their physical body at all if the astral body did not become so exhausted and depleted in the sense world that it urgently needed strengthening and refreshing through sleep. This drive, this yearning for their physical body, is what hinders human beings from experiencing consciously in the spiritual worlds during sleep. If they were clairvoyant, they would see how bright rays shine forth from their astral body and "I" to their etheric body and physical body. This yearning to be reunited is expressed in these rays.

Let us assume that people would suddenly become clairvoyant during sleep. What would they see there? When we meet people here on the physical plane, their physical form, in which an "I" lives, confronts us. It is different in the spiritual world; we must not think that we see the human being in the same form as on the physical plane. Here in the physical world we see things more with sharp contours. It is different in the spiritual world. What weaves and works there are moving images, and we recognize these moving images to be beings: the spirits of the higher hierarchies that send out their messengers, their helpers, to give the human form the right expression. These emissaries, these messengers of the spirits of form, are still at the stage of childhood, as it were. They will work their way upward to the same degree that they nurture the human "I." Another group of elemental beings, the guardians of the "I"-being, hover around the human head. They work on our thinking, and are sent out by the spirits of form and the spirits of movement. And yet other elemental beings, emissaries of the spirits of wisdom, work on the human heart and bring about the circulation of the blood.

Further, there are elemental beings that work on the human being's sense of warmth. We may not imagine this as being physical, where the warmth comes from a specific source; rather in the spiritual, the warmth arises out of the relationship between two beings.

Again other elemental beings work on the word-sense. This does not mean that these beings work on the spoken word that others can hear, but that they stand behind the individual consonants and vowels that build a word. They work on the composition of the letters and syllables. Those who are outside of their body cannot understand words that are being spoken, because they lack the physical organ necessary for it. They can, however, follow the work of the elemental beings as they bring together the individual letters in order to build a word.

The human being has twelve senses† and not just five, as the other science would have us believe. Our senses are: the light-sense (sight), thought-sense, warmth-sense, balance-sense, word-sense, life-sense, smell, taste, hearing, feeling, sense of movement, and "I"-sense.

Behind these twelve senses are elemental beings that are servants and helpers of the spirits of form, the spirits of movement, and the spirits of wisdom. Now, these elemental beings are still to a certain extent in the stage of childhood, but they will develop in the same measure as the human beings progress and develop themselves upward to the Jupiter condition.† These elemental beings will one day build the zodiac of Jupiter; they will be the zodiac constellations of Jupiter after the Earth has completed its seven periods, and has emerged from the pralaya again in a new configuration in the Jupiter planetary condition. It is exactly the same process as what formerly worked on us during the old Moon—and now stands behind our senses—and became [what is now] the zodiac of the Earth.

Jupiter will also have a sun. Behind it will stand the beings that work into our blood system today.

Only with the greatest as we and admiration can we look upon how whole groups of elemental beings are actively working on the wonderful temple of the human body. In earnest meditation, my dear sisters and brothers, put yourself into this mood, [of witnessing] how countless elementals construct the temple that shall build the home for the human "I."

Why is it that we do not see that these elemental beings are at work? It is because, in the moment of our waking up, the Guardian of the Threshold conceals the spiritual worlds from us. Waking up means nothing other than chasing away those elemental beings from their field of work. Just as soon as we are in our day-consciousness, Ahriman sees to it that the spiritual world is covered up for us. He paints the picture of this sense world, and because we give ourselves over to the great illusionist—the maya—the souls, the beings that work on the spiritual organization of the human being, become invisible for us.

What we know as the physical body is all a product of Ahriman. In contrast, we must recognize the work of Lucifer in what we experience as soul life exclusively in the physical body. Lucifer fills our soul with so much arrogance and delusion that it receives false ideas and feelings in relation to the spiritual world.

Ex Deo nascimur
In – – – morimur
Per Spiritum Sanctum reviviscimus.

From God we are born
In – – – we die
Through the Holy Spirit we come to life again.

* * *

RECORD B

The last esoteric lesson concerned itself with the efforts we must make in order to progress esoterically and ended with the threefold meditation. Today, we want to discuss more esoteric actualities and so treat a subject that we all already know: sleep. Why are we not conscious during sleep? It is because the astral forces do not allow it; they are so strong that they numb us. The astral forces express themselves in what fills us completely during sleep, namely, the burning wish to be in our physical body. It is this wish that darkens our consciousness.

If we could be conscious during sleep, we could look upon the wonder of the structure of our physical body and etheric body and would notice how legions of spiritual beings, elemental beings are working in this physical body. These elemental beings are servants and messengers, partly of the spirits of form and partly of the spirits of movement.

If we really want to contemplate the spiritual world correctly, we must think away out of the spiritual world everything that exists in the physical world, including the space. In the spiritual world, there are no things and facts like in the physical world, but only beings and relationships of beings with one another, deeds of the beings. If, for instance, we feel warmth in the spiritual world, this does not come from an object, but it radiates forth from a being; it signifies the relationship of one spiritual being with another. It is the same with a stream of light. Why do we not really perceive the physical body and etheric body? Why are we not conscious of the weaving, working, and living of countless elemental beings in us? We are not aware of them because the wish to be an "I," to live in our physical body, fills us so passionately (through Lucifer) during sleep, that we perceive absolutely nothing else. Otherwise, we would see the physical and etheric bodies as a wonder upon which legions of elemental spirits work. What do they work on? On our senses. We can differentiate twelve groups of elemental beings that work on our twelve senses. Human beings have twelve senses: the sense of "I," sense of life, sense of one's own movement, sense of balance, sight, hearing, touch, smell, taste, sense of speech, sense of thought, and sense of warmth. And now in order to live in our "I," every morning upon awakening and returning to our body, we drive away the beings that work on us in the night. In order to feel ourselves completely in our "I," we drive the hierarchies out of our physical and etheric bodies.

Who are you, O Human Being, that legions of spirits work on your physical and etheric bodies? The messengers and servants—some of the spirits of form and some of the spirits of movement—hover around our head. These messengers take care of our "I." In our brain work the elemental beings that make human thinking possible. Again other elemental spirits work on the organs that enable us to understand speech, but not to be able to speak, mind you. They are the elemental beings that stand as spiritual beings behind the sounds, behind the individual vowels and consonants. Thus, these twelve groups of servants of the hierarchies work out the forms in which the "I" can live. When we look into the spiritual world at these working beings themselves, we have the impression that they are young spirits that, in their childhood, have the task of nurturing and caring for the human "I." Later, when they are further along in their development, they are pre-destined for other evolutionary work. On Jupiter, they will be the servants of the zodiac and beings of Jupiter. One day they will work down from the zodiac of Jupiter. It is the same with the twelve groups of elemental spirits that now build our senses, as with those that built our senses on the old Moon and are today the beings of our zodiac. Just as a sun shines upon our Earth, so too, as surely as we develop ourselves into the Jupiter-existence, will a sun shine upon this Jupiter. The beings that will live and work in this sun are the beings that are now servants of the spirits of wisdom, and which live in our blood circulation. The spiritual beings that regulate the course of our blood will one day regulate the course of the sun of the Jupiter condition!

We are also in the spiritual world during the day when we are awake, but we do not know it because we do not see the wonder of our body, the world of the spiritual beings that, weaving and working, fill the space. Why do we not see the spiritual world around us during the day? Because Ahriman shoves the picture of the sense world in front it. Oh, he is a great artist, for this world is great and magnificent, but it is not the true world. We do not see Ahriman himself in the physical world, but only his work, his deed; we see him only in the spiritual world.

Lucifer is the one that does not allow us to become conscious of the spiritual world in the night. He blunts the feeling for the spiritual world while he endeavors to bring about the feeling and yearning for the physical world. That is why we see the physical body instead of the work of the beings on our senses; that is Lucifer's deed. Sense experience is Lucifer's deed; world experience is Ahriman's deed. During the day we are totally in our senses; we occupy them completely. During the night the servants of the hierarchies, the divine-spiritual elemental beings, are within and work on our senses. A wise cosmic guide allowed the intervention by Lucifer and Ahriman, so that we can properly attain our goal as human beings. A meditation that is especially effective for attaining a proper esoteric feeling and sensing is to imbue oneself before falling asleep with the feeling: I am now entering a spiritual world, a wonderful world of the gods, in which the divine-spiritual beings of the higher hierarchies live and work. They take loving care of me and send their forces out, and bear me upon their wings. And through them, I am a force in the spiritual world. They nurture me as soul. E.D.N.

If we, when outside of our physical and etheric bodies during sleep, can for moments suppress the wish to be in our body, so that it does not fill us completely, and so that not we but Christ is in us, then we get a sense of the I.C.M. This occurs when Christ, who is the power of all the hierarchies, is in our body, and not just we ourselves, who want to enter it and drive out the servants of the hierarchies that are working there on our sense organs.

If both feelings (E.D.N. and I.C.M.) are properly experienced, then the third feeling (P.S.S.R.) comes of itself. The Holy Spirit is born through the first two feelings. We can penetrate thus ever deeper into our Rosicrucian formulation (mantra) that the Masters of Wisdom and the Harmony of Feelings explain by saying to us:

> In the spirit lay the germ of my body.
> And the spirit has imprinted in my body
> The eyes of sense,
> That through them I may see
> The light of bodies.
> And the spirit has imprinted in my body
> Reason and sensation
> And feeling and will,
> That through them I may perceive bodies
> And act upon them.
> In the spirit lay the germ of my body.
>
> In my body lies the germ of the spirit.
> And I will incorporate into my spirit
> The supersensuous eyes,
> That through them I may behold the light of spirits.
> And I will imprint in my spirit
> Wisdom and power and love,
> So that through me the spirits may act
> And I become the self-conscious organ
> Of their deeds.
> In my body lies the germ of the spirit.

* * *

Record C

My dear sisters and brothers, we can know a great deal of Anthroposophy and be able to quickly answer all possible questions, and yet, must say to ourselves: Actually, if I want to be honest, I must admit that I do not progress well in my meditations. What should I do to better move forward? Quite often, the reason students must say such a thing is that they do not immerse their souls completely in the element of devoutness in relation to the spiritual beings. The deepest reverence must hold sway in their soul, if they want to raise themselves up to these beings. No thought or feeling from the daily life may be in the students; they must be totally still within themselves.

In such a mood, we want to contemplate human sleep from a certain side. We know that during sleep the astral body and "I" leave the physical body and etheric body. However, the "I" knows nothing of this; it remains unconscious. The consciousness of the "I" and astral body is awake only on the physical plane. Why is this? It is because the moment the "I" and astral body are outside, they have a burning desire to be reunited with the physical and etheric bodies. That is the reason consciousness does not awaken in the spiritual world. Just as soon as the "I" is back in the physical body, it awakens to the things presented to it by the senses. If human beings did not have this burning desire, they would immediately become conscious in the spiritual world. Then they would see a world full of life around them, but it would be totally different from the physical world. They would perceive a world of spiritual beings and forces. And the students would see that all of these beings and forces tend toward a single central point, and would see that this central point is their own physical body and etheric body.

If we as human beings would go further, and could make observations outside of our body in the spiritual world—to the point where we could observe our "I" or that of another—we would then see that the human "I" is the target of the spiritual beings' work. And we would recognize these beings as messengers and servants of the spirits of form and, in part, of the spirits of movement. And we would know that these beings working on the human "I" are in progress; they are involved in their own development. By nurturing and caring for the human "I," they develop themselves at the same time. Clairvoyants would see behind every human being such a group of beings taking care of the human "I." And if the clairvoyants would look at the physical body and etheric body, they would again see crowds of elemental beings that they would recognize as servants of the spirits of movement, spirits of wisdom, and spirits of form.

And human beings would recognize, in reverence and devoutness, that all of these elemental beings are working on the temple of the physical body and etheric body, while the human beings themselves are outside of their body-temple. Waking up is nothing other than driving these beings from their field of work, and taking their place with our egotistical earthly "I."

There are twelve categories of such beings. Human beings have twelve senses, and these beings work on them. We have the warmth-sense, the "I"-sense, the thought-sense, balance-sense, word-sense, life-sense, smell, taste, sight, hearing, touch, and movement-sense. The word-sense works in such a way that, when we hear another person speak, we do not hear the words spoken, but the individual vowels and consonants out of which the word was formed.

We know how these beings work upon the temple of humanity given to the human "I" by the Godhead. And we know that the human "I" destroys this temple again and again by allowing Ahriman and Lucifer to seduce us. Of course, it will be clear to the clairvoyant that what we consider to be the physical body—what we can touch and take hold of—is not the temple that is being referred to. The clairvoyant knows this temple to be the spiritual organization that stands behind the physical body. And these spiritual beings work on this spiritual organization.

What we call our physical body, what as such is in the physical surroundings, is all the product of Ahriman. We meet his products in everything that is physical. And we know, when we come to the point of experiencing ourselves outside the physical and etheric bodies, that our whole soul life that we bear within us through the physical body is the work of Lucifer. Lucifer is at work in all of our thinking, feeling, and willing that is stimulated only through the emotions caused by the sense world. The clairvoyant knows that these elemental beings strive to remove the effects of Lucifer and Ahriman. These effects exhibit themselves as physical illness, as well as psychologically as soul-pain, fear, anxiety, and mental illnesses. These elemental beings strive to heal the human being by removing these effects of Ahriman and Lucifer. These beings are servants of the lofty spirit beings that now shine upon our Earth and the human world from the forces of the zodiac. These elemental beings are the spirit-messengers of the forces of our zodiac, and out of this circumference they all work into the center point: our Earth.

All human beings may feel themselves as a center point of the work of these elemental beings and of the spiritual beings working upon their "I." Our Earth passes over into a spiritual condition, which is called the "pralaya," once it has gone through its prescribed seven evolutionary stages. It will then emerge again in a new configuration as Jupiter. The elemental beings that now are the messengers of our zodiac will then become the zodiac of Jupiter; that is their development. Now they are working on what stands spiritually behind our senses.

* * *

Record D

The last time, our esoteric lesson treated the spreading out of oneself in the etheric atmosphere, and it ended in the three mantric formulations. This time, we will start with life during sleep. When we sleep, our "I" and astral body are in the spiritual world, but we cannot perceive anything there. We could become almost fearful and ask whether it will also be the case after death that, although we are in the spiritual world, we will not be able to perceive anything. Spiritual researchers know, however, that we all have a drive, a wish, of which we ourselves are not conscious, but which asserts itself the moment we are outside of the body. This wish is to descend again into the body and to experience ourselves within it. If we were clairvoyant in our sleep, we would notice how we look back upon our body and see the body as a wonderfully beautiful world. The more we have an open eye for all the beauty in nature, the more we can marvel at the beauty of the bodily world in which divine beings are working, and which is a temple for these beings.

We see how twelve classes of elemental beings work on the twelve senses of the physical body, and that these beings are the servants of the elohim, which gave us our form on Earth. These spirits (the servants) are now still in their childhood, so to speak; but their work on our twelve bodily senses will help them develop, so that as the Earth evolves, they will become the forces of the zodiac for the Jupiter planetary condition.† They will be the direct mediators of the gods of the zodiac for Jupiter. There will also be a sun, and the beings that will work there in the Sun forces are the elemental beings that work now in our blood circulation. This can give us a feeling for the sacredness of our bodily temple, and it is good to feel within ourselves the knowledge of the cosmic forces working in this temple. But now, at the same time, if we were to perceive this clairvoyantly, we would see the wish arise in us to penetrate this body with our own "I"—to drive away the elemental beings and enter into it ourselves. How is it that when we stand on Earth in our usual consciousness, everything is different, and that we are so totally different from this divine, luminous temple? Ahriman throws the view of the material world as a veil over our eyes, and thus hides from us the divine world that weaves in the physical. And what allows us to experience our ordinary "I"-consciousness in this physical world is Lucifer, who brings us the feeling of the personal "I." Perhaps there is only one thing we can do, and that is to meditate, and thus... [The record breaks off here].

* * *

Record E

The last esoteric study was dedicated to the description of the processes of the etheric body on one hand, which spreads itself out more and more in meditation; and on the other hand, of the inward concentrating and contracting of the "I" within itself. Today's lesson shall be devoted to more such factual things. With sleeping human beings, we see the astral body and the "I" lifted out of the physical and etheric bodies and living in the spiritual world. Why can we not consciously know anything there? It is because our "I" and astral body continually yearn for the physical body and strive to reunite with it. This is also the case after death.

If we were to become suddenly clairvoyant during sleep, we would know how spiritual beings work on our physical body. These beings are elemental spirits, servants of the hierarchies. Certain spiritual beings work on a specific human sense, and certain others work on another sense. The human being has twelve senses, and so working upon the senses are twelve groups of elemental beings that are servants of the higher hierarchies.

When the Earth later advances to the Jupiter existence, the sky with its stars, Moon, and Sun will not be spread over it like today. Indeed, there will be a sun, but it will be emitting tones. The forces of the elemental spirits that now work upon our senses will then form the zodiac of Jupiter, just as, during the Moon existence, the forces of beings that worked on our senses now work down upon the Earth out of the twelve constellations of our current zodiac.

We should look up with gratitude to the gods that made this wonder of our body the purpose of their work.

* * *

Record F

Twelve kinds of elemental spirits take care of us and work on our twelve senses, sharpening them anew in our sleep. These beings serve the spirits of form and the spirits of movement. During the Jupiter existence, these beings will be the spirits of the twelve signs of the zodiac. The spirits of the twelve signs of the Earth's zodiac worked in this way during the old Moon existence. The sun spirits of Jupiter are today elemental spirits that are subordinate to the spirits of wisdom, and they work on the human blood circulation.

We do not perceive the spiritual world during sleep because astral forces give us a yearning for the physical body. Just as soon as the physical body lets the "I" and astral body in again, these [elemental beings] leave.

Ahriman paints the picture of the sense world as a veil before the spiritual world. Lucifer darkens the spiritual world itself before the human being.

Esoteric Lesson
KASSEL, MAY 9, 1914

Mantra for Saturday.

My dear sisters and brothers!

In the ordinary day-consciousness, we know nothing about what is behind our sensing, imagining, thinking, feeling, and willing. We are in our dream life in what stands behind our day-consciousness, in this living, weaving background. A part of this [living] world that we otherwise do not perceive reaches into our life in the chaotic images of our dreams. If we could awaken halfway out of the dream, we would then experience around us a surging wave, in which our soul has lived from the beginning of our sleep. And if we would fully awaken, we would then bring into our day-consciousness a consciousness, a memory, of the living, weaving dream life during sleep. It is physically impossible to wake up halfway, as described; we must pass immediately and completely into the consciousness of the senses. For this reason, we know nothing of that other world.

Actually, however, we always dream. This living, weaving dream-world is always around us, and we are in it. We just do not know it. It is a characteristic of the dream that we forget it quite easily, that we rarely can remember it. We forget it much more easily than anything we experience with our day-consciousness. We cannot bring up the dream again.

People dream of things that are connected only with their day-consciousness, because they actually think nothing that goes beyond this daily life. Only when they fill their thoughts with ideas, feelings, etc., that reach above and beyond their daily life, can they also dream of something that has its origin in the spiritual. Human beings know nothing of the spiritual behind all their thinking, feeling, and willing in the physical life.

We can manage to attain the consciousness of this spiritual from yet another side.

Stream of the spiritual until death

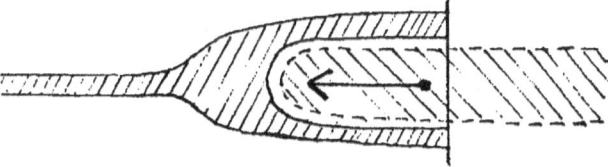

Birth or conception   New soul-seed

At birth or conception, the spiritual stream pours itself into the physical, builds up, and streams and pulsates through the whole organism.

During the course of life, there forms within this organism the soul-seed for the next life. This soul-seed continues beyond death. However, we know nothing of either the original spiritual element that streams out of the earlier life into the physical existence with birth or conception, or of the soul-seed that forms for the next life. What do we then actually know about? Our life falls into two parts: the one part is from birth to the point of our earliest memory, and the other is from this point of the earliest memory on to death.

When we are in our thirtieth year of life and remember back to the point [of our earliest memory], we come to a boundary—the boundary of the in-flowing spiritual.

And we perceive this boundary; through bumping into it, we become aware of it. Such bumps in life remain in our recollection and build our memories. Our memories collect together, and this is our consciousness in physical life.

Just as in the plant the seed for a new plant develops, so too do we work on the forces that will later form our new life. Good for those who have stored up good and beautiful memories! The spiritual element from the former life that built the new body from the time of birth and streams through it, gradually fades and passes away during life.

It has often been said that after death the great memory-tableau appears first. Upon leaving the physical body, we come first to this boundary where all the memories are stored.

We see these memories as a large tableau before us. The memory of some experience can be forgotten for a whole lifetime, until it is suddenly brought into the consciousness. It was always there. It is just like when one puts salt into water and it falls to the bottom as a sediment, as it were. It can be brought up from the bottom by stirring it. So too are our memories, so to speak, a sediment that can be brought to the surface again. When we pour seltzer in a glass, we see little bubbles rise. We do not see the water that is actually real, but only what is nothing, the bubbles of carbon dioxide. That we see. That appears to us as reality. Where nothingness bumps against something, we perceive this nothingness as something.

Thus, we become aware only of the boundary between the new soul essence and the old spiritual. Where they bump into each other, we become aware of something. And that makes up our day-waking consciousness. Consciousness arises through the touching or contact between the past and the future.

Now we can approach this from a third side to become aware of the spiritual. Not only do human beings think, and their thoughts and memories remain behind as a deposit, but also the spiritual beings thought and still think. What the lofty hierarchies thought in ages past, the memories that have remained from these thoughts are what we perceive here as mountains, clouds, streams—in short, what we have around us as nature. The physical Sun is the remaining memory of the

Sun leader, of Christ, who later with the event of Golgotha entered into the Earth and became the Spirit of the Earth. And the memories of what the lofty beings on the Moon thought are the plants, animals, and also the physical body of the human being. The spiritual beings there thought the error—there it had its rightful place—but they did not do [the error]. When we human beings think good, noble thoughts, they remain in existence; we see them in the distant future as having eternal existential worth. However, also what we think that is false, an error, or wicked, continues to exist. We see it in the distant future as a waste product that serves as nourishment for the seed, which proceeds out of the good that was thought—just as we now nourish ourselves from the error-thoughts of the spirits of the old Moon condition. In itself, this waste product is unfruitful. Yet, it serves as nourishment for the germ or seed that develops out of the good, just as the mineral kingdom provides the soil for the plants, and just as the one always nourishes the other. The good feeds itself from the evil like a sprouting seed that consumes the wickedness, and yet remains eternal itself. However, we may only think of the bad, the evil. We may not allow it to become deed, to become reality, because that is always luciferic and ahrimanic.

Lucifer, who is now at a similar stage as the elohim were on the Moon, wants to think the error now, just as those beings did then. For those beings at that time, it was the right thing to do; now it is wrong. Lucifer can cause the error to be thought only in human beings. Thus, we have error and illusion. We must become ever more conscious of them.

Where the memories of the lofty hierarchies are, we become aware of something. Because we hit our hand, which was built out of the memory of the gods, against a wall that also is memory, the boundaries of these realities crash into one another. Through this, we become aware of this object. Thus, where this reality ends and there is nothing there, we sense reality or matter in day-consciousness, and sense the other as nothing. We feel neither our hand nor the wall, but only the boundary between them. The table is not reality, but rather a hole in the spiritual world—a hole that is filled with wood. Only we, in our ordinary consciousness, take the table to be reality.

If, through meditation, we could make ourselves so strong that we could dampen down this day-consciousness, and that we become completely aware of the nothingness or void of the surroundings, then we would always experience ourselves with our soul in the spiritual world. To accomplish this strengthening of our soul, three verses for meditation were given to us. It matters that we meditate them in the right way; that we do not simply say the words, as it were, but that we hear the expression that must be put into them if they are to work in the right way upon our souls.

> I turn to things,
> I turn with my senses.
> Sense being, you deceive me!
> What flees existence as nothing
> Is being and essence to you.
> May what must seem to you worth nothing
> Reveal itself within me!

With the first verse, the first two lines are descriptive—and then comes repulsion or resistance. Then again, it becomes descriptive, and at the close comes a petition. Beginners can meditate this verse in the evening after their review of the day. Those who already have a practice can take up this verse at any time they wish.

> Spirit Light, warm me,
> Let me feel myself willing in you.
> What is well-thought, cognized truth,
> How does the luminous "I" experience you!
> Weaving error, badly thought out
> Show yourself to the beacon of my soul
> That I may be weaving in myself.

With the second verse, the question in the fourth line should be especially stressed. The verse closes with a plea. Beginners can do this first in the morning. Others may do it any time they wish.

Yet a third verse is given to us, to attempt a counsel from time to time in order to ask ourselves if we sense the spiritual world already as truth and reality.

> Luminous "I" and beacon-soul,
> Hover above true being of becoming
> What is thought out, what cognized
> Condenses now to spirit being.
> And like pearls of existence
> There dwells in the sea of divine truth
> What deceives the senses' existence.

(As Dr. Steiner received these words [from the spiritual world], he realized that the predicate in the second line of the third verse should actually be in the plural. Then he realized that *Luminous "I"* and *beacon-soul* are one and the same, and that it is quite correct that the verb [*schwebet* in the German] should be in the singular. When we receive such a thing as this, we must often learn from it, and realize only later from it what is meant.) These verses were given in three seven-line stanzas; this was not accidental or thought out by Dr. Steiner to make it work out that way. Everything that is inspired out of the spiritual world reveals itself in numbers. The words are merely the means and opportunity through which the spirits express themselves. The being that let these verses flow in gave thereby the promise to help with recognizing the difference between the real and the unreal. By letting these verses pass again and again through our soul, we give the being that gave these verses the opportunity to speak to our soul. This being helps us to bring about in ourselves the proper affect of the verses—in each and every one of us!

These verses are expressed in a shortened way in the Rosicrucian mantra:

> Verse I. *Ex Deo nascimur*
> Verse II. *In Christo morimur*
> Verse III. *Per Spiritum Sanctum reviviscimus*

They are also contained in the words with which we close our esoteric lessons:

> In the spirit lay the germ of my body.
> And the spirit has imprinted in my body
> The eyes of sense,
> That through them I may see
> The light of bodies.
> And the spirit has imprinted in my body
> Reason and sensation
> And feeling and will,
> That through them I may perceive bodies
> And act upon them.
> In the spirit lay the germ of my body.
>
> In my body lies the germ of the spirit.
> And I will incorporate into my spirit
> The supersensuous eyes,
> That through them I may behold the light of spirits.
> And I will imprint in my spirit
> Wisdom and power and love,
> So that through me the spirits may act
> And I become the self-conscious organ
> Of their deeds.
> In my body lies the germ of the spirit.

* * *

RECORD B

E.D.N.

I turn to things,
I turn with my senses.
Sense being, you deceive me!
What flees existence as nothing
Is being and essence to you.
May what must seem to you worth nothing
Reveal itself within me!

I.C.M.

Spirit Light, warm me,
Let me feel myself willing in you.
What is well-thought, cognized truth,
How does the luminous "I" experience you!
Weaving error, badly thought out
Show yourself to the beacon of my soul
That I may be weaving in myself.

P.S.S.R.

Luminous "I" and beacon-soul,
Hover above true being of becoming
What is thought out, what cognized
Condenses now to spirit being.
And like pearls of existence
There dwells in the sea of divine truth
What deceives the senses' existence.

Nature is the thinking or pondering, the memory, of the divine beings of the Sun and Moon. Our thinking, feeling, and sensing are different than they seem. Our life between birth and death alternates among sleep and waking and dreaming.

To the first stanza: We actually always dream. That is why we so easily forget what we have dreamed. We retain sense impressions so easily; why do we not remember the dream? Because we are always dreaming; we can never come out of the dream.

To the second stanza: What we perceive while we are awake is actually not there. What comes from the previous incarnation goes into the physical body; what we take into our life now will form our body in the following incarnation. What we perceive outwardly is neither the one [past], nor the other [future]; it is merely the meeting of both, where they come together.

To the third stanza: In a bottle of soda water we see the carbon dioxide, the gas bubbles, but not the water. What we perceive outwardly is like these bubbles. The reality, the actuality, remains hidden from us.

When hate is there, one bumps against something in the spiritual world.

Esoteric Lesson

BASEL, JUNE 3, 1914

RECORD A

Our exercises are predisposed to bring us into the spiritual world. We are also in the spiritual world in the night, but we are not conscious of it. Why not? Because we have the habit—the cosmic habit—to perceive through physical senses, and we are too weak to develop a consciousness without them. What are these sense perceptions actually? They contain also what we can attain from the higher consciousness: the imaginations, the images of the higher reality; the inspirations through which spiritual beings reveal themselves to us; and the intuitions, through which we become one with the divine beings. All of this is contained in the perception, but it does not come into us. When we seek the reason for this, we find that Lucifer burns it up with the fire of the passions, drives, and desires. Lucifer has taken up residence in the heart, and there performs the burning of the imaginations, inspirations, and the intuitions that lie at the foundation of everything of a sensory nature; for with every breath and with every perception, the images of the spiritual beings penetrate into us. In the beginning of the Lemurian epoch, during what the Bible describes as the battle between the elohim and Lucifer, Lucifer interfered in the human heart with his fire.

The heart was pre-determined to be something totally different. It was created by the elohim to be their place of residence. Something can be small in the physical world, and yet great in the spiritual world, and vice versa. Thus, the heart is physically only a small thing, and the anatomist believes that it is the same thing if it is taken out of the body. However, the heart is something very large or great in the spiritual world, and was intended to be the residence of the elohim. As Lucifer moved into the human heart, the elohim, however, preserved a place for themselves. The elohim can still live in this place in the heart, and that manifests in human life as the voice of the conscience. Where this voice speaks, there speaks something that does not belong to Lucifer with his consuming fire. In this voice, a direct divine inspiration reaches the human being. And we see that at important moments in history, this voice of conscience became actual for human beings and stood before them. This was the case with Moses, upon whose soul the destiny of his whole people pressed. He climbed Mount Sinai. In the burning bush (that is, in the fire that Lucifer had kindled) he perceived the voice of his God, who later on Mount Sinai gave him the Ten Commandments that became the foundation of all later human laws.

After Lucifer had seized the human heart in this way, the elohim had to lay a counterweight on the other side of the scale of cosmic world order to restore the balance. That took place in the Atlantean epoch when, through the elohim, Ahriman and all the ammunition he needed were entrenched in the human brain in order to bring there his cooling effect against the luciferic fire. And what Ahriman cooled down from the fire that burned the imaginations, inspirations, and intuitions, became thoughts and ideas in the human being. (There is one thing that is quite special fuel for Lucifer's fire: lovelessness.)

The old initiates have always had this knowledge that Lucifer with his fire is enthroned in our heart, and Ahriman cools down this fire in the head. We find a last remnant of this knowledge with Aristotle (who was not clairvoyant himself), who said that the warmth goes out from the heart up to the head, and is cooled down there.

No one could object that what is said is strange: that Lucifer and the Godhead both live in our heart! It sounds as if there were only one heart in the world, and yet there are actually so many hearts in the world as there are human beings. Yes, here we come to a riddle which is only one of the smaller ones that esotericists meet. The riddle is: how did the one become many? It is not the intention to answer this here, but one can try to penetrate it ever further through meditative contemplation.

(There follows the three seven-line verses as meditations.)

* * *

Record B

We must not believe that everything in the spiritual world is just as it is in the physical world. What is large or great in the physical world can be small in the spiritual world, and what is large or great in the spiritual world is often small in the sense world. We have an organ in us that is physically small: the heart. Seen spiritually, it is infinitely large because it is the home of the gods. The elohim chose it to be their residence, but in the Lemurian epoch Lucifer took possession of it. The elohim allow imaginations, inspirations, and intuitions to flow into him, but Lucifer burns them in his furnace of passions and makes them into the sense perceptions. In order that not everything was totally burned, the elohim created a counterweight by setting the ahrimanic beings into the human brain. These ahrimanic beings cooled down the luciferic heat with intellectual thinking and ideas. The elohim have retained a small part of the heart as a residence, and they planted therein, as a counterweight against Ahriman-Lucifer, the conscience.

This is a deep riddle: the elohim selected the human heart as their residence, and Lucifer nested there. How is it, then, instead of one heart there are many—instead of the one, the plurality?

Lovelessness is a great hindrance for our development.

Then follows the three verses.

* * *

Record C

The heart is a large cosmic structure wherein the elohim are active. The effect of Lucifer is that imaginations, inspirations, and intuitions are as if burned up and appear then as sense perceptions. These sense perceptions are the burned imaginations, and so on. The countereffect of the good gods is that they sent the ahrimanic powers, which now work in the brain in a cooling manner.

The effect of the elohim appeared to Moses in the burning thorn bush. He then [later] received the tablets of the law (Ten Commandments).

When we leave out the middle word of *In Christo morimur*, we can experience a world.

The heart is the residence of the gods.

Esoteric Lesson

NORRKÖPING, JULY 14, 1914

RECORD A†

One wishes, my dear sisters and brothers, that all who participate in an esoteric lesson would be quite properly permeated with the meaning of the lesson. We should consciously leave the daily life. It must be for us as if the veil separating us from the spiritual world were pulled away, so that we may find ourselves in the spiritual world. The same thing also happens in meditation. [With a real meditation] we should become free of our body; we should abandon everything that is connected with the bodily nature, extinguish all the interests of daily life, and devote ourselves only to the object of our meditation. We should leave our body completely; leave it totally behind, just as with sleep, only that with meditation it happens consciously. Yet, there is one thing we take with us: the breath—the effect of the lungs in the heart, the breath of life that Yahweh-Elohim once blew into the earthly human being.

When we are totally given over to our meditation, we will feel as if our brain were an etheric brain only. [We must become clear that] when human beings think, it has nothing to do with their brain. When they believe (sense), or feel, it has nothing to do with the organ of the heart. Just as when a wagon leaves deep ruts in the road, this has nothing to do with the wagon as such, but with how and of what the road was made, so too we may not judge the organs according to what we see outwardly—the way physiology and anatomy do. The organs themselves do not think or feel, but rather the spiritual beings and forces that work into them do. Just as letters are only signs for the content of word, so too are the organs only signs through which the higher beings express themselves in the human being.

We have an overview of three evolutionary periods of our Earth planet: the present one, the Earth; the previous one, the Moon; and the next one, the Jupiter condition. Most of you will know that human beings have, besides the cerebrum (the large brain) as the instrument through which they think, also the cerebellum (a small brain) that sits more underneath the other and at the back, near the neck. All physiologists and anatomists know this, but they do not know that the cerebrum is the remnant of the old Moon condition. It stands there as a document of the old Moon time, as a sign of the battle fought for us by the gods. What was thought on the Moon became the cerebellum. However, there was no error in our thoughts then, because the divine powers were the ones who thought for us and guided our thinking. At that time human beings were not free; divine beings guided and led them. On the Earth, human beings have now attained freedom, independence, and have taken onto themselves the responsibility for what they think.

Also in the cerebrum, there is something left over from the Moon condition: the pineal gland and the mucus gland. These glands were, on the Moon, what the lungs and heart are in the human being of today.

Through our life here on Earth, we are living upwards to Jupiter. (We are already preparing Jupiter, the future planetary condition of the Earth.) What human beings are in their actions, deeds, and their whole being will build their cerebrum on Jupiter. And what they now think in their cerebrum will one day build the cerebellum on Jupiter. No longer do the gods watch over human thinking; human beings became free on the Earth. We must bear the consequences of our thinking ourselves, and the cerebellum sits at the neck like a judge, for it will take the results of all that we thought on Earth over to the Jupiter condition.

And now I ask you, if we let this fact in its entire magnitude and responsibility work upon us, do we need yet another judgment? Is this judgment not more gripping, more powerful, than even what Michelangelo presented in his "Last Judgment"? Just consider the tragedy that lies in the fact that human beings themselves must bear the consequences of their own deeds, feelings, and thinking! However, in the midst of this tragedy we have one comfort, one support: Christ entered into Earth evolution. If we entrust ourselves to him, he will carry our deeds, feelings, and thoughts over to the Jupiter condition. For this reason, it is so important that spiritual science (Christ-science, the knowledge of Christ) enters precisely into our time (the time of the consciousness soul development), so that the understanding for the true Christ is again enlivened.

Already in her *Secret Doctrine*, Blavatsky spoke of Yahweh as Moon god.[†] However, because she mixed in her own feelings, much is incorrect in it, and through this, much of the bad karma came about that weighs upon the Theosophical Society. And since Yahweh was so little understood, it is no wonder that people also now understand the Christ being so little. In order to correct this, we had to speak of Lucifer and Ahriman immediately, at the beginning of our Movement, for only through a knowledge of their being and working can we value Yahweh correctly. One leads human beings into the spiritual worlds correctly only when one conducts them through Lucifer and Ahriman so that they may come to Christ there. If we do not place Christ in the center of every esoteric striving, we lead them (human beings) to Lucifer.

People do not like to call things by their rightful name; they deceive themselves concerning their true nature. Yet, what people in certain circles call so scientific is actually of ahrimanic nature. Thus, it was said in the leading magazine[†] of the Theosophical Society that "esoteric science" is psychic-mystical in nature, and that in contrast, the writings of Annie Besant and Leadbeater are scientific and esoteric. This, however, is ahrimanic; and what one calls psychic and mystical there should be called Christian. For the entire "esoteric science," and the totality of our work from the beginning, was founded on the knowledge of Christ; it was inspired by the Christ-being himself. We want to always keep this in mind, my dear sisters and brothers.

We came over here from the Moon condition, where we were in the bosom of the gods: *Ex Deo nascimur*. On Earth we are to unite with Christ and die into him: *In – – – morimur*. Thus will the Holy Spirit lead us over into the new Earth embodiment, the Jupiter condition: *Per Spiritum Sanctum reviviscimus.*

* * *

Record B

All truly earnestly striving esotericists who wish to make progress through meditation and concentration want basically nothing other than to become different, better human beings. In ordinary life, we think through the instrument of our brain, thus by means of our physical body. In meditation it is different. When esotericists give themselves over with devotion to their meditation, they enter a condition that is like sleep, but with retention of consciousness. We eliminate what is bound to the physical body. Only the breathing process remains. It is the breath breathed into the human being by Yahweh. In meditation, we think with our etheric body. Lungs and heart expand and become brain, but etheric brain; and as our head relates to the rest of the physical body, so does this etheric brain relate to the heavenly body. We cannot know the human being with the methods of science—not through physiology, anatomy, chemistry, etc. This would be as if we wanted to know what was written in the letters on a piece of paper by examining the paper itself and the ink. We cannot learn what is expressed in the letters in this way. The human organs are just such letters or signs through which the divine-spiritual beings speak. Our larynx, our heart, our lungs, our brain, are all such signs or letters. The thinking, by condensing the substance, builds the brain, and the feeling forms the heart. Human beings were not always as they are today. On the old Moon, they inhaled warmth. We have something in our head that we brought over into the Earth condition from the old Moon evolution. It is a remnant, a monument, of the Moon condition: the leaf-like cerebellum at the back of our head. Then, during the Moon period, it was not small; it is now shrunken. And what were lungs and heart in the Moon humans are now the pineal and mucus glands in our head. Lungs and heart of the Moon human beings transformed themselves and became brain for the Earth human beings. In like manner, the lungs and heart of the human beings on Earth will transform into the brain for the human beings of the Jupiter condition. This is prepared through our esoteric exercises.

The Godhead spoke to the human being through the cerebellum when it was the cerebrum in the Moon period. This is the Godhead that is called Yahweh, and which had connected itself with the Moon evolution. This may now be spoken. It was already expressed once by Blavatsky in the *Secret Doctrine,* where she called Yahweh a Moon god. It does not matter if a fact is merely expressed, but what matters is how one expresses it. A great deal of the bad karma of the Theosophical Society is the result of Blavatsky having spoken this in a derogatory manner. For this reason, the teaching about Ahriman and Lucifer had to be brought; these beings had to be put in the right place. Yahweh worked upon and led the human beings by means of the Moon-brain. However, the Earth human beings, because they take Christ into themselves, shall execute their actions and deeds in freedom. The Moon humans did not yet have freedom; it was brought to human beings first by Lucifer. Just as we today feel Yahweh sitting in our neck as our judge, so will the results of our deeds on Earth place before the Jupiter humans what is good and what is evil. They will see it. It will be a terrible judgment—more terrible than Michelangelo represented on the wall of the Sistine Chapel. Human beings will then no longer be led in the way Yahweh led them through his work on the cerebellum.

* * *

Record C

When we come together for such a lesson, we wish that it could be imparted to all human beings so that the veil that separates us from the spiritual world would be torn open. Such a mood of prayer is the right mood in which we should receive what is communicated in esoteric lessons.

In daily life, we live in our physical body and use our senses and our intellect. When we are meditating, we live in our etheric body. We must become completely free of the body in meditation. When we are meditating, we live in the heavenly body, in Christ. What do we do then when we meditate? We form something new, we create something new into the cosmos. We imprint a new etheric body upon the cosmos. When we bear this in mind, then we will gradually become aware of the great responsibility for what we do when we become a meditant.

We know that the previous embodiment of our Earth was the old Moon. Now we ask if everything that was our body on the old Moon is now gone. Is nothing of it physically present anymore? No, in no way is it gone; we still carry it in us. You still carry within you the whole Moon human. In your cerebellum, you bear what was once the brain of the Moon human being. And in your present-day cerebrum you carry, in a horizontal position in two organs that are no longer active today but are stunted and dried up, the rest of the old Moon human. You carry the old Moon human shriveled up within yourself in the pineal gland and mucus gland. The present-day pineal gland came into being out of the lungs of the old Moon human. We carry the heart from the old Moon human in our brain as the mucus gland. The present human being will become the brain of the Jupiter human being. And you will have trouble thinking on Jupiter if you have acted badly here on Earth. What today is the brain of the human being on Earth will be the cerebellum of the Jupiter human being.

Today there stand behind us—of which we are still unconscious—divine-spiritual beings who worked upon us on the old Moon, and who created us through the preceding stages of evolution. These beings say to us: you should follow the truth and not give in to error. They are our judges, and they warn us to become worthy of all that was brought to bear of force, of work, of offering, by the hierarchies for the becoming of humanity. They are the beings of the elohim, of Yahweh, that worked in us on the Moon without our being aware of them. They stand behind us today on the Earth as admonishers, as the judges.

On Jupiter, however, human beings—then conscious—will have a being sitting in the neck region that will tell them: that is good, and that is evil! It will be Christ, who will sit in our neck region as the judge (note Michelangelo's "The Last Judgment" in the Sistine Chapel in Rome). What humanity will experience on Jupiter as the judgment will be something totally different from what anyone has been able to think or imagine.

While you were un-free on the Moon, there worked upon you beings that you now have behind you as the admonishing gods here on Earth. Through the freedom of the Earth, you will know on Jupiter who sits in your neck region as judge.

The final decision for humanity, whether to walk with Christ in evolution or whether to remain behind, will take place on Venus; but the judgment will be fulfilled on Jupiter.

The lesson was closed by pointing out the inexhaustibility of our Rosicrucian mantra, E.D.N.—I.C.M.—P.S.S.R., which were explained in the three meditations given below. They should help us ascend faster into the spiritual world.

E.D.N.

I turn to the things,
I turn with my senses.
Sense being, you deceive me!
What flees existence as nothing
Is being and essence to you.
May what must seem to you worth nothing
Reveal itself within me!

I.C.M.

Spirit Light, warm me,
Let me feel myself willing in you.
What is well-thought, cognized truth,
How does the luminous "I" experience you!
Weaving error, badly thought out
Show yourself to the beacon of my soul
That I may be weaving in myself.

P.S.S.R.

Luminous "I" and beacon-soul,
Hover above true being of becoming
What is thought out, what cognized
Condenses now to spirit being.
And like pearls of existence
There dwells in the sea of divine truth
What deceives the senses' existence.

PART II
FROM THE ESOTERIC SCHOOL

1920 to the New Founding of the Esoteric School as
the "Independent School for Spiritual Science "
at the Goetheanum 1923/1924

Foreword

The outbreak of World War I in August 1914 caused Rudolf Steiner to close the Esoteric School. Thus, during the war there were no esoteric lessons. Later, Steiner said of this: "We have stopped our esoteric lessons since the outbreak of the war for the simple reason that it is necessary to adhere to the purpose of our Society. And then, of course, we must not hold any gatherings that are not public. This is equally true whether we are in a country that is an enemy or one that is neutral."(Lecture of August 22, 1915, in GA 253).

An exception was one lesson that was totally private. When on a trip to Austria in the summer of 1918, Rudolf Steiner and Marie Steiner visited the Polzer-Hoditz family at Tannbach near Gutau. Ludwig Polzer-Hoditz reported in his memoirs† that on this occasion an esoteric ceremonial act took place. He related the following:

"June 9, 1918 was a Sunday. Dr. Steiner and Marie Steiner went with us to Mass in Gutau. When we came back from there, Rudolf Steiner held a ceremony in the sign of the Rose Cross. Steiner spoke of how central European humanity would have been receptive to a spiritual impulse in the beginning of the seventeenth century, and of how the spiritual world wanted to approach humanity. The Thirty Years' War, however, prevented this impulse from being taken up by a larger group of human beings. He followed this with a reflection on the Chymical Wedding of Christian Rosenkreutz. He spoke of how Valentin Andreae, when he was quite young, could write it down out of inspiration, and of how then, at an advanced age, he became a well-behaved, materialistic pastor who could not understand his own meaningful work from his youth. He closed by comparing the spirit that is descending to humanity with the snow that lays its cover of purity over the cold surface of the Earth in the winter."

After the war ended at the end of 1918, members of the former Esoteric School asked Rudolf Steiner repeatedly to take up the esoteric lessons again. In the beginning of 1920, after a pause of five-and-a-half years, he began to meet these requests. According to the stenographer, Helene Finckh, Rudolf Steiner made the following announcement at the end of his lecture in Dornach, on February 7, 1920:

"Let me announce here that I would like those members whose names I will read aloud to come, when they wish to do so, not only tomorrow, but also Monday at 8:00 p.m. For the most part, it will be people who have already been in the Society for quite a long time and who are also involved in other ways. That is the basis for the list I have written. I want to stress the fact that, of course, those who do not wish to come do not need to. (Names are read. List is not available.).

Thus, I would ask those whose names I have read to come tomorrow and on Monday at 8:00 p.m. As I said, you do not have to come if you do not want to."

Helene Finckh noted in addition: "It began one day later, because all kinds of people whose names were not read wanted to come also."

Thus, the next evening after the lecture on February 8th, additional names were announced: "I will make up for the names I forgot yesterday." (A number of names were read. The names were not taken down in the notes.) Helene Finckh noted in addition: "Apparently, by far, not all of the names of those who had counted on coming were read. There were many tears, and when people came for the first lesson, several stood before the door of the carpentry studio (the Schreinerei—the lecture and meeting room at that time). Especially noticeable is that Frau *X* was there, completely bathed in tears because only her husband had been invited but not her. It was an attempt that, because of various circumstances, did not go beyond a second lesson at that time. Dr. Steiner was asked again and again by older members to hold more intimate lessons again. He alluded to this a few times, but always said that it was not yet the appropriate time for it."

These lessons in Dornach were not continued at that time. Also, when the question about esoteric lessons surfaced in the College of teachers in the Independent Waldorf School in Stuttgart (in the conference of November 16, 1921; GA 300, volume 2), Rudolf Steiner answered in a very reserved manner, stressing that first the adequate method must be found. Nevertheless, an esoteric lesson took place soon afterward, on December 4, 1921, in Christiania (Oslo), Norway. Written records from this do not exist. But, according to Helene Finckh, who participated in it, the lesson was similar in content to the Dornach lesson. Further, such lessons followed then at Easter, as well as in November of 1922 in England (London); again on May 18, 1923 in Christiania, Norway; and on September 30, 1923 in Vienna.

In addition, several esoteric lessons took place through the initiative of several members who were especially interested in the content of the earlier cognitive-ritual work. Rudolf Steiner named this group the Wachsmuth-Lerchenfeld Group, after the main speakers. This group of about fifteen people came together three times in "House Hansi," Rudolf Steiner's Dornach home. They met twice before, and once after the Christmas Conference: May 27, and October 23, 1923; and January 3, 1924 (The notes that exist from these lessons are in CW 265.). The list of participants that are known—though this is not exhaustive—were: Maria Röschl, Marie Steiner, Harriet von Vacano, Elisabeth Vreede, Ita Wegman, Margarita Woloschin, Jürgen von Grone, Kurt Piper, Otto von Lerchenfeld, Albert Steffen, Günther Wachsmuth, and Wolfgang Wachsmuth and his wife. Between the first and second lesson was scheduled yet another that was supposed to take place in Stuttgart in July 1923 (probably Sunday, July 15th), and to which Friedrich Rittelmeyer was invited. However, Rudolf Steiner canceled this lesson because he had to consider the publishing of the Rittelmeyer-Lempp discussion in the magazine *Anthroposophie* to be a grave error. (For details, see GA 259.) Just as with these three lessons (May 27, October 23, and January 3), so too was the lesson of September 30, 1923, in Vienna, more in accordance content-wise with the Cognitive-Ritual Section of the former Esoteric School.

The participants in all of these lessons of the post-war time were either members of the earlier Esoteric School or such people who had already received personal meditations from Rudolf Steiner.

Esoteric Lesson
DORNACH, FEBRUARY 9, 1920

One wishes, my dear sisters and brothers, that all who participate in an esoteric lesson would be quite properly permeated with the meaning of the lesson. We should consciously leave the daily life. It must be for us as if the veil separating us from the spiritual world were pulled away, so that we may find ourselves in the spiritual world. The same thing also happens in meditation. [With a real meditation] we should become free of our body; we should abandon everything that is connected with the bodily nature, extinguish all the interests of daily life, and devote ourselves only to the object of our meditation. We should leave our body completely; leave it totally behind, just as with sleep, only that with meditation it happens consciously. Yet, there is one thing we take with us: the breath—the effect of the lungs in the heart, the breath of life that Yahweh-Elohim once blew into the earthly human being.

It has already been said repeatedly in the exoteric lectures that our head is ordained to destruction, to death, and that out of the rest of the human being there flows upward the living stream that can awaken the dead again. In addition, however, human beings must not reject what descends out of the spiritual world and can unite with the living stream. Otherwise, this living stream would have to go back down, and the head, the brain, would remain a dead organism.

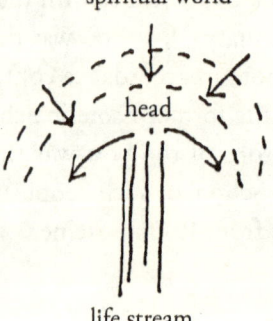 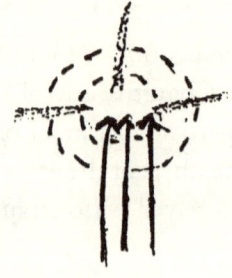

Humanity as a whole is different from the individual human being. Humanity belongs to the Earth organism and so takes part in the karma of the Earth; the individual human being has his or her own karma. We must differentiate this correctly. Today humanity as such is experiencing the meeting with the Guardian of the Threshold, and the crossing of the threshold has already begun in recent years. This is also the beginning of the split of humanity, and this signifies a critical point in time at which we have now arrived. The forces that formerly streamed out of the spiritual beings into humanity are used up, are exhausted. We are now on our own, and must now bring up these forces out of our subconsciousness. The Mystery of Golgotha will have happened for nothing if human beings do not use these inner forces, but reject them instead. That would bring about the total destruction of the Earth evolution. Souls would indeed still descend into bodies, but they would abandon them again in the thirty-third year of life, if they did not in their earlier years take in through their bodies the stream of the spiritual. Such thirty-three-year-olds who have taken in the spiritual stream should instruct the younger ones, so that the seed for grasping the Mystery of Golgotha will already be planted in the youth. And regarding those who die before their thirty-third year, they will be taken care of also.

If this were not fulfilled, then soul-less bodies would wander around on Earth. These bodies would only be able to work with an automaton-like intellect. During the catastrophe of the war, there have already appeared soul-less human beings, and more and more will come if the spirit that is pressing down to us is not taken up. These soul-less human beings are a welcome prize for demonic beings, who will use this automaton-working intellect for their purposes. If there is not a small number of human beings who permeate themselves with the meaning of this terrible thing that is now being said, if the necessary earnestness cannot be brought to it, then the further evolution of humanity is not possible.

I will give you a provision that can be of great help to you, if meditated, to bring to your consciousness the many secrets that lie in what was just said. (The mantras were written on the blackboard and could be copied.)

I imagine
That wakes my "I"
For mature, creative cosmic becoming;
That weaves etherically
Into cosmic being.

I think
That bears my "I"
Into long-past cosmic ages:
Preserved in image
By me.

I feel
That holds my "I"
In the present moment:
That, existing, weaves
As "I"-experience.

I dream
That leads my "I"
Through present events:
That weave etherically
As cosmic working.

I will
That works in me
In far-future cosmic ages:

That builds in seed
Through me.

I sleep
May that work me
  In promising cosmic
weaving
That conceals itself
From sense-nature.

If you permeate yourself completely with these words, you will come to a higher knowing.

Feeling is a reflection of the dreaming; and also the dreaming reflects itself in feeling.

To the mantras given: Only thinking is conscious. For this reason, *imagine* is written to the left of it. The others still work unconsciously (sleeping and dreaming in willing and feeling, respectively).

First, the middle three mantras were written on the board; then, beside *I feel...* was written *I dream...*, and beside *I will...* was written *I sleep....*

Dr. Steiner said that in feeling, we still dream; in willing, we still absolutely sleep; only in thinking, at this point, is something possible (imagining). For this reason, he wrote *I imagine...* to the left of *I think....*

At the beginning and the closing of the lesson, Rudolf Steiner spoke the following mantra:

> O Mensch erkenne dich selbst
> So tönt das Weltenwort
> Du horst es seelenkräftig
> Du fühlst es geistgewaltig
>
> Wer spricht so weltenmächtig?
> Wer spricht so herzinniglich?
>
> Wirkt es durch des Raumes Weitenstrahlung
> In deines Sinnes Seinserleben?
> Tönt es durch der Zeiten Wellenweben
> In deines Lebens Werdestrom?
>
> Bist du es selbst, der sich
> Im Raumesfühlen, im Zeiterleben
> Das Wort erschafft, dich fremd
> Erfühlend in Raumes Seelenleere
> Weil du des Denkens Kraft
> Verlierst im Zeitvernichtungsstrome.

*

O Human Being, know yourself
So resounds the cosmic Word
You hear it soul-forcefully
You feel it spirit-mightily

Who speaks so cosmic-powerfully?
Who speaks so heart-inwardly?

Does it work through space's expansive radiance
Into your senses' experience of being?
Does it resound through time's weaving waves
Into your life's stream of becoming?

You are yourself the one who,
In the feeling of space, the experience of time,
Creates the Word, feeling yourself
Estranged in space's soul-emptiness
Because you lost thinking's force
In time's annihilating stream.

Esoteric Lesson
DORNACH, FEBRUARY 17, 1920

It is necessary that we know that we live in three realms, three streams: namely, the physical world where we perceive and process the perceptions with our intellect that is brain-bound; then, the world at the threshold where the intellect is no longer adequate to explain the experiences; and lastly, the world on the other side of the threshold where one comes into contact with spiritual beings. Humanity as such stands at the threshold.

Everything of nature and the outer world that is around us is on this side of the threshold, but we can ask ourselves where we can find the experiences of the threshold revealed. We find these mainly in the religious confessions of the most varied kinds. Their rituals, practices, and so on, tell us what cannot be grasped by the intellect.

The experiences at the threshold have something confusing about them. That is because everything that we bring with us from the sense world loses its meaning there. The modern religious denominations have no religious impulses. For this reason, they want to penetrate everything with the intellect, which must fail there. Thus, they cannot understand Christ as an other-worldly or spiritual being, nor can they understand the Resurrection. When theologians speak of Jesus, as is common today, they actually deny that Christ is resurrected. Only when we comprehend the Event in Palestine as something that is not grasped with the intellect, as what we can understand only suprasensible, do we cross to the other side of the threshold.

The confusion, which arises because everything brought with us from the sense world loses its meaning, ceases only when the light from the other side of the threshold rays into this confusion. This is, however, not possible without Christ. If we do not unite with Christ in such a manner that we can say: "Not I, but Christ in me," then in the future we cannot even live on as human beings.

The Godhead that we call the Father God gave humanity the forces necessary for us to feel ourselves as an "I," an "I" that continues on through the incarnations. But these forces are used up, and the gods have ordained that each of us human beings, out of our own self and out of our own free will, leads our "I" further, so that we can feel ourselves as "I" in our further incarnations. Otherwise, we are subject to the danger that was spoken of last time: that human beings become soul-less, that the thread of the "I" breaks off. So that this would not happen in humanity, Christ descended out of the spiritual world, went through death, and resurrected. For this the meditation is given to us:†

> *Ein Ich gab mir das Göttliche*
> *Die Menschheit weist mir Christus*
>   —der Christus macht mich zum Menschen—
> *die Seele wird mir der Geist beleben.*

> *The divine gave me an "I"*
> *Christ shows me humanity*
>   —Christ makes me human—
> *The Spirit will enliven my soul*

Many secret societies know such truths, but want to keep them to themselves. For this reason, such secret societies want, not so much to deny these truths as to obtain them for themselves, to divert the truths away from their rightful stream, and to represent them in the world as having originated from themselves. There would be nothing easier than to make spiritual science popular. I would only have to withdraw and let the rumor spread that I were dead, and the secret societies would help the truths of spiritual science soon become popular. That would strengthen their (the secret societies) power. We should therefore not argue with, for instance, the Jesuits, who are now fighting so against spiritual science, the way we could with other opponents with whom we could take up an objective battle. It cannot be a matter of converting the Jesuits, of convincing them through arguments. What we bring as refutation is very valuable to them, because that is for them the weapon they will one day use when they want to represent the supersensible truths as coming from themselves. At most, we can try to inform other people about the manner of the

Jesuits' attacks, but not attempt a refutation of the Jesuits' attacks themselves.

Elaboration from Helene Finckh:
The "I" is actually still only a sheath; and it will become thinner and thinner; but Christ intercedes for this. Christ can, however, be found *only in humanity*, not with the individual human being.
At the beginning and closing of the lesson, Rudolf Steiner spoke following mantra:

O Human Being, know yourself
So resounds the cosmic Word
You hear it soul-forcefully
You feel it spirit-mightily

Who speaks so cosmic-powerfully?
Who speaks so heart-inwardly?

Does it work through space's expansive radiance
Into your senses' experience of being?
Does it resound through time's weaving waves
Into your life's stream of becoming?

You are yourself the one who,
In the feeling of space, the experience of time,
Creates the Word, feeling yourself
Estranged in space's soul-emptiness
Because you lost thinking's force
In time's annihilating stream.

From Rudolf Steiner's Notebook, Archive No. 82
Esoteric Lesson of February 17, 1920, in Dornach:
1) The forces of "I"-affirmation—exhausted—they must be newly grasped by human beings.
   The true will can reveal itself only in pure thoughts.
2) Father God—the healer—bestowing comfort—
   \# Mystery of Golgotha = death of Jesus
3) Religion: at the "Guardian"—stop before him.
   In the mirror: facts borne by the senses' experience—
The " Christ in me"   The abyss—
                                   The new logic.
4) That is "in advance"—

5) The truths about nature are such that they,
   when used in reference to the human being,
   give a false picture.
6) After I am no longer there,
   the matter would be brought by others—
   However, it is not yet time for that to happen;
   It is still necessary to do something myself.

The religions are given from out of the "boundary." They show the abysses of life—in image—they speak of the world for which "this" is untrue.—
Human beings have as their law of life to consciously deny "nature;" living nature denies also; but the denial does not lead back to the starting point.
An animal denies the physical organization; however, it does *not* deny the *present* organization, but only the past organization.—

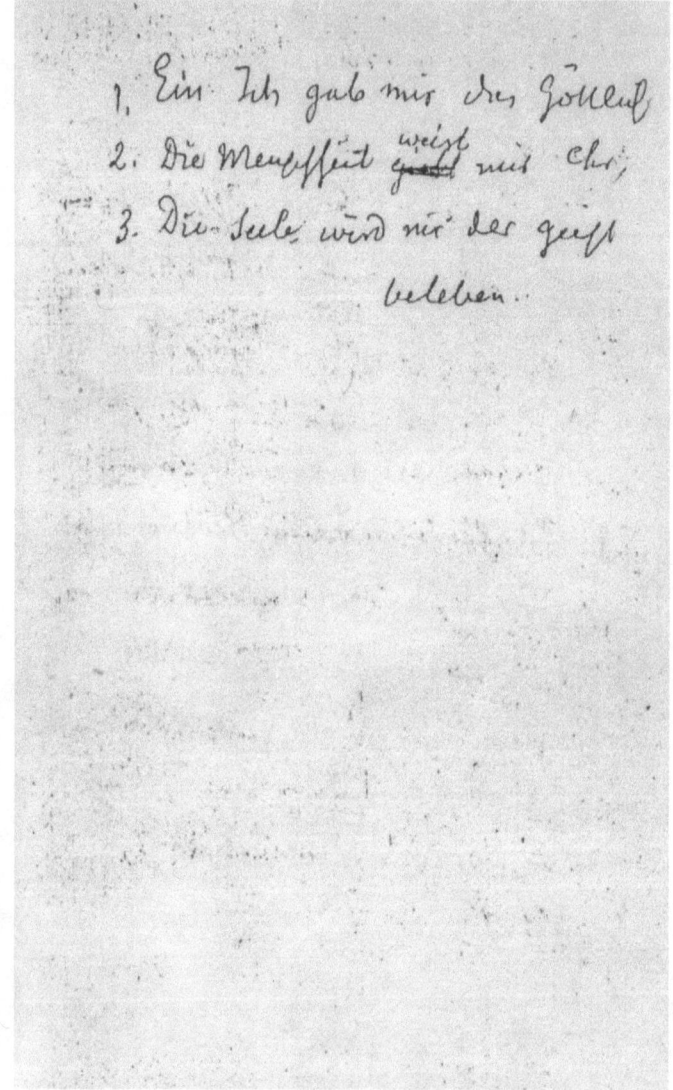

1. The divine gave me an "I."
2. Christ shows me humanity.
3. The Spirit will enliven my soul.

Esoteric Lesson

LONDON, APRIL 16, 1922

Dr. Steiner held an esoteric lesson in London, on the morning of April 16, 1922. (All who had received personal meditations from Rudolf Steiner were allowed to attend.) The lesson took place in the branch meeting room of the Zarathustra Group—founded by Mr. Heywood-Smith† and led many years by Mrs. Drury-Lavin†—at 47 Radcliffe Square, London, S W. In this same room, Rudolf Steiner had earlier given the lectures on Michael and the new Christ-event† (May 1-2, 1913).

Rudolf Steiner spoke, among other things, quite earnestly about the Academe of Gondhishapur† and the ahrimanic impact that was connected with it, and which is working into our time. The lesson peaked in the *first* and *third* of the "Three Tablets,"† which were spoken in many of the last class lessons in Dornach (until the beginning of August 1924): "O Human Being, know yourself," and the answer that the human being himself or herself speaks. Into this answer was woven the E.D.N. — I.C.M. — P.S.S.R. Afterward, those present were allowed to write down and keep the mantras.

Report from memory by George Adams
In a letter of October 8, 1954

From Rudolf Steiner's Notebook, Archive No. 304:

Esoteric Lesson for April 16, 1922
Mirror of the world / It lies in me / Power of thought / Grasps its images; / Behind it lies / The young soul. / It burns the stuff / And learns in the burning / The being of the world— / The soul weaves for it / The forming forces of the cosmos

For the human etheric being / That builds the head.

From Rudolf Steiner's Notebook, Archive No. 304:

Esoteric Lesson of April 16, 1922
1) Christ actually abandoned—
2) The School of Athens closed. Justinian.
   Then the mind of the West is guided in such a way that Ahriman receives the meaning of human thoughts—when human beings sleep—
3) Through that everything is led into the instincts.—There is fighting for fighting's sake.—
4) Research the will of Christ, in order to realize it.—

Form — unites the created
Burner — takes everything into itself.

Origenes = Christ integrated within
　　　　　　The physical—
　　　　　　The intellect—
　　　　　　The spiritual—

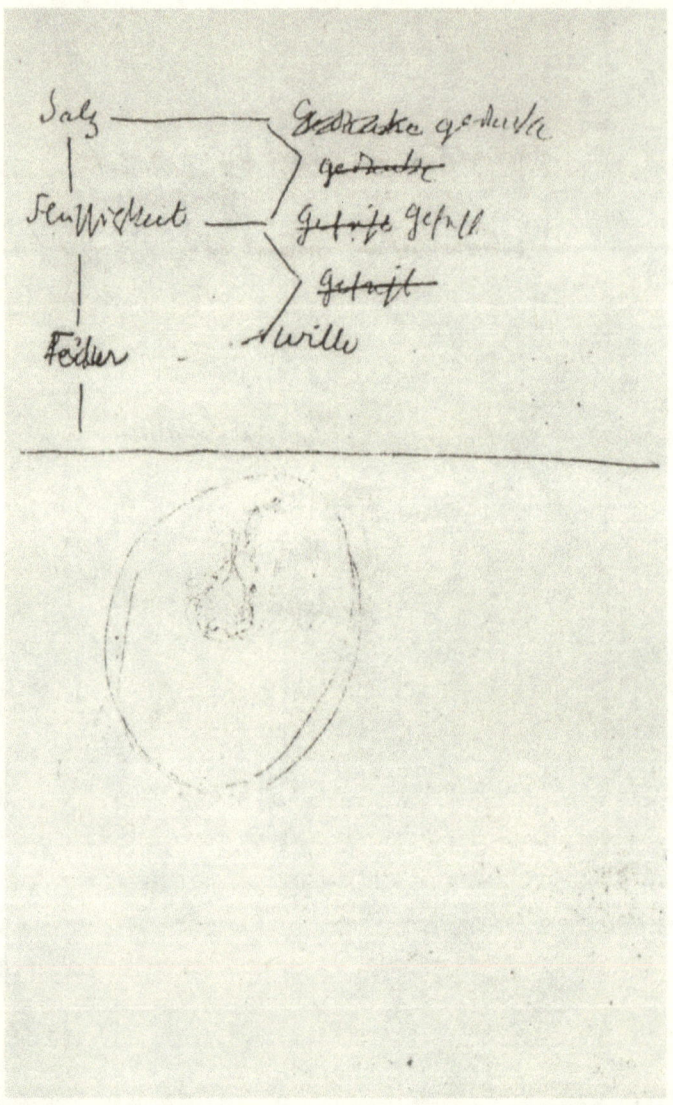

Salt ———— thought
Fluid ———— feeling
Fire ———— will

The skeletal system is formed in advance,
because the cosmic thoughts are creating within it:

Thoughts are creative = In the head
are the pictures of the bones
systems, etc.

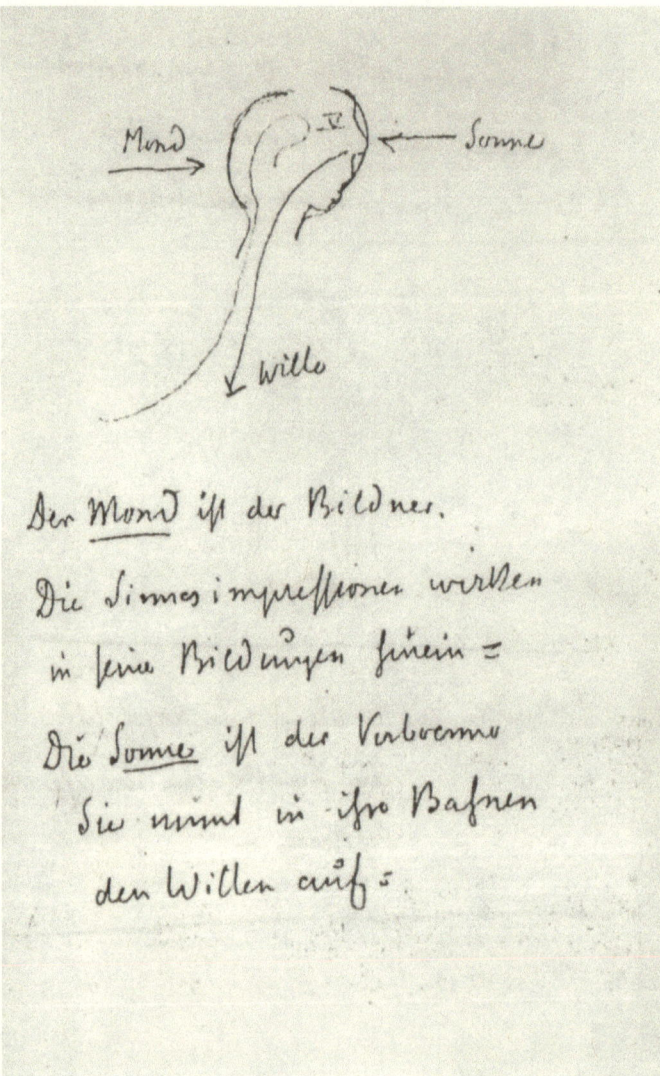

Moon / Sun / Will

The Moon is the sculptor.
The sense impressions work
Into its creations =
The Sun is the burner
It takes into its paths
The will.

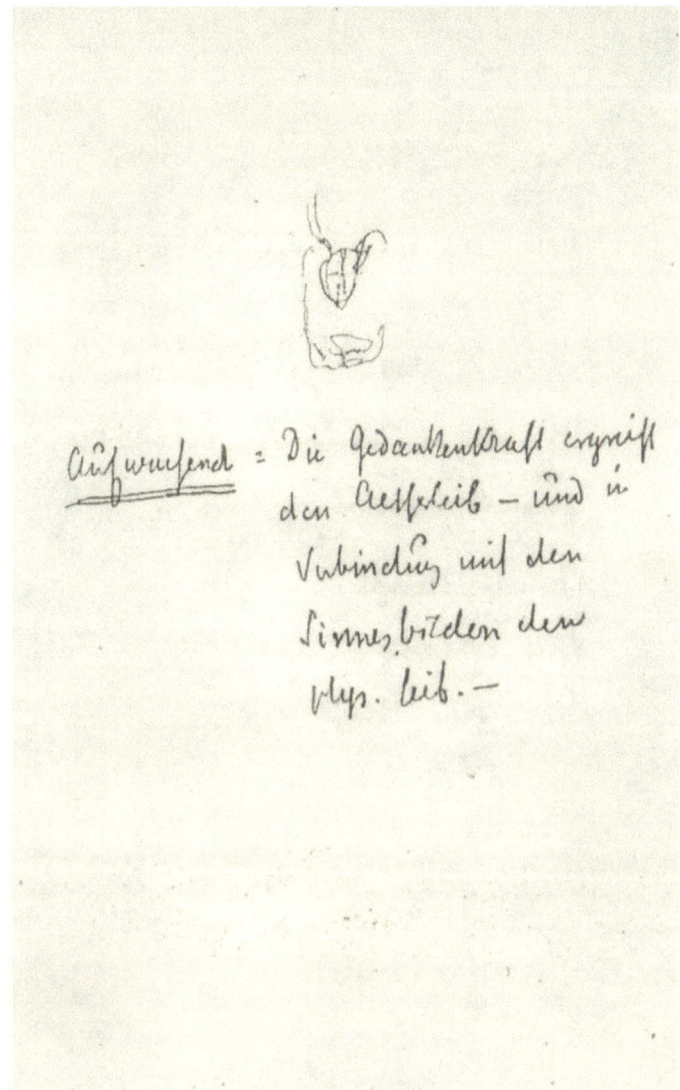

Waking up = the force of thought lays hold of
            the etheric body — and,
            in connection with the
            sense images,
            the physical body. —

Sun, you live in my heart
Moon, you carry the foreign element into me
Heart — it is the organ that
In the human being during earthly life
Enlivens the "I" —

In sleep = the organ
Of the "I" (heart)

In the light the love / Forming, growing round
Power of Moon — silver light
You rise up in me / Burning, consuming
Power of Sun — golden light
You sink down in me / Thus I become forevermore.

Fire
Meditation = on silver-blue ground
Within, I strew
Stars —

The meditation = it escapes Ahriman.
The ordinary egotistical prayer = it goes so into
    the sleep, that it, namely with adults,
    fights against Ahriman only cosmically:
    but does not free humanity from him. = Realm
    of the Sun and the Moon. —

Ahriman forms under the heart.
Lucifer forms above the heart.

Moon above the heart and in feminine figures
Sun under the heart and in masculine figures

Moon, burner under the heart.
Sun, burner above the heart.

Esoteric Lesson
LONDON, NOVEMBER 12, 1922

We have, besides knowledge of nature, moral responsibilities and the religious consciousness; this means: we feel that we rest with our whole being in a spiritual world. We have this religious consciousness while awake only because we are in our physical body. In our physical body, we are together with the spirits of higher cosmic order. And in our etheric body, we live together with what these spirits mean by the moral. Religious life depends on the physical body; moral life depends on the etheric body.

The cosmic ether, out of which our etheric body is taken, has two parts. The one part of this cosmic ether is made up of warmth ether, light ether, chemical ether, and life ether. Underlying all of this, as the second part, is a moral being of the cosmic ether. This moral being is, however, present only near the stars and planets. Thus, when you live on Earth, although you do not know it during the day, you are also within the cosmic ether as moral essence (thus in both parts). However, the moral is driven out from between the stars by the sunlight. The sunlight itself has within itself nothing less than the original source of the moral ether for us. Yet, while the Sun shines it drives, through its light, the moral essence out of the ether. And thus, when we look into the world with our eyes we see flowers, springs, etc., without weaving the moral into them, because the sunlight kills the moral.

When we go out of the physical and etheric bodies, we leave behind the religious and the moral. And because the moral cosmic order is gone from the ether, the ahrimanic being has access to this ether. This liar-spirit speaks to human beings during their sleep and represents the good as evil and the evil as good. With good people who have a good conscience, are devout, and have deeply moral feelings, the moral feeling goes so deep that they take it with them into sleep. Ahriman whispers to them that the good is evil, and they sleep poorly because they believe they have done much evil. Evil people often sleep so well because they are satisfied by the ahrimanic whisperings.

Esoteric Lesson
VIENNA, SEPTEMBER 30, 1923

During the lectures in September-October 1923 in Vienna, Rudolf Steiner held an esoteric lesson for a small group at the request of Ludwig Polzer-Hoditz. According to the record in Polzer-Hoditz's mantra book in the Rudolf Steiner Archive, the lesson took place on Sunday, September 30th. The mantras recorded were the following: "Satyam gnanam..." and the German translation: "Ewiges Sein, unendliche Gnade..." [Eternal being, unending grace], as well as the three-part mantra: "O Human Being, know yourself...."

According to the report available from Hans Erhard Lauer, approximately twenty people were present. Rudolf Steiner opened with an Indian mantra and closed with the class mantra: "O Human Being, know yourself..." and the Temple Legend.†

In a letter of February 27, 1930, to the Executive Council of the General Anthroposophical Society, Polzer related that in the fall of 1923, Rudolf Steiner allowed him, "when he held an esoteric lesson in Vienna at my request, to carry this lesson on and to expand the circle of esoteric students."

According to the report from Hans Ehrhard Lauer, Rudolf Steiner is supposed to have told Polzer he could, from time to time, repeat the lesson. He reported that Polzer did this only once or twice because shortly afterward came the Christmas Conference in Dornach and the setting up of the First Class.

In the handwriting of Ludwig Polzer-Hoditz: Vienna, Sunday, September 30, 1923

Eternal being, unending grace,
Fullness of wisdom, Brahma
Cosmic sheath of the cosmic soul,
Unlimited love, boundless,
Peace, salvation in the undivided
(In the cosmic harmony)
Aum.
Peace, Peace, Peace.

PART III

The Origin of the Esoteric Youth Group
with Records of the History of Its Origin
and Development

Two Esoteric Lessons
for the Esoteric Youth Group

The Youth Group Meditations

The Origin of the Esoteric Youth Group

Foreword by the Editor of the German Edition

In order to understand the history of the development of the Esoteric Youth Group, we must begin with the General Anthroposophical Youth Movement, because the idea of the "Group" is quite closely bound up with it.

The world war catastrophe had shown that the old social connections were no longer relevant, and that a completely new form was necessary. Thus, in spring 1919 the Movement for the Threefold Social Organism arose out of Rudolf Steiner's Anthroposophy. In the place of the centralized state, this Movement strove for the complete self-governing respectively of the spiritual life, the rights life, and the economic life. The great echo that made these strivings public consisted of the fact that more and more youth found their way to Anthroposophy. At the universities and other colleges in Germany— also in Switzerland and Austria—there arose the Anthroposophical student groups, which, in the summer of 1920, founded the Association for Anthroposophical College Studies. College courses were held at the Goetheanum in Dornach and in other cities with the intention of planting the seed of an independent college entity. People in the Anthroposophical Society apparently viewed this with skepticism, which caused Rudolf Steiner (at the first members' Annual Meeting of the Anthroposophical Society after 1914, held on September 4, 1921, in Stuttgart)† to react to the vote of a student of the Tübingen University† with the following words:

> Here has spoken a representative of the Youth Movement! Here sits a whole number of representatives of the student body! My dear friends, that members of such a Movement or body have come to our Anthroposophical Society, should be considered epoch-making in the history of our Anthroposophical Movement. We must do everything that can rightly be expected of the Anthroposophical Society by these youth.

Already before this, he had characterized the Youth Movement (Wandervogel [migratory bird]) that arose at the beginning of the twentieth century as a movement arising internationally out of elemental forces. In this Youth Movement, something lights up from the immensely significant turning point of the end of the nineteenth century: the end of Kali Yuga.†

Fired up by such elemental forces, the youth who were interested in Anthroposophy and who were partly still closely connected with the Wandervogel-Youth Movement, felt themselves deeply unsatisfied in the Anthroposophical Society. Thus, they sought possibilities to organize themselves in an Anthroposophical-social form.

A first circular dated March 17, 1921 ("An die Jugend der anthroposophischen Bewegung" [To the youth of the Anthroposophical Movement])† went out from Stuttgart with the call to unite, at the suggestion of Rudolf Steiner, for the founding of a general youth branch. Shortly afterward Otto Palmer, Jr. was given the opportunity to report on these efforts at the seventh regular General Meeting of the Association of the Goetheanum, the Independent School for Spiritual Science, on April 25, 1920, in Dornach. According to the minutes,† he said the following:

> To report on the Anthroposophical Youth Movement, about the positive things that have come about, we reach back briefly to the origin of this Movement and its development.
>
> If we are to understand this movement correctly, we must see it above all as a protest that came to life in the youth against the old branch life that has up until now been customary in the Anthroposophical Society. Indeed, there actually does live in the youth something that feels the need to have Anthroposophy not be just something we do on Sunday afternoons (not like wearing it as jewelry or decoration on Sunday), but rather to bring everything that is given in Anthroposophy into life and to make it into our practice. That at first, here and there, the mistake was made to approach the affair programmatically, rests perhaps partly on the fact that the need was felt so strongly that people should reach out to all sides to contact others, instead of starting on a single

facet of the work itself and then allowing the further development to crystallize out of this positive work. This gave rise to the controversy that, from the one side, special weight was given to the need to found a youth branch; and from the other side came the distrust that, through the founding of a branch, precisely those things would enter into it that were not wanted. This actually purely-supposed difference of opinion led to such a solution that we now have in Stuttgart a series of groups. They have grown out of the need of the Youth Movement in the sense that with their work, instead of one lecturer speaking from a podium, with an audience more-or-less listening, now people have joined together who want to work together on a theme.

The center-point of this work might be a book, a discussion-study, or a seminar-like study together of a specific theme with a specialized content. Working in this way creates, of itself, the basis for the lecturing. The presentations of these groups, which work individually, can be combined into a lecture cycle wherein a truly living connection is produced between the lecturer and the audience. And the members of the audience feel, through their preparatory work, that these lectures are the high point of their own work. This solution wishes, in a certain way, to come closer to the idea of freedom of the spiritual life, and cannot be boxed in. It strives—because the manner of the branch was felt as coercive—that in the place of this coercion, a creating and forming should take place out of what is truly living, and which cannot right up front be expressed in a specific program or plan.

It is a matter of attempting to carry out the freedom of the spiritual life as far as possible within this small parameter. It is necessary to overcome a certain fear, still reigning, that such a free spiritual life will awaken opposing forces that could and will cause difficulties. We can undertake such a task only if we believe to have within us something living, out of which the forces come that are able to conquer the counter-forces.

On April 16, 1920, Ehrenfried Pfeiffer sent out a circular that corresponded with the call of March 17, 1920. In this circular ("Entwurf über Grundzüge der Arbeit im Jugendzweig" [Draft of the essential aspects of the work in the youth branch]),† Pfeiffer writes: "The work in the youth branch should occur, above all, with the viewpoint that the youth can one day be carriers of the Anthroposophically-oriented spiritual science. If we ourselves add ability to our willing, then the fight against the old thinking can be taken up everywhere. If the work of the youth branch occurs in this sense, the form will come about on its own."

Such an outer form then came about first at the beginning of 1923, through Rudolf Steiner's help. He made it possible that, beside the official Anthroposophical Society, the Independent Anthroposophical Society could form for the youth themselves.†

The following stages led up to this: an Anthroposophical College Association was founded. Anthroposophical College courses and conferences were held. However, neither the young nor the old were satisfied with this development, and the conflict between the generations grew ever deeper. This led to the coming together, during the East-West Congress in Vienna, in June 1922, of some young people who made plans to try to set up a meeting of the youth with Rudolf Steiner concerning their problems.

Already in July, three of them (two friends, Ernst Lehrs and Fritz Kübler, as well as René Maikowski, the business manager of the College Association) could speak about this with Rudolf Steiner in Dornach. He agreed to have such a meeting at the beginning of October in Stuttgart. As a result, Ernst Lehrs traveled through northern Germany, and Fritz Kübler through southern Germany, to call the anthroposophically oriented youth to this meeting.

Ernst Lehrs reported his experiences in a letter to Rudolf Steiner as follows:†

Jena, September 18, 1922

Dear Dr. Steiner:

I am anxious, before we are together with you in Stuttgart, to tell you of my experiences in the meantime while with the friends in Bremen, Berlin, and Dresden, and through our written exchanges of opinion. To my great joy, I found everywhere a new current out of the same impulses that Kübler and I had when we came to you in Dornach. It has become generally apparent that every attempt at working together in the age of the consciousness soul, also in our group, was condemned to become a working beside one another, a co-existing beside one another. And it has become obvious that it is high time—especially in view of the collapse of the outer framework that can no longer be prevented—to train ourselves, through this working beside one another, for a brotherliness so that the working side-by-side, the co-existence, can become a working together and can serve as a model or ideal. Thus, it would be conceived of too narrowly to say that there will be coming together in Stuttgart a number of student teachers who wish to hear something from you for their professional training. Much more, there will come together scientifically, artistically, and pedagogically oriented people who for the most part are already working on a community form in the above sense. They all have in common the drive to be educators of the human being, because today *in all three areas* a learning or studying is not enough, but rather a self-education is desired—no longer a teaching but an educating. And to all of them came this year—as far as they are Anthroposophists—something like a "friend of God" out of the spiritual world; like the layman who came to Tauler! Thus, even if those present in Stuttgart are for the most part future school teachers, there is a sizable number of others; for instance, delegates from a group of sculptors and architects out of Dresden.

These people are working on forming a work community in which they wish to train themselves and others to become master builders on the basis of spiritual science. All of these, however, wish to be together in Stuttgart in such a way that, at their departure from one another, something remains together, as it were, in the spiritual world. They want this so that they can in earnest, heartfelt mutuality help and encourage one another from group to group; from place to place; from profession to profession. They wish to give, through their exemplary existence and work, their fellow human beings courage and trust for a freeing of the spiritual life at last. They wish to do this as a nameless, living association.

Greetings in gratitude and devotion,
Ernst Lehrs

P S: It would be appropriate not to schedule a presentation on October 1, so that the participants have time to get to know each other.

The letter makes it clear that the majority of these young people were interested in their future pedagogical profession. On the other hand, some of the others had more the intention to become a nameless, living association, independent of profession.

The indication of an association of this kind goes back to the meeting that Ernst Lehrs had with Wilhelm Rath and his study group in Berlin, in August 1922; therefore, shortly before the letter to Rudolf Steiner. During the work with the Berlin youth group on Rudolf Steiner's *Mystics after Modernism* (CW 7), Wilhelm Rath became inspired by the "Friend of God from Oberland" and his circle of twelve friends of God, from the Middle Ages. This kindled in him the ideal of building a similar brotherhood for the work of the Anthroposophical youth, only with the demands of the present time taken into account. The Berlin youth were further strengthened in this ideal through a call† to join the newly formed "Bund für freies Geistesleben." [Association for independent spiritual life]. This call appeared in the magazine *Anthroposophie, Wochenschrift für freies Geistesleben* [Anthroposophy, weekly for independent spiritual life] in the middle of July 1922. They were immediately of the opinion that they could not go forward in the way described in this appeal. And shortly afterwards, when Ernst Lehrs was on his organizational trip for the youth meeting and met with Wilhelm Rath and his study group in Berlin, also he became enthusiastic toward the ideal of an association similar to that of the friends of God. At that time, Wilhelm Rath told Ernst Lehrs about his idea of asking Rudolf Steiner for a meditation that could be done in common, through which all the youth could connect with each other daily in the spirit. Shortly before the departure for Stuttgart, Rath wrote to Lehrs regarding how he thought this idea could be brought forward at the youth meeting. It reads: "I have yet another suggestion: that the request can perhaps only be brought in personal conversations in the course of events, and then, should the occasion arise, it could be brought to Rudolf Steiner. The request is that, since we want for all the future to come to an intensive, living working-together, that Rudolf Steiner give us the possibility of uniting meditatively at a specific time in rhythmic sequence—even though we are separated in space—by giving us a unifying meditation into which we can immerse ourselves in the morning or in the evening. This idea seems important to me. If and how this takes place will become apparent. We must also think about the dangers associated with its realization." With this letter—according to Wilhelm Rath in his report, "Mein Weg zum Kreis" [My way to the group]—"the result was a long wrestling with the formulation of the question to be put to Dr. Steiner."

In addition, the relationship of trust that Wilhelm Rath had achieved with a few Berlin representatives of the older generation apparently contributed to [the formulation of the question]. They had reported to him a few things about the Esoteric School that existed before the war, and he was able likewise to speak to them about his idea for the formation of a community for esoteric striving. These people, with whom he spoke, were Wilhelm Selling and his wife, Karin Selling, as well as his brother-in-law, Kurt Walther, who was a member of the Executive Council of the Anthroposophical Society until the fall of 1921. These three became protectors of sorts of Wilhelm Rath's endeavor. They also went with him to Stuttgart in October 1922 and belonged then to the founding members of the Esoteric Youth Group.

On October 1, when approximately eighty people from eighteen to twenty-five years of age—whom a few older people joined—met in the Society house in Stuttgart for the meeting of the youth with Rudolf Steiner, the contrast between the older and younger generations became noticeable. The official Society representatives were offended that they were not included in the meeting.[†] They asked Rudolf Steiner why, and he answered that he himself did not know what the young people wanted from him. He said that a few of them had come to him and had discussed all kinds of things with him, and at their request, he had agreed to give this course. However, they had not told him what they really wanted. When this was told to the organizers of the youth meeting, they were shocked and had a friend ask Rudolf Steiner to explain it. Rudolf Steiner answered: "You said that you see fixed programs as something for which the time is past." Rudolf Steiner let them know that he agreed with them completely about this. Thus, they were to tell him, based on the work they had accomplished in the meantime, what they wanted him to speak about in the course. He let them know that Ernst Lehrs, in his letter, had suggested that he not come immediately on the first day, in order to let those who have come together have time to find their way to each other properly. Steiner suggested that they use this time to clarify the theme they want for his first lecture. After hearing the first lecture, they would then have the material to help clarify what they would want to hear from him in the second lecture. In this way—totally as was wished for—the course† without a set plan should arise in a quite living manner.

(According to the report, "Enstehungsgeschichte des Jugendkreises" [The history of the origin of the youth group] by Ernst Lehrs.)

In conversations in the organizing committee that followed Steiner's answer, two very opposite views formed. While the Rath-Lehrs group wanted to bring a question about building an esoteric community, the other group rejected this flatly and demanded that only a question that concerns the pedagogical realm should be brought. Finally, they agreed on a neutrally formulated question. When this question was then presented to Rudolf Steiner, after his arrival on October 3, and he appeared to be disappointed by it, Wilhelm Rath felt pressed to express the fact that for some the question that concerns them is about forming an esoteric community. Rudolf Steiner was immediately willing to do this, but suggested that it be discussed first among all the participants of the course. Those who feel sympathetic toward this would then find their way to it. He would then come himself and speak of it in such a way that then, at the next meeting, only those will come who really want this.

Several times all the course participants came together with Rudolf Steiner. In addition, there were discussions among only the participants themselves. After, quite intense arguments, the majority separated from the Rath-Lehrs group. The further discussions then took place in the smaller group without the opponents. When exactly these meetings took place, and what Rudolf Steiner spoke about at which meeting, cannot be any longer ascertained, due to contradictions in the records. It is known only that the date of the last preparatory discussion took place on October 12, 1922. On the following day, only those were present who had decided for the forming of the group. There were twelve to whom Rudolf Steiner gave the requested meditation,† and three days later, on October 16, the oath formulation.† October 16, 1922 is the founding day of the Esoteric Youth Group. Rudolf Steiner came, from the first meeting on, together with Marie Steiner, who participated in everything until 1924.

The next meeting of the group with Rudolf Steiner took place in Dornach, but a few days after the catastrophe of the burning of the first Goetheanum on the night of New Year's Eve 1922. Ernst Lehrs reported the following about this: "His (Rudolf Steiner's) open criticism in various directions concerning the Society and the various activities within it in the weeks leading up to the fateful Christmas-New Year's time, made one clear about the fact that it was due to the failure on the part of the Society that the necessary spiritual protection was missing from the building. Yet, it was out of an experience of this failure that the impulse for the Youth Course arose, as well as what led to the coming about of our specific endeavor. Thus the idea arose among us that we should ask Rudolf Steiner if and how we could contribute to the Anthroposophical Society 'consolidating' itself again—as one of us put it." With this in mind, they asked to be allowed to speak with him. As they then, in the Glass House, on January 3, 1923, asked about their helping toward the consolidation of the Society, Rudolf Steiner answered in a calm tone with emphatic earnestness: "Just keep yourselves consolidated, and the Society will be consolidated." Then he gave the advice that they should sit together on a regular basis and, in symposium-like conversations, reflect again and again upon the foundational impulse of their group.†

The next meeting with Rudolf Steiner occurred in Stuttgart on July 13, 1923. The group had asked to be able to bring questions. Rudolf Steiner did not allow for this, but held an esoteric lesson for them. A second lesson followed in Dornach, on December 30, during the time of the Christmas Conference. To this lesson Steiner brought Dr. Ita Wegman, in addition to Marie Steiner.

According to a record in 1963 by Ernst Lehrs on "Definition des Kreises" [Meaning of the group], Rudolf Steiner continued to be at the group's disposal with his advice orally until his illness, and then in writing until shortly before his death. There are, however, no records of this in the Rudolf Steiner Archive.

For the post-war time until the new founding of the earlier esoteric school as the "Freie Hochschule für Geisteswissenschaft." [Independent school for spiritual science] at the Goetheanum at Christmas 1923, it holds true generally—and for the Esoteric Youth Group specifically—that the initiatives for esoteric gatherings, as well as for the founding of The Christian Community, did not come from Rudolf Steiner himself. It was much more that he sought to meet the questions and requests that came toward him.

* * *

Some details about the 12 founding members:

Daniel van Bemmelen (1899-1982). Born in Dutch East Indies. A member of the Society since 1921. Teacher in the Waldorf School in The Hague, the first Dutch Waldorf school. He was a co-founder of this school (in 1923).

Georg Groot, MD (1899-1967). Born in Ronneburg, in the Baltic states. Became a member of the Society in May 1920 in Berlin. Became familiar with Anthroposophy through learning of the threefold social organism. Worked then as a co-worker in the Berlin group of the College Association, to which Wilhelm Rath belonged. Four years after the burning of the first Goetheanum, he was one of the guards who were responsible for the safety of the building and for Rudolf Steiner.

Herbert Hahn (1890-1970). Born in Pernau/Estland. Became a member in Berlin in March 1912. In 1919 he was called by Rudolf Steiner to teach at the Independent Waldorf School in Stuttgart.

Ernst Lehrs (1894-1979). Born in Berlin. Member since August 1921. At that time a student studying physics in Jena. Later a teacher at the Waldorf school in Stuttgart. Served on the committee for the Independent Anthroposophical Society founded in 1923 for youth. Later he taught in The Hague, London, and Aberdeen. After the war he and his wife, Maria Roeschl, taught in the Rudolf Steiner Seminar in Eckwälden.

René Maikowski (1900-1992). Born in Berlin. A member since 1921. Studied history and social science. As of March 10, 1922, he was the business manager of the Association for Anthroposophical College Studies. Later a teacher at various Waldorf schools.

Wilhelm Rath (1897-1973). Born in Berlin. Became a member in Berlin in June 1920. Bookseller, man of letters, and later farmer in Farrach in Kärnten. Was on the committee of the Independent Anthroposophical Society with Lehrs and Maikowski.

Wilhelm Selling (1869-1960). Born in Steinau on the Oder. Became a member in Berlin in April 1905. A mechanical engineer. He was for many years a colonial officer in Africa. Because of his early retirement for health reasons, he made himself completely available for Anthroposophical work. Thus, he was in charge of the Theosophical library in Motzstrasse and was considered to be the mentor of the youth work in Berlin. Was in Stockholm from 1931-1939.
Karin Selling, nee Flack (1880-1958). Swedish. Teacher. Was a member already in the Scandinavian Theosophical Society. Married Wilhelm Selling in 1920 and came to Berlin. Later a teacher in the Waldorf school in Stockholm.

Emma Smit (1896-1986). Dutch. Teacher. Along with her husband, Daniel van Bemmelen, she was among the organizers of the Independent school in The Hague.

Maria Spira (1895-1972). Became a member in April 1921 in Vienna. Came from the Zionist Youth Movement. Later married Wilhelm Rath and lived with him as of 1935 in Farrach in Kärnten.

Albrecht Strohschein (1899-1962). Born in Hamburg-Harburg. Became a member in Bremen in March 1920. A trained businessman. Was first a co-worker in the "Der Kommenden Tag" [The coming day] in Stuttgart. Then a student of psychology in Jena. A co-founder in 1924 of the therapeutic pedagogical movement.

Kurt Walther (1874-1940). Born in Frankfurt on the Oder. Postal official. Became a member in June or July 1904 in Hamburg. Transferred to Fürstenwalde by Berlin in 1908. In 1910, he married Wilhelm Selling's sister Clara who, as of 1905, belonged to Rudolf Steiner's household. After he was transferred to Berlin in 1913, Clara returned to Motzstrasse. Kurt Walther was a lecturer and the leader of many courses. From 1916-1921 he was the successor of Marie Steiner in the central Executive Council of the Anthroposophical Society.

Some Documents of the History of the Anthroposophical Youth Movement

1. Appeal for the Forming of a Youth Branch

The first appeal, of March 17, 1920, for the formation of an Anthroposophical Youth Movement was sent to Rudolf Steiner, along with the following letter by Robert Wolfgang Wallach:†

Stuttgart, March 18, 1920

Dear Dr. Steiner!

After working through it again, we finished the enclosed appeal to the young brothers and sisters of our Movement. We hope very much that it is to your liking. Concerning the form of the work of the youth branch, we have deliberated further and have come to several points that I would also like to submit to you. We will select, out of the circle of the older, recognized members of the Society, patrons or sponsors who will guide us spiritually. We will submit our endeavors and activities to them, and they will vouch for us with the Society. There will not be an Executive Council or anything like that. At every place where a working group arises, we will select someone from among us to serve as a kind of work-secretary. The wishes for the workgroups that are to be held will be given to the secretary. He or she will then seek, out of the circle of older members, an appropriate teacher for the given topic, and will ask that person to take on the task of teaching. The work in the Youth Movement group shall be managed by the secretary in a free manner that corresponds to our high goal. We are thinking further of doing circulars or newsletters, and later of doing newsletters that can be combined into a magazine, among individual working groups. We hope that we will be acting according to your wishes with this. Because I have been given the task of communicating our intentions to you, Dr. Steiner, I need to say that I feel infinitely indebted for having found you and for what you will yet bring.

Please accept my complete gratitude and devotion.

Your
Robert Wolfgang Wallach

Stuttgart, March 17, 1920

To the Youth of the Anthroposophical Movement!

Especially in the light of the living, spiritual striving in the younger generation, we have long, and to an ever increasing degree, felt the necessity to make the Anthroposophical worldview our own, to express it, and to live it in a manner that is in keeping with the inner and outer needs of our life and time. This need pressing for realization has allowed the stimulus to ripen that Rudolf Steiner himself gave for the founding of a general

YOUTH BRANCH

and has led to the following decision:

We call all youth who feel themselves to be a part of the Anthroposophical Movement, whether or not they are members of the Anthroposophical Society, to join together to form such a youth branch.

In this branch we want to work among ourselves, with teachers we choose, in a manner in accordance with what is right for our youth and what makes it a sacred duty in the dawning of a new age. In specifics, the work will be fully free individually and shall form as is suited to each location.

We want to reach out to all the youth groups we have not as yet reached, in the conviction that precisely they bear within themselves life possibilities for the future. It is also a call on the Anthroposophical Movement to rise up to its future world tasks. It needs, out of its own nature, its own path to this task. The only condition for acceptance in this youth branch shall be the pledge to put oneself with one's whole strength and devotion in the service of the Movement.

Walter Scheidegger, Rudolf Geering, Basel;
Ehrenfried Pfeiffer, Dornach; Anton Burg, Karlsruhe;
Hans Erhard Lauer, Heidelberg; Luise Kieser, Heilbronn;
Else Koch, Leipzig; Otto Senn, Munich;
Elisabeth Baumann-Dollfus, Paul Baumann, Freie Waldorfschule, Stuttgart;
Robert Wolfgang Wallach, staff of the Association for Threefolding, Stuttgart.

The members of the youth branch as such will be reported to the business office of the Anthroposophical Society in Berlin.

We ask that all join together soon, in the sense of the call, in the various locations, and that the lists of names and individual registrants be sent here to Dr. R. W. Wallach, Dobelstrasse 4/II, Stuttgart.

A circular with recommendations about the manner of the work together will follow shortly.

For Stuttgart, the union took place March 13, 1920.

Youth Branch: Stuttgart Group

2. Undated Circular, March/April 1920

Number II. Circular Concerning the Form of the Anthroposophical Youth Branch

The youth branch is a work-community. Its place of origin is Stuttgart. It has no Executive Council, but rather a business manager in Stuttgart and work/study leaders at the individual locations. These leaders can be selected annually.

The youth choose, from among the older Anthroposophists, their patrons or sponsors for whom they have the fullest trust. All the initiatives of the youth branch will be presented for them to examine. The term of service for the sponsors will be one year. There shall be no more than one sponsor per twelve young people.

The members of the youth branch will be reported to the business office of the Anthroposophical Society in Berlin, located at Mottstrasse. The membership cards for the youth branch will be issued from Stuttgart. All may become a member of the youth branch who are prepared to pledge to place their whole strength and devotion in the service of the Anthroposophical Movement.

There is no age limit; however, only those should become members who are willing to give the youngest involved their rights in the entirety of their learning and life. The pledge shall be given after a trial period of six weeks, except when the candidate for membership is already a member of the Anthroposophical Society. Upon acceptance and in the work together, all sympathies and antipathy should be set aside with regard to the matters at hand. The exclusion of members—in as much as it is not due to their retracting their pledge themselves—can only be done through the business office after a motion from the whole group, and with the approval of all the sponsors.

In the local group's discussions, which should occur monthly and which must take place upon the proposal of even one member, the votes of those members under thirty years of age count as two votes.

With respect to Rudolf Steiner as teacher, the members of the youth branch have the same rights as the members of the Society.

Above all, the initiative for study and work should be announced to the study-work leader by those wishing to learn. The leader then finds the appropriate teacher. As often as possible, the teacher should be sought for among the older Anthroposophists. However, the younger ones should also be given the possibility in developing themselves to become teachers.

In view of the ultimate truthfulness—real knowledge on the part of the teacher and the receptivity of those learning—the principle for the work should be that it takes place in free working groups and with mutual agreement. In the specifics, the work should adapt to the circumstances of the individual locations.

For outreach, it is a matter of working into all the youth groups. We must try to find an entry into the independent German associations, colleges, and youth organizations, and to hold lectures and introductory courses there. We should make an energetic attempt to draw individuals by coming closer to them on a personal basis. Exchange of literature. Essays in magazines for young Germans. Lay out our magazines in reading-rooms.

The connection among the local groups shall take place, according to need, through newsletters to be given out. Our insights and experiences are to be recorded in these circulars. In addition, when possible, meetings of the entire branch should be arranged.

The local groups will have to collect membership dues at a level that they themselves determine. We ask that a portion of these be transferred to the business office to help cover its costs.

We ask that this document be discussed in the local groups, and that your wishes for changes in the text, or your agreement with it, be communicated to the home office, at Dobelstrasse 4 II, Stuttgart. Afterward, we will then be able to disseminate it in greater number.

The Business Office of the Anthroposophical Youth Branch,
Otto Benn

3. Circular from Paul Baumann, April 1920

Paul Baumann, teacher at the Stuttgart Waldorf School and co-signer of the appeal of March 17, 1928 for the forming of a youth branch, distanced himself from a circular† concerning the youth branch with the following writing to the members of the Anthroposophical Society. This writing is not dated, but must have been sent before April 16, 1920, as can be seen in the reproduction of Ehrenfried Pfeiffer's letter that immediately followed it.

Anthroposophical Youth Movement: A Correction

As of a short time ago, a confused activity has been haunting us under the banner of the above title and appears, through a breach of trust and a misuse of my signature, to be more closely connected with my name that corresponds to reality.

Its organizational agenda is the opposite of everything I can represent. I do not intend to disrupt the positive work of the Anthroposophical Society by giving irresponsible elements—only because of their young years could these [aims] be thought of as essential—the opportunity to do their foul work in the name of the Society, and to misuse it for their own purposes. Just as little do I want to found a senseless youth movement that intoxicates itself on phrases. If there are young people, and people interested in the youth, who have a firm will for work and study in the Anthroposophical direction and who want to bring their striving to expression in a specific group, then it makes sense to form the group.

Two viewpoints come thereby into consideration: an extensive work outward in all—especially in youth groups—scientific, artistic, and promotional activity can be accomplished by individuals without any organization. Groups will rise first on the basis of accomplishments and can then enter into contact, in order to fructify themselves and to develop a common impetus. If there are today already independent groups in existence, their joining together into an Anthroposophical Youth Movement must bear the purpose of a strengthening. Large-scale initiatives should be made possible through them. The other viewpoint is that of an Anthroposophical Youth Branch within the scope of the Society. As a representative who is recognized by the Executive Council, I am forming such a branch at this time because a number of people have joined me under the prerequisites that justify its founding. Of course, this branch would set other requirements for its members than just a mere pledge of the young people. This branch would include the outer activity mentioned before and demand accomplishments in a yet higher degree. The special training of school graduates toward [an embodiment of] spiritual science in their personal interactions is the specific task of the branch. Goals of such a youth branch are: to further the educational work of the Independent Waldorf School; to support the spiritual scientific academic endeavors; and to find and guide people we can trust for the practice.

In the best case, the branch will be able to have only a small number of members. The will of the youngest will be most likely limited to learning. The regulating of their thinking, and the purification of their feeling life, can require all of their strength. And this is urgently necessary today. We can speak of a right to vote only when those involved are trustworthy; and the responsibility to judge this rests with the representative. On this basis, youth branches can arise and then unite.

I did not want to give programatic explanations here, but only brief tips for foundational elements that must be present for a fruitful Youth Movement. Above all, however, I wanted to correct the views that could be ascribed to me because of a second circular that bore my name and my address as that of the business office, without my being a part of it or being in agreement with it. It was written and sent in my absence. My activity here in Stuttgart already stands in the service of a comprehensive Anthroposophical Youth Movement that is present spiritually. If this finds the possibility also to take on outer organizational forms, then the youth will take, through this, a great step forward.

Paul Baumann, Teacher of the Independent Waldorf School.
Landhausstrasse 107 II, Stuttgart.

4. Circular from Ehrenfried Pfeiffer

Dornach, April 16, 1920.

To all who feel themselves to be youthful, who strive for the real renewal of spiritual life!

Almost too much has been written about the youth branch already. However, it seems to me, as a co-founder, necessary to take a position concerning two circulars, in order to bring the actual task of the youth branch to the fore again. The one circular (number 2) was sent from the business office of the Youth Branch in Stuttgart. It would have been impossible to send this circular if people had been clearly aware that the youth branch, above all, is a place of the most earnest effort and learning within, and of working toward the outside; and no organization should be created. The organization, like a rigid husk, would necessarily smother the good seed. The other circular is from Paul Baumann of Stuttgart. It appears to proceed directly from a spirit that shows itself as a senile youth. The task of the youth branch should be to overcome precisely this.

Instead of this, it seems necessary to create an association that will come about out of its own inner need, without sponsors or trusted representatives recognized by the Executive Council. The sponsor or representative could also hinder a living progress through a senile attribute.

There is no intention here to criticize these two circulars, but only to show that they do not contain the spirit that can support the youth in carrying out their mission. Their mission is to one day be the carriers of the Anthroposophical Movement, and already now to bring the renewal of spiritual life, out of youthful sensing and feeling, to the youth. However, how can the youth fulfill their mission if they are organized (per circular number two) or if they are placed under a guardian, such as Paul Baumann aspires to institute—in spite of all the good ideas and beautiful words contained in his circular?

The following draft should provide a stimulus for the work that will make this mission possible:

Outline of the Characteristics of the Work in the Youth Branch!

The work in the youth branch shall, above all, take place with the viewpoint that the youth can one day be the carriers of the anthroposophically oriented spiritual science. To enable the members of the youth branch to do this, there shall be, in regular meetings adapted to the local circumstances, an education in the spiritual scientific sense of the participants through appropriate reports, lectures, and the working together of those listening. This training would work especially on the strengthening of the will, and a sharpening and freeing of the thinking and the power of discernment.

Before the youth branch can do anything outside of its own group, it must have an energetic, knowledgeable core of people who are able, on the one hand, to represent the spiritual scientific standpoint in relation to the so-called exact science in a comprehensive and convincing manner. On the other hand, they need to be able to show the way to a clear intellectual activity, to active reason, to those people who have a right feeling for spiritual science but cannot express it in a logical, objective manner.

Each person must be conscious of the following: The future of Anthroposophy depends on me. I will to develop my capacities in such a way that I am in the position to stand up for and be an advocate for anthroposophically oriented spiritual science with my whole person. Only when there are trained personages permeated with such a consciousness, will it be possible to successfully approach the youth groups that are not yet a part of the Anthroposophical Movement, and to win them over for our cause. When we add ability to the forces of will, the battle against the old thinking can be taken up.

If the work of the youth branch happens in this sense, the outer form will rise of itself. Those who will to participate in such work will find their way to like-minded people. There will be in these youth groups those who are already able to give lectures and stimulus out of anthroposophically oriented spiritual science.

Should the youth find that their ability is not enough, there will surely be some out of the groups of older people who are willing to speak on a topic in the youth branch, or to teach in an area determined by the youth branch.

A local group does not need an Executive Council, or the like. The only need is for a business manager who takes care of the purely business matters for the local group. The manager is selected by a minimum of seven members. The manager can then connect with the central office. The selected manager remains in office for as long as he or she has the trust of at least seven members. The central office takes care of the forming of the groups and the connection among the individual local groups. The manager of the Central Business Office is selected by the spiritual center, Dr. Steiner.

It is the responsibility of the individual business office to arrange the lectures, courses, rentals of sites, the covering of costs, the reporting of the members' names to Executive Council of the Anthroposophical Society in Berlin and to the central business manager, etc.

If there are those who are not yet members of the Anthroposophical Society but show a firm will to work in the way outlined above, they can be accepted into the youth branch upon their application. The work of the local group will vouch for the new member, that he or she supports our cause in the right sense.

According to the expenses of the local groups, they may collect dues, a part of which should be deducted to pay the support of the Central Business Office.

Practical tips for successful work will be able to be given by every local group communicating the manner of its individual work to its business manager, who then passes it on to the Central Office, and then the Central Office passes this on to the other local groups. Through this constant contact, everyone can learn mutually from the successes and failures what is needed and which ways of working are especially effective.

This outline should only give the stimulus to work. What could be seen in it as organization is not intended as such, but should only be the thread of Ariadne that provides a common, goal-conscious unity of forces.

Those who are willing to work in a positive manner out of this viewpoint may send their written agreement to the address below. It is hoped that there will be youth found who are not permeated by senility and who are willing to work in the goal-conscious striving for renewal of the spiritual life.

Ehrenfried Pfeiffer
Haus Wendhof
Dornach, near Basel

5. Appeal of the Association for Independent Spiritual Life

Transition of the Association for the Threefold Social Organism into the Association for Independent Spiritual Life†

In Number 50 of the *Dreigliederungs-Zeitung* [Threefolding magazine], the change of name of this weekly† to *Anthroposophie, Wochenschrift für freies Geistesleben* [Anthroposophy, weekly for independent spiritual life] was announced, and details of the reason for the necessity of this were given precisely. This was the first step toward a re-forming of the foundations of the Threefold Movement in a way appropriate to the times and circumstances. A further step that proved to be necessary is the transition of the Association for the Threefold Social Organism into an Association for Independent Spiritual Life.

The Threefold Movement was introduced under the assumption that it would find a strong echo, because it comprise the impulses that lie in the will of the age and of modern humanity as a whole. It did not find this echo. As a result, its effectiveness for the future will extend to that area which is concerned with preparation for a new cultural element; and that is a free spiritual life.

The Threefold Movement came into being because a few Stuttgarters who belonged to the Anthroposophical Movement turned to Rudolf Steiner already in the spring of 1919 with a request for advice on the rebuilding of social life that was being sought everywhere. Dr. Steiner then wrote the well-known "Appeal to the German People and the Cultural World," behind which stood several hundred people out of all circles. This appeal was disseminated throughout Germany, Austria, and Switzerland. Subsequently the Threefold Movement arose. It built on ideas that Dr. Steiner had already presented in a number of lectures, and which he had laid down in *Towards Social Renewal* (CW 23).

The impulse of the Threefold Social Organism, when understood correctly, cannot be identified with, or confused with, any other direction of social ideas. What is intended with it lies within the tendency of modern humanity's development. This is only to express clearly what wants to emerge in general out of historical necessities. This impulse will work its way upward under all circumstances—perhaps even more difficult ones than exist now—because it actually lives in the unconscious depths of modern humanity's consciousness. We will see the truth of this fact, as some manifestations today already bear witness to it.

The Threefold Movement was never directed against the state. It wanted much more to give the state a secure foundation by bringing the spiritual-cultural life and economic life into a more appropriate relationship to it than was the case—to its own detriment—as a result of modern development.

Within the Anthroposophical Movement, people attempted to nurture a spiritual life that is able to give the present-day spiritual life those impulses needed for its continued development. The Threefold Movement did not meet with enough response; but in contrast, there is extensive understanding for Anthroposophy in all circles, even in the proletariat. These are the reasons for the retreat to the area of free spiritual life, which was always represented and belongs to the cultural task of the Threefold Movement. In this area a practical beginning was made for the current important question of education through the founding of the Independent Waldorf School in Stuttgart, and for the general progress of culture as such with the Goetheanum, the Independent School for Spiritual Science.

There is, among a great many people at the present time, due to the international situation, a deep need for a new spiritual, soul-bearing worldview. Anthroposophy believes that it meets this need in a manner truly appropriate for our time. It is a worldview that is scientifically sound. It shows itself to be artistically fruitful in all realms. With respect to the religious aspect, Anthroposophy leads to a deepening, and this is effective in the social aspect. It has at its disposal a comprehensive body of literature. There have been many editions printed of Rudolf Steiner's works, which proves that there is interest in Anthroposophy in the widest circles.

Such a Worldview-Movement demands, if it is to prove fruitful for the progress of humanity, that it enters fully into public life. The possibility must be given for it to be debated in the broadest measure and in an appropriate manner. The Association for an Independent Spiritual Life wants to create such a forum. The Association wants to provide a ground upon which new co-workers out of all areas of life can stand. The periodicals like the weekly *Anthroposophie* and the monthly *Die Drei* [The three] make themselves available for the tasks of the Association. A Worldview-Movement such as the Anthroposophical one will show itself to be more capable of life the more it sees itself faced by a free, unbiased, neutral judgment, and the more it helps as many people as possible, for whom a new form of the spiritual life matters, enter into a free relationship to it out of their life situation, their experiences, and their capacities. Dogmatic and unproductive supporters can only be a hindrance to the tasks of such a Movement. It also does not need to shy away from a fight, but it should not fight the battle with poisonous weapons. It must use honest weapons, not the opposite.

The Association for Independent Spiritual Life wants to provide a framework for this. It will lead further the current beginnings of a Movement for Independent Schools, and further all the scientific, artistic, and social striving that lie in the direction of a free spiritual life. For this it needs the cooperation of wider circles in a spiritual, as well as a financial connection.

Membership in the Association may be attained by registering with the Association leaders whose signatures are below, or with one of the local groups that are forming and are announced in the weekly periodical. Membership dues are 25 Marks per year. The local groups will charge, in addition, whatever is necessary to cover their own costs.

The undersigned express the expectation that the Association for Independent Spiritual Life, which meets a far-reaching need of our time, will meet with response in wider circles so that a free spiritual life can prove itself to be an appropriate cultural element demanded by the world situation.

Ernst Uehli, as leader of the Association for Independent Spiritual
    Life, Champignystrasse 17.
Rector Moritz Bartsch, Gottschallstrasse 8, Breslau.
Michael Bauer, Breitbrunn on the Ammersee.

Hermann Beck, Ph.D., professor, Doctor of philosophy and law, Marientorgraben 1, Nuremberg.
Herbert Hahn, Ph.D.. Teacher at the Independent Waldorf School, Kanonenweg 44, Stuttgart.
Eugen Kolisko, M.D., teacher at the Independent Waldorf School, Kanonenweg 44, Stuttgart.
Emil Leinhas, General Manager, Champignystrasse 17, Stuttgart.
Emil Molt, Counselor of Commerce, Spittlerstrasse 8, Stuttgart.
Rudolf Meyer, Kottbuser Ufer 25, Berlin SO.
Ludwig Polzer-Hoditz, Kösttlergasse 6/8, Vienna VI.
Friedrich Rittelmeyer, Ph.D., Lic. Theology, Kronenstrasse 70, Berlin W 8.
Walter Johannes Stein, Ph.D., teacher at the Independent Waldorf School, Kanonenweg 44, Stuttgart.
Carl Unger, Dr. of Engineering, Werastrasse 13, Stuttgart.
Ludwig Werbeck, Holzdamm 34, Hamburg.
H. Wohlbold, Ph.D., Adalbertstrasse 55, Munich.

6. Memorandum for the Committee of the Independent Anthroposophical Society for its Orientation†

Rudolf Steiner, March 1923

In Number 50 of the *Dreigliederungs-Zeitung* [Threefolding magazine], the change of name of this weekly† to *Anthroposophie, Wochenschrift für freies Geistesleben* [Anthroposophy, weekly for independent spiritual life] was announced, and details of the reason for the necessity of this were given precisely. This was the first step toward a re-forming of the foundations of the Threefold Movement in a way appropriate to the times and circumstances. A further step that proved to be necessary is the transition of the Association for the Threefold Social Organism into an Association for Independent Spiritual Life.

1. In reference to the outer constitution of the Independent Anthroposophical Society, you should work toward making this Society correspond to the "Outline of Statutes."† Through this, it is possible to unite in a Society those people who feel themselves free as individuals, without the Society being threatened by dissolution. Those who livingly understand the outline in the correct sense will have to find that everything is fulfilled in them.

2. First it is necessary to bring together all of those people who are already members of the Anthroposophical Society and who, according to the Committee, are proceeding with the viewpoint that the Society must be separated into two groups in a justifiable manner. Mere dissatisfaction with the old leadership cannot be enough, but only the positive orientation to an Anthroposophical goal that cannot be attained by the old leadership.

3. To begin with, out of this so-formed circle of the Independent Anthroposophical Society, select trusted representatives who are recognized by the Committee. Only such persons should be selected as representatives who are interested in giving Anthroposophy to the present civilization. Then there will come to those who are already in the Anthroposophical Society those who will have yet to be accepted. However, precisely with these, it is necessary to be sure that they have made the positive aspects of the Anthroposophical the direction of

their own life. Those who have *only* a general social interest, without an intensive Anthroposophical impulse, should not be selected as representatives, even if they are accepted into the Society with the idea that they will become real Anthroposophists.

4. For acceptance itself [as a member], standing within the Anthroposophical worldview to a certain extent should be decisive. Above all, for acceptance into the general Independent Anthroposophical Society, broad-mindedness must reign. Strictness *should* enter in first with the forming of the more restricted communities.

5. The Independent Anthroposophical Society should become an instrument for spreading Anthroposophy into the world. The lectures and all other work of spreading Anthroposophy should come out of it; also, institutes and other such things should be formed by it.

6. The general Independent Anthroposophical Society is one thing; the life-communities, or communities of life, that are to be built within it, are quite another thing. In these life-communities—whether exoteric or esoteric—people must come together who feel that they belong together and want to experience the spirit in common with one another. Alongside of such life-communities, it is thoroughly possible that a branch life, in the sense of the "Outlined of Statutes," forms. Branches would then be groups of the Independent Anthroposophical Society in general. It could, however, absolutely be that members of the Independent Anthroposophical Society join the branches of the Anthroposophical Society, and do this work together with the members there.

7. The work in the life-communities will be such that it remains within the corresponding community. Its goal is the improvement and perfection of those united within it. What those members of such a life-community undertake outside the community, they do as representatives of the general Independent Anthroposophical Society. Of course, such a life-community can step up to a specific outer work. However, it is to be desired that then its individual members act as representatives of the general Independent Anthroposophical Society. This does not necessitate the founding of a bureaucratic administration of an organizational activity, but it can absolutely be a free, conscious matter of fact for the individual.

8. Each of the committees (that of the Anthroposophical Society and that of the Independent Anthroposophical Society) should form a representative committee. These representative committees have the obligation to take care of the affairs of the general or entire Anthroposophical Society.

9. All institutions of the general or entire Anthroposophical Society should fall within the scope of interest of the Anthroposophical Society and the Independent Anthroposophical Society. This can well be, when we create a central administrative position that manages the affairs of the entire Society on behalf of both committees (communicated through their committees of representatives). The division of the Society into two groups should absolutely not lead to any one Anthroposophical institution—especially such a one that already exists—being seen as the affair or concern of only one of the groups.

A portion—to be determined by the committees—of the membership dues should come to the central fund, so the business of the entire Society can be supported.

10. The opinion should be understood that both groups came into being because there are among the members actually already two distinctly different groups that indeed want the same Anthroposophy, yet want to experience it in different ways. If this is correctly understood, then the relative separation can lead, not to a split, but rather to a harmony that would not be possible without the separation.

11. The Independent Anthroposophical Society should in no way attempt to destroy the Anthroposophical Society's developmental forces *from the past*. Those who want freedom for themselves should leave others free. That there are imperfections in the old Anthroposophical Society should not lead to a feud, but to the building of an Independent Anthroposophical Society that, according to those responsible, avoids these imperfections.

12. It is expected that through the separation, especially the youth in the Independent Anthroposophical Society will find a state of well-being. For the life-communities can be free groups of people who understand one another. This will be able to build the foundation upon which no one will feel their freedom limited, also in the general Independent Anthroposophical Society.

Reports from the Founding Members of the Youth Group Concerning Rudolf Steiner's Presentations for the Esoteric Youth Group

Preliminary Remarks from the Editor of the German Edition about the Text Records and Their Authenticity

The preparation of a reliable text of what Rudolf Steiner said at the meetings for the founding of the [Youth Group] is more difficult than for the other reports in this volume. Three circumstances contribute to the difficulty.

First, unlike with the lectures, there was no stenographer present. Some records were much later constructed from memory. Very few notes were taken at the time itself, and even those were quite incomplete. The original notes taken during the sessions no longer exist. We must, therefore, always take into account that what is reported is at least not exactly word-for-word; that the attitude and expectation of the listener changed what was heard; and that even in good faith, misunderstandings were passed on.

Second, at that time the reports and all that go with them were not regularly openly available but were passed on as private copies—partly undated—to relatively few people within the Youth Group itself. Members could go to these people to read the copies or to borrow them for a short time. What exist today are often photocopies of handwritten copies. The authenticity is not readily ascertainable.

Third, this situation made it possible for there to come into circulation a text that was manipulated—out of personal antipathy against the Youth Group and The Christian Community—apparently in order to set certain positions and arguments into the world. It contains statements that are incorrect or interpretations that could not have come from the founders of the Youth Group.† Because the Lehrs report is mentioned in it, it must have come into being after that report was written. The author, however, does not give his or her name and does not give any information about how this report came to be. The reason for this is that the text evidently comes from a source that is also otherwise known for its dubious handling of Rudolf Steiner's texts. This report was only disseminated around 1985, years after the death of most of the founders of the Youth Group. No small part of the texts that circulated within, and especially outside of, the Esoteric Youth Group came directly from this source or was infected by it. (This text is also the basis of the publication by the Cagliostro-Verlag [Cagliostro Press]: *Der Esoterische Jugendkreis—Dr. Rudolf Steiner* [The esoteric youth group—Rudolf Steiner], Rotterdam o.J. [1986].) The authenticity of Ernst Lehrs' report was disputed without any foundation, and the author's own view was implicitly maintained. In reality, it was a matter only of a coarsening of excerpts of Ernst Lehrs' report, but then expanded with statements falsely attributed to Rudolf Steiner. When we compare this in detail with Lehrs' original, we see how primitively the whole thing was done. The fact is that what is contained in this text, and is not borrowed from Lehrs, comes from the above-mentioned source and not from eyewitnesses. This holds true especially for a two-page passage about the priesthood that maintains that every active Anthroposophist is a priest. This may have been the main motive for the manipulation.

* * *

For this publication, in addition to Rudolf Steiner's own written pieces, the following documents whose authenticity could be ascertained were taken into account and at times quoted:

1. The report by Ernst Lehrs: "Entstehungsgeschichte des Jugendkreises" [The history of the origin of the youth group]. Private printing.

In 1974 Lehrs gives information about this report in his "Beilage zum Entstehungsbericht des Kreises" [Supplement to the report of the origin of the group]:

"The original record of the report of the Group was done in 1933...." The original version came about by Ernst Lehrs giving the report to Maria Röschl in shorthand, and she typed it. Afterward, it could be brought into better form through several stylistic changes and a rearranging of the order of the paragraphs. At the same time could be included what participants at the founding of the Group could contribute from memory. This is the way the present version of the report has been done. After forty years (from 1933) the need has recently arisen to bring out a different version of a certain part of the report. It has to do with the section titled, up until now, "Auseinandersetzung mit der Christengemeinschaft." [Argument or discussion with The Christian Community]. "[...] I ask that the new version of the section be given the title, 'Begegnung mit der jungen Bewegung für religiöse Erneuerung' [Encounter with the new Movement for Religious Renewal] and to cross out the old title." Changes in the text—but not those in the title—are insignificant.

The original version from 1933 does not exist in the archives. Probably it was hardly circulated; and most likely, it does not exist anymore. The first reproduction of this version originated presumably in the 1950s; the paper quality and method of reproducing it support this assumption. In the final version of 1974, the typing errors of the earlier version were corrected by hand and the section about The Christian Community was replaced by a text newly typed on a different typewriter, and then the result was photocopied. For this reason, the lines and page-breaks are identical in both versions. That the copies are genuine is confirmed also by a circular from Fritz Götte: "Nach 50 Jahren" [After 50 years], dated Easter 1975. It includes fifteen quotes from the report, and the page numbers cited correspond exactly. Lehrs read this circular and then, in a letter bearing his signature, he thanked Götte for it.

2. Two smaller circulars from Lehrs:

a) "Aus der Anfangzeit unseres Kreises." [From the beginnings of our Group] reports about the realization of the two Esoteric Lessons for the Youth Group in 1923. It is in this respect, in a certain way, a continuation of the Lehrs-report that ended with [the events of] October 16, 1922. This circular likewise is undated, but a comment in it shows that it was written in 1952 or somewhat later.

b) The circular already mentioned: "Beilage zum Entstehungsgeschichte des Kreises." [Supplement to the report of the origin of the Group], dated 1974.

3. A short memo from Lehrs for orientation of the Group. One copy bears the handwritten title "Definition des Kreises." [Definition of the Group]. According to tradition, this dates from 1963.

4. The report form Wilhelm Rath: "Mein Weg zum Kreis." [My way to the Group]. Private reproduction.

Regarding the report: According to the introductory remarks, Wilhelm Rath wrote his report in 1964 or shortly thereafter. It contains mainly personal memories, but not, like the Lehrs report, a private rendering of Rudolf Steiner's remarks at the various meetings. Wilhelm Rath refers to the Lehrs report, but not in detail.

5. Two collections of Rudolf Steiner's comments at the various meetings. The names of the writers are not known. It is probably a matter of notes taken at the meeting and notes made right after the discussions. Lehrs and Rath must have had these notes, as they both included them almost word-for-word in their reports. In this way their authenticity is to a certain extent confirmed by the eyewitnesses. (In one place in his report, Rath refers to this explicitly.)

6. The report by Herbert Hahn, "Notizen aus der Erinnerung (Zum 16. Oktober 1922)." [Notes from memory for October 16, 1922]. Its contents were told to C. Brumberg Hansen in Copenhagen, and he wrote them down immediately. Herbert Hahn signed the original and wrote the date August 12-14, 1963 on it. This is the document that was then photocopied.

7. Regarding the two Esoteric Lessons of July 13, 1923, in Stuttgart, and December 30, 1923, in Dornach:

The record of the *second* lesson is from a document signed by Maria Röschl. According to her notation, the text is put together out of her own notes made immediately afterwards, and out of those from several friends who quite especially remembered the composition.

For the record of the *first* lesson there is no signature or name given, but it may have been accomplished in a similar manner.

The slight differences in the texts that are circulating are certainly to be because of the frequent copying of the text by hand.

8. A notebook from Lili Kolisko, in which she wrote various verses and meditations. Among them were also those of the Youth Group.

Because Ernst Lehrs' report gives the clearest presentation, an excerpt of it is placed here at the beginning, even though it is not the oldest document in existence.

1. Rudolf Steiner's Presentations for the Founding of the Esoteric Youth Group

Excerpt from the report by Ernst Lehrs: "History of the Origin of the Youth Group"

Only the part of the following report is excerpted that has to do directly with Rudolf Steiner. The secondary title is from Ernst Lehrs. The parts that have been blocked or crossed out or underlined, and which did not change the meaning, have been omitted. Some of Lehrs' own commentary that was in brackets has been left out without giving any editorial markings. Other parts of the text that were omitted because they were not important have been indicated with ellipses (...). All comments or additions by the editor are enclosed in brackets. Also, the page numbers of the original document are enclosed in brackets for cross-referencing.

[Translator's note: some additions from the translator to better clarify the content are also enclosed in Brackets.]

Again, these records were given out of a more or less distant memory, and so some of the details may not be correct. One can see this from the few passages that can be compared and examined.

Editor of the German Edition

* * *

364 ❋ Esoteric Lessons

*Rudolf Steiner's Words from the Various Preparatory
Discussions for the Founding of the Group*

[p. 15] This presentation of the further events leading to the founding of the community is a compilation of Dr. Steiner's statements in reference to the question [concerning the forming of an esoteric community] that was sent to him ahead of time, beginning with the first meeting dedicated to handling this question. At this meeting, according to his instructions, first the question was expressed by each participant. The form in which these expressions are given here correspond to the notes of one or another friend who either took notes as Dr. Steiner spoke or who wrote them down later out of memory. Though they may be incomplete and not what he said word-for-word because of this, they do contain all the essentials and give a clear picture of the manner in which he led us through the preparatory work. With this [p. 16] guidance, he wanted to help us become as clear as possible in our active thinking about what we were striving for. Thereby also were stripped away many illusions we had about the coming times and the task we had to fulfill. It was a time of cares and pain—even after the settling of the argument with the others—yet also a time of joy and the good fortune of having been given a gift that we experienced through this.

At the first meeting that, according to Dr. Steiner's instruction took place with all the participants, he himself spoke very little. After a few of us tried to describe what we saw as the nature and task of a community for which we were striving, he said: "I would like to say up front that I would be very glad to hear from various sides how you imagine that your community, which is to come into being, is to be held together; how it shall work; and what unity will actually mean for you. Do not misunderstand me. Naturally, out of what is intended here can develop only what is well-grounded in the cause. However, it will be a matter of people from the various sides sharing what they imagine shall develop here, so that we can see to what extent a totally free personal will exists, and not merely an imagined free will. You can, of course, work together in the most varied ways in the sense of the general goals that are discussed here during our common campaign. However, several of you have more specific goals; or I will say that you intend to attain the common goal in a specific way. I must hear absolutely from the various sides what is wanted before it will be possible to frame objectively what you yourselves imagine that you want.

One can join such a cause only as a completely free human being. For this reason, I ask that you use this time to discuss everything in a frank, free, and unperturbed manner. At the same time, however, take into account what needs to be considered in order to come to a free decision. The rest I shall then say after everything has been discussed from the various sides."

As in the second meeting, the discussion came to a standstill—because a significant part of the assembly was in pronounced opposition or at least did not understand the issue at all—and Dr. Steiner said: "A number of you know quite energetically what you want. Another part does not yet know. A group is supposed to be formed. The scope and nature of the group is not yet determined. Those who want to do something in a specific sense—represented in Mr. Rath's statements (October 3, in the evening before Rudolf Steiner's first lecture)—want to form a group that contains a real spiritual substance within it, making it into a bearer of a spiritual reality. That gives the group an esoteric character, although I ask you not to misuse this word. People imagine all kinds of things with the term "esoteric group." I do not mean you, but others do. It is a matter of what one wants. What it is called does not matter much. If I am to go into what I understand with the term "esoteric group," then let me say that if you want to take the esoteric earnestly, you must say to yourself that it is an action out of impulses from the spiritual world. One can strive toward this. Anthroposophy is a path to this end. To build such a community would constitute a decision to set out upon this path. This would then lead to various measures which are suited to lead to this goal.

When you speak about spiritual content, you must be aware that it has to do with something living. The spiritual is a living element and so, such a group must not be something dead. In other words, the group must be a force-group. It then has the characteristic [p. 17] of being alive. Then there comes out all kinds of things that are analogous with an organism. The health of each part is the health of the whole. This is true also with illness. The little finger suffers when something in the small toe is not in order. If you want a real community, then you must want that the whole is just as influenced by the individual as the individual is by the whole. It is a mutual taking on of karma that is created in such a community. There is then mutual suffering to live through, but also mutual joys. (Rudolf Steiner stressed this strongly with a warm voice.)

Such a thing then requires that we not handle this as we usually do today with organizations. In those, one speaks of paragraph 1 or paragraph 2 of the program, and then all of the members are united under a program. People must be treated like human beings—and not like parts of a program-community or organization—like human beings, fellow human beings with all their imperfections. Therefore, it is a fundamental task that people are found who want to unite with the viewpoints that Mr. Rath, Mr. Lehrs, and Mr. Maikowski stated. When you have found such a group, it can then go its path esoterically. We will see, when the group really exists. We must first have the group, in order to be able to say whether or not it can follow an esoteric path. We do not yet have such a group; it will presumably present itself, however. This is the reason I said that there are those who know energetically what they want. An example is Mr. Lehrs, who expressed this in a letter to me. Not everyone has done this. You must attain this clarity; you must work toward this."

In order to characterize the nature of a real community, Dr. Steiner recalled in one of the beginning discussions, how Hermann Grimm[†] spoke of the friendship between Goethe and Schiller. If we wanted to express this friendship in a mathematical formula, we would not say, "G + S," but rather, "(G + S) + (S + G)." A true community is more than the mere sum of its members. To what two such people represent, there comes a new, third element in addition.[†]

The following also belongs with the first foundational words from Rudolf Steiner about the real nature of what we sought there.

"I will see to it that you receive a content for what you want. We will indeed come to build such a community. Let me yet today tell you the following as a piece of advice: It will be a matter [p. 18] of people of the most varied life paths coming together. The one will go this way; the other will go that way in life. Life will simply bring this with it. Very soon, life will become very, very complicated. We will have to frame this community in such a way that people with the most varied professions and ways of life can be included. What is involved is that each individual takes as concretely as possible the spirit that we seek through the community. That means that you understand the following.

What you seek is to find a friend in the spiritual world. To find such a friend is not actually difficult. The important thing is to remain spiritually true to the friend once found. (This was said with infinite warmth in his voice.).

Therefore, the first requirement of which I must speak to you (and I am always communicating requirements to you) is that you learn quite precisely what spiritual loyalty is. You must be capable of making a promise to yourself and remaining loyal to yourself. You will be able to receive all kinds of advice from me; yet that can only be half of what is necessary for what you are seeking. It will indeed be what you need as a foundation, but you will have to bring the other half yourself. For everything we want to attain in the spirit, loyalty to what we have set as intentions for ourselves in the spirit is necessary. What are the detriments today? People do not expect loyalty of themselves. This loyalty to a promise given to oneself or others is the firm staff in life.

The spirit that is full of life in Anthroposophy is not a doctrine. It is much more an actuality, a real being, that guides us through life. What you want is to find a community that has something of such a friendly guidance through life. We experience such things when we take the concrete spiritual as extended over the whole of life.

Your community will have in it something of the primordial mystery of all human community. This mystery is that, what we ourselves do within the community bears no fruit for us ourselves but for others, and that the fruits for us come from others."

Once during this conversation with all of us, he gave an example of what he understood—in the sense of the goal of our striving as we had expressed it—by "speaking concretely out of the spiritual." He had already spoken of this in general terms in one of his lectures. A youth, a friend who was an active farmer, had attempted in an earlier discussion to say something about Christ. It was more or less a helpless stammering, but in our effort to be positive, we thought we had to inwardly acknowledge his attempt. In addition, he told something about his work with agriculture, including his experience with manure. We found these comments to be a bit out of place, but did not speak of it. However, the next day, when some of us were with Dr. Steiner to discuss the progress of the meetings, he said suddenly: "What the young man said yesterday about Christ was quite insignificant. Yet, what he said about the manure was excellent. I would like to say something more about it myself in today's meeting." The following is an attempt to tell how he did that. It is to be noted that the Agriculture Course† had not yet occurred.

Dr. Steiner said: "What you said yesterday as a farmer was interesting. I do not have time to stay here for long, and therefore want to at least briefly say the following: We seek the spiritual also in agriculture. Also there it is believed that we must find new methods that reach as far as right into the way we handle matter. When you turn to modern materialistic science, you do not find [p. 19] much love for agriculture. Modern science believes that when we need a certain amount of nitrogen in the soil, we must add it, in that amount, to the soil. They do not know that one only has to plant sainfoin† around the field in order for the soil to receive the necessary nitrogen through what radiates out from this plant. It is already enough to plant a single row of sainfoin around the field." One courageous fellow among us, who did not know this plant, asked what this plant is. Dr. Steiner answered immediately, and indeed in such a way that we experienced that he did not speak about the plant as if it were not present. Through the intimate tone of his voice and the inwardness, the thoughtfulness, of his bearing, the direct spiritual presence of what he was describing could be experienced. The sainfoin came into being, as it were, through his words and gestures. One must try to feel this between the words that follow. "Sainfoin—they are plants—that have flower stands—butterfly blossoms—they are lilac-colored—they have pinnate petals—." And now continuing to speak about the plant made present to us, he said: "This plant has the peculiar power to penetrate wide areas of soil with what people want to add to it as artificially as possible. Do you think that (the effect of sainfoin) is absurd? No! These are things, of course, that one understands when one is able to press forward with spiritual insight."

* * *

The following are notes out of the discussions in the meetings that took place after the separation from those opposed. The discussions took place first in a wider compass, and then, later, with only those who participated in the founding of the group. Dr. Steiner designed the meetings to a certain extent like a seminar, in that he asked us questions that we were to answer either immediately or the next day. One of the first questions was what we imagine the task of the future Youth Movement to be. Among others, a young friend who had belonged to a Zionist Youth Movement for a while spoke about her experience and what she had learned there. Dr. Steiner listened with visible interest, but then said: "It would be good if you would mention in your talking something of the positive task you want to set for yourself. There flows in the Youth Movement something of a certain vagueness. It is characteristic that most who speak out of the Youth Movement do not speak decidedly, but out of a certain feeling. Yet out of feeling, too, one can specify many things with certainty. It would be good if such concrete, positive feelings were to come to expression at this time. You have characterized well the two Movements you have been involved with (Zionism and the Wandervogel). In the Zionist Movement there exists a certain yearning for the renewing of Judaism. However, so that this community does not get itself into something vague but rather into something clearly determined, it would be good to outline what you have imagined. Thus, for example, it will be good if you would talk about what you sought originally in the Youth Movement. It is not that I am looking for the information; it is so that you have to say to yourself: I sought this and that specific element in the Youth Movement. Such things do indeed grow out of the unspecific, and yet you can attempt to characterize more exactly what you are striving for."

Then something was said about the contrast between the older and younger generations—how one experiences the older generation—and at the same time, the significance of Nietzsche and Spitteler[†] for the opposition by the younger generation was mentioned. Dr. Steiner then spoke again: [p. 20] "You see, does this not tell us something which, according to its own nature, can only be a transition? For is it not true that we cannot avoid growing older? It is therefore a question of whether we may continue striving for something that belonged to a particular time and which is already completed, when we are actually moving forward. When you take the characteristic that you have just given, we see that it belongs to a particular time and was finished within that time. The objection that the next generation will have it easier is not valid. They will have it easier in part, if those who are growing older look back at their own youth, and then do not behave toward their children the way the older generation did. On the other hand, you may not forget that you have the opposition you faced to thank for the enthusiasm, the great inspiration that you had. These existed in you as fire. The next generation will not be able to have precisely this fire, if you make it easier for them. For this reason, difficulties will soon arise that must be compensated for by something you have been able to get from the forces of opposition.

Life goes forward and creates ever new conditions. It is always good when a generation, namely the one at the beginning of this (twentieth) century, has attained something through fighting for it—which has its inner character through a purely inner foundation. It is so that, with the end of the nineteenth century, totally new conditions emerged. The children who were born in 1897, 1898, and 1899 were born under totally different cosmic conditions from those born earlier. Actually, the modern opposition-mood can be traced to this. There has always been a contrast between the younger and older generations, but not these special opposition spirits. Precisely this led to seeing great difficulties for the coming generations. They are in danger of becoming unstable, of having no inner core. I wish to hear what thoughts you have about how the next generation can receive an inner core. The next generation will no longer want to know anything of Nietzsche or Spitteler. When you think back to how you were with the Youth Movement, and how you found something in the mysticism of Baal Schem,† you will have to admit that the next generation will not be able to be inspired the way you were. This is the difficulty that stands before us now.

How can we picture the next generation? We must work for the progress of humanity. For this reason, I would like for you to speak about the positive aspects. For this, it is not necessary to think up all-encompassing ideals or to say something all-comprehensive. Rather, it depends often on seemingly small, insignificant things that are in reality of great significance."

(Rudolf Steiner discussed the same thing then in the sixth lecture,† in which at the end, he said that the Youth Movement must have a Janus head. It must look not only at the responsibility and demands it has in relation to the older generation, but also at the undetermined demands "that are storming toward us with a mighty power and that the youth will put to us.")

When we came to speak in this sense, Dr. Steiner said: "Among the many criticisms leveled against the Waldorf school is that some children cannot yet read and write perfectly at nine years of age. There is nothing to say against this. They really cannot. However, we ourselves do not have the view that eight or nine-year-olds should be skilled readers or writers. This is because those who know the nature of the human being completely see that this skill that is being developed in the modern elementary school makes the human being half-way into a thinking-automaton. Instead of giving the children letters to copy, we let them putter about with color. Through the fact that they learn to feel or sense something through this, they retain the life of their soul, whereas otherwise it dies.."

[p. 21] Being asked to speak about the tasks of the Youth Movement made us aware, for the first time, of how difficult it was to arrive at real concepts of what we ourselves wanted. In relation to the strong youthful tendency that reigned among us of remaining with mere feelings, Dr. Steiner made the demand that always seems so un-youthful: "Formulate what you want in more exact terms!"

In this sense, Steiner gave one of us the task to think about and then present concrete ideas about the goals of the striving of the Anthroposophical Youth, with regard to a transformation of the present-reigning relationships among people in the outer social life. This friend worried and wrestled in search of the answer that he was to give the next day. He sought help from us in vain. At our next meeting, he looked fairly disheartened. He felt a hint could be given through a comparison between the other offices and a friendly reception given at the Anthroposophical initiative that existed at that time: Der Kommende Tag [The coming day]. Thus, he brought this with the remark that we should set ourselves the social goal that such friendly faces would be found in all the offices in the world. Dr. Steiner listened to this with an unconcealed little smile and said with a smile: "Now, not taking into account whether the example is really totally correct," (Anyone who was aware of the inner life of Der Kommende Tag knew what great human difficulties were to be dealt with there), and then Steiner became suddenly quite earnest and continued, "what matters is really something completely different. The social life up to this point has been like a mechanism, and nothing is accomplished when the levers and cranks of the existing mechanism is put into motion with somewhat smiling faces. Rather, it is important that this mechanism be replaced with an organism." And with an urgent tone he continued: "You must be clear that what you will want can be nothing more than the growing of a delicate, little plant. Imagine what is dead in modern social life as great stones, and imagine the little plant among the stones. What is dead has a much more tenacious hold in life than something living, because it cannot die. At most it can be ground or crushed. (With emphasis)—And the stones *will* be ground or crushed. However, you must take care that the delicate, little plant is not ground up along with the stones.

In the midst of the ever-repeated signs of being dissatisfied, he could immediately show his enthusiasm and affirmation, when the occasion for it arose. Once one of us said, in the view of the description Dr. Steiner had given during the course of the instability of the future youth due to a lack of opposition, that spiritual content must be brought to the souls of the young people, because through this there would arise new riddles which can ignite impulses and strength to penetrate further to the spiritual. Steiner showed special joy as the following was expressed: just as the physical social life consists of deeds done together, so too we strive for common deeds in the spirit—thus actually, for a social working in the suprasensible. Immediately Steiner wanted to know what we imagine or think spiritually with the concepts "deeds," and especially with the concept "common." When we quite timidly answered that such common deeds could perhaps arise through meditating spiritual contents in common, he showed his satisfaction openly.

In this way, we found ourselves—later, this would happen often—confirmed in our view of meditation, which we did not want to see as a method of private, self-perfection, but as a deed that works into a objective spiritual sphere.

* * *

[p. 22] The following are statements of Dr. Steiner's, according to the notes of the individual friends who could no longer remember to which conversation they belong:

"The souls of modern human beings come, as a result of the general development of the being of the human, to the boundary between intellect and the spirit. It is for people as it is for the fish. When it comes to the surface of the water, jumps out of the water, and feels the air, it reacts to this with the impulse to dive back down especially deep into the water. Thus, you will see in the coming time that people will have the urge, when they accidentally come against the boundary of the intellect, to dive down quite deeply into the intellect. In the face of this, it will be your task to penetrate through the intellect to the supra-intellect (over-intellect), through the clarity to the supra-clarity (over-clarity)."

*

"On the path you have resolved to go, you will become more sensitive to the ahrimanic effect in the world. And there you will have to be careful that you do not succumb to the temptation to escape this experience through the same method you used in attaining this sensitivity." (We understand this to mean that we should not retreat into a meditative life like a protective haven in order to escape.)

*

To the question from one of us about where the ahrimanic forces assert themselves most strongly, Dr. Steiner answered: "As far as I have been able to see, it is the case in the cinema and with the typewriter. It is not that there are no other machines, with respect to their construction, that are more ahrimanic. However, as regards the effect on the human being, it is as I have said."

*

At one occasion, he said to us with great urgency: "Become seekers of human beings!" (We felt this to be a time-appropriate metamorphosis of the words Christ spoke to the disciples: "Become fishers of men." In the age of the freedom of the individuality, "fishers" become "seekers.")

*

The comprehensive nature of what we were striving for (for humanity) came to expression in connection with the discussion about the Zionist Youth Movement: "You do not want to found something as small as is the case in Zionism."

*

We were reminded strongly of the strivings of the friends of God through the following explanation: "There are two parallel streams of history or evolution flowing.† The one is visible, apparent; and the other is un-revealed, unseen. Generally, people know only the first one. Yet, behind it there runs the other hidden stream. This stream is the actual one that brings things about. It must never dry up or fail. And to assure this, groups of human beings must come together from time to time and work further in this stream, forming it further. It is in this stream that you want to place yourself through your community."

*

"When people come and ask a spiritual researcher for a common meditation content, and when their really earnest will leads them to this, then a greater force can arise in order to accomplish something in the world than is the case with an oh-so-powerful statesman."

*

"It appears at present that much goes smoothly because it is done by a machine. However, the machine is beyond our heads. It becomes an ever-more gigantic force that works of itself, and which human beings can no longer stop with their existing forces. We can only be a match for this power of the machine through a striving that endeavors to carry spirit into the furthest consequences of our actions. This alone—that we bring spirit and love into our will—will make it possible to stand firmly against being overrun by the cultural machine. Too few people today develop real initiative. There is a lot of wishfulness, but little will."

*

"One must differentiate between prayer and meditation. The ordinary prayer serves today mostly as a satisfying of one's own self. The true meditation, however, is a fulfilling of the spiritual will that the time spirit bears within itself. Where such meditation is practiced, a spiritual force is able to work into the earthly events. Spiritual worlds want to work into earthly events today, but they can do this only when, through human meditation, space is created for it. Through meditation, something like an empty space comes about. Into this space, the spiritual beings can enter with their effects."

*

"Even though much is destroyed physically, even though outwardly little appears to be attained, what is created spiritually remains. It retains its value for the future."

*

"Now a time has come in which materialism has hardened the bodies so much that the individuality cannot incarnate enough. Many people go around today in such a way that they have a part of their being beside them like a companion. This part, this companion, cannot reside in the body. It remains hidden behind the sense world. It is necessary to penetrate through to this part, and meditation is a method for doing this."

* * *

Last Phase of the Preparation

After a few meetings, the smaller group came one day—Wednesday, October 11—to Dr. Steiner. He let us know that he did not have time for conversation. Seen outwardly, the reason was the extraordinary, many-sided demands on his time. We ourselves found, however, that we had to see in this a spiritual sign that something decisive was expected of us, and that we had to come to this out of ourselves.

[....]

In looking back at the coming about of the course and the gradual arising of the idea for the new community that we now took on, our thoughts had to stop at one thing. This was the anchoring that we were striving for of our community in the spiritual world: our striving, through this, to serve Michael, the guiding spirit of our time.

[...]. [p 24] [...].

In our distress, we turned to Marie Steiner after a Creative Speech class.† Without giving concretely the name before our mind's eye (Michael), we explained our situation briefly. Without hesitation, she made a corresponding movement over her head and said: "Yes, yes, the Doctor wants indeed to hear something from you about him." We had the immediate impression that she was informed by Dr. Steiner, out of foresight of our wrestling and the expectation that we would turn to her.

Immediately we came back together and discussed excitedly in what way each of us, when Dr. Steiner would call us back together again, could try to satisfy his expectation. It was now clear that one of us would have to speak about our will toward Michael. Because Wilhelm Rath was the one who, during the time of preparation for the course, was the first to speak this name in the sense of the orientation of our spiritual striving, we were all agreed that he should express this to Rudolf Steiner on our behalf. Rath took this on with the deepest earnestness.

As we left the room where we had discussed this, Rudolf Steiner passed by us. We asked him timidly about the possibility of a next meeting. Without hesitation, he scheduled it for the next day.

Thursday, October 12, 1922

Dr. Steiner began immediately with the question: "Now, what do you still have to say to me?" We each tried to say something about the spiritually essential side of our goals, whereupon Rath spoke the name Michael at the end. The following is some of the exchange that took place at that time.

One said that he thought that we must learn to speak just as spiritually about tables and chairs as we speak about the hierarchies. All of us were convinced that, with that, for once something was said with which Rudolf Steiner would agree. Instead, he smiled and shook his head, saying: "No, you should set yourself the task rather to speak as naturally about the hierarchies as you do otherwise about tables and chairs." He then gave a highly surprising example. He said we should become able to know and then, out of such insight, be able to say that Ibsen wrote out of an inspiration of the Archangel Gabriel, who had become luciferic. And he added that we may not understand this to mean that Gabriel himself is a luciferic being. However, Gabriel was taken hold of by the impulse to extend his influence beyond the time that was available for his reign. His age was to end in 1879, but he did not want to give up his reign over culture.

Thus, there came about such a drama as Ibsen's *Gespenster* [Ghosts] that is based on the idea of heredity. [p. 25] To keep something in effect in this manner beyond the time allotted to it is always luciferic. Thus, Gabriel was taken hold of by a luciferic impulse. And Dr. Steiner added: "Out of the un-rightful continuation of Gabriel, cultural deformities arise. These deformities then bring it about that in a mystical manner, wishes of a merely intellectual nature seek their way into the suprasensible."

The friend who had—as mentioned earlier in this report—participated in one of the Priest Courses, connected his comments with what Dr. Steiner said about the being of Anthroposophy. He thought that in order for this being to be effective on Earth, a body would have to be prepared for it. May we possibly think that our requested community should become an organ of this body? Dr. Steiner agreed fundamentally with this, yet he said that is not a matter of an incarnation of this being but rather of an incorporation. "In the Earth existence, this being can come only as far as incorporation. An incarnation of this being will be possible only in circumstances other than the earthly ones."

[Here a passage about the living together of the European peoples was left out. In the form given, it was certain that it was not authentic.]

About the comment of one of the friends that we were striving for guidance or leadership in common with one another, Steiner said: "Yes, you want to become a conscious group soul."

After each of us had spoken about what we thought he wanted to hear from us, it was Rath's turn. With almost quivering lips, he spoke the decisive words by saying that we wanted to place ourselves with this community under the leadership of *Michael*. All that came from Dr. Steiner after that was that he looked at his watch and said: "I must, unfortunately, leave you today, because I have another commitment. However, we will meet together again tomorrow evening. Then you will receive from me what you have requested of me."

Friday, October 13, 1922

We gathered at the appropriate time in the room made available to us and waited for Dr. Steiner in a festive, expectant mood. He entered the room, together with Frau Dr. Steiner, with a noticeably earnest bearing. He held in his hand a violet leather-bound [linen] book, out of which he later read the meditations and let them be copied. Upon entering the room, he paused a moment in the doorway and counted us as he pointed a finger at each of us [p. 26]. Thereby, we ourselves became aware for the first time that there were twelve of us.

He went to the table prepared for him and sat down, asking us to sit down likewise. Then he opened the book and said with a deep, calm voice: "I have the task of communicating the following to you." He read the words, having instructed one of us to write them down.[†] Afterward, he gave instructions for the practice of the exercises in general and for specific passages of the meditations given to us. These are in a separate part that is added to this report.[†] Finally, he gave indications about the nature and significance of such a community.

He spoke about the effect that meditating such a meditation in common has. "Assume that there were ten of you, and each of you were to summon up in your meditation the power of 'two'. Then the total effect is not 2×10, but 2^{10}. In other words, the increase in the power does not happen by multiplication, but by potentization."

Of our behavior toward each other as members of the group he said: "You will each come to have different cultural tasks. Not all of your work will be toward the outside in the same degree. Some will stand further in the foreground, while others are more in the background, according to destiny and talent. Each of you must feel joy for the success of the other. You must avoid every feeling of rivalry and have the awareness that what each of you accomplishes, you accomplish through the power of all of the others.

"Uniting yourself through a mutual promise to strive toward a common spiritual goal—and leaving one another completely free in actions and judgments in life—such a community based on this is something completely new in the evolution of humanity. And it is what is most necessary today."

"For someone who comes to specific results on the esoteric path, there always exists the danger of delusions of grandeur. Such a community as yours can be a protection against this. For in it, you strive together to cross the threshold of the spiritual world. And there each of you has to say that you have the efforts of all the others to thank for what you have achieved personally."

In connection with this, Dr. Steiner gave a corresponding instance in the Catholic Church. Once in the circle of priests, the thought arose that the individual priest, through his word, could summon Christ into the tabernacle; in other words, Christ obeys the word of the priest. As the bishop of the diocese in question noticed that this thought began to bring confusion, he wrote a pastoral letter[†] to explain that the individual priest has this power only as a member of the whole cleric body of the Church. The spirit of the Church is Christ, and he is also the spirit of the whole cleric body. In truth, in the sacred act Christ summons himself through the individual priest.

Concerning how to fit the meditative life into the outer, daily life, he said: "Now you must divide your life into two parts!" (He stressed this sharply.) "In the one part your exercises take place, and the other part is your outer life. In the first part you draw in the spirit; then in the second, the spirit will flow of itself into life. For this, however, it is necessary that you enter into the outer life completely."

[p. 27] As the last thing in this meeting, he came back to the necessity of persevering with the exercises once they have been undertaken. He described the significance of the deeds that we are able to perform through such conduct. "On the physical field, the ahrimanic power is so strong today that not one single human 'I' is equal to it. For this reason, no human 'I' today can guarantee that it can really fulfill its resolve, so far as it concerns a physical deed. Ahriman, however, has no access to the realm in which you now have resolved to execute deeds. Therefore, the fulfillment of these deeds depends on you yourselves. For this reason, you have here the first opportunity to execute deeds in freedom and consequently, the first opportunity to practice loyalty."

Again, as in the first meeting with him, the word "loyalty" was spoken with special warmth. With this, a detour was made back to the other indication of the necessary loyalty and devotion to the friend found in the spiritual world.

Here it should be added that before Dr. Steiner read the meditations, he gave an introduction, but no one could recall it in detail.

Only one individual thought to have remembered clearly that during this introduction Dr. Steiner spoke, at intervals, the Rosicrucian mantras as if out of primeval depths.

In closing, Dr. Steiner said he wanted to give us yet, in the next few days, something through which we would be able to expand our group in the future. "We will form your community according your heart's desire." He departed from us for this time by warmly giving us his hand, and Frau Dr. Steiner, who left with him, did the same. In his last words, we experienced the answer to what we had noticed in the course of the preparatory conversations. This was that we had thought the significance and meaning of the community we were seeking would have to come to expression through the act of its founding and through the form of membership.

For this founding, we were summoned quite early on Monday, October 16, before Rudolf Steiner's departure for Dornach.

Before the founding is described, an incident that took place in the meantime must be reported, because this caused Dr. Steiner to begin the foundation in a specific way and to indicate an incumbent task for the whole of the Anthroposophical Movement.

Encounter with the New Movement for Religious Renewal

[pp. 27/28] Here is reported that a few of those founding the Youth Group had the intention—with the agreement of Dr. Rittelmeyer and Dr. Steiner—to participate in the first Act of Consecration of Man, at which others in addition to just priests could be present, on Sunday, October 15. This was the preparation by the inner circle of priests for the first public celebration of the Act of Consecration of Man, which would be held on the first of Advent in the Communities. In the conversation beforehand, in which the details of the service were made known, Lic. Emil Bock called for all the participants, through their participation in the service, to commit themselves to building up The Christian Community. As a result of this, the [Youth] Group founders withdrew from their intention to participate.

Founding of the [Youth] Group, Monday, October 16, 1922

[p. 28] Because of Dr. Steiner's early-scheduled departure [for Dornach], the gathering took place at 7:00 a.m. We waited for him on the landing of the staircase outside the room to which we were called. He met us there and asked with the interested anticipation before entering the room, if we had participated in the Act of Consecration of Man the day before. We told him we had not, because of a difficulty that came from the side of the priests. About this, he stressed several times that he would not have had anything against our participating. "Come in. We want to discuss this right now. You must tell me what stood in your way."

Thus, the meeting that was dedicated to the festive founding of the Group began with our report of what we experienced that evening and the decision imposed upon us. This was followed by Dr. Steiner's presentation of his relationship to The Christian Community and, in comparison, his position in the Anthroposophical Movement. He made it clear that he had a thoroughly different opinion and judgment about the condition for participation in the ritual than what had been brought there. However, The Christian Community was founded in such a way that it is the decision of the priests that counts and not his. He himself was not responsible for decisions in the life of that Movement. He did not found The Christian Community, nor was he responsible to be its leader. Subtle differences of concepts are necessary in order to see his relationship to it correctly. He had only *demonstrated* the ritual for the priests; he himself had never *celebrated* the ritual. It was celebrated the first time by Dr. Rittelmeyer. It is different with his relationship to the Anthroposophical Movement. There he is responsible for seeing that correct judgments and decisions reign in it. "The following is, however, often the case: All in this [p. 29] Movement proceeded out of clear impulses, but often these are then later—and sometimes precisely with the best of intentions of the members—brought into unclarity. A group such as yours should help to keep the original impulses clear; or where they have become unclear, to lead them back to clarity."

Then he went on to something else. We remember that he took the opportunity to speak of H. P. Blavatsky, in connection with a description of the esoteric Movement (Theosophical Movement) of recent years that preceded Anthroposophy. No one can remember the details of this, except that Rudolf Steiner spoke of this personality as a "world-historical" medium.

Next, he explained some things about being in the world as members of our community or group. From now on, it will be for every human group in the outer world—thus, for instance, for students in a teachers' training institute, at which one of us studies—of karmic significance that at one time a member of this Group was a part of it. Also, effects would arise in the destiny between us and human beings who are connected with us physically or physical-spiritually. These effects would be of a good or bad nature, according to whether we were good or bad in our affairs. Yet, he warned us that this is not so easy to judge. For that, we would need a capacity that one can better express in the English language: esoteric discernment.

He said in view of future growth: "Consider yourselves as the root of the Group." About the accepting of future members, he said only that we should not take anyone who is younger than twenty-one years old. They are minors legally, and you could have a conflict with parents and because of that, with the law. The Group must at all costs, however, avoid any contact with the public officials. Further, he advised us not to take, when possible, a married woman whose husband is not joining, or with whom you must expect that he will not find a relationship with or access to the Group.

Dr. Steiner closed this part of the conversation when, with a noticeable change of his bearing, he said that he now wanted to give us a formulation of an oath.† Through the reading of this oath in the presence of the others, the admittance into the community would be effected. Thus, we were first to accept one another mutually through each of us reading the oath aloud to the others. From then on, the oath should serve to expand the Group through our own responsibility. He asked that someone write down what he then dictated freely by speaking the oath word-for-word, as if bringing it out of the spiritual world in the moment. All the while, he held his gaze meditatively before him. Then he paused briefly, laid his hands and arms quietly in front of him, and said with deep earnestness in a voice in which cosmic firmness and humble quiet appeared to be paired: "And now consider your community as having been founded by the spiritual world itself." At that, he got up, and we did also. He then came to each one of us, stood quietly before each, took our right hand in both of his, and looked us briefly in the eyes with a gaze that cannot be described in words. Perhaps we may say, thinking of a term used later in one of his Rosicrucian lectures,[†] of January 1924, that his was a star-gaze. Here we were allowed to look into eyes from which no personal gaze proceeded, but rather through which starry worlds looked and rayed forth.

[p. 30] Before he left he asked us to please report it to him, should anyone decide in the end not to join to Group. This surprised us, because we all thought such a thing unimaginable. Later, looking back at emerging difficulties led us to understand his precaution. At that time, however, no one made use of this available freedom. Nonetheless, it told us that in the future we should give those seeking admittance the opportunity for a last examination of their decision, after they have come to know what is involved with our Group.

It was important to us that we had, from the very beginning in our thoughts of such a group, no mutual soul-sympathy. Thus, we believed that also for the future, we should not strive to become closer to one another in this part of our being. How surprised we were when Dr. Steiner turned back to us as he was leaving and said warmly: "And now get to know one another well!" This gave us the idea to tell each other our biography that same evening at our mutual acceptance into membership. This then became a permanent practice with admittance to membership.

During the rest of the time before his departure, Dr. Steiner allowed us to ask him any kind of questions of more or less personal nature. One person asked for advice about his studies and received the topic for a doctoral dissertation. Another received pointers for his historical research. Yet another was given medical instructions for an ailment plaguing him. Among these questions was one that, because of its general significance, is communicated here.

The question was about Dr. Steiner's position in relation to both the School that was a kind of Esoteric Section† that existed in the Society until 1914 and to what has been newly formed here. About this he said: "As I began teaching, I had to connect my work with the thread of the old tradition. What came thusly into being had to be broken off due to outer circumstances.† What has taken place now is a first in the post-Christian age; human beings themselves chose, out of freedom before the spiritual world, to join together esoterically."

Here is added something that we experienced later. As at the end of World War I, some of the older Esoteric School members asked Dr. Steiner about the possibility of taking up what had been interrupted by the beginning of the war, he said that the old could no longer be taken up. Though, it could come to a new esoteric form within the Society. However, that would depend first upon people coming to him out of freedom and asking for an esotericism in common with one another. Such could only happen in central Europe, and from those belonging to the younger generation. He would have to wait for this.† We then understood his so surprisingly positive demeanor as Rath spoke the question in the committee discussion before the first lecture of the course.

As Rudolf Steiner finally left the room in order to travel to Dornach with the car that was already waiting for him, he turned several times at the door and waved warmly with both hands.

[End of the report by Ernst Lehrs]

2. Notes from Rudolf Steiner's Comments at Two Meetings with All Participants of the Pedagogical Youth Course†

According to a photocopy in the Rudolf Steiner Archive, the typed original document from which the photocopy was made bears the stamp, "Anthroposophische Vereeniging, Archief," [Anthroposophical Association, archive] and at the top right was the name of Daniel van Bemmelen. He was most likely the owner of the document and not its author. Minor corrections in the text were probably made by van Bemmelen.

It is probably an edited copy of notes taken by individual participants, either during or immediately after the discussions. Ernst Lehrs and Wilhelm Rath must have had access to this text as they wrote their reports, because they used it almost word for word. The places that had no meaning, which arose through being copied down, were corrected according to Lehrs' report and are marked with brackets.

Editor of the German Edition

Discussion on October 6, 1922
Pedagogical Course, October 2-15, 1922

Dr. Steiner: "I would like to say up front that I would be very glad to hear from various sides how you imagine that your community, which is to come into being, is to be held together; how it will work; and what unity will actually mean for you. Do not misunderstand me. Naturally, out of what is intended here can develop only what is well-grounded in the cause. However, it will be a matter of people from the various sides saying what they imagine shall develop here, so that we can see how much of a totally free personal will exists, and not merely an imagined free will. You can, of course, work together in the most varied ways in the sense of the general goals that are discussed here during our common campaign. However, you have, in addition, yet more specific goals; or I will say that you intend to attain the goals in a specific way. I must hear absolutely from various sides what is wanted before it will be possible to frame these things objectively. It is not what you yourselves imagine that you want. One can join such a cause only as a completely free human being. For this reason, I ask that you use this time to discuss everything in a frank, free, and unperturbed manner. At the same time, however, take into account what needs to be considered in order to come to a free decision. The rest I shall then say when everything has been discussed from the various sides."

Dr. Steiner: "It would be good if you would mention in your talking something of the positive task you have set for yourself. There flows in the Youth Movement something of a certain vagueness. It is characteristic that most who speak of the Youth Movement do not speak decidedly, but out of a certain feeling. Yet, out of feeling, too, one can specify many things with certainty. It would be good if, at this moment, such concrete, positive feelings came to expression. You have characterized well the two Movements you have been involved with (Zionism and the Wandervogel). In the Zionist Movement there is a certain yearning for the renewing of Judaism. However, so that this community here does not get itself into something vague, but rather into something clearly determined, it would be good if you would really try to rewrite what you have imagined. Thus, for example, if you would talk about what you actually sought originally in the Youth Movement. It is not that I am looking for the information; it is so that you have to say to yourself: I sought this and that specific element in the Youth Movement. Such things grow out of the unspecific, yet you can attempt to characterize some of what you were striving for."

Miss Spira: [No text]

Dr. Steiner: "You see, does that not tell us something that, according to its own nature, can only be a transition? For is it not true that we cannot avoid growing older? Now it is a question of whether we may remain with striving—it should be put as a question—for a thing that belongs to a particular time and is finished, when we ourselves are actually moving forward in time simply due to the natural course of things. When you take the characteristic that you have just given, it belongs to a particular time and was finished within that time. The objection that the next generation will have it easier is not valid. They will in part have it easier, if those who are growing older look at their own youth, and then do not behave toward their children the way the earlier elders did. But you may not forget that you have the opposition you faced to thank for the enthusiasm, the great inspiration, you have had. And this existed as fire in you. The next generation will not be able to have this fire; they will then be unable to have it precisely if you make it easier for them. Thus, for the next years new difficulties must arise, difficulties [that must be compensated for by something you have been able to get from the forces of opposition].

Yet, life goes forward and creates new conditions. And whoever can observe in life must say: it is a good thing that a new generation from the beginning of this century once achieved something. I can also quite honestly say what they accomplished. It had the right characteristic for an inner reason. With the end of the nineteenth century, new conditions emerged within human soul development. The children who were born from 1897-1899 were born under cosmically different conditions than those born earlier. It is from this that the mood of opposition first began. There has always existed a contrast between the younger and older generations, but these specific spirits of opposition did not always exist. This led to the anticipation of great difficulties coming soon and with the next generation. The next generation will face the great danger, in spite of everything, of becoming unstable, of not receiving an inner core. I would like to know if you are thinking about how the next generation can receive an inner core. You had an inner core, because without it, you would never have come to the opposition mood. The next generation will no longer know about Nietzsche or Spitteler. And when you think back to how you were with the Youth Movement and found something in the mysticism of Baal Shem,† you will have to say to yourself: the next generation will not be able to be inspired in such a way as you were. So, the difficulty now is: what picture can we make of the next generation?

We must work for the progress of humanity, and for that reason, I want you to say something about the positive aspects. This does not depend on making comprehensive statements or forming all-encompassing ideals. It depends rather on seemingly small, insignificant things that are in reality of great significance. Among the many criticisms leveled against the Waldorf School is that the children cannot yet read and write at the age of nine years. There is no objection to be made to this. They can...."

[The heading for the second meeting was written incorrectly and was corrected by hand, probably by van Bemmelen.]

8. X. 22 [October 8, 1922]

"A number of people know quite energetically what they want. Another part does not yet know. A group is to be formed. However, what the group is to encompass is not yet decided. Those individuals who want something energetically in a certain way—that lay in Mr. Rath's explanation—want to form a group that bears within it a spiritually essential substance that makes the group a carrier of a spiritual essence. This gives the group an esoteric character, although I would ask you not to misuse these things—as word. People imagine all kinds of things by the term 'esoteric group.' I do not mean you, but others. It is a matter of what you want. What name is chosen is insignificant. When I myself want to, or should, go into the esoteric, I must say that what matters is [to take the esoteric earnestly]. For when the esoteric is taken seriously, it is an acting or doing according to concrete impulses out of the spiritual world. One can strive to do this. Anthroposophy is a path for this. To build such a community would constitute the resolve to enter upon this path. This would result in various measures suited to lead to this goal. When you speak of spiritual content, you must be aware that it is a matter of something living. The spiritual must be a living essence, and the group cannot be dead; in other words, it must be a force-group. It then has the characteristic of being a living entity. You can set as a requirement everything that has already been said by various people here and by me. Yet, you must be clear about the fact that out of the common body, come common pains and common connections of destiny. All kinds of things occur for which, in a certain sense, an analogy would be that of an organism, in which when the finger suffers, the brain feels something of it. This requires that you do not proceed in the way other Societies tend to do where one says: paragraph 1, paragraph 2 of the program or the plan—and then all the differences are united under the plan. Human beings must take themselves as human beings and not as members of a program-society. They must be able to exist as fellow human beings with all their imperfections. For that reason, it is a quite fundamental task for you to form the group in such a way that you are clear about how the people who are united with the viewpoint laid out by Mr. Rath, Mr. Lehrs, and Mr. Maikowski come together. This group can then proceed to work esoterically. That will become clear when the group is formed. You must first have the group, in order to determine whether it can follow an esoteric path. You do not yet have the group. It will present itself, though. It is for this reason that I think there are or those who know energetically what they want, but have not yet expressed it. You must achieve this clarity before you are done with the preparations. You must work toward this. Perhaps you will come first and foremost to such things when you connect with the starting point." [Lehrs pp. 16f]

[In the report by Wilhelm Rath, he says: "... and Dr. Steiner turned to me with the request, for the purpose of better clarity, that I connect with the starting point." These words by Rudolf Steiner were written down at that time:].

"It is perhaps quite easy to connect with the starting point that you have touched upon. You pointed out an acquaintance with the Bundes für freies Geistesleben [Association for independent spiritual life]† and have said of it that what you want cannot be done in the same way. It is quite surely true that the Association for Independent Spiritual Life was also founded out of the premise to realize something similar [to what you are wanting], even though in a different way. And now, without my judging anything about the Association for Independent Spiritual Life, it would be good for the sake of reaching inner clarity, if you would elaborate further about your concern with the Association. It would be of interest to hear what instantly repelled you. Then one would see what crystallizes out of it as will. It would quite certainly be something interesting and stimulating for everyone.

From the manner [of your presentation], one would perhaps be able to know a lot. You do not have to think that you need to go easy on the Association for Free Spiritual Life just because I am here."

[Then the report from Rath relates further: "I described how at that time the style of this appeal (from the Association) estranged us young people in Berlin. We found it to be like 'advertising.' Anthroposophy could not be spread in the world in this manner. A spiritual substance was missing. A truly free spiritual life must be founded in the spirit, and an association that wanted to proclaim it to the world would itself have to stand together in a brotherly attitude, and not be united by an organizational, but rather by a spiritual bond. This awakened in us the idea of a living, spiritually united association like we found presented exemplarily in the writings of the Friend of God from Oberland; it is just that such an association would now have to be formed according to the demands of the present time. This spiritual background was not clearly recognizable in the appeal (of the Association)." To this Dr. Steiner said the following:].

"That is just what must be determined from the very beginning: a certain clarity about the matter. Perhaps I may bring out one thing that you said about spreading the word. Something totally different was behind this than the impression it made upon you. What was behind it is as follows. Let us take it completely objectively. Take my *Outline of Esoteric Science*, which is not exactly a conversational content. That book has reached so many souls in such a short time that one would have to say that a great deal of people know the content of this book." (At that time it was in its twelfth printing; thus 12,000 copies had been printed,[†] and that means four to five times that many people had read it. From experience, it is probably a much higher number.) "We must say: The number of people who have a desire for what they can experience through Anthroposophy is very large. Large groups of souls desire it to be such that the passive yearning for Anthroposophy imposes a duty upon one to do something, so that Anthroposophy can be effective on Earth. And the number of people entering actively into the service of a cause for which there is such a great yearning has never been so small as with Anthroposophy. When you look at any impulse arising in humanity, you will find, as a rule, that only small groups have the desire to spread the word about it. With Anthroposophy, it is true that it sits in many souls, but in order for these people to gain access to this content, there have to be enough people working actively to help this happen. This would already justify the way the Association for Independent Spiritual Life strives to bring activity into the passivity. One can say that such a thing must be. You will no longer find this to be like advertising.

"However, you will also see how terribly difficult it is to express yourself clearly. Through the way they spoke, what they said took on the form you characterized. The lack of clarity in its representation, whether in internal instances or more toward the outside, has created great hindrances for Anthroposophy. Clarity is required. You understand what I mean. It is just that I am not in the position to say what would be necessary." [Rath, p. 31]

"You should not think that I want to criticize what you have said about the Association for Independent Spiritual Life. I wanted only to tell how that came about. It happened because there was no clarity with the appeal from the Association. There was indeed good will behind it. Perhaps you could add that the result shows that it was not done right. The appeal had no effect." [Rath, p. 33]

"I would like to give you one thing to think about. This is whether there are a number of you who expected some things from the Pedagogical Youth Course in Stuttgart and are of the opinion today that what you expected still should be realized, but because you pass over your intentions and simply go into the day's business and omit them tomorrow, you then bring forth a reproach. That accusation is: They called us, invited us, and then they left us standing. They did not concern themselves with us any further, because we wanted to work in a different way.

"One thing is certain: a group will form out of those who are here today and who work as they have resolved to do."

3. Further Notes from Presentations by Rudolf Steiner in the Preparatory Conversations for the Founding of the Youth Group

[Note from the editor of the German Edition: The following is most likely also a very old compilation of statements by Rudolf Steiner. They were often copied by hand. Lehrs put them pretty much word-for-word into his report.[†] The paragraph added at the end during the copying shows that this copy is from after 1950.]

About the Nature and Effect of Our Community

(Presentations by Rudolf Steiner in conversations preparing for the foundation, written down from memory immediately afterwards.)

"A true community is always more than the mere sum of its members. Hermann Grimm said about the friendship between Goethe and Schiller: 'If one wants to express it in a mathematical formula, it is not enough to say G + S, but rather it must be G + S + S + G. There always comes a third element[†] to what is between two people who are together in such a manner.'" [Lehrs p. 17].

"With what you wish to form, it is a matter of people from the most varied walks of life coming together. The one will go this way, and the other will go that way in life. Life will very soon become very complicated. It will be necessary that each individual takes as concretely as possible the spirit that is sought through the community. This means that you understand the following: What you are seeking is a *friend* in the spiritual world. Finding such a friend is not difficult. What matters is that, once the friend is found, you remain true in soul to this friend. You must be able to promise yourself something and to remain true to what you have promised. What I will be able to give you will always be only half of what is needed. It will be what you need as a foundation. You yourselves must bring the other half. The loyalty to what you promise to yourself and others is the firm staff and support in life." [Lehrs, p. 18].

"What is living as spirit in Anthroposophy is not a 'doctrine.' It is much more a real being that leads one through life. What you want is to found a community that has something of such a friendly guidance through life. We experience such things when we accept the concrete spiritual as expanded or spread over the whole of life." [Lehrs, p. 18].

"Your community will have something in it that is of the primordial mystery of all human community. That is, what we ourselves do within the community does not bear fruit for ourselves, but for the others; and all the fruits for us come from the others." [Lehrs, p. 18].

To Rudolf Steiner's question of what we imagine concretely the goal of the Anthroposophical youth striving to be, a friend answered that one should find in all the offices in the world such friendly faces as she found on a visit to "Der Kommende Tag" [The coming day] in Stuttgart. Rudolf Steiner then answered: "That is not what matters, but something else does. Social life up to now is like a mechanism, and it is not our task to set all the cranks and levers of the existing mechanism in motion with smiling faces. Rather, the goal must be to replace this mechanism with an organism. With this, what you want to do can be nothing other than the growing of a delicate, little plant. Think of the dead aspects of modern social life as large stones, and of the little plant between these stones. What is dead has, so to speak, a much more tenacious hold in life than the living because it cannot die. At most it can be ground up. And the stones will be ground up! And then you must take care that the little plant is not ground up along with the stones." [Lehrs, p. 21].

"The souls of modern human beings come, as a result of the general development, on the boundary between intellectuality and the spirit. For you, it is as it is with a fish. When a fish comes to the surface of the water, jumps out of the water, and feels the air, it reacts with the impulse to dive back down especially deep into the water. So too, in the coming time, will people who accidentally come to the boundary of the intellect have the desire to dive quite deeply into the intellectual. In relation to this, it will be your task to penetrate through the intellectuality to supra-intellectuality, through clarity to supra-clarity." [Lehrs, p. 22].

As concerns the possibility of expanding the community in the future, he said: "Become seekers of human beings!" (We felt this statement to be a modern metamorphosis of the words of Christ to the disciples: "Become fishers of men!" In the age of the development of personal freedom, "fishing" is replaced with "seeking.") [Lehrs, p. 22].

In view of the earlier membership of one of the participants in the Zionist Youth Movement, in whose report of her experiences he was visibly interested, he said to us all: "You do not want to found something as small as Zionism." [Lehrs, p. 22].

"There are two spiritual streams that run parallel to each other: the one is open, revealed; and the other is hidden, unrevealed. Generally, people know only the first one. The hidden one, the one that actually brings things about, must never fail or dry up. To this end there must come together, from time to time, groups of human beings who work further in it. You want to place yourself in this stream through your community." [Lehrs, p. 22].

When people come and ask a spiritual researcher for a meditation in common, and when their really earnest will leads them to this, then a greater force can arise to accomplish something in the world than an oh-so-great statesman could achieve." [Lehrs, p. 22].

"So much at the present time appears to go so smoothly because it proceeds mechanically. However, the operation of the machine runs beyond the heads of the human beings, beyond their understanding. It is becoming an ever more gigantic force that runs on its own, and human beings can no longer stop it with their existing forces. People can be equal to this force only through a striving that makes an effort to carry spirit right into the most outer consequences of actions.

When we bring spirit and love into our will, this alone will make it possible to stand against being overpowered by the culture-machine. Too few people today develop real initiative. There is much desire, but too little will." [Lehrs, p. 22].

"You must differentiate between prayer and meditation. The ordinary prayer today serves mostly to satisfy one's own self. The true meditation, however, is a fulfilling of the spiritual will that the time spirit bears within himself. Where such a meditation is practiced, a spiritual force is able to work into earthly happenings. Today, spiritual worlds want to work into earthly events, but they can do this only when space is made for it through human meditation. There occurs something like an empty space in the physical field into which the spiritual beings can enter with their effects. Even when much is destroyed physically, and even though it appears that little is achieved outwardly, what is accomplished in such a spiritual way remains. This retains its worth for the future." [Lehrs, p. 23].

"Now the time has come when materialism has so hardened the bodies that the individuality cannot incarnate sufficiently. Many people walk around today with one part of their being beside them like a companion that cannot reside in the body. This part remains hidden behind the sense world. It is necessary to penetrate through to this part, and meditation is a means for this." [Lehrs, p. 23].

A friend expressed the opinion that our goal should be to be able to speak about tables and chairs just as spiritually as we otherwise speak of the hierarchies. To this he said: "No, rather you should give yourselves the task to learn to speak of the hierarchies just as naturally as you otherwise speak of tables and chairs." [Lehrs, p. 24]

A friend asked whether our community was meant to build an organ of the body that must be prepared for the being of Anthroposophy, in order for it to be able to be effective on Earth. He answered: "Certainly, but not for an incarnation, rather for an incorporation. This being can come only as far as an incorporation in Earth existence.

An incarnation will be possible only under other conditions than the Earth conditions." [Lehrs, p. 25].

To the question about experiences in common among the members of the community, he said: "Yes, you want to become a conscious group soul." [Lehrs, p. 25].

With regard to the effect of such meditation done in common, he said: "Assume that you are a group of ten, and that each of you brings forth the power of two. Then the total effect is not 2 X 10, but 2¹⁰. In other words, the increase of power takes place not according to the law of multiplication, but to that of potentization." [Lehrs, S. 26].
Concerning the necessary matter of our mutual behavior, he said: "Individually, you will come to have very different cultural tasks from one another. Not all of you will have to work toward the outside to the same degree. Some will stand more in the forefront and others more in the background, according to destiny and talent. Each of you must have joy for the success of the others. Every feeling of rivalry must be kept far away. In the consciousness of each of you must live the awareness that what you accomplish, you accomplish through the power of all of the others." [Lehrs, p. 26].

"To join together through a mutual promise to strive toward a common spiritual goal, and thereby to leave one another mutually free in action and judgment—a community founded on this is something new in the evolution of humanity. And today it is what is most needed." [Lehrs, p. 26].

"For someone who comes to specific experiences on the esoteric path, the danger of illusions of grandeur arises easily. A community such as yours can be a protection against this. This is because in the community you strive together to cross the threshold of the spiritual world. And there, each of you has to say that you have the efforts of all of the others to thank for what you have achieved personally."
After giving the texts for the meditations, he said: "Now you must divide your life into two parts. The one part takes place in your

meditations. The other part takes place in outer life. In the first, you draw in the spirit; and then in the other, the spirit flows of itself into life. For this, it is necessary that you stand fully in this outer life." [Lehrs, p. 26]

"On this path that you have resolved to take, human beings become more sensitive than previously to the ahrimanic effects in the world. Thus, you will have more to suffer through than other people do. And thereby you will have to take care that you do not succumb to the temptation to flee from this experience by using the same means through which you attained this sensitivity in the first place." (We thought this meant that we should take care not to use meditation as a protective haven.) [Lehrs, p. 22].

"In the physical realm today, the ahrimanic power is so strong that no single human 'I' is equal to it. Therefore, no human 'I' can guarantee, where a physical deed is concerned, that it can really execute its resolve. The arena in which you have intended to work and fulfill deeds is one to which Ahriman has no access. Therefore, the fulfillment of what you have resolved to do depends solely upon you. You have the first opportunity to enact deeds in freedom; and the first opportunity to practice loyalty and devotion." [Lehrs, p. 27].

Here is added a statement we received from Rudolf Steiner at a meeting a few days after the burning of the first Goetheanum. (More details of this gathering are to be found in the special report,[†] "Aus der Anfangszeit unseres Kreises." [From the beginnings of our Group].) In connection with his request that we always again think about the original impulse of the group, Rudolf Steiner said: "You must understand that you have resolved to sacrifice freedom for the sake of a higher freedom."

4. Notes from Memory by Herbert Hahn

From a photocopy of a memorandum signed and dated by Herbert Hahn in 1963.

[Letterhead:] C. Brumberg Hansen

[In unknown handwriting:] told by Herbert Hahn to this friend who wrote it down at the same time.

Notes from Memory (for October 16, 1922)

Among other things, Rudolf Steiner spoke about being young and growing old. He said for instance: "It is unavoidable that you will one day get gray hair here and a wrinkle there, as the physical body shall and must become old. But keep in mind that there is no reason for the soul to grow old. For every gray hair that appears and for every wrinkle that imprints itself, the soul can add a fresh, young 'something.' Only then does aging proceed the way it is willed by the spirit."

In connection with this, he said that we should again and again enliven the impulse that led us to founding a community, so that it lives as it did on the first day. He said: "You see, in the day to day world the old adage, 'new brooms sweep well,' holds true. It means that the bristles of the broom gradually wear, even though in the beginning they were ever so good. That must not be the case with you! Your 'broom' must receive new bristles every day."

* * *

Another time, he spoke of enthusiasm and said that true enthusiasm is very rare. For real enthusiasm does not consist of our being fired up in ourselves and for ourselves. Only then is the enthusiasm real and strong when the flame in us burns so strongly that others can be inwardly enkindled by it. This is what, according to my memory, he meant with the words: "Develop the grips [slang for: ability to understand]." At first we understood him to mean this word in the trivial sense of intelligence or smartness. But then he gave the above as explanation.

* * *

In connection with the modern intellectual culture, he told us that it is not just a few people who see the one-sidedness and dangers of this culture today. However, the tendency arises to set aside the head and to immerse themselves in the feel-good, non-rational regions of feeling and the depths of the dark will. In order to experience themselves fully as human being, they choose the path from the head downwards. He said we should become conscious of the dangers and illusions that are connected with this downward path. It is a wrong way, which fully contradicts what the time spirit wants.

Rudolf Steiner stressed that it was not for nothing that the head has acquired clarity in relation to all one-sidedness. This clarity must not be lost, but must be taken along on the spiritual path intended by the time spirit. And indeed it must be taken along on the path from the head upwards beyond the head. On this path, what is beyond the rational is achieved through supra-clarity. This is the path that wants to be taken by a Michaelic thinking.

* * *

About meditation and meditating, Rudolf Steiner said, among other things: "The meditations are indicated for specific day-situations, or times of day. And when circumstances allow, they should be done at definite, specific times. Yet, one member of the community that is forming will do the first meditation as the morning meditation, and another will do the last one. But both meditations—indeed all the morning meditations of the community—approach one another, belong to one another. It happens such that the meditation that is done first is written into the ether. All the rest that then follow, crystallize around the first. In a certain sense, a 'virtual time' applies to the meditations. This virtual time is the result of the situation and allows the last of these morning meditations, which out of unforeseen circumstances is perhaps done late, still to be a 'morning meditation.'"

Rudolf Steiner said something very decisive that was a summoning to obligation concerning the task and effect of the meditations.

While, on the one side, they are for the individual and the community an organ of higher spiritual development, they also serve, on the other side, the whole Earth. He explained that the moral forces of the Earth today are so threatened with corruption, ruination, that this meditative activity has an immensely significant healing effect for the Earth. This is especially true when, as happens in a spiritual community, the meditative forces potentize in their effect.

In this connection Rudolf Steiner also mentioned The Christian Community that was starting. It is to be thanked as a helper in this service for the preservation of the moral forces of the Earth. This indication of the significance of The Christian Community has ever more meaning, because Rudolf Steiner stressed in another place that The Christian Community is an independent Movement, at the founding of which he played only a mediating role. About the effect of the meditation in the community that was coming into being, he said, among other things: "With the appropriate spiritual attitude there will result, in connection with the spiritual substance built through meditation, a relationship of every individual to the whole. This relationship will form in such a manner that at given times and for specific tasks, everything that the community has attained will concentrate itself on an individual. The individual will then, to a certain extent, be blessed for his or her task with the entire spiritual substance of the community.

When the others who belong to the community correctly understand what is happening, they do not become envious but look with justified feelings of mutual joy upon how, at this moment, everything is given to the one individual. And vice versa, this individual will not ascribe the success to his or her own virtues or talents. The individual will be aware that he or she works and has effect essentially through what others have given. And this will summon modesty and gratitude."

As the conversations for the founding of the community became still more concentrated, Rudolf Steiner said one day that we should see how the meditative activity, in the sense of the new esotericism now arising, has a specific connection with a time-phenomenon known only to the initiate. Then he characterized this time-phenomenon as follows: "Today there are only a few people who are well-incarnated—who are really in their body. Human bodies have become more and more difficult to fully incarnate into." He went on to say that when we do this community-meditation, it will bring about a deeper connection of the core of our being with our sheaths. This can, however, because it is the birth process, be connected with feelings of suffering and pain. He said word for word: "For a time, an unexplainable melancholy can overwhelm one or the other of you." He stressed that we should not shrink back from this melancholy. We should understand it for what it is: the shadow of an incarnation process that we are catching up on. A danger can arise for those who do not recognize this darkening of the soul for what it is. This danger will exhibit itself in the sudden arising of the tendency to want to make oneself numb. And it will not be a matter of numbing oneself in the trivial sense, but rather a clever, refined numbing such as through exaggerated busyness, and similar things.

Rudolf Steiner said all of this with especially great earnestness. One had the impression of looking at great dangers that are coming toward us out of a time that is striding on into one-sidedness. As he gave us the meditations in an unforgettable spirit-mood—a description of this mood follows—and spoke about the meditations, he said something deeply stimulating. These meditations, when used correctly, could become something like windows into the spiritual world. The words and pictures given form only half of what was to be entrusted to us. The other half we were to find ourselves through spiritual activity.

In the moment in which the meditations were given, the following took place. While Rudolf Steiner had the violet-colored notebook that contained the meditations either in his hand or lying before him, he said: "You can consider this thusly, that I was given the charge to bring this to you."

For the writer of these lines, this was the highest impression that he ever received of the person of Rudolf Steiner. More and more he was allowed to experience how the suprasensible world revealed its full power in the work and appearance of Rudolf Steiner himself, as a high spiritual individuality. In this moment [of the giving of the meditations], however, as if through a bolt of lightning, a spiritual background—which one can only divine—behind the bearer of the modern initiation was torn open. In this experience, there was an indescribable spirit-aroma that remains connected with these meditations forever.

* * *

Among the many presentations Rudolf Steiner gave concerning our being in modern culture and the world civilization, one very earnest appeal rises up as special in my memory. Rudolf Steiner warned us not to build up our initiatives and activities, which are directed toward great goals, on forms that exist in the outer world and are created out of routine. He said that these forms had grown old and brittle; they cannot be saved from perishing. We must see that we achieve a new basis and ground upon which we can move, borne by the spirit.

This comment, like all of the others he made in connection with the foundation of the community, was brought into a very large perspective. The largest perspective that opened up may well have been as he said in view of the future of the community: "When this is founded, then you can think of it as determined for a wide-reaching working. It could, for instance, be the case that, at a given time, none of the members of the community are living on Earth; in the ordinary sense, the community would count as having died out. Yet, it will not be wiped out. With the first community members who reincarnate, the community returns to Earth."

The final comment given answers in a totally satisfying manner a question that was often asked by those joining the community later. The question was whether the Esoteric Youth Group were not to be considered dissolved by the Christmas Conference.

Aside from the fact that Rudolf Steiner again confirmed and gave the call to the community through a new, essential meeting during the Christmas Conference, what was said above removes any doubt. The indication of the carrying of the community impulse through the incarnations speaks for itself. More precise is the idea that the founding of the Esoteric Youth [Group] community in October 1922 may be considered to be one of the preparatory steps for the Christmas Conference of 1923. And still more certain is that this community is given an inner obligation for the carrying through of the great impulse of the Christmas Conference.

Herbert Hahn
Copenhagen-Charlottenlund.
August 12-14, 1963.

Two Esoteric Lessons for the Youth Group

For these two lessons there are seven documents. Six are typed; and one, copy C, is handwritten. Two copies contain both lessons, while the other five each contain only one. Only Record A of the second lesson is signed, and that was signed by Maria Röschl. The others bear no names.

The variations in the actual texts are minimal. Only in the note-takers' inserted comments are there greater differences in the formulation, but not in the content of the text itself. The comments of the note-takers are given in parentheses.

First Esoteric Lesson

STUTTGART, JULY 13, 1923

[This text follows Record B, unless otherwise noted.]

(Record E: Rudolf Steiner came somewhat earlier than expected, about 8:00 p.m., while we waited for him in the library on Landhausstrasse. We had asked Rudolf Steiner for a meeting as a result of our being acutely at odds and depressed because of the withdrawal of our friend [name unknown]. While we waited, we came into discussion again about our difficulties. Then Rudolf Steiner came in unexpectedly. We were prepared to describe our plight and to be permitted to ask his advice. Instead of this, once he and Marie Steiner had taken their places, he immediately began speaking to us out of his own self, addressing us with the following words:)

My dear sisters and brothers!

The meditations you have received for your inner work will be valid for a long time yet. Today, something is to be given that can contribute to the infinite deepening of the mood with your practicing.

(He described what we would receive as a kind of accompaniment, or supplement, for the daily exercises. Then he began, explaining:)

The meditation consists of words that you must first live into. However, people today sleep in relation to the word. For example, they think the word "Wachs" [wax] comes from "wachsen" [to grow or expand], while in reality it comes from "weich sein." [To be soft]. Today yet in the dialect of some regions the word for "weich" is "waach." What does someone actually experience today with such an expression as: "Deine Worte haben mein Gemüt erweicht" [Your words have softened my mind and heart]?

(The soft, penetrating tone with which this sentence, and especially the last word, was spoken pressed deeply into the minds and hearts of those listening.)

(Record E: One must imagine how the seal is pressed into the wax—that is how the talk imprinted itself into my soul.)

One must come to a completely different relationship to the word. There are, for example, the words "to sleep" and "to wake." They mean something totally different from what is usually thought. Those sleeping and those who are awake are in the same outer surroundings. It is just that those who are awake know this world, and those who are sleeping know nothing of it. Correspondingly, it is also the same with the Anthroposophists in relation to the non-Anthroposophists. The Anthroposophists know of a world, the spiritual world, in which the non-Anthroposophists also live without knowing anything of it. This is true to yet a greater extent with the meditants. For this reason, they must become modest in the use of the word.

(This last sentence could not help but find an especially earnest resonance in our souls, remembering the discussion that had taken place among us just before this.)

(Record E: The difference between the earnest, subdued mood in which Rudolf Steiner spoke and the mood into which we ourselves had come, was very great.)

A further such word is "I." Among all of the words of human speech, this word has a special place. In approximately the third year of life, the human being learns to use this word. That is an age, however, in which there is as yet no actual "I"-consciousness present. Therefore, one learns at first to speak this word only *automatically*. Only in the twenty-first year of life does the birth of the "I" take place. However, what appears there is still, even through the whole of life, not the true "I." The ordinary human being meets the "I" again only after death. So, until death, all human beings use the word "I" always only *provisionally*. The meditants must become especially conscious of this provisional use of the word "I." Meditants must learn that they must find their way to the true "I" gradually, by learning first to experience it through all their three sheaths.

(Rudolf Steiner now began to describe the three sheaths in sequence, beginning with the physical body.)

The physical body is subject to gravity, just as the mineral is. Opposite to the force of gravity is the force of light. In the heart, both of these work against each other; the gravity pulls downward, and the light draws upwards. In order to correctly experience gravity, hold a crystal in your hand and examine it. Do not look at the transparency, i.e., its light-nature, but rather let its weight work on you.

(Immediately, the words "gravity/weight" and "light" were spoken in such a manner that the real weight and light could be experienced in the words. Now Rudolf Steiner seemed to be weighing a crystal in his hand, such that one experienced the weight of it in the movement of his hand. From then on his devotion to sound and gesture became ever stronger and more expressive.)

You must learn to experience your relationship to your physical body in the same way that you experience an outer body. It must become all the same to you whether you shovel a pile of sand from one side to the other (he made the gesture of shoveling with all devotion), or whether you are moving your own body through space. Thus must the meditant regain the experience that is natural in the East and is described there in the words: "I carry my body through the door."

Individual things of the Earth do not have weight because the Earth pulls each of them toward it, but because they are all subject together to the unified gravity-being of the Earth. Our task consists of consciously living into this gravity-being of the Earth. May the following mantra serve to deepen this experience:

My own being is interwoven with the Earth gravity

(Record E: Rudolf Steiner used an ever stronger sound-gesture in his speech. Thus, real weight or gravity was at work in the individual words he used to characterize the Earth gravity. The words he used then to describe the lightness of the light were a great contrast:)

Only when you immerse yourself completely in the element of weight or gravity can you advance to the experience of lightness. In a dream of flying, this element presses into human experience. The interpretation of this dream by modern psychology is totally wrong, because it calls it an anxiety dream. Anxiety has to do with becoming small and cramped. In the dream of flying one dreams precisely of becoming wide, of lightness.

The force of lightness is connected with the Sun. It is the force that causes water to ascend and to evaporate. This evaporated water condenses again into clouds and returns to the Earth again as rain. It is, however, not correct to think that the force of lightness lifts the water only to this sphere, where it condenses and returns to Earth. Actually, the substance of the water is led still much further;

it is fully dematerialized by the lightness. When the clouds ascend and then disappear, the water ceases to be matter. The force of the Sun that brings this about can, however, work so intensely that too much Earth-water is taken up and etherized. Then, too much foreign ether collects in the surroundings of the Earth. Then the congested, damned-up ether suddenly breaks back into the material Earth-sphere again. We experience this as the phenomenon of lightning. In lightning the etheric substance lights up, in order to condense into a watery form as rain, or even into a solid form as hail. In lightning the sky tears and the damned-up ether breaks and descends. What happens in this way suddenly and therefore perceptibly, also takes place quietly in the constant rhythm in the evaporating water and the forming of the clouds.

In order to live into this element of lightness, it is helpful to place a cosmic picture before the soul. You can imagine, for example, a dark, heavy mountain or forest. Floating in front of this there are clouds that ascend and, gradually dissipating, disappear. For deepening in this element, may the following mantra serve:

My own being is interwoven with the lightness of the light

The plant is fixed between the Earth and the Sun. Gravity works on it from below, and the light from above. This light streams from the universe down upon the Earth, and is taken in by the Earth and preserved within it. At the same time, along with the light, the warmth enters into the Earth. This streaming-in takes place during the summer and autumn. During the winter, the light and warmth rest in the Earth. In the spring the light frees itself and pulsates elastically back to the cosmos. Thereby, it brings about the growth of the plants. People do not know much about the warmth that is preserved in the Earth during the winter. Only the farmer uses it, for instance, when he stores his potatoes in a silo. The light streams thus elastically—downward, upward, downward.

(Again, this was accompanied by impressive gestures.).

The plant lives in this pulsating. For this reason, it can move vertically; it can grow and shrivel. But it cannot move horizontally from its place. In contrast, the animals and human beings can move freely in the horizontal. This freedom from their place on the Earth is given by the breathing. The breath makes it possible for them to move about on the Earth. Also, the atmosphere spreads itself out horizontally, encompassing the whole Earth. Only those beings that can breathe freely can walk freely. When you think about this, every step must become a mystery of walking. May the following saying serve to deepen in this element:

My own being is interwoven with the strength of the breath

(Now all three sheaths and the cosmic forces that are interwoven with them are gone through a second time. The connection was still more deeply illumined, and then led on to the grasping of the "I.")

If you want to understand the nature of gravity as it works in the human body, you must look at the development of the embryo. During this development, gravity plays no part in the human body, in the embryo. The embryo floats in the amniotic fluid. Only through the physical birth does the human being come under the influence of gravity. It is also exactly the same for the body of the Earth. The gravity-being becomes connected with it also only over time [Record E: in the course of its evolution]. When you immerse yourself spiritually in gravity, you are led back to the cosmic past of the Earth and thereby to the experience of that moment when the Earth was born out of the divine Father-forces. Thus you are led on this path to the meeting with these divine Father-forces themselves.

The following saying:

My being is interwoven with the Earth gravity

leads to the experience of:

Ex Deo nascimur [Out of God we are born]

Every time, when you go to sleep, you enter into the world in which the lightness of the light reigns. [Record E: "When you learn to go to sleep consciously, you will perceive this."]. It is the same world that you enter through the portal of death. It is the realm where Christ lives today. We reach him through dying out of the physical. The following mantra:

My own being is interwoven with the lightness of the light

leads to the experience of:

In Christo morimur [In Christ we die]

Darkness and light, gravity and lightness, work in opposition on the plant. Both are combined with each other in the element of air. We experience this clearly in the phenomena of the red glow of dawn and of sunset. Yet, what is perceptible for ordinary sight in the East and West, a finer vision also notices in the North and the South, and actually all the way around in the horizontal in all directions. The element of air surrounds the whole Earth. Thus, in this sphere the human being becomes a member of, belongs to, the whole Earth. The mantra: *My own being is interwoven with the Earth gravity* connects us with the physical in the world. The force of the etheric lives in the lightness of the light. Through the breath we connect our self with the astral that gives us the free mobility of our limbs and the strength of will. Being born and waking up are connected with the inhaling; dying and going to sleep are connected with exhaling. We breathe living air in and breathe dead air out. In the exhaled air, we form speech. This is a spiritual act of will through which the dead air is again enlivened. Therefore, deepening in the mantra:

My own being is interwoven with the strength of the breath

leads to the experience of:

Per Spiritum Sanctum reviviscimus [Through the Spirit we are reborn]

The "I" of the human being is surrounded by three sheaths. The "I" itself is not egotistical. Only the sheaths are egotistical. If the "I" is freed from its sheath, it wants immediately to spread or expand itself out to the whole cosmos. However, it is enclosed in its three sheaths. In the East, the image of this being-enclosed is the lotus flower. Also in the lotus flower, the innermost core is surrounded by three circles of blossom petals.

(As Rudolf Steiner spoke this, he supported his elbows on the table and, with both hands, he made the gesture of the form of a flower bud. His gestures and voice had a special delicacy and devotion [Record G: delicacy and inwardness]. Then he said:)

In India this was expressed with the words:

Aoum mani padme aoum†

Mein Ich ist beschlossen in der Lotusblüte
[My "I" is enclosed in the lotus flower]

If you want to come to the true "I," you must go through all three sheaths. There are three stages that lead to the "I."

(The following was spoken with a ritual-intonation. With each stage, he let his arms fall heavily onto the table—to the right and to the left. He then brought them back up for building the flower form again.)

One enters the first stage and experiences:

My own being is interwoven with the Earth gravity
Ex Deo nascimur
The first sheath falls

One enters the second stage and experiences:

My own being is interwoven with the lightness of the light
In Christo morimur
The second sheath falls

One enters the third stage and experiences:

My own being is interwoven with the strength of the breath†
Per Spiritum Sanctum reviviscimus
The third sheath falls

(Record C: Every time Rudolf Steiner mentions the falling of the sheaths, he lets his forearms and hands fall heavily upon the table. The way he spoke the word "falls," he again sculpted in sound the falling of the sheath in question. He closed the session by speaking the Indian mantra once again. He said it could be practiced either in the original or in the German translation.).

Aoum mani padme aoum [hum]

(In the meantime, it had become dark. In the last light, only the white of Rudolf Steiner's face and hands was visible. After he gave a sign that the lesson was ended, the light was turned on. He got up and said goodbye to us by shaking the hand of each of us and of Marie Steiner.)

[Remark of the note-taker: of the words in the Sanskrit, Rudolf Steiner said one could meditate them in the original form or in the translation in one's own language.]

In explanation: Of the syllable "Aoum," he said in another connection that it had sounded this way originally—in as far as we can imitate it.† The *A* is the sound of awe; *O* is the sound of reverence; and the *U* is the sound of fear. All three together results in the sound of *Ehrfurcht* [a solemn, respectful reverence and awe].

"Mani" is the phonetic expression of the purest, the most inward, the essential. And so in the mineral kingdom, it expresses the pure crystal, especially the quartz crystal; in the plant, especially the lotus, the innermost part of the flour where the fragrance arises; and in the human being, the "I." "Padme" means "in the lotus."]

Second Esoteric Lesson

DORNACH, DECEMBER 30, 1923, 8:30 AM

[This report corresponds in all details to Record A, which was signed by Maria Röschl and bears the name of Fritz Götte stamped on it.]

Under the impression of the new esoteric form of the Anthroposophical Society through the Christmas Conference,[†] we went to Dr. Steiner with the question of whether he had in this time something to say to us that concerned our work specifically. He said he did, and after a few days told us the place and time of the meeting. This time we gathered in a mood that attempted to correspond to the responsibility of the moment that was approaching.

We gathered in the middle room of the Glass House.[†] We sat on benches that were arranged in a half-circle, so that no one sat behind anyone else. Before us stood a table. Dr. Steiner sat at the long side of the table, and Marie Steiner and Ita Wegman sat at either end. Rudolf Steiner was in front of the arch of the east wall of the room.

Dr. Steiner entered the room in accompaniment of the two guests. He greeted us with a special ceremonial solemnity. He then explained that the two ladies would be present as guests: "Marie Steiner, because she is present for everything; Dr. Wegman, because there are also other groups of the same kind as yours that nurture the inner life. These must now be integrated into the general esoteric life, naturally according to strict esoteric laws. For this, there must be a person who connects all of this. That is the reason Dr. Wegman is here." He described the two ladies as "auditors."

From the first moment on, one experienced that Dr. Steiner had a bearing that was quite specially earnest and of a ceremonial-like solemnity. He got up from his seat and, standing the whole time and turned completely toward us, he spoke quite solemnly. Thereby his gesture and power of speech was such that his voice was as if writing the words into the far-reaching distances, not just for the present.

Let us, my dear sisters and brothers, hear in standing the words of self-knowledge that resound to human beings out of stone and mountain; out of forests and clouds; out of all the forms of the world that surround them; and that have resounded as words of self-knowledge in all the ages wherein a spiritual striving existed. These words resound:

O Mensch erkenne dich selbst
So tönt das Weltenwort
Du hörst es seelenkräftig
Du fühlst es geistgewaltig

Wer spricht so weltenmächtig?
Wer spricht so herzinniglich?

Wirkt es durch des Raumes Weitenstrahlung
In deines Sinnes Seinserleben?
Tönt es durch der Zeiten Wellenweben
In deines Lebens Werdestrom?

Bist du es selbst, der sich
Im Raumesfühlen, im Zeiterleben
Das Wort erschafft, dich fremd
Erfühlend in Raumes Seelenleere
Weil du des Denkens Kraft
Verlierst im Zeitvernichtungsstrome.

O Human Being, know yourself
So resounds the cosmic Word
You hear it soul-forcefully
You feel it spirit-mightily

Who speaks so cosmic-powerfully?
Who speaks so heart-inwardly?

Does it work through space's expansive radiance
Into your senses' experience of being?
Does it resound through time's weaving waves
Into your life's stream of becoming?

Are you yourself the one who,
In the feeling of space, the experience of time,
Creates the Word, feeling yourself
Estranged in space's soul-emptiness
Because you lost thinking's force
In time's annihilating stream.

— Now he motioned with his hand for us to sit down. He remained standing.

The human being is losing the force of thought. I turn today to the youth in you, since you have come together as esoteric youth, for you are the Esoteric Youth Group.

The human being is losing the force of thought. However, the time has come when humanity must re-conquer this force. I gave this to you as a task when you connected with one another as an esoteric Youth Group. And you must strive toward this. The youth should not want to know more than the rest of the members of the Anthroposophical Society. And your striving should not be to know something different, but rather to know the same thing *differently*.

We are led to a different kind of knowing, however, when we strive to experience the *Earth as a star*—as a star among stars. For thinking, feeling, and willing, the Earth must be conquered anew.

What makes something a star? Something is a star when it rays out, gleams, and has form and weight in it that holds the body together.

But what is it that *rays out* from the star? It is the *will* of the beings that reside in the star. You will—and the Earth radiates out into the universe.

It is the *feeling* of the beings that reside in a star that makes it gleam and sparkle. You feel, and the Earth gleams as star into the universe.

It is the *thinking* that wraps light-filled around the star. You think, and your thinking allows the Earth to shimmer in waves of light.

In the perceiving and touching of the beings that reside in the star, the star builds its density. Through your touch, the Earth achieves its form.

(Record B: Rudolf Steiner said that here, "touch" refers to all perception.)

It is just that you must so train your consciousness that your thinking, feeling, and willing is not for you, but is for the cosmos; so that it rays out, gleams, and shines into the widths of the cosmos. Through your thinking, feeling, and willing, the Earth becomes visible to the beings on the other stars. But also the evil that human beings think, feel, and will radiates out into the cosmos. It is still visible in the starry space after millions of years.

A star radiates; a star gleams; a star shines; a star has density:

In dem Strahle lebt mein Wollen – denn Güte strahlt vom Sterne
In dem Glanze lebt mein Fühlen – denn Liebe glänzt am Sterne
In der Hülle lebt mein Denken – denn Licht wirkt in dem Sterne
In der Schwere lebt mein Tasten – denn Dichte bildet den Stern.

In the ray lives my will – for the good rays forth from the star
In the gleam lives my feeling – for love gleams on the star
In the sheath lives my thinking – for light works in the star
In the gravity lives my touch – for density builds the star.

[In F. Götte's handwriting:]

In dem Strahle lebt mein Wollen – denn Güte strahlt vom Sterne
In dem Glanze lebt mein Fühlen – denn Liebe glänzt am Sterne

In the ray lives my will – for the good rays forth from the star
In the gleam lives my feeling – for love gleams on the star[†]

Yes, dear sisters and brothers, cosmic responsibility should awaken in your souls. Love gleams from the star, and truth forms on the star. The ancient sacred wisdom of the Indians already spoke of this. And it is again time for today's youth to bring the oldest wisdom of humanity back into consciousness.

Yasmajjatam jagat sarvam yasminneva praliyate
Yenedam dharyate chaiva tasmai gnanatmane namah.

Von dem die ganze Welt stammt, zu dem sie wieder
    zurückkehrt, durch den sie sicher gestützt ist
Ihm dem Selbst, welches weiss / sei alle Ehre.

To him out of which the whole world comes, to whom
    it returns again, and through whom it is safely supported,
To him the self who knows, all honor be given.[†]

Kali Yuga has now ended—a span of 5000 years. And our whole experience today must again pick up the thread of the Light Age that ended 5000 years ago. In this new age, humanity must come to experience the Earth in a completely new way. Humanity is now being led to cross over the threshold of the spiritual world. This means that human beings between their thirtieth and fortieth year of life meet the Guardian of the Threshold. Many people experience the Guardian unconsciously, and that is something terrible. Then consequences will come for human beings of such a kind: Elemental beings will make themselves noticeable. Then everything that becomes enlivened out of the realm of nature crawls around them as the spiritual. Everything out of the solid element—especially out of the horned and hoofed animals—becomes free and interferes in a terrible, demonic manner in the human soul, and the whole life of the nerves is ruined. For this reason, it is necessary at the turning point of Kali Yuga to cross the threshold consciously:

> Erkenne erst den ernsten Hüter
> Der vor des Geisterlandes Pforten steht
> Den Einlass deiner Sinnenkraft
> Und deines Verstandes Macht verwehrend
> Weil du im Sinnesweben
> Und im Gedankenbilden
> Aus Raumeswesenlosigkeit
> Aus Zeiten Truggewalten
> Des eignen Wesens Wahrheit
> Dir kraftvoll erst erobern mußt.

> Know first the earnest guardian
> Who stands before the door of spirit land
> Refusing entrance to your senses' power
> And your understanding's might
> Because in your senses' weaving
> And your thoughts' forming
> From space's beinglessness

> And time's powers of illusion
> The truth of your own being
> You must first raise.

It is the destiny of humanity to stand before the Guardian of the Threshold at the turning point of Kali Yuga.

If you approach the Earth from out of the cosmos, you experience it as closed within an atmosphere of human karma. It surrounds the Earth like a warmth-love cloak, out of which your own karma speaks to you world-mightily. When you learn to meet the Guardian, you will experience how your karma wraps itself around you like a warmth cloak, how it blows lovingly upon you.

[In handwriting from F. Götte:]

> In dem Glanze lebt mein Fühlen
>   denn Liebe glänzt am Sterne
>
> In the gleam lives my feeling
>   for love gleams on the star

Our thinking should radiate, should shine into the cosmos. When, however, human beings do not think, feel, and will spiritually, when they refuse to meet the Guardian consciously, then no human experience shines into the cosmos. In the nineteenth century, as human beings stopped thinking spiritually, human thinking was not sufficient to let the Earth radiate. Yet, a star must radiate. Because of that, in the last third of the nineteenth century, the higher animal group souls had to step in and send out their light. At that time the cosmic disgrace of humanity began to radiate into the cosmos.

For that reason, there must be found in humanity souls whose spiritual knowledge allows the Earth to shine out as star into cosmic space for the residents of the other stars.

> In dem Strahle lebt mein Wollen – denn Güte strahlt vom Sterne
> In dem Glanze lebt mein Fühlen – denn Liebe glänzt am Sterne

In the ray lives my will – for the good rays forth from the star
In the gleam lives my feeling – for love gleams on the star

The Light Age has begun, and the relation of the spiritual world to the physical has become completely different. When I sit with the spirits and minds of the nineteenth century and words resound, for instance of a Herman Grimm, they sound quite spiritually sensitive. But when I sit with the spirits that your souls want to become, it makes those fine, sensitive words sound like empty word-chiming. This is because at the present time such a great wealth streams down out of the spiritual world. One can experience this as spiritual snow flurries falling softly onto the souls of human beings.

The youth must find their way in what spurs them on to spiritual deeds. Up until now the youth have learned some things from us about the nature of their youth. That was enough. Now they must learn to experience this nature of youth themselves. Now it is a matter of winning the Earth anew for thinking, feeling, and willing. It is a matter of your finding the development-stream of the world.

Then you will experience that the Earth-being disappears. The time will come when the ground is taken from beneath your feet. And when the moment comes in your life when everything physical plunges into the abyss, because the abyss opens up and the firm ground under your feet disappears, then the spirit light that shines in the development-stream of the world will become weaker and weaker. It will become like a thin thread, and you will experience that this thread burns. Then, however, you must have the courage to take hold of this thread, even though it burns. You must hold firmly onto this glowing, burning thread of the spiritual, and you must say to yourselves: we want to create a *new* ground under our feet.

Thus, you must learn to have soul courage!

There was an ancient sacred knowledge in humanity. You must have the courage to pick up the thread of this knowledge. This knowledge lived once in Aristotle. It disappeared. People did not understand Aristotle anymore. Only in certain Catholic Orders was it known yet in the nineteenth century that the wisdom of Aristotle was, in truth, a path of meditation. There they still knew how to read his books in this manner. Vincenz Knauer† was among those who still knew this.

Only with aching heart did I decide to say what I said in the evening lectures.† Often the ancient sacred knowledge was not to be found among the scholars, but among the poor, simple people. It was one of the most deeply moving events of my life when I met such a human being: the herb gatherer.† He spoke in words that went deeply to the heart about plants, stones, animals, stars, Sun, and Moon. The living stream of the old knowledge still lived in him. And it is a special destiny that I could meet these two people—Vincenz Knauer and the herb gatherer—that in the last moment of humanity I could connect with both of these streams,† through which the dwindling ancient knowledge could still trickle into the nineteenth century.

Yes, the youth must learn to reach into that fiery thread, even though it burns. When everything sinks into the abyss, we must learn to find *ourselves* in the development-stream of the world. When earlier in ancient times, there sounded forth to human beings out of stone and spring, out of tree and flower, the exhortation: "O Human Being, know yourself," the answer was then the sacred AOUM. The human being went into the sacred stillness to receive the Word of the gods. Now that the world has entered the age, however, in which human deeds are expected in the cosmos, when the human beings are called to their own activity, this sacred AOUM is no longer the answer that should resound. It should now sound forth to the spirits that want to become the spirits of your souls, as the answer:

> Ja, da bin ich für Eure Welten-Taten.
>
> Yes, I am there for your cosmic deeds.

The youth must make this come true.

Dr. Steiner closed the lesson by speaking the words of the Guardian once again:

Erkenne erst den ernsten Hüter
Der vor des Geisterlandes Pforten steht
Den Einlass deiner Sinnenkraft
Und deines Verstandes Macht verwehrend
Weil du im Sinnesweben
Und im Gedankenbilden
Aus Raumeswesenlosigkeit
Aus Zeiten Truggewalten
Des eignen Wesens Wahrheit
Dir kraftvoll erst erobern mußt.

Know first the earnest guardian
Who stands before the door of spirit land
Refusing entrance to your senses' power
And your understanding's might
Because in your senses' weaving
And your thoughts' forming
From space's beinglessness
And time's powers of illusion
The truth of your own being
You first must raise.

And the answer of the human soul:

Ich trat in diese Sinnes-Welt
Des Denkens Erbe mit mir führend
Eines Gottes Kraft hat mich hereingeführt
Der Tod, er steht an des Weges Ende –
Ich will des Christus Wesen fühlen –
Es weckt in Stoffes-Sterben Geistgeburt
Im Geiste find ich so die Welt
Und erkenne mich im Weltenwerden.

I stepped into this sensory world
Bringing with me thinking's harvest
A god's power has brought me in

Death stands at the path's end—
I feel the being of Christ—
It awakens in matter's dying spirit birth.
In spirit I find the world
And know myself in world becoming.

At the end Rudolf Steiner made the same sign† in front of him in the space that he made later at the Christmas Conference, and spoke with this the words:

"Ja, so sei es!"
[Yea, so be it!]

* * *

(The notes reproduced here do not come from a direct stenographic record. They are put together from my notes made immediately afterwards and from those of several friends, where the composition was quite specially remembered. From other remarks by Rudolf Steiner, it follows that the term "youth" naturally does not mean the physical, chronological age, but the characteristic of being a post-Kali Yuga soul. Dr. M. R. [the characteristic signature of Maria Röschl])

The Youth Group Meditations

Meditation given on October 13, 1922

```
(Sonne)          uns    (Mond)
Es wärme       | Gemeinsames Fühlen
die Sonnenseele| befeuere uns mit heiligem Feuer
In Meinem Haupt|        lebe auch euer Denken
                        uns
Es leuchte     | Gemeinsames Licht
                        uns
der Sonnengeist| erhelle mit reinem Licht
In meinem Herzen| lebe auch euer Wollen
So bin Ich     | mit Euch, Ihr mit mir
                          blauer Himmel
                    ┌ Ich bin
                    │ Seele lebt
                    │ Geist wirkt
                    │ Ich im Weltensein
   Erholung! —     │ Seele im Geisteswollen
                    └ Geist im Gottes-Ihm
                          ----
```

Notebook Archive No. 282

| Zu Menschen taten (Sterne)
| in allen Lebenslagen
| und trage geistige Wesen
| ~~in allem Lebensstreben~~ für ~~alle~~ Menschenziele
| in allem Lebensstreben
| und wirke göttliches Wollen
| und ~~des Geistes~~ Christi Kraft im Erdensein

) Erfüllung.—

Annotation of the editors [of the German edition] for the facsimile on pages 426 and 427:

The word Erhellung [Illumination] below on the left side is written in pencil by Marie Steiner. Two further comments that belong to it are on the right side of the original but are not visible in the facsimile, because the back side of the page shone through and therefore the page had to be cleaned up. These comments that were also written in pencil and are as follows: (above right), "do not type this page — M.St." and (below right), "not copied —J.M." The latter is the handwriting of Johanna Mücke. This has to do with the fact that in the first years after Rudolf Steiner's death, Marie Steiner allowed the mantras and other notes be copied out of his notebooks so that they would be on hand for publishing purposes.

According to the handwritten entry of Lili Kolisko in her notebook, she was given the mantra on November 11, 1924 as follows:

For the first part:
>
> *Evenings* (Sun shining mildly in the sky.)
> May it warm
>
> . . .
>
> *Mornings* (Sun and Moon in the sky.)
> May it warm feeling in common for us.
>
> . . .
>
> *Mid-day* (Starry heavens. Moon among the stars. Sun shining
> through the Earth.)
> May it warm our feeling in common to human deeds.

For the second part:
>
> *Wakeful expectation* (blue sky)
> I am.
>
> . . .
>
> *Illumination*
> I am in World-existence.
>
> . . .

Transcription of the facsimile on pages 426 and 427:

Sonne	Mond	Sterne
Es wärme	| uns gemeinsames Fühlen	| zu Menschentaten
die Sonnenseele	| befeuere uns mit heiligem Feuer	| in allen Lebenslagen
In meinem Haupt	| lebe auch euer Denken	| und trage geistige Wesen
Es leuchte	| uns gemeinsames Licht	| für Menschenziele
der Sonnengeist	| erhelle uns mit reinem Licht	| in allem Lebensstreben
In meinem Herzen	| lebe auch euer Wollen	| und wirke göttliches Wollen
So bin Ich	| mit Euch, Ihr mit mir	| und Christi Kraft im Erdensein

Sun	Moon	Stars
May there warm	| for us common feeling	| to human deeds
The Sun's soul	| kindle us with holy fire	| in all life circumstances
In my head	| may there live your thinking	| and bear spiritual beings
May there shine	| for us common light	| for human goals
The Sun spirit	| illumine us with pure light	| in all life's striving
In my heart	| may there live also your willing	| and work divine willing
Thus I am	| with you, you with me	| and Christ's power in Earth-existence

          Blue Sky
I am
Soul lives
Spirit works
"I" in world existence
Soul in spirit-willing   Illumination. —
Spirit in deed of God

- - - -

The mantras given in the Esoteric Lesson in Dornach, on December 30, 1923:

> Yasmajjatam jagat sarvam yasminneva praliyate
> Yenedam dharyate chaiva tasmai gnanatmane namah.*

In German:
Von dem die ganze Welt stammt, zu dem sie wieder
Zurückkehrt, durch den sie sicher gestützt ist
Ihm dem Selbst, welches weiss | sei alle Ehre.

In English:
From which the whole world comes, to which
It returns again, through which it is safely protected
To him, the Self which knows | be all honor.

> In the rays lives my willing — for the Good
>   rays in the stars
> In the shine lives my feeling — for love
>   shines in the stars
> In the sheaths lives my thinking — for light
>   works in the stars
> In the gravity lives my touching — for density
>   builds the stars.

---

*Rudolf Steiner took the Sanskrit from the translation of G.R.S. Mead and Jagadisha Chandra Chattopadhyaya of *The Upanishads*, translated into English with a preamble and arguments. Published in 1896. The authors close their Foreword as follows: "For those who approach the study of the Upanishads with minds of devotion, three mantras are here appended," and then they give this and two further mantra without citing the sources.

Yasmajjatam jagat sarvam [yasminneva praliyate

Yenedam dharyate chaiva tasmai gnanatmane namah.

Von dem die ganze Welt stammt, zu dem sie wieder zurückkehrt, durch den sie viele gestützt ist

Ihm dem Selbst, welches weiss | sei alle Ehre.

In dem Strahle lebt mein Wollen — denn Güte strahlt vom Sterne

In dem Glanze lebt mein Fühlen — denn Liebe glänzt am Sterne

In der Hülle lebt mein Danken — denn Luft wirbelt in dem Sterne

In der Schwere lebt mein Tasten — denn Dichte bildet den Stern

Notebook Archive No. 281

Entry in Rudolf Steiner's notebook (Archive No. 850) for the Esoteric Lesson of December 30, 1923.

These must be connected with this Lesson, because it is included in the notes for the December 1923 lectures.

Esot.

The more the human being can avoid
the melding with the earthly system —
For the head:
For the breast: courage
For the limbs:

Know that courage carries
the Earth upwards through you —
Spirit carries the spirit light
toward you; soul is the inner
shelter of the light.

The human being is, above, completely independent
of the outer world — below, completely surrendered to it
1) The "I" can live only in the rays of the stars
2) The astral body can live only in the shine of the stars
3) The etheric body lives in the sheaths of the stars
4) The physical body lives in the gravity of the stars

The Three-Part Mantra

(Three Tablets)

All of the Esoteric Lessons that were held from the end of WWI to the new founding of the Esoteric School as the Independent School for Spiritual Science were opened and closed with the first of these three mantras. (Prior to WWI other meditative verses were used; see CW 266/I.) This practice was then continued in the new Esoteric School. However, all three mantras were only rarely spoken together. In London, on April 16, 1922, and in Vienna, on September 30, 1923, the Rosicrucian sentences were interwoven with the third mantra (see the facsimile on pages 444-445).

The original document, with many corrections, is to be found in Rudolf Steiner's notebook for the year 1920 (Archive No. 98).

The facsimile given in this volume comes from Rudolf Steiner's notebook for the year 1923 (Archive No. 281).

Included also is the handwritten record of the mantras by Ludwig Polzer-Hoditz from the Lesson in Vienna on September 30, 1923.

Esot.   I.

O Mensch erkenne dich selbst
So tönt das Weltenwort
Du hörst es seelenkräftig
Du fühlst es geistgewaltig

Wer spricht so weltenmächtig?
Wer spricht so herzinniglich?

Wirkt es durch des Raumes Weitenstrahlung
In deines Sinnes Seinserleben?
Tönt es durch der Zeiten Wellenweben
In deines Lebens Werdestrom?

Bist du es selbst, der sich
Im Raumesfühlen, im Zeiterleben
Das Wort erschafft, dich fremd
Erfühlend in Raumes Seelenleere
Weil du des Denkens Kraft
Verlierst im Zeitvernichtungsstrome

II

Erkenne erst den ernsten Hüter
Der vor des Geisterlandes Pforten steht
Den Einlass deiner Sinnenkraft
Und deines Verstandes Macht verwehrend
Weil du im Sinnesweben
Und im Gedankenbilden
Aus Raumes wesenlosigkeit
Aus Zeiten Trüggewalten
Des eignen Wesens Wahrheit
Dir kraftvoll erst erobern musst.

III.

Ich trat in diese Sinnes-Welt
Des Denkens Erbe mit mir führend
Eines Gottes Kraft hat mich hereingeführt
Der Tod, er steht an des Weges Ende —
Ich will des Christus Wesen fühlen —
Es weckt in Stoffes-Sterben Geist-Geburt
Im Geiste find ich so die Welt
Und erkenne mich im Weltenwerden.

I

O Mensch erkenne dich selbst
So tönt das Weltenwort
Du hörst es seelenkräftig
Du fühlst es geistgewaltig

Wer spricht so weltenmächtig?
Wer spricht so herzinniglich?

Wirkt es durch des Raumes Weitenstrahlung
In deines Sinnes Seinserleben?
Tönt es durch der Zeiten Wellenweben
 In deines Lebens Werdestrom?

Bist du es selbst, der sich
Im Raumesfühlen, im Zeiterleben
Das Wort erschafft, dich fremd
Erfühlend in Raumes Seelenleere
Weil du des Denkens Kraft
Verlierst im Zeitvernichtungsstrome.

I

Human being, know yourself
So resounds the cosmic Word
You hear it soul-forcefully
You feel it spirit-mightily

Who speaks so cosmic-powerfully?
Who speaks so heart-inwardly?

Does it work through space's expansive radiance
Into your senses' experience of being?
Does it resound through time's weaving waves
Into your life's stream of becoming?

You are yourself the one who,
In the feeling of space, the experience of time,
Creates the Word, feeling yourself
Estranged in space's soul-emptiness
Because you lost thinking's force
In time's annihilating stream.

II

Erkenne erst den ernsten Hüter
Der vor des Geisterlandes Pforten steht
 Den Einlass deiner Sinnenkraft
Und deines Verstandes Macht verwehrend
Weil du im Sinnesweben
Und im Gedankenbilden
Aus Raumeswesenlosigkeit
Aus Zeiten Truggewalten
Des eignen Wesens Wahrheit
Dir kraftvoll erst erobern mußt.

II

Know first the earnest guardian
Who stands before the door of spirit land
Refusing entrance to your senses' power
And your understanding's might
Because in your senses' weaving
And your thoughts' forming
From space's beinglessness
And time's powers of illusion
The truth of your own being
Must raise you first.

III

Ich trat in diese Sinnes-Welt
Des Denkens Erbe mit mir führend
Eines Gottes Kraft hat mich hereingeführt
Der Tod, er steht an des Weges Ende —
Ich will des Christus Wesen fühlen —
Es weckt in Stoffes-Sterben Geistgeburt
Im Geiste find ich so die Welt
Und erkenne *mich* im Weltenwerden.

III

I stepped into this sensory world
Bringing with me thinking's harvest
A god's power has brought me in
Death stands at the path's end —
I feel the being of Christ —
It awakens in matter's dying spirit birth.
In spirit I find the world
And know *myself* in world becoming.

From the Lesson of December 30, 1923, in the handwriting of Ludwig Polzer-Hoditz

> Wien, Sonntag 30._IX_.1923.
> u. für die Classe später.
>
> O Mensch erkenne dich selbst,
> So tönt das Weltenwort
> Du hörest es seelenkräftig
> Du fühlest es geistgewaltig,
> Wer spricht so weltenmächtig?
> Wirkt es durch des Raumes Weiten-
> strahlung
> In deines Sinnes Seinserleben?
> Tönt es durch der Zeiten Wellenweben
> In deines Lebens Werdestrom?
> Bist du es selbst, der sich
> Im Raumesfühlen
> Im Zeiterleben
> Das Wort erschafft?
> Dich fremd erfühlend
> In Raumes Seelenleere
> Weil du des Denkens Kraft verlierst
> Im Zeitvernichtungs Strome.

Erkenne erst den ernsten Hüter,
Der vor des Geisterlandes Pforten
                                steht,
Den Einlass deiner Sinneskraft
und deiner Verstandesmacht er-
                                wehrend
Weil du im Sinnesweben
und im Gedankenbilden
aus Raumes Wesenlosigkeit
aus Zeiten Truggewalten
des eigenen Wesens Wahrheit
die kraftvoll erst erobern musst.

Ich trat in diese Sinneswelt
des Denkens Erbe mit mir führend
Eines Gottes Kraft hat mich herein=
                                geführt.
     EDN.
Der Tod er steht an des Weges Ende,
Ich will des Christus Wesen fühlen
Es weckt in Stoffes Sterben Geistgeburt.
    J. CH. M.
Im Geiste find ich so die Welt
Und erkenne mich im Weltenwerden
    P. S. S. R.

EDITORIAL AND REFERENCE NOTES

GENERAL EDITORIAL NOTES

The title of the volume, the table of contents, and the references were provided by the two publishers.

Concerning the text documents: Most of the notes taken from memory were typed; the rest were handwritten. The names of the note-takers are given on the documents. It is, however, questionable whether the original notes were taken by the one whose name was on the document, because it was quite apparent that a lively exchanging of notes went on among the participants. For this reason, there exist for the same lesson several identical records, each in a different handwriting. Therefore, a handwritten or typed text that bears a particular name might have been copied by another participant other than the original note-taker. Proof of this is to be found, in fact, in the texts in Mathilde Scholl's handwriting. For instance, for the Lesson of February 26, 1908, in Berlin, there is a handwritten record from Mathilde Scholl, but also an identical record from Lilla Harris that bears the note: "Notes not from Mathilde Scholl." This is also confirmed by Mathilde Scholl herself in a letter to Marie Steiner on January 6, 1928, in which she wrote: "Today I am sending you a couple of Esoteric Lessons and one record of a Freemasonry Lesson [for this, see CW 265] that I copied from Mrs. Behrendts." Nevertheless, many of the existing records in Mathilde Scholl's handwriting were indeed taken down by her.

While it is noted for each Lesson in this volume which record was used, it still remains a question as to whether the text really came from the person named. The exceptions to this are the notes by Louise Clason and Alice Kinkel, as well as the records that are ascribed to Günther Wagner, his daughter Ida Knoch-Wagner, Wilhelm Hübbe-Schleiden, and his adopted daughter Paula Stryczek from whom no handwriting, however, is available.

This process of being copied many times explains also why there are slight differences in the texts that are otherwise essentially identical.

Arrangement of the text: There are multiple records of many of the lessons. Some of the records differ greatly; some have a few more sentences or paragraphs; some are only slightly different because of a different word or sentence placement. It was attempted to include all of these various nuances in the following way:

1. Where there are significant differences in the various records for the same Lesson, each of the various records are given in their entirety.

2. Where the differences are minor (individual words or sentences), and yet significant, they are indicated in the the text in [ ] and in Reference Notes.

3. The best record, relatively, is placed at the beginning. Where other notes expand on this record or give other nuances—but the records are otherwise identical—they are added as excerpts at the end of the record. Because the authorship of the various texts is so uncertain, the variations are indicated simply as "Record A," "Record B," and so on. However, in the Reference Notes the names that appeared on the respective records are listed.

Concerning the drawings and diagrams: Rudolf Steiner often drew on the blackboard in the Esoteric Lessons, as well as in his other lectures. The original drawings from the Lessons do not exist. The drawings and diagrams in this text have been reproduced just as they were taken down by the individual note-takers, and shown, as much as possible, as a facsimile.

Of the Lessons collected in this volume, only the Lessons from January 2 and January 4, 1913, in Cologne were published in another volume (in CW 264).

Editorial notes concerning terminology and phrases used repeatedly in the Esoteric Lessons:

My dear sisters and brothers:
As stated by others, and as can be seen in some of the records, Rudolf Steiner always addressed the participants in this way.

Rasse [Race] ... Unterrasse [Sub-race] ... Wurzelrasse [Root race] ... Hauptrasse [Main race]:
The use of these designations was customary in Theosophical literature from the end of the nineteenth century and the beginning of the twentieth century, and they were used to indicate the various phases of the great evolution of humanity. Rudolf Steiner, too, used them in the first years of his work within the Theosophical Society. Gradually, he replaced the designation "sub-race" with "cultural epoch" or "cultural period." "Root race" or "main race" he replaced with "main age" or "main era." Compare the lectures of 1908 in *The Apocalypse of St. John* (CW 104) and *Outline of Esoteric Science* (CW 13), originally published in 1909/10.

Esoteric training/schooling... exercises... meditations... subsidiary exercises:
In reference to the various exercises, compare CW 264, as well as the German volumes GA 267 and GA 268. A selection of exercises can be found in the small volume titled *Guidance in Esoteric Training.* For the subsidiary exercises, see Rudolf Steiner's fundamental presentations in the chapter "Some Effects

of Initiation" in *How to Know Higher Worlds* (CW 10) and in the chapter "Knowledge of Higher Worlds — Initiation" in *Outline of Esoteric Science* (CW 13).

Master... Masters of Wisdom and Harmony of Feelings:
Rudolf Steiner is referring to highly evolved individualities who are of the greatest significance for the evolution of humanity. In a letter dated January 2, 1905, that was published in CW 264, he says: "These lofty beings have already gone the path that the rest of humanity has yet to go. They work as great teachers of wisdom and harmony of humanity's feelings."

Spirits of time — archangel epochs:
Indications appear repeatedly in Rudolf Steiner's lectures of the seven archangels and their periods of rulership—chronologically for the first time in the Esoteric Lessons. The names of the seven archangels and the connection of each with their respective planet, as well as the span of time of their rulership, stems from Johannes Trithemius. In 1508 he made public a mystical chronology in the article "Von den syben Geysten oder Engel" [Concerning the seven spirits or angels.] of spirits that should rule the world in accordance with God. In the dedication's epistle to Emperor Karl Maximilian: "...that it is the belief of ancient wise ones that the world, as arranged by God, should be ruled by subordinate spirits. The seven planets of world creation were determined for the seven spirits respectively. Each would reign the world from his planet for 354 years and four months (in the Foreword of the sixth book of the *Polygraphy*, another four days and four hours are added to this), and should rule four times in the sequence of these spirits' rulership. This view is taken from the book of the ancient philosopher Menastor mentioned by Trithemius in the third book of his stenography." (Quoted according to Isodore Silbernagel in *Johannes Trimethius*, Regensburg, 1885.)

The designation "Theosophy" and "Theosophical":
Because Rudolf Steiner was general secretary of the German Section of the Theosophical Society from 1902-1912/13, he used the terminology that was customary at that time, but always in the sense that he characterized in his introduction to his book *Theosophy*, published in 1904, as follows: "As human beings we call the highest thing that we can look up to 'the Divine,' and we must imagine that our highest aim and calling have something to do with this divine element. This may well be why wisdom that transcends the sense-perceptible world, that reveals to us both our essential nature and our destiny, is called *theosophy*, or 'divine wisdom.' The name 'spiritual science' can be given to the observation of spiritual processes in human life and in the cosmos. If, as has been done in this book, we extract from spiritual science the phenomena pertaining especially to the essential spiritual core of the human being, then we use the term "theosophy" for this particular subject area, since it has been applied in this sense for centuries."

After the separation from the Theosophical Society, Rudolf Steiner went back to using the designations "Anthroposophy" and "anthroposophically-oriented spiritual science," as he had done at the beginning of the twentieth century.

"Not I, but Christ in me":
This quotation of the Apostle Paul is used often in the Esoteric lessons. It comes from Galatians 2:20. It reads as follows: "I am crucified with Christ: nevertheless I live; yet not I, but Christ liveth in me: and the life which I now live in the flesh I live by the faith of the Son of God, who loved me, and gave himself for me."

Reference Notes for the Esoteric Lessons

PART I

Notes of Esoteric Lessons 1913 and 1914

Cologne, January 2, 1913

Record A: in the handwriting of Alice Kinkel; Record B: in the handwriting of Mathilde Scholl; Record C: record from Margrethe Morgenstern; Record D: record from Helene Röchling.

Page 23, "that we have to separate ourselves completely … "
This refers to the agitation caused by the Star of The East about the alleged appearance of a world teacher in the person of Krishnamurti. More details can be found in CW 264, Part II.

Page 23, "words of Mrs. Besant from 1906 are read"
"Judge has fallen on this perilous path of occultism; Leadbeater has fallen on it; very likely I too shall fall; but we shall all come back and work again. If the day of my fall should come, I ask those who love me not to shrink from condemning my fault, not to attenuate it, or say that black is white; but rather let them lighten my heavy karma as I am trying to lighten that of my friend and brother, by saying that black is black, by proclaiming the unshaken purity of the ideal, and by declaring that the fall of an individual leaves shattered their trust in the Masters of Purity and Compassion. On that rock we rest." (Esoteric Lesson circular from Annie Besant from Simla, India, dated June 9, 1906). Rudolf Steiner translated this into German (Archive No. 6961).

Compare also the chapter, "Mrs. Besant's Verfahren. Der Konvent von 1912," [Mrs. Besant's transgression. The convent in 1912] in Eugène Levy's book *Mrs. Annie Besant und die Krisis in der Theosophischen Gesellschaft* [Mrs. Annie Besant and the crisis in the Theosophical Society], Berlin, 1913. See also CW 264.

Page 23, "Watch and pray"
Translator's note: Matthew 28:20, Revised Standard Version.

Page 23, "Essene Order"
The Essenes built several remote communities in Israel, in which they lived ascetically—often in poverty and celibacy. They had a mystery teaching that was only for initiates. Basic information about them was given by Philo of Alexandria (20 B.C.E.–30 C.E.) in his *Vom beschaulichen Leben* [Concerning contemplative life]. In this work, he also speaks of the two rules or regulations of the Essenes that are mentioned in the Lesson. See also Emil Bock's translation in his *Caesars and Apostles*. For more on the Essenes, see also Rudolf Steiner's statements in *According to Matthew* (CW 123).

Page 23, "the Nathan Jesus"
In reference to the two Jesus boys, see Rudolf Steiner's fundamental presentation in his book *The Spiritual Guidance of the Individual and Humanity* (CW 15), third lecture; as well as the lecture cycles: *According to Luke* (CW 114) and *According to Matthew* (CW 123).

Page 25, "Rather a beggar in the overworld"
In Homer's *Odyssey*, the shadow of Achilles among the dead complains in the 11th Book: "'Say not a word,' he answered, 'in death's favour; I would rather be a paid servant in a poor man's house [a beggar] and be above ground than king of kings among the dead....'" [Rendered into English prose by Samuel Butler. Published in the *Great Books* series by William Benton, Encyclopaedia Britannica, Inc., Chicago: 1952, nineteenth printing, 1971.

Page 27, "Leadbeater"
Charles Webster Leadbeater (1847-1934). Formerly a priest of the High Anglican Church, he became a member of the Theosophical Society in 1883 and accompanied Blavatsky to India in 1884. After his return, he worked with Sinnett in London. In 1906 he withdrew from the Society after various reproaches led to his "demise." However, already in 1909 Annie Besant called him back again, and he discovered the child Krishnamurti. Thus, he actually inspired the founding of the order of the Star of the East. In 1913, he went to Australia and took part in the founding of the Liberal Catholic Church, where he became a bishop. This did not lessen his influence in the Theosophical Society.

Page 27, "must remain closed to the followers of her esoteric direction"
The Executive Council of the German Section of the Theosophical Society decided on December 8, 1912, to call upon the members of the Star of the East to leave the Theosophical Society; otherwise they would be shut out of the Section. (Compare Mathilde Scholl in the *Mitteilungen* [News], XV, January 1913.

Page 30, "when an esoteric movement arises"
This probably refers to the founding of the Anthroposophical Society that had taken place a few days before.

Page 30, "Wisdom is only in the truth"
According to J. W. Goethe: "Wisdom is only in the truth." From "Maximen und Reflexionen" [Maxims and reflections] in *Kunst und Altertum* [Art and antiquity], volume 3, first book: "Eigenes und Angeignetes in Sprüchen" [Personal and the appropriated aphorisms]). This was placed by Rudolf Steiner as the motto at the beginning of "Entwurf der Grundsätze einer Anthroposophischen Gesellschaft" [Outline of the bylaws of an Anthroposophical society] that he gave for the Anthroposophical Society. In *Awakening to Community* (CW 257).

Page 30, "Judge"
William Quan Judge (1851-1896). Co-founder and vice-president of the Theosophical Society. General Secretary of the American Section. When he was attacked in 1894 from Adyar, almost the whole American Section separated itself from the central leadership and formed itself autonomously as the Theosophical Society in America.

Page 30, "Judge has fallen and Leadbeater has fallen ..."
Annie Besant's words in 1906. See the corresponding note above for this Lesson. The part of the sentence having to do with Judge was maintained by Annie Besant and had its effect, not through its truth, but through its being repeated. See Chapter VII in Hella Wiesberger's *Rudolf Steiners esoterische Lehrtätigkeit* [Rudolf Steiner's teaching activity], Dornach, 1997.

Cologne, January 4, 1913

Record A: in the handwriting of Mathilde Scholl; Record B: record from Hendrika Hollenbach; Record C: in the handwriting of Alice Kinkel; Record D: in the handwriting of Louise Clason.

Page 34, "what Mrs. Besant said in 1909 is a contradiction of what she maintained in 1912"
This has to do with the contradictory letter that Annie Besant wrote in reference to Dr. Hugo Vollrath. Vollrath (born 1877) was a Theosophical bookseller and publisher (Theosophisches Verlag [Theosophical press], Leipzig). Because Vollrath wanted to use the German Section for his personal purposes, working with him was quite difficult. Mainly through pressure by the Leipzig Branch he was, according to the decision of the seventh General Meeting of the German Section, excluded from the German Section in October 1908.

Rudolf Steiner came to an understanding about this matter with Annie Besant. See his letter of 1909 printed in CW 264. In spite of this, in the summer of 1911, Besant named Vollrath as secretary for the representative of the Star of the East, Wilhelm Hübbe-Schleiden.

In May 1912, Annie Besant wrote a letter to the *Mitteilungen für die Mitglieder der deutschen Sektion der Theosophischen Gesellschaft* [News for members of the German section of the Theosophical Society] (edited by Mathilde Scholl), in which she denied things she had written in 1908, or 1909. Rudolf Steiner wrote a response to this (Mathilde Scholl—*Mitteilungen*, No. XIV, Cologne, December 1912). In order to document Annie Besant's contradiction, an excerpt of Steiner's response is given here as an example:

"I am obliged to clarify things concerning Mrs. Besant's letter to the members. I will do this totally objectively on the basis of the facts. Mrs. Besant wrote in May of 1912: 'Dr. Vollrath made no appeal to me. Therefore, I had no obligation to take heed of correctness or incorrectness in this matter, and even as yet I do not recognize it.' Exactly the opposite is the objective truth! The facts are as follows: already on December 1, 1908, Dr. Vollrath directed an appeal to Mrs. Besant in the form of a letter that was five quarter-pages long, about his having been excluded [from the German Section] in October 1908. Mrs. Besant sent me this letter from Dr. Vollrath enclosed in a letter she wrote to me on January 7, 1909, and in which Mrs. Besant wrote: 'Dr. Vollrath sends me various complaints. I am enclosing his letter. Let me know if it is your opinion that, in his case, there is something that would be a hindrance to his remaining a member in the broader sense. A person who is harmless as a member in the Theosophical Society can be disruptive at times in a lodge or section, and a section can exclude a person from itself but not from the Theosophical Society, just as a lodge can exclude a person from its body but not from the section. I am not inclined to exclude a member from the general Theosophical Society; however, I will not answer Dr. Vollrath definitely before I have heard from you.'"

[Translator Note: This letter from Annie Besant was originally in English and was then translated into German. The above is a literal translation of the German rendering of her statements.]

To this letter from Mrs. Besant and to the appeal from Dr. Vollrath to Mrs. Besant—his appeal already contained things of the same kind that he wrote in his pamphlet in 1911—Steiner answered Mrs. Besant thoroughly and described the situation. He also wrote her about the reasons that led, not him, but the Executive Council of the Section to take the step of excluding Dr. Vollrath.

"Besant then answered me on March 18, 1909 [again a literal translation of the rendering into German]: "With regard to Dr.Vollrath, I acknowledge fully that occasionally it is necessary to exclude a person from the closer work of a lodge or a section. Because an appeal was made to me (underlining by me—R. Steiner), I as president, agree with the action of the German Section and enclose a note that you may use officially as his you see fit. I am writing at the same time to Dr. Vollrath to inform him of this."

The note mentioned above and which was enclosed with this letter reads as follows [literal translation]:

To Dr. Rudolf Steiner,
General Secretary of the German Theosophical Society
My Dear Colleague,
In the sense of Rule 36 of the General Constitution of the Theosophical Society, which gives the president alone the power to grant charters and diplomas or to invalidate them, and in view of Rule 37, which grants the national Societies the right to form their own regulations, I decide, as president, since Dr. Vollrath of Leipzig appealed to me (These words underlined by me—Dr. Steiner.) because of his exclusion from the German Theosophical Society, and having heard all the details of the matter (words underlined by me—Dr. Steiner), that his exclusion from the German Theosophical Society is well-founded, and that Dr. Vollrath is no longer a member of this body.'

"With regard to this fact, I wish to say yet in summary: On March 18, 1909, Mrs. Besant writes: 'since Dr. Vollrath appealed to me and after having heard all the details of the matter....' On May 8, 1912, the *same* Mrs. Besant writes: 'Dr. Vollrath made no appeal to me; therefore, I have no obligation to pay heed to the correctness or incorrectness in this matter; and as yet I do not recognize it'. "

Page 34, "that a general secretary (the English secretary) writes that Mrs. Besant must have forgotten her letter of 1909"

Rudolf Steiner reports about this in a letter to the members of the Theosophical Society (*Mitteilungen für die Mitglieder der deutschen Sektion der Theosophischen Gesellschaft* [News for members of the German section of that Theosophical Society], No. XV, Cologne, January 1913): "Another leading personality of the Theosophical Society [this was J.I. Wedgwood, General Secretary of the Theosophical Society in England and Wales.], who was advised, through extensive writing, how the statements of Mrs. Besant stand in absolute contradiction to what was written in 1909, surprised me because she was actually in a position to fell the following judgment: 'Mrs. Besant must have forgotten her letter of 1909; and of course, wrote in perfect good faith that she did not know the ins-and-outs of the Vollrath case. She has a mass of correspondence from all over the world, and much public, non-Theosophical work in England and India, so that forgetfulness is readily pardonable.' [Wedgwood's letter from London to Rudolf Steiner on December 17, 1912]. Now it appears to me that a system that makes *such* a judgment possible should be impossible in the Theosophical Society. The gentleman in question must know that Mrs. Besant cannot just have forgotten what happened in 1909, but rather that in 1912 she not only denied what happened in 1909, but in this denial she accused a general secretary of giving an untrue description of a situation."

Page 34, "H. P. Blavatsky ... the correct idea of what an avatar is"
See *The Secret Doctrine* by H. P. Blavatsky, volume 3, chapter XLI: "The Doctrine of the Avatars."

Page 35, "Within your thinking cosmic thoughts live"
See "The Souls' Probation" in the *Four Mystery Dramas* (CW 14), first scene; and "The Guardian of the Threshold," sixth scene, in the same volume.

Page 36, "the human being is the result of the working together of all the gods"
Felix Balde or Capesius in the fifth scene of "The Souls' Probation."

Page 36, "apostle Paul speaks of the first Adam"
1 Corinthians 15:45-49 and Romans 5:14.

Page 36, "Renounce God and die"
Book of Job 2:9.

Page 37, "Where two or three are gathered together in my name ..."
Matthew 18:20.

Berlin, January 6, 1913

Record A: in the handwriting of Lilla Harris; Record B: record from Hendrika Hollenbach.

Page 43, "wish to say along with Meister Eckardt: 'What good is it if I am a King, if I do not know it'"
The quote in literal translation: "For if I were a king who did not know it, I would be no king." Sermon 36, "Scitate, qui prop est regnum dei," in *Deutsche Predigten und Trakate* [German Sermons and treatises], published by Josef Quint, Munich, 1963.

Page 45, "Better a beggar in the overworld ..."
See the corresponding note for page 25.

Berlin, February 8, 1913

Record A: record from Günther Wagner ; Record B: record from the collection of Elisabeth Vreede; Record C: record from Hendrika Hollenbach; Record D: record from Mathilde Scholl.

Page 56, "presented or intimated in the third Mystery Drama with the two paintings by Raphael and Leonardo da Vinci"
According to oral communication from Henry Collison—and passed on by Michael Blume in Dornach—during the first production of the third mystery drama, "The Guardian of the Threshold," in the third scene (in Lucifer's realm), paintings were projected onto the background. They were as follows: in the center and above was the Leonardo da Vinci's *Last Supper*; above and left was Raphael's *School of Athens*; and above and right was Raphael's *Disputa*. Below, sculptures were projected as follows: from left to right was one of the Michaelangelo Slaves; in the center, the Laocoön Group; and finally, Venus de Milo.

Page 56, "Pleasure (?)"
Compare this with Record A of the same Lesson.

Stuttgart, sometime between February 17–20, 1913

Record A: record from Ida Knoch; Record B: record source is not known; Record C: in the handwriting of Camilla Wandrey.

Page 58, "Thus the divine thinks us in the 'I'"
In Record B it reads: "Thus the divine thinks my 'I.'"

Page 59, "Better a beggar in the over-world"
See the corresponding note for page 25.

Page 60, "the feeling of deepest reverence and devotion"
There then follows text in Record B that is exactly the same as in Record A from the fourth paragraph onward. It is, therefore, not repeated here.

Munich, March 12, 1913

Record A: in the handwriting of Mathilde Scholl and Barbara Wolf; Record B: in the handwriting of Alice Kinkel.

Berlin, March 16, 1913

Record A: record from Hendrika Hollenbach; Record B: record from the collection of Elisabeth Vreede; Record C: in the handwriting of Camilla Wandrey; Record D: record from Günther Wagner; Record E: in the handwriting of Nelly von Lichtenberg.

Page 69, "Oda Waller"
Oda Waller (ca. 1880–March 8, 1913). Sister of Mieta Waller. See Rudolf Steiner's lectures of January 18, 1914, and May 9, 1914, in *Our Dead* (CW 261).

The Hague, March 21, 1913

Record A: in the handwriting of Lilla Harris and Nelly von Lichtenberg; and the records of Mathilde Scholl and Günther Wagner.

Page 79, "living in the consonants and vowels"
In another record that is otherwise the same, there follows here: E.D.N. – I. – M. – P.S.S.R.

The Hague, March 21 and 25, 1913

Record from Hendrika Hollenbach.

The Hague, March 25, 1913

Handwritten records in the handwriting of Lilla Harris and Nelly von Lichtenberg; notes from Mathilde Scholl and Günther Wagner.

Page 82, "earthly development"
In another record, that is otherwise the same, the term is "earthly being."

Page 85, *"Per Spiritum Sanctum reviviscimus"*
In another record, that is otherwise the same, is added as the final phrase: "The Grail: chalice entwined by purified serpents."

Berlin, April 11, 1913

Record A: record from the collection of Elisabeth Vreede; Record B: in the handwriting from an unknown source; Record C: record of Hendrika Hollenbach; Record D: in the handwriting of Louise Clason.

Page 89, "Record B"
This record states that the obituary of Julius Bittmann was read before the beginning of the Lesson. See what Rudolf Steiner said about him in the lecture of January 18, 1914, in *Our Dead* (CW 261).

Straßburg, May 14, 1913

Record A: record from Emma Klein; Record B: record from the collection of Elisabeth Vreede, in the handwriting from an unknown source.

Page 97, "Plato already said: 'God is the good'"
See Plato's "The State," Volume III of Collected Works of Plato, as well as "Theaitos" in Volume IV.

Page 97, "No one is good but God alone:"
Mark 10:18 and Luke 18:19.

Page 98, "You will be like the gods"
Genesis 3:5.

Page 98, "You are gods"
John 10:34.

Page 99, "Nature is sin, spirit is devil"
Quote from Goethe's *Faust*, Part I, Act I: Imperial palitanate.

Stuttgart, May 18, 1913

Record A: in the handwriting of Mathilde Scholl; Record B: in the handwriting of Barbara Wolf; Record C: record of Ida Koch; Record D: record from the collection of Elisabeth Vreede, in the handwriting of unknown source; Record E: in handwriting of Camilla Wandrey; Record F: source of record is unknown.

Page 100, "what was discussed yesterday in the public lecture"
Lecture of May 17, 1913, in Stuttgart: "Ergebnisse der Geistesforschung für Lebensfragen und das Todesrätsel" [Results of spiritual research for life questions and the riddle of death]. (As of 1998 not yet published in the German collected works).

Page 104, "Mercury (the Venus of today)"
Rudolf Steiner spoke several times about the fact that in ancient times the planet we call Mercury was called Venus and the planet we call Venus was called Mercury. See the lectures of June 20, 1908, in *The Apocalypse of St. John* (CW 104); of September 5, 1908, in the *Egyptian Myths and Mysteries* (CW 106); and of April 15, 1909, in *Spiritual Hierarchies and the Physical World* (CW 110).

Page 106, "third Sun"
For the mystery of the three Suns, see Rudolf Steiner's lectures of August 24, 1918, in *Die Wissenschaft vom Werden des Menschen* [The science of the development of the human being] (GA 183); and of April 24, 1922 in *The Sun Mystery: and the Mystery of Death and Resurrection* (CW 211).

Page 106, "Not I, but Christ in me"
Galatians 2:20.

Page 106, "Julian the Apostate"
Julianus Flavius Claudius (331-363 c.e.). Roman Caesar. Although raised as a Christian, he turned to the ancient Mysteries again, for which reason Christian authors called him "the apostate," which means the unfaithful. When he was thirty-two years old, he was murdered during a campaign in Asia. See the detailed comments by Rudolf Steiner, in his lecture of December 30, 1910,

in *Occult History* (CW 126); of April 19, 1917, in *Building Stones for an Understanding of the Mystery of Golgotha* (CW 175); and of September 16, 1924, in *Karmic Relationships*, volume IV (CW 238).

Page 110, "green ... violet" (In diagram)
In another record, that is otherwise the same, the colors of the circles, from inside out, are as follows: violet, reddish, yellow, blue, red, violet, green.

Helsingfors (Helsinki), June 1, 1913

Record from Hendrika Hollenbach.

Helsingfors (Helsinki), June 5, 1913

Record from Hendrika Hollenbach.

Page 124, "The events of Adyar"
At the end of 1912 in Adyar, it was decided to exclude the German Section from the Theosophical Society, and this was settled in March 1913. For this Wilhelm Hübbe-Schleiden wrote a memorandum: "Denkschrift über die Abtrennung der Anthroposophischen Gesellschaft von der Theosophischen Gesellschaft" [Memorandum about the severance of the Anthroposophical Society from the Theosophical Society]. It was full of untruths, such that Rudolf Steiner saw himself forced to publish a correction. This was printed in the July edition of the Scholl-*Mitteilungen* [News], No. III, 1913.

Stockholm, June 8, 1913

Record from the collection of Elisabeth Vreede, and a handwritten record from an unknown source.

Munich, September 3, 1913

Record A: record from Paula Hübbe-Schleiden; Record B: record source unknown; Record C: in the handwriting of Barbara Wolf; Record D: in the handwriting of Louise Clason.

Page 129, "that we experienced during our time together"
From August 19-23, 1913, performances of both Mystery Dramas, *The Guardian of the Threshold* and *The Soul's Awakening* took place. Immediately afterward, from August 24-31, 1913, Rudolf Steiner held the lecture cycle "The Secrets of the Threshold" (CW 147).

Page 129, "Leibniz's philosophy"
Gottfried Wilhelm Leibniz (1646-1716). German mathematician and philoso-

pher. With his "Monadologie" [Monadology] and "Theodizee" in which he attempted to unite universal mathematics and theological philosophy into a world system, he was one of the forerunners of the "Aufklärung" [Age of Enlightenment] in Germany. Leibniz conceives of the world as a system of original forces that he calls monads. These monads—each closed within itself—have various degrees of consciousness. Compare in Rudolf Steiner's book *The Riddles of Philosophy* (CW 18) the chapter: "The World Conceptions of the Modern Age of Thought Evolution."

Page 129, "Haeckel's materialism"
Ernst Haeckel (1834-1919). Medical doctor and natural scientific researcher. Professor of Zoology in Jena. Haeckel represented vehemently the monistic approach, wherein everything in existence precedes out of one and the same principle. Concerning Haeckel, see also Rudolf Steiner's essay, "Haeckel und seine Gegner" [Haeckel and his opponents] in *Methodische Grundlagen der Anthroposophie. Gesammelte Aufsätze zur Philosophie, Naturwissenschaft, Ästhetik und Seelenkunde 1884-1901* [Methodical foundations of Anthroposophy. Collected essays on philosophy, natural science, aesthetics, and psychology; 1844-1901], (GA 30); and his lecture of October 5, 1905, in *Die Welträtsel und die Anthroposophie* [The World Riddle and Anthroposophy] (GA 54).

Page 129, "Spinoza's philosophy"
Baruch Spinoza (1632-1677). Leading Dutch philosopher of rationalism. Mathematician and optician. Spinoza wrote—proceeding from Neo-platonism and from Descartes—a pantheistic philosophy of necessity. According to him, there is only one solitary substance, and it has its beginning and being out of itself and cannot be substantiated by anything; that one substance is God. See Rudolf Steiner's *The Riddles of Philosophy* (CW 18) the chapter: "The World Conceptions of the Modern Age of Thought Evolution."

Page 129, "Hegel's worldview"
Georg Wilhelm Friedrich Hegel (1770-1831). Philosopher of German idealism. For Hegel, the absolute (idea, God) is the foundation and principle of the entire world. See Rudolf Steiner's statements about him in *The Riddles of Philosophy* (CW 18), the chapter: "Reactionary World Conceptions" and in his *The Riddle of Man* (CW 20), the chapter: "German Idealism as Conception of Thought."

Page 129, "one of them came to me"
Details of this are not known.

Page 130, "The Soul's Awakening"
Rudolf Steiner's fourth Mystery Drama. In *Four Mystery Dramas* (CW 14).

Page 132, "*Theosophy*"
(CW 9), first published in 1909.

Editorial and Reference Notes ✳ 461

Page 138, "in this lecture cycle"
Secrets of the Threshold (CW 147). Held in Munich from August 24-31, 1913.

Munich, September 4, 1913
Record A: in the handwriting of Nelly von Lichtenberg; Record B: record from the collection of Elisabeth Vreede, and also a handwritten record of unknown source; Record C: records from Clara Motzkus and Anna Riebensahm; Record D: in the handwriting of Louise Clason; Record E: record from the collection of Fred Poeppig.

Page 140, "Meister Eckardt"
Meister Eckardt (1260-1327). Dominican and Mystic. Lectures in Paris, Straßburg, and Cologne. He was accused of being a heretic. Well-known are his *Deutsche Predigten und Trakate* [German sermons and treatises], translated and published by Josef Quint, Munich 1963 and Zürich 1979. See also the chapter "Meister Eckardt" in Rudolf Steiner's *Mystics after Modernism* (CW 7), first published in 1901.

Page 140, "Ruysbroek"
Jan van Ruysbroek (1294-1381). Mystic, vicar, and a priest in Brussels. Retreated in 1354 into the Augustine Cloister in Groenendal (near Waterloo). He died as it's prior. The nature of his mysticism earned him the name, "Doctor ecstaticus" [Dr. ecstasy]. See also Rudolf Steiner's *Mystics after Modernism* [CW 7], the chapter: "Friend of God."

Page 140, "Tauler"
Johannes Tauler (1300-1361). Mystic. Preacher in Straßburg. Pupil of the "Unknown Friend of God from Oberland." See also in Rudolf Steiner's *Mystics after Modernism* (CW 7), the chapter: "Friend of God," first published in 1901.

Page 140, "Suso"
Heinrich Suso (1295-1366). Dominican monk in Constance, and a pupil of Eckardt. See also the chapter "Friend of God," in Rudolf Steiner's *Mystics after Modernism* (CW 7).

Page 141, "Swedenborg's worldview"
Emanuel Swedenborg (1688-1772). Swedish scientist and Mystic. His works are: *Vom Himmel* [Of heaven], 1784; *Der Verkehr zwischen Seele und Leib* [The association between soul and body]; and *Himmel und Hölle* [Heaven and hell]. Compare Rudolf Steiner's lecture of September 23, 1923: "Jacob Boehme, Paracelsus, Swedenborg" in *Three Perspectives of Anthroposophy: Cultural Phenomenon* (CW 225).

Page 141, "what Kant ... took from Swedenborg's writings"
Immanuel Kant (1742-1804). See *Träume eines Geistersehers* [Dreams of a seer],

462 * Esoteric Lessons

Königsberg, 1766. See also his letter to Miss Charlotte von Knobloch about Swedenborg on August 10, 1763, in *Kant's Briefe* [Kant's letters], Leipzig, 1911.

Page 142, "how Maeterlinck wanted proof of the spiritual life"
See the lecture of August 27, 1913, in *Secrets of the Threshold* (CW 147), in which Rudolf Steiner spoke about Maeterlinck's *Vom Tode* [About death], Jena 1913.

Maurice Maeterlinck (1862-1949). Belgian poet.

Page 143, "irrefutable proof of the immortality of the soul"
Compare this with the formulation in Record D.

Page 143, "The Soul's Awakening"
The fourth Mystery Drama, first performed in 1913; in *Four Mystery Dramas* (CW 14).

Page 147, "in the thirteenth chapter of the John Gospel"
The Washing of the Feet.

Page 147, "the Sermon on the Mount or the Beatitudes"
Matthew 5:3 – 7:27; Luke 6:20-49.

Page 147, "Cusanus"
Nicholas of Kues (1401-1464).

Christiania (Oslo), October 5, 1913

Record A: record from the collection of Elisabeth Vreede and a record in an unknown handwriting; Record B: in the handwriting of Alice Kinkel.

Page 150, "William Crookes"
William Crookes (1832-1909). English physicist and chemist. Discovered Thallium. Member of the Theosophical Society. He organized many experiments with mediums. Crookes wrote *Spiritualism and Science*, published in German in Leipzig, 1871 and *Materialization Experiments*, published in German in Leipzig, 1923.

Page 151, "And they hid their face."
Which ancient document is referred to here could not be ascertained. The statement was not taken down in its entirety in this record. Compare Record B of the lesson of October 6, 1913. See also the lecture of March 24, 1908, in *The Influence of Spiritual Beings on Man* (CW 102).

Page 152, "Anaxagoras"
Anaxagoras [ca. 500-428 B.C.E.]. Klazomena, Asia Minor. The pre-Socratic natural philosopher. He was exiled from Athens due to his maintaining that

the Sun is a glowing stone mass. His doctrine is based on the assumption of an eternal "primordial material" (Homoiomerien). See also Rudolf Steiner's *Riddles of Philosophy* (CW 18), the chapter: "The World Conception of the Greek Thinkers."

Page 152, "Empedocles"
Empedocles (483-424 B.C.E.). Born in Agrigent. Greek nature philosopher and statesman. He is supposed to have died by falling into Mt. Etna. His philosophy proceeds from the four elements, which build physical matter through the forces of love and hate. See also Rudolf Steiner's brief outline of his philosophy in *Riddles of Philosophy*, in the chapter: "The World Conception of the Greek Thinkers."

Page 152, "Leibniz"
See the note for page 129 (for the Lesson of September 3, 1913).

Page 152, "a bowl filled with oil"
See, in relation to this, the esoteric exercises given in *Seelenübungen mit Wort- und Sinnbildmeditationen* [Soul exercises with word and image meditations] (GA 267).

Christiania (Oslo), October 6, 1913

Record A: record from Paula Hübbe-Schleiden and a record in an unknown handwriting; Record B: in the handwriting of Alice Kinkel.

Page 156, "The people never feel the devil"
Quote of Mephisto in Goethe's *Faust*, Part I: "Auerbach's Tavern."

Page 156, "Be pleased with what is given to you"
Presumably a free rendering of Christian Fürchtegott Gellert (1715-1769). In his "Zufriedenheit mit seinem Zustande" [Satisfaction with his situation]: "Enjoy what God gives you,/Gladly go without what you do not have."

Page 157, "Schiller let his *Wilhelm Tell* say things"
Friedrich Schiller (1759-1805). In his *Wilhelm Tell*, 1804.

Page 157, "Gerhard Hauptmann"
Gerhart Hauptmann (1862-1946). Main representative of German naturalistic drama. He wrote *Die Weber* [The weavers] in 1892 and *Der Biberpelz* [The beaver pelt] in 1893. See also Rudolf Steiner's essays and reviews in *Gesammelte Aufsaetze zu Dramaturgie* [Collected essays on drama] (GA 29).

Bergen, October 11, 1913

Record A: record from the collection of Elisabeth Vreede and a record in handwriting, source not known; Record B: in the handwriting of Alice Kinkel.

Page 159, "hindrances from the physical body"
See the Esoteric Lessons of January 2, October 27, October 30, and November 19, 1911; as well as the Esoteric Lessons of January 1 and January 16, 1912, in *Esoteric Lessons 1904-1905* (CW 266/2).

Page 160, "given recently as *The Fifth Gospel*"
See Rudolf Steiner's *The Fifth Gospel* (CW 148), especially the lectures of October 1, 2, 3, 5, and 6 in Christiania (Oslo).

Page 161, "phantom"
See the lectures of October 10-14, 1911, in *From Jesus to Christ* (CW 131).

Copenhagen, October 15, 1913

Record A: record from the collection of Elisabeth Vreede and a record in an unknown handwriting; Record B: in the handwriting of Alice Kinkel; Record C: in the handwriting of Camilla Wandrey; Record D: in the handwriting of Louise Clason.

Page 162, "the Fall of humanity"
Genesis 3.

Page 162, "You will become like the gods"
According to Genesis 3:5.

Page 163, "in the form of a serpent in the temptation"
Genesis 3:4.

Page 163, "concepts like 'light', 'warmth' ... our exercises"
See *Seelenübungen mit Wort- und Sinnbildmeditationen* [Soul exercises with word and image meditations] (GA 267).

Page 168, "(Tower of Babel)"
Genesis 11:1-9.

Nuremberg, November 9, 1913

Record from Margareta Morgenstern.

Nuremberg, November 10, 1913

Record from Margareta Morgenstern.

Berlin, November 17, 1913

Record A: in the handwriting of Mathilde Scholl from a record from Mrs. Behrendts; Record B: record from Mathilde Scholl; Record C: records from

Hendrika Hollenbach and from the collection of Elisabeth Vreede — the source of the handwriting is unknown; Record D: in the handwriting of Louise Clason.

Page 175, "In the lecture before the last one in the Lodge"
The lecture of October 21, 1913, in Berlin. Can be found in *The Fifth Gospel* (CW 148).

Page 175, "the women at the grave sought him and found that the grave was empty"
Luke 24:1-3.

Page 176, "Kant"
Immanuel Kant (1742-1804). Königsberg philosopher. His most important works, in which he laid out his doctrine of the boundaries of knowledge are: *Critique of Pure Reason* (written in 1781/1786); *Critique of Practical Reason* (written in 1788); and *Critique of the Power of Judgment*.

Page 177, "between birth and the seventh year of life is the first moment that we can recall"
For this, see Rudolf Steiner's writing, "The Education of the Child in Light of Spiritual Science," included in *The Education of the Child and Early Lectures on Education* (CW 34); and the lecture of April 16, 1912, in *Erfahrungen des Übersinnlichen. Drei Wege der Seele zu Christus* [Experiences of the supersensible. Three paths of the soul to Christ] (GA 143).

Stuttgart, November 23, 1913

Record A: in the handwriting of an unknown source; Record B: in the handwriting of Alice Kinkel.

Page 187, "conversation that a student of Schopenhauer's had with Nietzsche"
Arthur Schopenhauer (1788-1860). Philosopher. See also the biography of him that Rudolf Steiner wrote as the introduction for the Cotta Edition of *Arthur Schopenhauers sämtlichen Werken* [Arthur Schopenhauer's collected works]; also contained in Steiner's *Biographien und biographischer Skizzen* [Biographies and biographical sketches] (GA 33). See also "Reactionary World Conceptions" in *Riddles of Philosophy* (CW 18), as well as the lecture of December 4, 1920, in *The Bridge between Universal Spirituality and the Physical Constitution of Man* (CW 202).

Friedrich Nietzsche (1844-1900). See Rudolf Steiner's *Friedrich Nietzsche: A Fighter against His Time* (CW 5). Written in 1895.

Page 187, "Deussen maintained in relation to Nietzsche"
Could not be ascertained.

Paul Deussen (1845-1919). Sanskrit expert. Professor in Kiel. Friend of Nietzsche.

Munich, December 9, 1913

Record A: records in the handwriting of Mathilde Scholl and Barbara Wolf; Record B: records from the collection of Elisabeth Vreede and a record in an unknown handwriting.

Page 192, "Maeterlinck maintained in his last book"
Vom Tode [On death], Jena 1913. Rudolf Steiner speaks about this in more detail in his lecture of August 27, 1913, in *Secrets of the Threshold* (CW 147). Compare also, the Esoteric Lesson of September 4, 1913, in this volume.

Page 194, "Wallace"
Alfred Russel Wallace (1823-1913). British natural scientist. Co-worker and friend of Darwin. Adherent of spiritism.

Page 194, "This help is always present"
In a record that is otherwise the same, it reads here: "these impulses are always there!"

Cologne, December 18, 1913

Record in the handwriting of Louise Clason.

Leipzig, December 30, 1913

Record A: in the handwriting of Camilla Wandrey, and in an unknown handwriting; Record B: records from the collection of Elisabeth Vreede, and in an unknown handwriting; Record C: record from Hendrika Hollenbach; Record D: record from unknown source (perhaps Margareta Morgenstern). Christian Morgenstern was present at this Esoteric Lesson.

Page 207, "[streaming to us]"
The notes are actually illegible here, but the context indicates that perhaps "streaming into us" fits.

Leipzig, January 2, 1914.

Record A: in the handwriting of Camilla Wandrey; Record B: record from Paula Hübbe-Schleiden, records from the collection of Elisabeth Vreede, and record in an unknown handwriting; Record C: record from Hendrika Hollenbach; Record D: record from an unknown source.

Page 211, "Legend of the dog is told"
A legend that Rudolf Steiner often used to show what he understood by positivity.

In *Outline of Esoteric Science* (CW 13), in the chapter: "Knowledge of Higher Worlds–Initiation": "there is a beautiful legend that tells of Christ Jesus and several other people walking past a dead dog. The others all turned away from the ugly sight, but Christ Jesus spoke admiringly of the animal's beautiful teeth." The legend comes from a poem by the Persian poet Nizeni (1141-1203). In the German translation it is called: "Herr Jesus, der die Welt durchwandert..." [Lord Jesus, who wandered through the world]. Also included in Goethe's "Noten und Abhandlungen zu besseren Verständnis des West-östlichen Divan," [Notes and treatments for a better understanding of the West-East Divan], in the author's final version (1827) of "West-östlichen Divan," now to be found in *Goethe's Werke* [Goethe's Works], Volume 7. Weimar Edition: Hermann Böhlan, 1888.

Page 212, "Swan"
In his lecture of March 28, 1905, Rudolf Steiner says the following: "The third stage is the one where human beings—just as they in ordinary life say 'I' to themselves—now can say 'I' to all beings of the world; where they are raised to encompass the All. In mysticism, the pupil at this stage is called *Swan*. They become the mediator between the teacher and the people." This was printed in the newssheet, "Was in der Anthroposophischen Gesellschaft vorgeht" [What is happening in the Anthroposophical Society], no.44/1936. See also the lectures of June 8, 1906, in *Cosmogonie* [Cosmogony] (GA 94) and of March 29, 1906, "Parzival und Lohengren" in *Die Welträtsel und die Anthroposophie* [The world riddle and Anthroposophy] (GA 54).

Page 212, "these five exercises"
See the note under "Notes on esoteric training/schooling...exercises..." on page 448 of this volume.

Page 215, "[There stood in olden times...]"
First line of the poem "Das Schloss am Meer." [The Castle on the sea] by Ludwig Uhland, German poet.

Bremen, January 24, 1914

Record in the handwriting of Camilla Wandrey.

Berlin, January 24, 1914

Record A: records from the collection of Elisabeth Vreede, and in an unknown handwriting; Record B: record from Hendrika Hollenbach.

Hannover, February 7, 1914

Record from the collection of Elisabeth Vreede.

Stuttgart, March 5, 1914

Record A: record from the collection of Elisabeth Vreede, and in an unknown handwriting; Record B: in the handwriting of Nanna Thorne; Record C: record of unknown source, but in the handwriting of Günther Schubert, and the mantra is from Rudolf Steiner's notebook, Archive No. 499: "I turn to things...."

Page 228, *"How to Know Higher Worlds"*
(CW 10). Published in parts, 1904/05, then later as a book.

Page 229, "lines of the following verses"
The mantras differ slightly in the various students' records. The version here is Rudolf Steiner's original.

Berlin, March 27 (and Vienna, April 14), 1914

Record A: in the handwriting of Louise Clason; Record B: records from the collections of Elisabeth Vreede and Hendrika Hollenbach; Record C: in the handwriting of Camilla Wandrey; Record D: record from Günther Wagner.

The notes for these two Esoteric Lessons are summarized together in all the records, which is why they are included together here. The Lesson of April 14, 1914, in Vienna, was figured falsely at times as having been held on April 11, 1914.

Page 235, "how difficult it was going to be that he (Rudolf Steiner) could not be with us anymore this winter"
This comment probably referred to an announcement by Rudolf Steiner that he must in the future direct his activity more and more toward Dornach where the first Goetheanum was being built.

Page 240, "Record C"
This record bears the following locations and dates: Berlin and Vienna; March 27 and April 14, 1914.

Page 247, "the verb in line two is in the singular"
Actually the verb *schwebet* is in the plural of the subjunctive mood. Being in the subjunctive mood, it was used for the singular as well as the plural. This does not negate Rudolf Steiner's statement that the two subjects are really one.

Page 247, "There, everything is experienced and felt"
See, in addition, the Esoteric Lesson in Munich, on March 31, 1914.

Page 247, "Record D"
This record bears the locations and dates: Berlin, March 27, 1914; and Vienna, April 11, 1914.

Munich, March 31, 1914

A record in the handwriting of Barbara Wolf and a record from Mathilde Scholl.

Page 258, *"Outline of Esoteric Science"*
(CW 13).

Berlin, April 25, 1914

Record A: record from Günther Wagner and a record in an unknown handwriting; Record B: in the handwriting of Alice Kinkel; Record C: in the handwriting of Camilla Wandrey; Record D: record from Hendrika Hollenbach; Record E: record from Mathilde Scholl, according to notes by Mrs. Berhrendts; Record F: in the handwriting of Emil Leinhas.

Page 261, "The human being has twelve senses"
Concerning the senses, see especially chapter IV, "About the Real Bases of the Intentional Relationship," in *Riddles of the Soul* (CW 21); *Anthroposophy: A Fragment* (CW 45); the lecture cycle, *A Psychology of Body, Soul & Spirit* (CW 115); the lecture of June 20, 1916, in *Weltwesen und Ichheit* [Cosmic being and "I"] (GA. 169); the lectures of August 12, 1916, and September 2, 1916, in *The Riddle of Humanity* (CW 170); the lecture of August 25, 1918, in *Die Wissenschaft vom Werden des Menschen* [The science of the development of the human being] (GA 183); and the lecture of July 22, 1921, in *Menschenwerden, Weltenseele und Weltengeist* [Human development, world-soul, and world-spirit] Part II (GA 206). In addition, booklets, 14, 34, and 58/59 in the series: *Beiträge zu Rudolf Steiners Gesamtausgabe* [Contributions to Rudolf Steiner's collected works].

Page 262, "the Jupiter condition"
In the original record-document, instead of "Jupiter condition," it says "fourth condition." This is certain to be an inadvertent error. It is presumed that the note-taker put in the astrological sign for Jupiter instead of the actual word "Jupiter" and that this was later read as "four." It has been corrected here.

Kassel, May 9, 1914

Record A: record from the collection of Elisabeth Vreede; Record B: in an unknown handwriting.

Basel, June 3, 1914

Record A: records from Günther Wagner, and in an unknown handwriting; Record B: in the handwriting of Louise Clason; Record C: record from Mathilde Scholl.

Norrköping, July 14, 1914

Record A: one record from Paula Hübbe-Schleiden, one in the handwriting from Camilla Wandrey, and one in an unknown handwriting; Record B: record from Mathilde Scholl, according to notes from Mrs. Behrendts; Record C: record from an unknown source, but in the handwriting of Günther Schubert.

Page 285, "Record A"
The insertions here in parentheses come from another record that is otherwise identical.

Page 287, "Blavatsky spoke of Yahweh as Moon god"
For example, in volume 1 of the German edition (Leipzig, O.J.). It reads, in the literal translation: "Yahweh, who is to an outstanding degree a Moon god."

Page 287, "leading magazine of the Theosophical Society that 'esoteric science' is psychic-mystical."
Presumably *The Theosophist* is meant. The statement could not be found.

PART II

Notes of Esoteric Lessons 1920–1923

Foreword

Page 295, "in his memoirs"
From "Errinerungen an der großen Lehrer Dr. Rudolf Steiner, Lebensrückschau eines Österreichers" [Remembrances of the great teacher Rudolf Steiner, a life-review of an Austrian], by Ludwig Graf Polzer-Hoditz. Typescript, Prag, 1937. Published later as *Erinnerungen an Rudolf Steiner* [Remembrances of Rudolf Steiner], Dornach, 1985.

Dornach, February 9, 1920

Record from Helene Finckh. Facsimile of the mantra from Rudolf Steiner's notebook, Archive No. 3316.

Dornach, February 17, 1920

Record from Helene Finckh; and from Rudolf Steiner's notebook, Archive No. 82.

Page 305, "meditation is given to us"
The meditation was written on the blackboard and could be copied.

London, April 16, 1922

Report from memory by George Adams, in a letter on October 8, 1954. Also from Rudolf Steiner's notebook, Archive No. 304.

George Adams-Kaufmann (1894-1963). Member of the Anthroposophical Society in the Emerson Group in London. He translated into English the lectures that Rudolf Steiner held in England, as well as some of Steiner's writings.

Page 311, "Mr. Heywood-Smith"
H.J. Heywood-Smith died in 1951. Member of the Anthroposophical Society in England. Translator of Rudolf Steiner's lectures into English. See also his obituary in "Nachrichtenblatt" [Newssheet] in *Das Goetheanum*, XXVIII, No. 35, 1951.

Page 311, "Mrs. Drury-Lavin"
Ada Drury-Lavin (1858-1931). One of the earliest members of the Anthroposophical Society in England and the leader of the "Zarathustra-Group" in London. See also her obituary in the "Nachrictenblatt" [Newssheet] in *Das Goetheanum*, VIII, No. 45, 1931.

Page 311, "lectures on Michael and the new Christ-event"
Lectures of May 1 and 2, 1913, in *Approaching the Mystery of Golgotha* (CW 152).

Page 311, "the Academe of Gundishapur"
See the lectures of October 12 and October 16, 1918, in *Die Polarität von Dauer und Entwickelung im Menschenleben* [The polarity between duration and development in human life] (GA 184); the lectures of May 1, 1921, and June 5, 1921, in *Materialism and the Task of Anthroposophy* (CW 204); and the lecture of September 12, 1924, in *The Book of Revelation* (CW346).

Page 311, "the Three Tablets"
See **pp. 437-443** of this volume for these mantras.

London, November 12, 1922

Record in the handwriting of Camilla Wandrey.

Vienna, September 30, 1923

The content is as was handed down by Ludwig von Polzer-Hoditz and from a personal conversation on January 28, 1973, between Helga Wiesberger and Hans Erhard Lauer, Polzer-Hoditz's secretary at the time the Lesson was given.

PART III

The Esoteric Youth Group

Page 329, "held on September 4, 1921, in Stuttgart"
The minutes of this meeting were not made public.

Page 329, "vote of a student of the Tübingen University"
Alfred Heidenreich (1898-1969). See his "Jugendbewegung und Anthroposophie" [Youth movement and Anthroposophy], Stuttgart 1922.

Page 330, "end of Kali Yuga"
Talk given to the youth in Stuttgart on March 20, 1921. In *Youth and the Etheric Heart* (CW 217a).

Page 330, "circular:…[To the youth of the Anthroposophical Movement]"
See page 342.

Page 330, "According to the minutes"
Not yet made public.

Page 332, "Draft of the essential aspects of the work in the youth branch"
See page 349.

Page 332, "Independent Anthroposophical Society could form for the youth themselves"
For the memorandum for the forming of this Society, see page 356. More details are in *Das Schicksalsjahr 1923* [The year of destiny 1923], (GA 259).

Page 332, "in a letter to Rudolf Steiner as follows"
Ernst Lehrs included this letter almost word-for-word in his memoirs: *Gelebte Erwartung* [Lived expectation], Stuttgart 1979, without having the original in front of him. The original is handwritten and is in the Rudolf Steiner Archive. He mistakenly gives the date of September 3 instead of September 18th.

Page 334, "through a call"
This call or appeal is given in its entirety, with a chapter heading of it own, in this volume. See p. 352.

Page 335, "official Society representatives were offended that they were not included in the meeting"
At Rudolf Steiner's recommendation, the Executive Council of the Society and the college of teachers of the Independent Waldorf School were invited to his lectures.

Page 336, "the course"
The Youth Course held in Stuttgart, October 3–5, 1922, See *Becoming the Archangel Michael's Companion*, (CW 217).

Page 337, "There were twelve to whom ... the oath formulation"
The number twelve and an oath played a role already from the beginning of the Youth Movement, see pages 334 and 383. Apparently for this reason, the originators of the Esoteric Youth Group felt that an oath would be good. Rudolf Steiner's comment at the close of the meeting of October 13, 1922, may have been in connection with this.

Page 337, "reflect again and again upon the foundational impulse of their group"
From a circular by Ernst Lehrs, "From the Beginnings of our Group."

Page 341, "along with the following letter by Robert Wolfgang Wallach"
The original is in the Rudolf Steiner Archive.

Page 346, "distanced himself from a circular"
It is not clear from which circular Paul Baumann distanced himself. Content-wise and through the indication, "second circular," it could be the preceding one in this volume.

However, the following passage does not fit: "views, that one could ascribe to me on the basis of a (second) circular that bears my name as the contact for the Society." Either he did not express himself clearly and meant the presence of his name on the first circular, or there was another version of the second circular that is not in the Rudolf Steiner Archive.

Page 352, "Transition of ... Spiritual Life"
From the weekly news report *Anthroposophie, Wochenschrift für freies Geistesleben* [Anthroposophy, weekly for independent spiritual life], Volume 4, Number 2, July 13, 1922.

Page 352, "this weekly"
Formerly, *Dreigliederung des sozialen Organismus* [Threefolding of the social organism].

Page 356, "Memorandum ... Orientation"
From *Youth and the Etheric Heart* (CW 217a); also in *Das Schicksalsjahr 1923 in der Geschichte der Anthroposophischen Gesellschaft* [The year of destiny 1923 in the history of the Anthroposophical Society] (GA 259).

Page 356, "Outline of the Statutes"
What is meant are the separately-existing statutes of the old Anthroposophical Society. See GA 259.

Page 359, "could not have come from the founders of the Youth Group"
For instance, the record in question puts the giving of the formulation of the oath on October 12, and then in an illogical context. All the founding members knew, naturally, that the formulation was given on October 16. Further, he brought the question—from Hedwig Hauck, the handwork teacher at the Waldorf School—that was asked on November 16, 1921, after the Esoteric Lesson in *Faculty Meetings Part II* (CW 300b) into connection with the Esoteric Youth Group. This was a totally arbitrary statement, as the idea of an Esoteric Youth Group was not yet born at that time. Finally, Rudolf Steiner's statements of October 16 about the Christian Community were brought in, and these were not included at all in the reports by Lehrs and Rath. Had Rudolf Steiner really said what was maintained there, it would be unthinkable that Rath and Lehrs would not take it up.

Page 366, "a new third element in addition"
Herman Grimm, *Goethe Vorlesung an der Königlichen Universität zu Berlin* [Goethe lectures at the royal university in Berlin], Berlin, 1877. From the twenty-first lecture: "When two men of exceptional means unite for an activity in common, their power does not double, but rather quadruples. Each of them has the other invisibly beside them. The formula would not be G + S, but (G + S) + (S + G). Each adds to the power of the other."

Page 368, "Agriculture Course"
Koberwitz, June 7-16, 1924 (CW 327).

Page 370, "Spitteler"
Carl Spitteler (1845-1924). Swiss poet and winner of the Nobel Prize in 1919.

Page 371, "mysticism of Baal Schem"
This refers either to the kabbalistic mysticism in the name of God, or to the Rabbi who founded the Hassidic sect in the Ukraine around 1740.

Page 371, "in the sixth lecture"
Stuttgart, October 8, 1922 (CW 217).

Page 374, "two parallel streams of history or evolution flowing"
Rudolf Steiner indicated this often, for instance, in the lecture of December 14, 1918, in Dornach: *Die soziale Grundforderung unserer Zeit—In geänderter Zeitlage* [The fundamental social demands of our time—in changed situations] (GA 186), partially translated and published as *The Challenge of the Times*.

Page 376, "after a Creative Speech class"
Rudolf Steiner had Marie Steiner hold a Creative Speech (speech formation) course for the participants of the Youth Course.

Page 379, "having instructed one of us to write them down"
See the facsimile and transcription of the mantra on pages 426-429.

Page 379, "a separate part that is added to this report"
This part is not included here, as the instructions therein add nothing new to this volume. The specific information for the Youth Group meditation is on page 428 in the form that Lili Kolisko recorded.

Page 380, "pastoral letter"
This memory related by Ernst Lehrs is misleading. The confusion was not cleared up, but rather caused by the pastoral letter: "Die dem katholischen Priester gebührende Ehre" [The honor due to the Catholic priests], dated February 2, 1905, by the Archbishop of Salzburg, J.B. Katschthaler. Printed in Carl Mirbt's *Quellen zur Geschichte dea Papstums und des römischen Katholizismus* [Sources for the history of the papacy and Roman Catholicism], Fourth Edition, Tübingen 1924; and also in the end notes of *Polarities in the Evolution of Mankind* (CW197). Rudolf Steiner quoted this pastoral letter often (in the lectures of March 9, 1920, [CW 197]; and July 17, 1920, [CW 198]; as well as in GA 343) as an illustration of the absurdities that arise "when the modern consciousness takes hold of something that should be grasped in a completely different mood." He did this without giving the solution to the problem that arose through this.

Page 383, "a formulation of an oath"
An original by Rudolf Steiner is obviously not available, due to the way he gave it. Lili Kolisko wrote it in her notebook on November 11, 1924, as follows:

> "I promise herewith that I enter, as far as I am aware of, into this community with pure thinking and pure will, and that I acknowledge that the judgment of my being through the acceptance into the community is left to spiritual beings. I want to bring to my consciousness that, through every transgression against this promise, I act against the spiritual being in whose service this community places itself. My soul would succumb to the consequences of such a transgression."

Page 384, "Rosicrucian lectures"
See CW 233a, published in English in three parts: *Mystery Centers of the Middle Ages*; *Rosicrucianism and Modern Initiation*; and *The Easter Festival*.

Page 385, "a kind of Esoteric Section"
See *From the History and Contents of the First Section of the Esoteric School 1904-1914*. (CW 264).

Page 385, "He would have to wait for this"
Rudolf Steiner cannot have meant this the way it is recorded here, as is made clear by the Esoteric Lessons of 1920-1923/24. See part II of this volume.

Page 388, "mysticism of Baal Schem"
See the note for page 371.

Page 390, "Association for independent spiritual life"
Rath commented in his report: "I spoke in my first presentation of the idea of the Group, that our occupying ourselves in Berlin with the 'Call' for this association gave the first impulse." This Call is given as a separate chapter in this volume.

Page 391, "12,000 copies printed"
The existing edition at that time was the 1920 edition and bore the description: 7th-15th editions.

Page 393, "always comes a third element"
See the note for page 366.

Page 398, "special report"
This report was written in the 1950s. It was one of the documents used in the preparation of this volume. See also in part III of this volume:, p. 359, "Reports from Founding Members of the Youth Group Concerning Rudolf Steiner's Presentations for the Esoteric Youth Group: Preliminary Remarks from the Editor of the German Edition...."

Stuttgart, July 13, 1923

First of the two Esoteric Lessons for the Youth Group. No documentation exists concerning the source of records.

Page 412, *"Auom mani padme aoum"*
There may be an error in memory or understanding with what was spoken here. The Indian formulation is: *"Aum mani padme hum."* In another situation Rudolf Steiner translated it in the same sense: "I am the jewel in the Lotus flower. *Aum mani padme hum. Aum*, the most inner part, the actual life force in the human being, which one touches only with tone; *mani*: what has become stone, the jewel, manas; *padme*: the astral; *hum*: once more, 'I am.'" According to Marie Steiner's notes in Berlin, on August 17, 1904.

Page 412, "My own being is interwoven with the strength of the breath"
There are some differences in various records of the exact formulation of the three mantric sentences: some words are hyphenated and others are separated into two words rather than being one word. There is no original from Rudolf Steiner.

Page 413, "Of the syllable *'AOUM,'* he said in another connection"
For example, see the lecture of April 1, 1922 in *The Sun Mystery* (CW 211).

Dornach, December 30, 1923

Second of the two Esoteric Lessons for the Youth Group. The content of the record in this volume was prepared and signed by Maria Röschl. According to her comments, the record is a compilation of her notes that she made immediately after the lesson and of the notes by several friends. The structure of the Lesson was especially remembered.

Page 414, "Christmas Conference"
See *The Christmas Conference for the Foundation of the General Anthroposophical Society 1923/24* (CW 260).

Page 414, "Glass House"
The building on the Goetheanum grounds that was so named because it was specially constructed and used for the production of the colored windows for the first Goethanum.

Page 417, "for love gleams on the star"
It is not certain, but perhaps Rudolf Steiner spoke only two lines of the mantra each time at first, and then the third time all of the lines of the mantra were spoken.

Page 417, "out of which the whole world comes"
For a somewhat different German translation of the Indian mantra see, for example, the Esoteric Lesson of April 18, 1906, in CW 266/I, or the Esoteric Lesson of May 27, 1923, in CW 265.

Page 420, "Herman Grimm"
Herman Grimm (1828-1901). Literary and art historian. Son of the linguist and collector of fairy tales, Wilhelm Grimm. Professor in Berlin. Concerning Herman Grimm, see Rudolf Steiner's remembrances in his Autobiography (CW 28); his essays in *Der Goetheanumgedanke inmitten der Kulturkrisis der Gegenwart. Gesammelte Aufsätze aus der Wochenschrift "Das Goethanum"* [The Goetheanum, idea in the midst of the cultural crisis of the present. Collected essays from the periodical, "The Goetheanum"] (GA 36) and in *Methodische Grundlagen der Anthroposophie* [Methodical foundations of Anthroposophy], (GA 30). See also Steiner's lecture on Herman Grimm, on January 16, 1913, in *Results of Spiritual Research* (CW 62).

Page 412, "Vincenz Knauer"
Knauer (1828-1894). Philosopher. Private lecturer in Vienna.

Page 421, "only with aching heart did I decide ... in the evening lectures"
See the lecture of December 9, 1923, in *World History in Light of Anthroposophy* (CW 233).

Page 421, "when I met ... the herb gatherer"
Felix Koguzki (1833-1909). In Koguzki's journal, which remains in existence, the following entry is to be found: "Mr. Steiner, student, living in Inzersdorf,

came to see me on Sunday, August 21, 1881 A.D. Unfortunately, I was not at home. Mr. Steiner came to see me a second time on Friday, May 26th." (in Emil Bock's *Rudolf Steiner. Studien zu seinem Lebensgang und Lebenswerk* [Rudolf Steiner: studies in his life and work], Stuttgart, 3rd edition, 1990. There is a detailed description of this meeting in Rudolf Steiner's *Autobiography* (CW 28).

Page 423, "made the same sign"
According to other documents, Rudolf Steiner made the often-used sign of the Rose Cross:

RUDOLF STEINER'S COLLECTED WORKS

The German Edition of Rudolf Steiner's Collected Works (the Gesamtausgabe [GA] published by Rudolf Steiner Verlag, Dornach, Switzerland) presently runs to over 354 titles, organized either by type of work (written or spoken), chronology, audience (public or other), or subject (education, art, etc.). For ease of comparison, the Collected Works in English [CW] follows the German organization exactly. A complete listing of the CWs follows with literal translations of the German titles. Other than in the case of the books published in his lifetime, titles were rarely given by Rudolf Steiner himself, and were often provided by the editors of the German editions. The titles in English are not necessarily the same as the German; and, indeed, over the past seventy-five years have frequently been different, with the same book sometimes appearing under different titles.

For ease of identification and to avoid confusion, we suggest that readers looking for a title should do so by CW number. Because the work of creating the Collected Works of Rudolf Steiner is an ongoing process, with new titles being published every year, we have not indicated in this listing which books are presently available. To find out what titles in the Collected Works are currently in print, please check our website at www.steinerbooks.org, or write to SteinerBooks 610 Main Street, Great Barrington, MA 01230:

Written Work

CW 1	Goethe: Natural-Scientific Writings, Introduction, with Footnotes and Explanations in the text by Rudolf Steiner
CW 2	Outlines of an Epistemology of the Goethean World View, with Special Consideration of Schiller
CW 3	Truth and Science
CW 4	The Philosophy of Freedom
CW 4a	Documents to "The Philosophy of Freedom"
CW 5	Friedrich Nietzsche, A Fighter against His Own Time
CW 6	Goethe's Worldview
CW 6a	Now in CW 30
CW 7	Mysticism at the Dawn of Modern Spiritual Life and Its Relationship with Modern Worldviews
CW 8	Christianity as Mystical Fact and the Mysteries of Antiquity
CW 9	Theosophy: An Introduction into Supersensible World Knowledge and Human Purpose
CW 10	How Does One Attain Knowledge of Higher Worlds?
CW 11	From the Akasha-Chronicle
CW 12	Levels of Higher Knowledge

CW 13	Occult Science in Outline
CW 14	Four Mystery Dramas
CW 15	The Spiritual Guidance of the Individual and Humanity
CW 16	A Way to Human Self-Knowledge: Eight Meditations
CW 17	The Threshold of the Spiritual World. Aphoristic Comments
CW 18	The Riddles of Philosophy in Their History, Presented as an Outline
CW 19	Contained in CW 24
CW 20	The Riddles of the Human Being: Articulated and Unarticulated in the Thinking, Views and Opinions of a Series of German and Austrian Personalities
CW 21	The Riddles of the Soul
CW 22	Goethe's Spiritual Nature And Its Revelation In "Faust" and through the "Fairy Tale of the Snake and the Lily"
CW 23	The Central Points of the Social Question in the Necessities of Life in the Present and the Future
CW 24	Essays Concerning the Threefold Division of the Social Organism and the Period 1915-1921
CW 25	Cosmology, Religion and Philosophy
CW 26	Anthroposophical Leading Thoughts
CW 27	Fundamentals for Expansion of the Art of Healing according to Spiritual-Scientific Insights
CW 28	The Course of My Life
CW 29	Collected Essays on Dramaturgy, 1889-1900
CW 30	Methodical Foundations of Anthroposophy: Collected Essays on Philosophy, Natural Science, Aesthetics and Psychology, 1884-1901
CW 31	Collected Essays on Culture and Current Events, 1887-1901
CW 32	Collected Essays on Literature, 1884-1902
CW 33	Biographies and Biographical Sketches, 1894-1905
CW 34	Lucifer-Gnosis: Foundational Essays on Anthroposophy and Reports from the Periodicals "Lucifer" and "Lucifer-Gnosis," 1903-1908
CW 35	Philosophy and Anthroposophy: Collected Essays, 1904-1923
CW 36	The Goetheanum-Idea in the Middle of the Cultural Crisis of the Present: Collected Essays from the Periodical "Das Goetheanum," 1921-1925
CW 37	Now in CWs 260a and 251
CW 38	Letters, Vol. 1: 1881-1890
CW 39	Letters, Vol. 2: 1890-1925
CW 40	Truth-Wrought Words
CW 40a	Sayings, Poems and Mantras; Supplementary Volume
CW 42	Now in CWs 264-266

CW 43   Stage Adaptations
CW 44   On the Four Mystery Dramas. Sketches, Fragments and Paralipomena on the Four Mystery Dramas
CW 45   Anthroposophy: A Fragment from the Year 1910

Public Lectures

CW 51   On Philosophy, History and Literature
CW 52   Spiritual Teachings Concerning the Soul and Observation of the World
CW 53   The Origin and Goal of the Human Being
CW 54   The Riddles of the World and Anthroposophy
CW 55   Knowledge of the Supersensible in Our Times and Its Meaning for Life Today
CW 56   Knowledge of the Soul and of the Spirit
CW 57   Where and How Does One Find the Spirit?
CW 58   The Metamorphoses of the Soul Life. Paths of Soul Experiences: Part One
CW 59   The Metamorphoses of the Soul Life. Paths of Soul Experiences: Part Two
CW 60   The Answers of Spiritual Science to the Biggest Questions of Existence
CW 61   Human History in the Light of Spiritual Research
CW 62   Results of Spiritual Research
CW 63   Spiritual Science as a Treasure for Life
CW 64   Out of Destiny-Burdened Times
CW 65   Out of Central European Spiritual Life
CW 66   Spirit and Matter, Life and Death
CW 67   The Eternal in the Human Soul. Immortality and Freedom
CW 68   Public lectures in various cities, 1906-1918
CW 69   Public lectures in various cities, 1906-1918
CW 70   Public lectures in various cities, 1906-1918
CW 71   Public lectures in various cities, 1906-1918
CW 72   Freedom – Immortality – Social Life
CW 73   The Supplementing of the Modern Sciences through Anthroposophy
CW 73a   Specialized Fields of Knowledge and Anthroposophy
CW 74   The Philosophy of Thomas Aquinas
CW 75   Public lectures in various cities, 1906-1918
CW 76   The Fructifying Effect of Anthroposophy on Specialized Fields
CW 77a   The Task of Anthroposophy in Relation to Science and Life: The Darmstadt College Course
CW 77b   Art and Anthroposophy. The Goetheanum-Impulse

CW 78   Anthroposophy, Its Roots of Knowledge and Fruits for Life
CW 79   The Reality of the Higher Worlds
CW 80   Public lectures in various cities, 1922
CW 81   Renewal-Impulses for Culture and Science–Berlin College Course
CW 82   So that the Human Being Can Become a Complete Human Being
CW 83   Western and Eastern World-Contrast. Paths to Understanding It through Anthroposophy
CW 84   What Did the Goetheanum Intend and What Should Anthroposophy Do?

Lectures to the Members of the Anthroposophical Society

CW 88   Concerning the Astral World and Devachan
CW 89   Consciousness–Life–Form. Fundamental Principles of a Spiritual-Scientific Cosmology
CW 90   Participant Notes from the Lectures during the Years 1903-1905
CW 91   Participant Notes from the Lectures during the Years 1903-1905
CW 92   The Occult Truths of Ancient Myths and Sagas
CW 93   The Temple Legend and the Golden Legend
CW 93a   Fundamentals of Esotericism
CW 94   Cosmogony. Popular Occultism. The Gospel of John. The Theosophy in the Gospel of John
CW 95   At the Gates of Theosophy
CW 96   Origin-Impulses of Spiritual Science. Christian Esotericism in the Light of New Spirit-Knowledge
CW 97   The Christian Mystery
CW 98   Nature Beings and Spirit Beings – Their Effects in Our Visible World
CW 99   The Theosophy of the Rosicrucians
CW 100   Human Development and Christ-Knowledge
CW 101   Myths and Legends. Occult Signs and Symbols
CW 102   The Working into Human Beings by Spiritual Beings
CW 103   The Gospel of John
CW 104   The Apocalypse of John
CW 104a   From the Picture-Script of the Apocalypse of John
CW 105   Universe, Earth, the Human Being: Their Being and Development, as well as Their Reflection in the Connection between Egyptian Mythology and Modern Culture
CW 106   Egyptian Myths and Mysteries in Relation to the Active Spiritual Forces of the Present
CW 107   Spiritual-Scientific Knowledge of the Human Being
CW 108   Answering the Questions of Life and the World through Anthroposophy

Rudolf Steiner's Collected Works

CW 109	The Principle of Spiritual Economy in Connection with the Question of Reincarnation. An Aspect of the Spiritual Guidance of Humanity
CW 110	The Spiritual Hierarchies and Their Reflection in the Physical World. Zodiac, Planets and Cosmos
CW 111	Contained in 109
CW 112	The Gospel of John in Relation to the Three Other Gospels, Especially the Gospel of Luke
CW 113	The Orient in the Light of the Occident. The Children of Lucifer and the Brothers of Christ
CW 114	The Gospel of Luke
CW 115	Anthroposophy – Psychosophy – Pneumatosophy
CW 116	The Christ-Impulse and the Development of "I"- Consciousness
CW 117	The Deeper Secrets of the Development of Humanity in Light of the Gospels
CW 118	The Event of the Christ-Appearance in the Etheric World
CW 119	Macrocosm and Microcosm. The Large World and the Small World. Soul-Questions, Life-Questions, Spirit-Questions
CW 120	The Revelation of Karma
CW 121	The Mission of Individual Folk-Souls in Connection with Germanic-Nordic Mythology
CW 122	The Secrets of the Biblical Creation-Story. The Six-Day Work in the First Book of Moses
CW 123	The Gospel of Matthew
CW 124	Excursus in the Area of the Gospel of Mark
CW 125	Paths and Goals of the Spiritual Human Being. Life Questions in the Light of Spiritual Science
CW 126	Occult History. Esoteric Observations of the Karmic Relationships of Personalities and Events of World History
CW 127	The Mission of the New Spiritual Revelation. The Christ-Event as the Middle-Point of Earth Evolution
CW 128	An Occult Physiology
CW 129	Wonders of the World, Trials of the Soul, and Revelations of the Spirit
CW 130	Esoteric Christianity and the Spiritual Guidance of Humanity
CW 131	From Jesus to Christ
CW 132	Evolution from the View Point of the Truth
CW 133	The Earthly and the Cosmic Human Being
CW 134	The World of the Senses and the World of the Spirit
CW 135	Reincarnation and Karma and their Meaning for the Culture of the Present
CW 136	The Spiritual Beings in Celestial Bodies and the Realms of Nature

CW 137	The Human Being in the Light of Occultism, Theosophy and Philosophy
CW 138	On Initiation. On Eternity and the Passing Moment. On the Light of the Spirit and the Darkness of Life
CW 139	The Gospel of Mark
CW 140	Occult Investigation into the Life between Death and New Birth. The Living Interaction between Life and Death
CW 141	Life between Death and New Birth in Relationship to Cosmic Facts
CW 142	The Bhagavad Gita and the Letters of Paul
CW 143	Experiences of the Supersensible. Three Paths of the Soul to Christ
CW 144	The Mysteries of the East and of Christianity
CW 145	What Significance Does Occult Development of the Human Being Have for His Sheaths–Physical Body, Etheric Body, Astral Body, and Self?
CW 146	The Occult Foundations of the Bhagavad Gita
CW 147	The Secrets of the Threshold
CW 148	Out of Research in the Akasha: The Fifth Gospel
CW 149	Christ and the Spiritual World. Concerning the Search for the Holy Grail
CW 150	The World of the Spirit and Its Extension into Physical Existence; The Influence of the Dead in the World of the Living
CW 151	Human Thought and Cosmic Thought
CW 152	Preliminary Stages to the Mystery of Golgotha
CW 153	The Inner Being of the Human Being and Life Between Death and New Birth
CW 154	How does One Gain an Understanding of the Spiritual World? The Flowing in of Spiritual Impulses from out of the World of the Deceased
CW 155	Christ and the Human Soul. Concerning the Meaning of Life. Theosophical Morality. Anthroposophy and Christianity
CW 156	Occult Reading and Occult Hearing
CW 157	Human Destinies and the Destiny of Peoples
CW 157a	The Formation of Destiny and the Life after Death
CW 158	The Connection Between the Human Being and the Elemental World. Kalevala – Olaf Asteson – The Russian People – The World as the Result of the Influences of Equilibrium
CW 159	The Mystery of Death. The Nature and Significance of Middle Europe and the European Folk Spirits
CW 160	In CW 159
CW 161	Paths of Spiritual Knowledge and the Renewal of the Artistic Worldview
CW 162	Questions of Art and Life in Light of Spiritual Science

CW 163	Coincidence, Necessity and Providence. Imaginative Knowledge and the Processes after Death
CW 164	The Value of Thinking for a Knowledge That Satisfies the Human Being. The Relationship of Spiritual Science to Natural Science
CW 165	The Spiritual Unification of Humanity through the Christ-Impulse
CW 166	Necessity and Freedom in the Events of the World and in Human Action
CW 167	The Present and the Past in the Human Spirit
CW 168	The Connection between the Living and the Dead
CW 169	World-being and Selfhood
CW 170	The Riddle of the Human Being. The Spiritual Background of Human History. Cosmic and Human History, Vol. 1
CW 171	Inner Development-Impulses of Humanity. Goethe and the Crisis of the 19th Century. Cosmic and Human History, Vol. 2
CW 172	The Karma of the Vocation of the Human Being in Connection with Goethe's Life. Cosmic and Human History, Vol. 3
CW 173	Contemporary-Historical Considerations: The Karma of Untruthfulness, Part One. Cosmic and Human History, Vol. 4
CW 174	Contemporary-Historical Considerations: The Karma of Untruthfulness, Part Two. Cosmic and Human History, Vol. 5
CW 174a	Middle Europe between East and West. Cosmic and Human History, Vol. 6
CW 174b	The Spiritual Background of the First World War. Cosmic and Human History, Vol. 7
CW 175	Building Stones for an Understanding of the Mystery of Golgotha. Cosmic and Human Metamorphoses
CW 176	Truths of Evolution of the Individual and Humanity. The Karma of Materialism
CW 177	The Spiritual Background of the Outer World. The Fall of the Spirits of Darkness. Spiritual Beings and Their Effects, Vol. 1
CW 178	Individual Spiritual Beings and their Influence in the Soul of the Human Being. Spiritual Beings and their Effects, Vol. 2
CW 179	Spiritual Beings and Their Effects. Historical Necessity and Freedom. The Influences on Destiny from out of the World of the Dead. Spiritual Beings and Their Effects, Vol. 3
CW 180	Mystery Truths and Christmas Impulses. Ancient Myths and their Meaning. Spiritual Beings and Their Effects, Vol. 4
CW 181	Earthly Death and Cosmic Life. Anthroposophical Gifts for Life. Necessities of Consciousness for the Present and the Future.
CW 182	Death as Transformation of Life
CW 183	The Science of the Development of the Human Being
CW 184	The Polarity of Duration and Development in Human Life. The Cosmic Pre-History of Humanity

CW 185	Historical Symptomology
CW 185a	Historical-Developmental Foundations for Forming a Social Judgment
CW 186	The Fundamental Social Demands of Our Time–In Changed Situations
CW 187	How Can Humanity Find the Christ Again? The Threefold Shadow-Existence of our Time and the New Christ-Light
CW 188	Goetheanism, a Transformation-Impulse and Resurrection-Thought. Science of the Human Being and Science of Sociology
CW 189	The Social Question as a Question of Consciousness. The Spiritual Background of the Social Question, Vol. 1
CW 190	Impulses of the Past and the Future in Social Occurrences. The Spiritual Background of the Social Question, Vol. 2
CW 191	Social Understanding from Spiritual-Scientific Cognition. The Spiritual Background of the Social Question, Vol. 3
CW 192	Spiritual-Scientific Treatment of Social and Pedagogical Questions
CW 193	The Inner Aspect of the Social Riddle. Luciferic Past and Ahrimanic Future
CW 194	The Mission of Michael. The Revelation of the Actual Mysteries of the Human Being
CW 195	Cosmic New Year and the New Year Idea
CW 196	Spiritual and Social Transformations in the Development of Humanity
CW 197	Polarities in the Development of Humanity: West and East Materialism and Mysticism Knowledge and Belief
CW 198	Healing Factors for the Social Organism
CW 199	Spiritual Science as Knowledge of the Foundational Impulses of Social Formation
CW 200	The New Spirituality and the Christ-Experience of the 20th Century
CW 201	The Correspondences Between Microcosm and Macrocosm. The Human Being – A Hieroglyph of the Universe. The Human Being in Relationship with the Cosmos: 1
CW 202	The Bridge between the World-Spirituality and the Physical Aspect of the Human Being. The Search for the New Isis, the Divine Sophia. The Human Being in Relationship with the Cosmos: 2
CW 203	The Responsibility of Human Beings for the Development of the World through their Spiritual Connection with the Planet Earth and the World of the Stars. The Human Being in Relationship with the Cosmos: 3
CW 204	Perspectives of the Development of Humanity. The Materialistic Knowledge-Impulse and the Task of Anthroposophy. The Human Being in Relationship with the Cosmos: 4

CW 205	Human Development, World-Soul, and World-Spirit. Part One: The Human Being as a Being of Body and Soul in Relationship to the World. The Human Being in Relationship with the Cosmos: 5
CW 206	Human Development, World-Soul, and World-Spirit. Part Two: The Human Being as a Spiritual Being in the Process of Historical Development. The Human Being in Relationship with the Cosmos: 6
CW 207	Anthroposophy as Cosmosophy. Part One: Characteristic Features of the Human Being in the Earthly and the Cosmic Realms. The Human Being in Relationship with the Cosmos: 7
CW 208	Anthroposophy as Cosmosophy. Part Two: The Forming of the Human Being as the Result of Cosmic Influence. The Human Being in Relationship with the Cosmos: 8
CW 209	Nordic and Central European Spiritual Impulses. The Festival of the Appearance of Christ. The Human Being in Relationship with the Cosmos: 9
CW 210	Old and New Methods of Initiation. Drama and Poetry in the Change of Consciousness in the Modern Age
CW 211	The Sun Mystery and the Mystery of Death and Resurrection. Exoteric and Esoteric Christianity
CW 212	Human Soul Life and Spiritual Striving in Connection with World and Earth Development
CW 213	Human Questions and World Answers
CW 214	The Mystery of the Trinity: The Human Being in Relationship to the Spiritual World in the Course of Time
CW 215	Philosophy, Cosmology, and Religion in Anthroposophy
CW 216	The Fundamental Impulses of the World-Historical Development of Humanity
CW 217	Spiritually Active Forces in the Coexistence of the Older and Younger Generations. Pedagogical Course for Youth
CW 217a	Youth's Cognitive Task
CW 218	Spiritual Connections in the Forming of the Human Organism
CW 219	The Relationship of the World of the Stars to the Human Being, and of the Human Being to the World of the Stars. The Spiritual Communion of Humanity
CW 220	Living Knowledge of Nature. Intellectual Fall and Spiritual Redemption
CW 221	Earth-Knowing and Heaven-Insight
CW 222	The Imparting of Impulses to World-Historical Events through Spiritual Powers
CW 223	The Cycle of the Year as Breathing Process of the Earth and the Four Great Festival-Seasons. Anthroposophy and Human Heart (Gemüt)

CW 224	The Human Soul and its Connection with Divine-Spiritual Individualities. The Internalization of the Festivals of the Year
CW 225	Three Perspectives of Anthroposophy. Cultural Phenomena observed from a Spiritual-Scientific Perspective
CW 226	Human Being, Human Destiny, and World Development
CW 227	Initiation-Knowledge
CW 228	Science of Initiation and Knowledge of the Stars. The Human Being in the Past, the Present, and the Future from the Viewpoint of the Development of Consciousness
CW 229	The Experiencing of the Course of the Year in Four Cosmic Imaginations
CW 230	The Human Being as Harmony of the Creative, Building, and Formative World-Word
CW 231	The Supersensible Human Being, Understood Anthroposophically
CW 232	The Forming of the Mysteries
CW 233	World History Illuminated by Anthroposophy and as the Foundation for Knowledge of the Human Spirit
CW 233a	Mystery Sites of the Middle Ages: Rosicrucianism and the Modern Initiation-Principle. The Festival of Easter as Part of the History of the Mysteries of Humanity
CW 234	Anthroposophy. A Summary after 21 Years
CW 235	Esoteric Observations of Karmic Relationships in 6 Volumes, Vol. 1
CW 236	Esoteric Observations of Karmic Relationships in 6 Volumes, Vol. 2
CW 237	Esoteric Observations of Karmic Relationships in 6 Volumes, Vol. 3: The Karmic Relationships of the Anthroposophical Movement
CW 238	Esoteric Observations of Karmic Relationships in 6 Volumes, Vol. 4: The Spiritual Life of the Present in Relationship to the Anthroposophical Movement
CW 239	Esoteric Observations of Karmic Relationships in 6 Volumes, Vol. 5
CW 240	Esoteric Observations of Karmic Relationships in 6 Volumes, Vol. 6
CW 243	The Consciousness of the Initiate
CW 245	Instructions for an Esoteric Schooling
CW 250	The Building-Up of the Anthroposophical Society. From the Beginning to the Outbreak of the First World War
CW 251	The History of the Goetheanum Building-Association
CW 252	Life in the Anthroposophical Society from the First World War to the Burning of the First Goetheanum
CW 253	The Problems of Living Together in the Anthroposophical Society. On the Dornach Crisis of 1915. With Highlights on Swedenborg's Clairvoyance, the Views of Freudian Psychoanalysts, and the Concept of Love in Relation to Mysticism

CW 254   The Occult Movement in the 19th Century and Its Relationship to World Culture. Significant Points from the Exoteric Cultural Life around the Middle of the 19th Century
CW 255   Rudolf Steiner during the First World War
CW 255a   Anthroposophy and the Reformation of Society. On the History of the Threefold Movement
CW 255b   Anthroposophy and Its Opponents, 1919-1921
CW 256   How Can the Anthroposophical Movement Be Financed?
CW 256a   Futurum, Inc. / International Laboratories, Inc.
CW 256b   The Coming Day, Inc.
CW 257   Anthroposophical Community-Building
CW 258   The History of and Conditions for the Anthroposophical Movement in Relationship to the Anthroposophical Society. A Stimulus to Self-Contemplation
CW 259   The Year of Destiny 1923 in the History of the Anthroposophical Society. From the Burning of the Goetheanum to the Christmas Conference
CW 260   The Christmas Conference for the Founding of the General Anthroposophical Society
CW 260a   The Constitution of the General Anthroposophical Society and the School for Spiritual Science. The Rebuilding of the Goetheanum
CW 261   Our Dead. Addresses, Words of Remembrance, and Meditative Verses, 1906-1924
CW 262   Rudolf Steiner and Marie Steiner-von Sivers: Correspondence and Documents, 1901-1925
CW 263/1 Rudolf Steiner and Edith Maryon: Correspondence: Letters, Verses, Sketches, 1912-1924
CW 264   On the History and the Contents of the First Section of the Esoteric School from 1904 to 1914. Letters, Newsletters, Documents, Lectures
CW 265   On the History and Out of the Contents of the Ritual-Knowledge Section of the Esoteric School from 1904 to 1914. Documents, and Lectures from the Years 1906 to 1914, as well as on New Approaches to Ritual-Knowledge Work in the Years 1921-1924
CW 266/1 From the Contents of the Esoteric Lessons. Volume 1: 1904-1909. Notes from Memory of Participants. Meditation texts from the notes of Rudolf Steiner
CW 266/2 From the Contents of the Esoteric Lessons. Volume 2: 1910-1912. Notes from Memory of Participants
CW 266/3 From the Contents of the Esoteric Lessons. Volume 3: 1913, 1914 and 1920-1923. Notes from Memory of Participants. Meditation texts from the notes of Rudolf Steiner

CW 267	Soul-Exercises: Vol. 1: Exercises with Word and Image Meditations for the Methodological Development of Higher Powers of Knowledge, 1904-1924
CW 268	Soul-Exercises: Vol. 2: Mantric Verses, 1903-1925
CW 269	Ritual Texts for the Celebration of the Free Christian Religious Instruction. The Collected Verses for Teachers and Students of the Waldorf School
CW 270	Esoteric Instructions for the First Class of the School for Spiritual Science at the Goetheanum 1924, 4 Volumes
CW 271	Art and Knowledge of Art. Foundations of a New Aesthetic
CW 272	Spiritual-Scientific Commentary on Goethe's "Faust" in Two Volumes. Vol. 1: Faust, the Striving Human Being
CW 273	Spiritual-Scientific Commentary on Goethe's "Faust" in Two Volumes. Vol. 2: The Faust-Problem
CW 274	Addresses for the Christmas Plays from the Old Folk Traditions
CW 275	Art in the Light of Mystery-Wisdom
CW 276	The Artistic in Its Mission in the World. The Genius of Language. The World of the Self-Revealing Radiant Appearances – Anthroposophy and Art. Anthroposophy and Poetry
CW 277	Eurythmy. The Revelation of the Speaking Soul
CW 277a	The Origin and Development of Eurythmy
CW 278	Eurythmy as Visible Song
CW 279	Eurythmy as Visible Speech
CW 280	The Method and Nature of Speech Formation
CW 281	The Art of Recitation and Declamation
CW 282	Speech Formation and Dramatic Art
CW 283	The Nature of Things Musical and the Experience of Tone in the Human Being
CW 284/285	Images of Occult Seals and Pillars. The Munich Congress of Whitsun 1907 and Its Consequences
CW 286	Paths to a New Style of Architecture. "And the Building Becomes Human"
CW 287	The Building at Dornach as a Symbol of Historical Becoming and an Artistic Transformation Impulse
CW 288	Style-Forms in the Living Organic
CW 289	The Building-Idea of the Goetheanum: Lectures with Slides from the Years 1920-1921
CW 290	The Building-Idea of the Goetheanum: Lectures with Slides from the Years 1920-1921
CW 291	The Nature of Colors
CW 291a	Knowledge of Colors. Supplementary Volume to "The Nature of Colors"
CW 292	Art History as Image of Inner Spiritual Impulses

CW 293	General Knowledge of the Human Being as the Foundation of Pedagogy
CW 294	The Art of Education, Methodology and Didactics
CW 295	The Art of Education: Seminar Discussions and Lectures on Lesson Planning
CW 296	The Question of Education as a Social Question
CW 297	The Idea and Practice of the Waldorf School
CW 297a	Education for Life: Self-Education and the Practice of Pedagogy
CW 298	Rudolf Steiner in the Waldorf School
CW 299	Spiritual-Scientific Observations on Speech
CW 300a	Conferences with the Teachers of the Free Waldorf School in Stuttgart, 1919 to 1924, in 3 Volumes, Vol. 1
CW 300b	Conferences with the Teachers of the Free Waldorf School in Stuttgart, 1919 to 1924, in 3 Volumes, Vol. 2
CW 300c	Conferences with the Teachers of the Free Waldorf School in Stuttgart, 1919 to 1924, in 3 Volumes, Vol. 3
CW 301	The Renewal of the Pedagogical-Didactical Art through Spiritual Science
CW 302	Knowledge of the Human Being and the Forming of Class Lessons
CW 302a	Education and Teaching out of a Knowledge of the Human Being
CW 303	The Healthy Development of the Human Being
CW 304	Methods of Education and Teaching Based on Anthroposophy
CW 304a	Anthroposophical Knowledge of the Human Being and Pedagogy
CW 305	The Soul-Spiritual Foundational Forces of the Art of Education. Spiritual Values in Education and Social Life
CW 306	Pedagogical Praxis from the Viewpoint of a Spiritual-Scientific Knowledge of the Human Being. The Education of the Child and Young Human Beings
CW 307	The Spiritual Life of the Present and Education
CW 308	The Method of Teaching and the Life-Requirements for Teaching
CW 309	Anthroposophical Pedagogy and Its Prerequisites
CW 310	The Pedagogical Value of a Knowledge of the Human Being and the Cultural Value of Pedagogy
CW 311	The Art of Education Out of an Understanding of the Being of Humanity
CW 312	Spiritual Science and Medicine
CW 313	Spiritual-Scientific Viewpoints on Therapy
CW 314	Physiology and Therapy Based on Spiritual Science
CW 315	Curative Eurythmy
CW 316	Meditative Observations and Instructions for a Deepening of the Art of Healing
CW 317	The Curative Education Course
CW 318	The Working Together of Doctors and Pastors

CW 319	Anthroposophical Knowledge of the Human Being and Medicine
CW 320	Spiritual-Scientific Impulses for the Development of Physics 1: The First Natural-Scientific Course: Light, Color, Tone, Mass, Electricity, Magnetism
CW 321	Spiritual-Scientific Impulses for the Development of Physics 2: The Second Natural-Scientific Course: Warmth at the Border of Positive and Negative Materiality
CW 322	The Borders of the Knowledge of Nature
CW 323	The Relationship of the various Natural-Scientific Fields to Astronomy
CW 324	Nature Observation, Mathematics, and Scientific Experimentation and Results from the Viewpoint of Anthroposophy
CW 324a	The Fourth Dimension in Mathematics and Reality
CW 325	Natural Science and the World-Historical Development of Humanity since Ancient Times
CW 326	The Moment of the Coming Into Being of Natural Science in World History and Its Development Since Then
CW 327	Spiritual-Scientific Foundations for Success in Farming. The Agricultural Course
CW 328	The Social Question
CW 329	The Liberation of the Human Being as the Foundation for a New Social Form
CW 330	The Renewal of the Social Organism
CW 331	Work-Council and Socialization
CW 332	The Alliance for Threefolding and the Total Reform of Society. The Council on Culture and the Liberation of the Spiritual Life
CW 332a	The Social Future
CW 333	Freedom of Thought and Social Forces
CW 334	From the Unified State to the Threefold Social Organism
CW 335	The Crisis of the Present and the Path to Healthy Thinking
CW 336	The Great Questions of the Times and Anthroposophical Spiritual Knowledge
CW 337a	Social Ideas, Social Reality, Social Practice, Vol. 1: Question-and- Answer Evenings and Study Evenings of the Alliance for the Threefold Social Organism in Stuttgart, 1919-1920
CW 337b	Social Ideas, Social Realities, Social Practice, Vol. 2: Discussion Evenings of the Swiss Alliance for the Threefold Social Organism
CW 338	How Does One Work on Behalf of the Impulse for the Threefold Social Organism?
CW 339	Anthroposophy, Threefold Social Organism, and the Art of Public Speaking
CW 340	The National-Economics Course. The Tasks of a New Science of Economics, Volume 1

CW 341	The National-Economics Seminar. The Tasks of a New Science of Economics, Volume 2
CW 342	Lectures and Courses on Christian Religious Work, Vol. 1: Anthroposophical Foundations for a Renewed Christian Religious Working
CW 343	Lectures and Courses on Christian Religious Work, Vol. 2: Spiritual Knowledge – Religious Feeling – Cultic Doing
CW 344	Lectures and Courses on Christian Religious Work, Vol. 3: Lectures at the Founding of the Christian Community
CW 345	Lectures and Courses on Christian Religious Work, Vol. 4: Concerning the Nature of the Working Word
CW 346	Lectures and Courses on Christian Religious Work, Vol. 5: The Apocalypse and the Working of the Priest
CW 347	The Knowledge of the Nature of the Human Being According to Body, Soul and Spirit. On Earlier Conditions of the Earth
CW 348	On Health and Illness. Foundations of a Spiritual-Scientific Doctrine of the Senses
CW 349	On the Life of Human Being and of the Earth. On the Nature of Christianity
CW 350	Rhythms in the Cosmos and in the Human Being. How Does One Come To See the Spiritual World?
CW 351	The Human Being and the World. The Influence of the Spirit in Nature. On the Nature of Bees
CW 352	Nature and the Human Being Observed Spiritual-Scientifically
CW 353	The History of Humanity and the World-Views of the Folk Cultures
CW 354	The Creation of the World and the Human Being. Life on Earth and the Influence of the Stars

SIGNIFICANT EVENTS IN THE LIFE OF RUDOLF STEINER

1829: June 23: birth of Johann Steiner (1829-1910)—Rudolf Steiner's father—in Geras, Lower Austria.

1834: May 8: birth of Franciska Blie (1834-1918)—Rudolf Steiner's mother—in Horn, Lower Austria. "My father and mother were both children of the glorious Lower Austrian forest district north of the Danube."

1860: May 16: marriage of Johann Steiner and Franciska Blie.

1861: February 25: birth of *Rudolf Joseph Lorenz Steiner* in Kraljevec, Croatia, near the border with Hungary, where Johann Steiner works as a telegrapher for the South Austria Railroad. Rudolf Steiner is baptized two days later, February 27, the date usually given as his birthday.

1862: Summer: the family moves to Mödling, Lower Austria.

1863: The family moves to Pottschach, Lower Austria, near the Styrian border, where Johann Steiner becomes stationmaster. "The view stretched to the mountains...majestic peaks in the distance and the sweet charm of nature in the immediate surroundings."

1864: November 15: birth of Rudolf Steiner's sister, Leopoldine (d. November 1, 1927). She will become a seamstress and live with her parents for the rest of her life.

1866: July 28: birth of Rudolf Steiner's deaf-mute brother, Gustav (d. May 1, 1941).

1867: Rudolf Steiner enters the village school. Following a disagreement between his father and the schoolmaster, whose wife falsely accused the boy of causing a commotion, Rudolf Steiner is taken out of school and taught at home.

1868: A critical experience. Unknown to the family, an aunt dies in a distant town. Sitting in the station waiting room, Rudolf Steiner sees her "form," which speaks to him, asking for help. "Beginning with this experience, a new soul life began in the boy, one in which not only the outer trees and mountains spoke to him, but also the worlds that lay behind them. From this moment on, the boy began to live with the spirits of nature...."

1869: The family moves to the peaceful, rural village of Neudorfl, near Wiener-Neustadt in present-day Austria. Rudolf Steiner attends the village school. Because of the "unorthodoxy" of his writing and spelling, he has to do "extra lessons."

1870: Through a book lent to him by his tutor, he discovers geometry: "To grasp something purely in the spirit brought me inner happiness. I know that I first learned happiness through geometry." The same tutor allows him to draw, while other students still struggle with their reading and writing. "An artistic element" thus enters his education.

1871: Though his parents are not religious, Rudolf Steiner becomes a "church child," a favorite of the priest, who was "an exceptional character." "Up to the age of ten or eleven, among those I came to know, he was far and away the most significant." Among other things, he introduces Steiner to Copernican, heliocentric cosmology. As an altar boy, Rudolf Steiner serves at Masses, funerals, and Corpus Christi processions. At year's end, after an incident in which he escapes a thrashing, his father forbids him to go to church.

1872: Rudolf Steiner transfers to grammar school in Wiener-Neustadt, a five-mile walk from home, which must be done in all weathers.

1873-75: Through his teachers and on his own, Rudolf Steiner has many wonderful experiences with science and mathematics. Outside school, he teaches himself analytic geometry, trigonometry, differential equations, and calculus.

1876: Rudolf Steiner begins tutoring other students. He learns bookbinding from his father. He also teaches himself stenography.

1877: Rudolf Steiner discovers Kant's *Critique of Pure Reason*, which he reads and rereads. He also discovers and reads von Rotteck's *World History*.

1878: He studies extensively in contemporary psychology and philosophy.

1879: Rudolf Steiner graduates from high school with honors. His father is transferred to Inzersdorf, near Vienna. He uses his first visit to Vienna "to purchase a great number of philosophy books"—Kant, Fichte, Schelling, and Hegel, as well as numerous histories of philosophy. His aim: to find a path from the "I" to nature.

October 1879-1883: Rudolf Steiner attends the Technical College in Vienna—to study mathematics, chemistry, physics, mineralogy, botany, zoology, biology, geology, and mechanics—with a scholarship. He also attends lectures in history and literature, while avidly reading philosophy on his own. His two favorite professors are Karl Julius Schröer (German language and literature) and Edmund Reitlinger (physics). He also audits lectures by Robert Zimmerman on aesthetics and Franz Brentano on philosophy. During this year he begins his friendship with Moritz Zitter (1861-1921), who will help support him financially when he is in Berlin.

1880: Rudolf Steiner attends lectures on Schiller and Goethe by Karl Julius Schröer, who becomes his mentor. Also "through a remarkable combination of circumstances," he meets Felix Koguzki, an "herb gatherer" and healer, who could "see deeply into the secrets of nature." Rudolf Steiner will meet and study with this "emissary of the Master" throughout his time in Vienna.

1881: January: "... I didn't sleep a wink. I was busy with philosophical problems until about 12:30 a.m. Then, finally, I threw myself down on my couch. All my striving during the previous year had been to research whether the following statement by Schelling was true or not: *Within everyone dwells a secret, marvelous capacity to draw back from the stream of time—out of the self clothed in all that comes to us from outside—into our innermost being and there, in the immutable form of the Eternal, to look into ourselves.* I believe, and I am still quite certain of it, that I discovered this capacity in myself; I had long had an inkling of it. Now the whole of idealist philosophy stood before me in modified form. What's a sleepless night compared to that!"

Rudolf Steiner begins communicating with the leading thinkers of the day. They send him books in return, which he reads eagerly.

July: "I am not one of those who dives into the day like an animal in human form. I pursue a quite specific goal, an idealistic aim—knowledge of the truth! This cannot be done offhandedly. It requires the greatest striving in the world, free of all egotism, and equally of all resignation."

August: Steiner puts down on paper for the first time thoughts for a "Philosophy of Freedom." "The striving for the absolute: this human yearning is freedom." He also seeks to outline a "peasant philosophy," describing what the worldview of a "peasant"—one who lives close to the earth and the old ways—really is.

1881-1882: Felix Koguzki, the herb gatherer, reveals himself to be the envoy of another, higher initiatory personality, who instructs Rudolf Steiner to penetrate Fichte's philosophy and to master modern scientific thinking as a preparation for right entry into the spirit. This "Master" also teaches him the double (evolutionary and involutionary) nature of time.

1882: Through the offices of Karl Julius Schröer, Rudolf Steiner is asked by Joseph Kurschner to edit Goethe's scientific works for the *Deutschen National-Literatur* edition. He writes "A Possible Critique of Atomistic Concepts" and sends it to Friedrich Theodore Vischer.

1883: Rudolf Steiner completes his college studies and begins work on the Goethe project.

1884: First volume of Goethe's *Scientific Writings* (CW 1) appears (March). He lectures on Goethe and Lessing, and Goethe's approach to science. In July, he enters the household of Ladislaus and Pauline Specht as tutor to the four Specht boys. He will live there until 1890. At this time, he meets Josef Breuer (1842-1925), the coauthor with Sigmund Freud of *Studies in Hysteria*, who is the Specht family doctor.

1885: While continuing to edit Goethe's writings, Rudolf Steiner reads deeply in contemporary philosophy (Edouard von Hartmann, Johannes Volkelt, and Richard Wahle, among others).

1886: May: Rudolf Steiner sends Kurschner the manuscript of *Outlines of Goethe's Theory of Knowledge* (CW 2), which appears in October, and which he sends out widely. He also meets the poet Marie Eugenie Delle Grazie and writes "Nature and Our Ideals" for her. He attends her salon, where he meets many priests, theologians, and philosophers, who will become his friends. Meanwhile, the director of the Goethe

Archive in Weimar requests his collaboration with the *Sophien* edition of Goethe's works, particularly the writings on color.

1887: At the beginning of the year, Rudolf Steiner is very sick. As the year progresses and his health improves, he becomes increasingly "a man of letters," lecturing, writing essays, and taking part in Austrian cultural life. In August-September, the second volume of Goethe's *Scientific Writings* appears.

1888: January-July: Rudolf Steiner assumes editorship of the "German Weekly" (*Deutsche Wochenschrift*). He begins lecturing more intensively, giving, for example, a lecture titled "Goethe as Father of a New Aesthetics." He meets and becomes soul friends with Friedrich Eckstein (1861-1939), a vegetarian, philosopher of symbolism, alchemist, and musician, who will introduce him to various spiritual currents (including Theosophy) and with whom he will meditate and interpret esoteric and alchemical texts.

1889: Rudolf Steiner first reads Nietzsche (*Beyond Good and Evil*). He encounters Theosophy again and learns of Madame Blavatsky in the Theosophical circle around Marie Lang (1858-1934). Here he also meets well-known figures of Austrian life, as well as esoteric figures like the occultist Franz Hartman and Karl Leinigen-Billigen (translator of C.G. Harrison's *The Transcendental Universe*.) During this period, Steiner first reads A.P. Sinnett's *Esoteric Buddhism* and Mabel Collins's *Light on the Path*. He also begins traveling, visiting Budapest, Weimar, and Berlin (where he meets philosopher Edouard von Hartman).

1890: Rudolf Steiner finishes volume 3 of Goethe's scientific writings. He begins his doctoral dissertation, which will become *Truth and Science* (CW 3). He also meets the poet and feminist Rosa Mayreder (1858-1938), with whom he can exchange his most intimate thoughts. In September, Rudolf Steiner moves to Weimar to work in the Goethe-Schiller Archive.

1891: Volume 3 of the Kurschner edition of Goethe appears. Meanwhile, Rudolf Steiner edits Goethe's studies in mineralogy and scientific writings for the *Sophien* edition. He meets Ludwig Laistner of the Cotta Publishing Company, who asks for a book on the basic question of metaphysics. From this will result, ultimately, *The Philosophy of Freedom* (CW 4), which will be published not by Cotta but by Emil Felber. In October, Rudolf Steiner takes the oral exam for a doctorate in philosophy, mathematics, and mechanics at Rostock University, receiving his doctorate on the twenty-sixth. In November, he gives his first lecture on Goethe's "Fairy Tale" in Vienna.

1892: Rudolf Steiner continues work at the Goethe-Schiller Archive and on his *Philosophy of Freedom*. *Truth and Science*, his doctoral dissertation, is published. Steiner undertakes to write introductions to books on Schopenhauer and Jean Paul for Cotta. At year's end, he finds lodging with Anna Eunike, née Schulz (1853-1911), a widow with four daughters and a son. He also develops a friendship with Otto Erich Hartleben (1864-1905) with whom he shares literary interests.

1893: Rudolf Steiner begins his habit of producing many reviews and articles. In March, he gives a lecture titled "Hypnotism, with Reference to Spiritism." In September, volume 4 of the Kurschner edition is completed. In November, *The Philosophy of Freedom* appears. This year, too, he meets John Henry Mackay (1864-1933), the anarchist, and Max Stirner, a scholar and biographer.

1894: Rudolf Steiner meets Elisabeth Förster Nietzsche, the philosopher's sister, and begins to read Nietzsche in earnest, beginning with the as yet unpublished *Antichrist*. He also meets Ernst Haeckel (1834-1919). In the fall, he begins to write *Nietzsche, A Fighter against His Time* (CW 5).

1895: May, *Nietzsche, A Fighter against His Time* appears.

1896: January 22: Rudolf Steiner sees Friedrich Nietzsche for the first and only time. Moves between the Nietzsche and the Goethe-Schiller Archives, where he completes his work before year's end. He falls out with Elisabeth Förster Nietzsche, thus ending his association with the Nietzsche Archive.

1897: Rudolf Steiner finishes the manuscript of *Goethe's Worldview* (CW 6). He moves to Berlin with Anna Eunike and begins editorship of the *Magazin fur Literatur*. From now on, Steiner will write countless reviews, literary and philosophical articles, and so on. He begins lecturing at the "Free Literary Society." In September, he attends the Zionist Congress in Basel. He sides with Dreyfus in the Dreyfus affair.

1898: Rudolf Steiner is very active as an editor in the political, artistic, and theatrical life of Berlin. He becomes friendly with John Henry Mackay and poet Ludwig Jacobowski (1868-1900). He joins Jacobowski's circle of writers, artists, and scientists—"The Coming Ones" (*Die Kommenden*)—and contributes lectures to the group until 1903. He also lectures at the "League for College Pedagogy." He writes an article for Goethe's sesquicentennial, "Goethe's Secret Revelation," on the "Fairy Tale of the Green Snake and the Beautiful Lily."

1898-99: "This was a trying time for my soul as I looked at Christianity.... I was able to progress only by contemplating, by means of spiritual perception, the evolution of Christianity.... Conscious knowledge of real Christianity began to dawn in me around the turn of the century. This seed continued to develop. My soul trial occurred shortly before the beginning of the twentieth century. It was decisive for my soul's development that I stood spiritually before the Mystery of Golgotha in a deep and solemn celebration of knowledge."

1899: Rudolf Steiner begins teaching and giving lectures and lecture cycles at the Workers' College, founded by Wilhelm Liebknecht (1826-1900). He will continue to do so until 1904. Writes: *Literature and*

Spiritual Life in the Nineteenth Century; Individualism in Philosophy; Haeckel and His Opponents; Poetry in the Present; and begins what will become (fifteen years later). *The Riddles of Philosophy* (CW 18). He also meets many artists and writers, including Käthe Kollwitz, Stefan Zweig, and Rainer Maria Rilke. On October 31, he marries Anna Eunike.

1900: "I thought that the turn of the century must bring humanity a new light. It seemed to me that the separation of human thinking and willing from the spirit had peaked. A turn or reversal of direction in human evolution seemed to me a necessity." Rudolf Steiner finishes *World and Life Views in the Nineteenth Century* (the second part of what will become *The Riddles of Philosophy*) and dedicates it to Ernst Haeckel. It is published in March. He continues lecturing at *Die Kommenden*, whose leadership he assumes after the death of Jacobowski. Also, he gives the Gutenberg Jubilee lecture before 7,000 typesetters and printers. In September, Rudolf Steiner is invited by Count and Countess Brockdorff to lecture in the Theosophical Library. His first lecture is on Nietzsche. His second lecture is titled "Goethe's Secret Revelation." October 6, he begins a lecture cycle on the mystics that will become *Mystics after Modernism* (CW 7). November-December: "Marie von Sivers appears in the audience...." Also in November, Steiner gives his first lecture at the Giordano Bruno Bund (where he will continue to lecture until May, 1905). He speaks on Bruno and modern Rome, focusing on the importance of the philosophy of Thomas Aquinas as monism.

1901: In continual financial straits, Rudolf Steiner's early friends Moritz Zitter and Rosa Mayreder help support him. In October, he begins the lecture cycle *Christianity as Mystical Fact* (CW 8) at the Theosophical Library. In November, he gives his first "Theosophical lecture" on Goethe's "Fairy Tale" in Hamburg at the invitation of Wilhelm Hubbe-Schleiden. He also attends a tea to celebrate the founding of the Theosophical Society at Count and Countess Brockdorff's. He gives a lecture cycle, "From Buddha to Christ," for the circle of the *Kommenden*. November 17, Marie von Sivers asks Rudolf Steiner if Theosophy does not need a Western-Christian spiritual movement (to complement Theosophy's Eastern emphasis). "The question was posed. Now, following spiritual laws, I could begin to give an answer...." In December, Rudolf Steiner writes his first article for a Theosophical publication. At year's end, the Brockdorffs and possibly Wilhelm Hubbe-Schleiden ask Rudolf Steiner to join the Theosophical Society and undertake the leadership of the German section. Rudolf Steiner agrees, on the condition that Marie von Sivers (then in Italy) work with him.

1902: Beginning in January, Rudolf Steiner attends the opening of the Workers' School in Spandau with Rosa Luxemburg (1870-1919).

January 17, Rudolf Steiner joins the Theosophical Society. In April, he is asked to become general secretary of the German Section of the Theosophical Society, and works on preparations for its founding. In July, he visits London for a Theosophical congress. He meets Bertram Keightly, G.R.S. Mead, A.P. Sinnett, and Annie Besant, among others. In September, *Christianity as Mystical Fact* appears. In October, Rudolf Steiner gives his first public lecture on Theosophy ("Monism and Theosophy") to about three hundred people at the Giordano Bruno Bund. On October 19-21, the German Section of the Theosophical Society has its first meeting; Rudolf Steiner is the general secretary, and Annie Besant attends. Steiner lectures on practical karma studies. On October 23, Annie Besant inducts Rudolf Steiner into the Esoteric School of the Theosophical Society. On October 25, Steiner begins a weekly series of lectures: "The Field of Theosophy." During this year, Rudolf Steiner also first meets Ita Wegman (1876-1943), who will become his close collaborator in his final years.

1903: Rudolf Steiner holds about 300 lectures and seminars. In May, the first issue of the periodical *Luzifer* appears. In June, Rudolf Steiner visits London for the first meeting of the Federation of the European Sections of the Theosophical Society, where he meets Colonel Olcott. He begins to write *Theosophy* (CW 9).

1904: Rudolf Steiner continues lecturing at the Workers' College and elsewhere (about 90 lectures), while lecturing intensively all over Germany among Theosophists (about a 140 lectures). In February, he meets Carl Unger (1878-1929), who will become a member of the board of the Anthroposophical Society (1913). In March, he meets Michael Bauer (1871-1929), a Christian mystic, who will also be on the board. In May, *Theosophy* appears, with the dedication: "To the spirit of Giordano Bruno." Rudolf Steiner and Marie von Sivers visit London for meetings with Annie Besant. June: Rudolf Steiner and Marie von Sivers attend the meeting of the Federation of European Sections of the Theosophical Society in Amsterdam. In July, Steiner begins the articles in *Luzifer-Gnosis* that will become *How to Know Higher Worlds* (CW 10) and *Cosmic Memory* (CW 11). In September, Annie Besant visits Germany. In December, Steiner lectures on Freemasonry. He mentions the High Grade Masonry derived from John Yarker and represented by Theodore Reuss and Karl Kellner as a blank slate "into which a good image could be placed."

1905: This year, Steiner ends his non-Theosophical lecturing activity. Supported by Marie von Sivers, his Theosophical lecturing—both in public and in the Theosophical Society—increases significantly: "The German Theosophical Movement is of exceptional importance." Steiner recommends reading, among others, Fichte, Jacob Boehme, and Angelus Silesius. He begins to introduce Christian themes into Theosophy. He also begins to work with doctors (Felix Peipers and Ludwig Noll). In July, he is in London for the Federation of European Sections, where he attends a lecture by Annie Besant: "I have seldom seen Mrs. Besant speak in so inward and heartfelt a manner...." "Through Mrs. Besant I have found the way to H.P. Blavatsky." September to October, he gives a course of thirty-one lectures for a small group of esoteric students. In October, the annual meeting of the German Section of the Theosophical Society, which still remains very small, takes place. Rudolf Steiner reports membership has risen from 121 to 377 members. In November, seeking to establish esoteric "continuity," Rudolf Steiner and Marie von Sivers participate in a "Memphis-Misraim" Masonic ceremony. They pay forty-five marks for membership. "Yesterday, you saw how little remains of former esoteric institutions." "We are dealing only with a 'framework'... for the present, nothing lies behind it. The occult powers have completely withdrawn."

1906: The expansion of Theosophical work. Rudolf Steiner gives about 245 lectures, only 44 of which take place in Berlin. Cycles are given in Paris, Leipzig, Stuttgart, and Munich. Esoteric work also intensifies now. Rudolf Steiner begins writing *An Outline of Esoteric Science* (CW 13). In January, Rudolf Steiner receives permission (a patent) from the Great Orient of the Scottish A & A Thirty-Three Degree Rite of the Order of the Ancient Freemasons of the Memphis-Misraim Rite to direct a chapter under the name "Mystica Aeterna." This chapter will become the "Cognitive Cultic Section" (also called "Misraim Service") of the Esoteric School. (See: *From the History and Contents of the Cognitive Cultic Section* (CW 264). During this time, Steiner also meets Albert Schweitzer. In May, Steiner is in Paris, where he visits Edouard Schuré. Many Russians attend Stewiner's lectures (including Konstantin Balmont, Dimitri Mereszkovski, Zinaida Hippius, and Maximilian Woloshin). He attends the General Meeting of the European Federation of the Theosophical Society, at which Col. Olcott is present for the last time. He spends the year's end in Venice and Rome, where he writes and works on his translation of H.P. Blavatsky's *Key to Theosophy*.

1907: Further expansion of the German Theosophical Movement according to the Rosicrucian directive to "introduce spirit into the world"—in education, in social questions, in art, and in science. In February, Col. Olcott dies in Adyar. Before he dies, Olcott indicates that "the Masters" wish Annie Besant to succeed him: much politicking ensues. Rudolf Steiner supports Besant's candidacy. April-May: preparations for the Congress of the Federation of European Sections of the Theosophical Society—the great, watershed Whitsun "Munich Congress," attended by Annie Besant and others. Steiner decides to separate Eastern and Western (Christian-Rosicrucian) esoteric schools. He takes his esoteric school out of the Theosophical Society (Besant and Rudolf Steiner are "in harmony" on this). Steiner makes his first lecture tours to Austria and Hungary. That summer, he is in Italy. In September, he visits Edouard Schuré, who will write the introduction to the French edition of *Christianity as Mystical Fact* in Barr, Alsace. Rudolf Steiner writes the autobiographical statement known as the "Barr Document." In *Luzifer–Gnosis*, "The Education of the Child" appears.

1908: The movement grows (membership: 1150). Lecturing expands. Steiner makes his first extended lecture tour to Holland and Scandinavia, as well as visits to Naples and Sicily. Themes: St. John's Gospel, the Apocalypse, Egypt, science, philosophy, and logic. *Luzifer-Gnosis* ceases publication. In Berlin, Marie von Sivers (with Johanna Mücke (1864-1949) forms the *Philosophisch-Theosophisch* (after 1915 *Philosophisch-Anthroposophisch*) *Verlag* to publish Steiner's work. Steiner gives lecture cycles titled *The Gospel of St. John* (CW 103) and *The Apocalypse* (104).

1909: *An Outline of Esoteric Science* appears. Lecturing and travel continues. Rudolf Steiner's spiritual research expands to include the polarity of Lucifer and Ahriman; the work of great individualities in history; the Maitreya Buddha and the Bodhisattvas; spiritual economy (CW 109); the work of the spiritual hierarchies in heaven and on Earth (CW 110). He also deepens and intensifies his research into the Gospels, giving lectures on the Gospel of St. Luke (CW 114) with the first mention of two Jesus children. Meets and becomes friends with Christian Morgenstern (1871-1914). In April, he lays the foundation stone for the Malsch model—the building that will lead to the first Goetheanum. In May, the International Congress of the Federation of European Sections of the Theosophical Society takes place in Budapest. Rudolf Steiner receives the Subba Row medal for *How to Know Higher Worlds*. During this time, Charles W. Leadbeater discovers Jiddu Krishnamurti (1895-1986) and proclaims him the future "world teacher," the bearer of the Maitreya Buddha and the "reappearing Christ." In October, Steiner delivers seminal lectures on "anthroposophy," which he will try, unsuccessfully, to rework over the next years into the unfinished work, *Anthroposophy (A Fragment)* (CW 45).

1910: New themes: *The Reappearance of Christ in the Etheric* (CW 118); *The Fifth Gospel; The Mission of Folk Souls* (CW 121); *Occult History* (CW 126); the evolving development of etheric cognitive capacities. Rudolf Steiner continues his Gospel research with *The Gospel of St. Matthew* (CW 123). In January, his father dies. In April, he takes a month-long trip to Italy, including Rome, Monte Cassino, and Sicily. He also visits Scandinavia again. July-August, he writes the first mystery drama, *The Portal of Initiation* (CW 14). In November, he gives "psychosophy" lectures. In December, he submits "On the Psychological Foundations and Epistemological Framework of Theosophy" to the International Philosophical Congress in Bologna.

1911: The crisis in the Theosophical Society deepens. In January, "The Order of the Rising Sun," which will soon become "The Order of the Star in the East," is founded for the coming world teacher, Krishnamurti. At the same time, Marie von Sivers, Rudolf Steiner's coworker, falls ill. Fewer lectures are given, but important new ground is broken. In Prague, in March, Steiner meets Franz Kafka (1883-1924) and Hugo Bergmann (1883-1975). In April, he delivers his paper to the Philosophical Congress. He writes the second mystery drama, *The Soul's Probation* (CW 14). Also, while Marie von Sivers is convalescing, Rudolf Steiner begins work on *Calendar 1912/1913*, which will contain the "Calendar of the Soul" meditations. On March 19, Anna (Eunike) Steiner dies. In September, Rudolf Steiner visits Einsiedeln, birthplace of Paracelsus. In December, Friedrich Rittelmeyer, future founder of the Christian Community, meets Rudolf Steiner. The *Johannes-Bauverein*, the "building committee," which would lead to the first Goetheanum (first planned for Munich), is also founded, and a preliminary committee for the founding of an independent association is created that, in the following year, will become the Anthroposophical Society. Important lecture cycles include *Occult Physiology* (CW 128); *Wonders of the World* (CW 129); *From Jesus to Christ* (CW 131). Other themes: esoteric Christianity; Christian Rosenkreutz; the spiritual guidance of humanity; the sense world and the world of the spirit.

1912: Despite the ongoing, now increasing crisis in the Theosophical Society, much is accomplished: *Calendar 1912/1913* is published; eurythmy is created; both the third mystery drama, *The Guardian of the Threshold* (CW 14) and *A Way of Self-Knowledge* (CW 16) are written. New (or renewed) themes included life between death and rebirth and karma and reincarnation. Other lecture cycles: *Spiritual Beings in the Heavenly Bodies and the Kingdoms of Nature* (CW 136); *The Human Being in the Light of Occultism, Theosophy, and Philosophy* (CW 137); *The Gospel of St. Mark* (CW 139); and *The Bhagavad Gita and the Epistles of Paul* (CW 142). On May 8, Rudolf Steiner celebrates White Lotus Day, H.P. Blavatsky's death day, which he had faithfully observed for the past decade, for the last time. In August, Rudolf Steiner suggests the "independent association" be called the "Anthroposophical Society." In September, the first eurythmy course takes place. In October, Rudolf Steiner declines recognition of a Theosophical Society lodge dedicated to the Star of the East and decides to expel all Theosophical Society members belonging to the order. Also, with Marie von Sivers, he first visits Dornach, near Basel, Switzerland, and they stand on the hill where the Goetheanum will be. In November, a Theosophical Society lodge is opened by direct mandate from Adyar (Annie Besant). In December, a meeting of the German section occurs at which it is decided that belonging to the Order of the Star of the East is incompatible with membership in the Theosophical Society. December 28: informal founding of the Anthroposophical Society in Berlin.

1913: Expulsion of the German Section from the Theosophical Society. February 2-3: Foundation meeting of the Anthroposophical Society. Board members include: Marie von Sivers, Michael Bauer, and Carl Unger. September 20: Laying of the foundation stone for the *Johannes Bau* (Goetheanum) in Dornach. Work on building begins immediately. The third mystery drama, *The Soul's Awakening* (CW 14), is completed, and the book *The Threshold of the Spiritual World* (CW 147). Lecture cycles include: *The Bhagavad Gita and the Epistles of Paul* and *The Esoteric Meaning of the Bhagavad Gita* (CW 146), which the Russian philosopher Nikolai Berdyaev attends; *The Mysteries of the East and of Christianity* (CW 144); *The Effects of Esoteric Development* (CW 145); and *The Fifth Gospel* (CW 148). In May, Rudolf Steiner is in London and Paris, where anthroposophical work continues.

1914: Building continues on the *Johannes Bau* (Goetheanum) in Dornach, with artists and coworkers from seventeen nations. The general assembly of the Anthroposophical Society takes place. In May, Rudolf Steiner visits Paris, as well as Chartres Cathedral. June 28: assassination in Sarajevo ("Now the catastrophe has happened!"). August 1: War is declared. Rudolf Steiner returns to Germany from Dornach—he will travel back and forth. He writes the last chapter of *The Riddles of Philosophy*. Lecture cycles include: *Human and Cosmic Thought* (CW 151); *Inner Being of Humanity between Death and a New Birth* (CW 153); *Occult Reading and Occult Hearing* (CW 156). December 24: marriage of Rudolf Steiner and Marie von Sivers.

1915: Building continues. Life after death becomes a major theme, also art. Writes: *Thoughts during a Time of War* (CW 24). Lectures include: *The Secret of Death* (CW 159); *The Uniting of Humanity through the Christ Impulse* (CW 165).

1916: Rudolf Steiner begins work with Edith Maryon (1872-1924) on the sculpture "The Representative of Humanity" ("The Group"—Christ, Lucifer, and Ahriman). He also works with the alchemist Alexander von Bernus on the quarterly *Das Reich*. He writes *The Riddle of Humanity* (CW 20). Lectures include: *Necessity and Freedom in World History and Human Action* (CW 166); *Past and Present in the Human Spirit* (CW 167); *The Karma of Vocation* (CW 172); *The Karma of Untruthfulness* (CW 173).

1917: Russian Revolution. The U.S. enters the war. Building continues. Rudolf Steiner delineates the idea of the "threefold nature of the human being" (in a public lecture March 15) and the "threefold nature of the social organism" (hammered out in May-June with the help of Otto von Lerchenfeld and Ludwig Polzer-Hoditz in the form of two documents titled *Memoranda*, which were distributed in high places). August-September: Rudolf Steiner writes *The Riddles of the Soul* (CW 20). Also: commentary on "The Chemical Wedding of Christian Rosenkreutz" for Alexander Bernus (*Das Reich*). Lectures include: *The Karma of Materialism* (CW 176); *The Spiritual Background of the Outer World: The Fall of the Spirits of Darkness* (CW 177).

1918: March 18: peace treaty of Brest-Litovsk—"Now everything will truly enter chaos! What is needed is cultural renewal." June: Rudolf Steiner visits Karlstein (Grail) Castle outside Prague. Lecture cycle: *From Symptom to Reality in Modern History* (CW 185). In mid-November, Emil Molt, of the Waldorf-Astoria Cigarette Company, has the idea of founding a school for his workers' children.

1919: Focus on the threefold social organism: tireless travel, countless lectures, meetings, and publications. At the same time, a new public stage of Anthroposophy emerges as cultural renewal begins. The coming years will see initiatives in pedagogy, medicine, pharmacology, and agriculture. January 27: threefold meeting: " We must first of all, with the money we have, found free schools that can bring people what they need." February: first public eurythmy performance in Zurich. Also: "Appeal to the German People" (CW 24), circulated March 6 as a newspaper insert. In April, *Toward Social Renewal* (CW 23)—"perhaps the most widely read of all books on politics appearing since the war"—appears. Rudolf Steiner is asked to undertake the "direction and leadership" of the school founded by the Waldorf-Astoria Company. Rudolf Steiner begins to talk about the "renewal" of education. May 30: a building is selected and purchased for the future Waldorf School. August-September, Rudolf Steiner gives a lecture course for Waldorf teachers, *The Foundations of Human Experience (Study of Man)* (CW 293). September 7: Opening of the first Waldorf School. December (into January): first science course, the *Light Course* (CW 320).

1920: The Waldorf School flourishes. New threefold initiatives. Founding of limited companies *Der Kommenden Tag* and *Futurum A.G.* to infuse spiritual values into the economic realm. Rudolf Steiner also focuses on the sciences. Lectures: *Introducing Anthroposophical Medicine* (CW 312); *The Warmth Course* (CW 321); *The Boundaries of Natural Science* (CW 322); *The Redemption of Thinking* (CW 74). February: Johannes Werner Klein—later a cofounder of the Christian Community—asks Rudolf Steiner about the possibility of a "religious renewal," a "Johannine church." In March, Rudolf Steiner gives the first course for doctors and medical students. In April, a divinity student asks Rudolf Steiner a second time about the possibility of religious renewal. September 27-October 16: anthroposophical "university course." December: lectures titled *The Search for the New Isis* (CW 202).

1921: Rudolf Steiner continues his intensive work on cultural renewal, including the uphill battle for the threefold social order. "University" arts, scientific, theological, and medical courses include: *The Astronomy Course* (CW 323); *Observation, Mathematics, and Scientific Experiment* (CW 324); the *Second Medical Course* (CW 313); *Color*. In June and September-October, Rudolf Steiner also gives the first two "priests' courses" (CW 342 and 343). The "youth movement" gains momentum. Magazines are founded: *Die Drei* (January), and—under the editorship of Albert Steffen (1884-1963)—the weekly, *Das Goetheanum* (August). In February-March, Rudolf Steiner takes his first trip outside Germany since the war (Holland). On April 7, Steiner receives a letter regarding "religious renewal," and May 22-23, he agrees to address the question in a practical way. In June, the Klinical-Therapeutic Institute opens in Arlesheim under the direction of Dr. Ita Wegman. In August, the Chemical-Pharmaceutical Laboratory opens in Arlesheim (Oskar Schmiedel and Ita Wegman, directors). The Clinical Therapeutic Institute is inaugurated in Stuttgart (Dr. Ludwig Noll, director); also the Research Laboratory in Dornach (Ehrenfried Pfeiffer and Gunther Wachsmuth, directors). In November-December, Rudolf Steiner visits Norway.

1922: The first half of the year involves very active public lecturing (thousands attend); in the second half, Rudolf Steiner begins to withdraw and turn toward the Society—"The Society is asleep." It is "too weak" to do what is asked of it. The businesses—*Die Kommenden Tag* and *Futura A.G.*—fail. In January, with the help of an agent, Steiner undertakes a twelve-city German tour, accompanied by eurythmy performances. In two weeks he speaks to more than 2,000 people. In April, he gives a "university course" in The Hague. He also visits England. In June, he is in Vienna for the East-West Congress. In August-September, he is back in England for the Oxford Conference on Education. Returning to Dornach, he gives the lectures *Philosophy, Cosmology, and Religion* (CW 215), and gives the third priest's course (CW 344). On September 16, The Christian Community is founded. In October-November, Steiner is in Holland and England. He also speaks to the youth: *The Youth Course* (CW 217). In December, Steiner gives lectures titled *The Origins of Natural Science* (CW 326), and *Humanity and the World of Stars: The Spiritual Communion of Humanity* (CW 219). December 31: Fire at the Goetheanum, which is destroyed.

1923: Despite the fire, Rudolf Steiner continues his work unabated. A very hard year. Internal dispersion, dissension, and apathy abound. There is conflict—between old and new visions—within the society. A wake-up call is needed, and Rudolf Steiner responds with renewed lecturing vitality. His focus: the spiritual context of human life; initiation science; the course of the year; and community building. As a foundation for an artistic school, he creates a series of pastel sketches. Lecture cycles: *The Anthroposophical Movement; Initiation Science* (CW 227) (in England at the Penmaenmawr Summer School); *The Four Seasons and the Archangels* (CW 229); *Harmony of the Creative Word* (CW 230); *The Supersensible Human* (CW 231), given in Holland for the founding of the Dutch society. On November 10, in response to the failed Hitler-Ludendorf putsch in Munich, Steiner closes his Berlin residence and moves the *Philosophisch-Anthroposophisch Verlag* (Press) to Dornach. On December 9, Steiner begins the serialization of his *Autobiography: The Course of My Life* (CW 28) in *Das Goetheanum*. It will continue to appear weekly, without a break, until his death. Late December-early January: Rudolf Steiner refounds the Anthroposophical Society (about 12,000 members internationally) and takes over its leadership. The new board members are: Marie Steiner, Ita Wegman, Albert Steffen, Elizabeth Vreede, and Guenther Wachsmuth. (See *The Christmas Meeting for the Founding of the General Anthroposophical Society* (CW 260). Accompanying lectures: *Mystery Knowledge and Mystery Centers* (CW 232); *World History in the Light of Anthroposophy* (CW 233). December 25: the Foundation Stone is laid (in the hearts of members) in the form of the "Foundation Stone Meditation."

1924: January 1: having founded the Anthroposophical Society and taken over its leadership, Rudolf Steiner has the task of "reforming" it. The process begins with a weekly newssheet ("What's Happening in the Anthroposophical Society") in which Rudolf Steiner's "Letters to Members" and "Anthroposophical Leading Thoughts" appear (CW 26). The next step is the creation of a new esoteric class, the "first class" of the "University of Spiritual Science" (which was to have been followed, had Rudolf Steiner lived longer, by two more advanced classes). Then comes a new language for Anthroposophy—practical, phenomenological, and direct; and Rudolf Steiner creates the model for the second Goetheanum. He begins the series of extensive "karma" lectures (CW 235-40); and finally, responding to needs, he creates two new initiatives: biodynamic agriculture and curative education. After the middle of the year, rumors begin to circulate regarding Steiner's health. Lectures: January-February, *Anthroposophy* (CW 234); February: *Tone Eurythmy* (CW 278); June: *The Agriculture Course* (CW 327); June-July: Speech [?] Eurythmy (CW 279); *Curative Education* (CW 317); August: (England, "Second International Summer School"), *Initiation Consciousness: True and False Paths in Spiritual Investigation* (CW 243); September: *Pastoral Medicine* (CW 318). On September 26, for the first time, Rudolf Steiner cancels a lecture. On September 28, he gives his last lecture. On September 29, he withdraws to his studio in the carpenter's shop; now he is definitively ill. Cared for by Ita Wegman, he continues working, however, and writing the weekly installments of his *Autobiography* and *Letters to the Members/Leading Thoughts* (CW 26).

1925: Rudolf Steiner, while continuing to work, continues to weaken. He finishes *Extending Practical Medicine* (CW 27) with Ita Wegman.
On March 30, around ten in the morning, Rudolf Steiner dies.

INDEX

Act of Consecration of Man, 381-382
Academe of Gondhishapor, 311
Adam, 36, 38, 41-42, 45
Adams, George, 311
Ahriman, 68, 70, 72-73, 81, 83, 124, 126-127, 129-133, 136, 138-143, 145-149, 155-158, 162-164, 168-171, 186-187, 189, 196, 256, 262, 265, 268, 270-271, 182, 287, 289, 314, 322-324, 380, 398
  as Lord of Death, 143, 155
ahrimanic, 65-66, 124, 127, 130-131, 135-139, 145-149, 168, 244, 250, 275, 283, 287, 311, 324, 373-374, 380, 396
akashic chronicle, 127
Anaxagoras, 152
Andrae, Valentin, 295
  author of the "Chymical Wedding," 295
angel, 24, 28, 31, 43-44, 46, 48, 77, 80, 82, 87, 91, 94, 150, 155, 158, 160, 163, 169-170, 176, 179, 181, 184, 199, 203, 206-207, 220-221, 256
  guardian angel, 87, 91-92, 94
  as messengers, 80, 82
Anthroposophical/Anthroposophy, xiv, xvii, xxii-xxv, xxix, 87, 111, 149, 241, 266, 286-287, 305, 320, 330, 332-334, 338-339, 342, 345-347, 349, 353-354, 356-358, 360, 365, 367, 372, 378, 383, 389, 391-392, 394, 396, 407
Anthroposophical Movement, 69, 72, 287, 329-330, 342-344, 348-349, 352-353, 381-382
Anthroposophical Society, xv, xxii, xxviii, 295-296, 329-330, 332, 337, 342-344, 346, 350, 356-358, 414, 416
  Zarathustra group, 311
Anthroposophical Youth Branch, 344-345, 347-348
Anthroposophical Youth Movement, 330, 341, 346
antipathy, 101, 107, 112, 115, 119, 131, 137, 344
aoum/aum, 326, 412-413, 421
archangel, 78, 80, 82, 155, 160, 199, 203, 207
archetypes, 65, 70, 73
Ariadne, thread of, 351
Aristotle, 282, 420
art/artist, 50, 53, 55-56, 66, 141, 156-157, 346
Association for Anthroposophical College Studies, 329, 332, 339
Association for Independent Spiritual Life, 352, 354, 356, 390-392
Association for the Threefold Organism, 352, 356
astral, 58, 60-61, 155, 158, 210, 216, 260, 271, 411
  body, xxvi, 24, 32, 59, 61, 65, 68, 95, 99, 152, 154, 171, 174, 176, 192-193, 196, 198-199, 202-203, 205-207, 210-211, 216-218, 241, 260, 267, 269-271, 433
astronomer/astronomy, 164, 174
Atlantean/Atlantis, 59, 61
  epoch, 282
atoms/atomism, 136, 139, 255
auras, 163-165, 170, 174-177, 206, 224
awe, sacred, 71, 73-76, 83-84, 104-105, 413

Baptism in the Jordan, 183
Bartsch, Moritz, 354
Bauer, Michael, 354
Baumann, Paul, 343, 346,-348
Bauman-Dolfus, Elisabeth, 343
beacon (soul), 21, 230-231, 233, 236, 239-240, 246, 251, 257-258, 276-277, 279, 291

Beatitudes, 147
beinglessness, 418, 422, 442
Bemmelen, van, Daniel, 338-339, 386, 389
Benn, Otto, 344
Besent, Annie, 23, 27, 30, 34, 40, 287
Bible, 151-152, 162, 193
Blavatsky, Helena P., 287, 289, 383
   Secret Doctrine, 287, 289
Beck, Hermann, 355
blessedness, 11, 13, 15
bliss/blissfulness, 77, 80
blood, 36, 38, 49, 52, 54, 56, 158-159, 168, 199, 202-203, 206, 256, 261-262, 264, 270-271
   prickling of, 159, 161-162, 168
Bock, Emil, 381
boundary, 273, 275, 309
   spiritual boundary at birth, 273
brain, 25, 33, 385-286, 288-290, 298, 389
   cerebellum, 286, 288-290
   cerebrum, 285-286, 288, 290
breath/breathing, 36, 100, 107, 111, 121-122, 159, 161, 159, 281, 285, 288, 298, 410-412
bubbles (in club soda), 242, 248, 255, 258, 274, 280
Burg, Anton, 343
burning bush, 282, 284

carpentry studio/hall (Schreinerei), 296
Catholic Church, 380, 420
cerebellum. See brain, cerebellum
cerebrum. See brain, cerebrum
chalice, 31-32, 43-44, 46, 247, 252
Chattopadhyaya, J.C., 430
choking (during meal), 161
Christ, 26, 29, 33-34, 36-37, 39, 41-42, 45, 51, 59-61, 67, 71, 74-75, 84-85, 96-99, 106, 109-110, 113, 117-118, 120, 128, 164, 169, 172, 175-180, 182-184, 189-190, 193-194, 196, 201, 205, 211, 221, 224, 240, 246, 251, 259, 265, 275, 286-287, 289-291, 304-306, 310-311, 314-315, 368, 374, 380, 395, 410-411, 423, 443

Christ-circle, 110
Christ principle, 106, 109
Christ-event, 60, 311
Christ force, 45, 123
Christ impulse, 26, 33, 36-38, 42, 72, 170, 179-180, 184
Christ power, 39
Christ substance, 26, 29, 33, 42, 45, 47, 75, 85
Christ-Sun, 106
Christ as unspeakable name, 26, 29, 31, 33, 45, 67, 74, 79, 81, 84, 106, 110, 182, 201, 246, 251, 262-263, 284, 287
   in the etheric (Etheric Christ), 177
   as the highest truth, 98
   as the leader, 1, 13, 15
   as Light of the World, 143
   as Lord of Karma, 41
   as the New Adam, 36
   Resurrection, 04
   as the Son, 222
   as Spirit of the Earth, 75
   as Sun leader, 275
   as the Sun-Spirit, 99, 117
   will of Christ, 314
   the Word, 17, 143, 146-147, 415, 421, 441
Christian/Christianity, 193, 221, 287
Christian Community, 338, 359, 361, 381-382, 401
   as Movement for Religious Renewal, 361
Christmas Conference, 297, 325, 338, 403-404, 414, 423
clairvoyance/clairvoyant, 23, 61, 65, 126, 149, 156-157, 176, 180, 183, 188, 234, 260, 267-271, 282
cognize/cognition, 9, 11, 230-231, 233, 236, 239-240, 246, 251, 257-258, 276, 291
consciousness, 24-26, 28-29, 31-33, 40, 43, 45-47, 49, 59, 61, 63, 65, 72, 75-77, 79, 82-85, 93, 100-102, 104-105, 118, 159, 171-172, 175, 180-183, 191, 204, 215, 218-219, 222, 254, 263, 267, 270, 272-275, 281, 288-299, 324, 349, 397, 416-417
clairvoyant, 61

day, 43, 46, 50, 82, 178, 207, 260, 262, 272, 274, 276
earthly, 76, 79, 84-85
picture-consciousness, 82
post-mortem, 76, 84-85
self-consciousness, 26, 29, 31, 33, 45, 47, 71, 74-76, 79, 85, 102-103, 156, 175-176, 179, 182
community impulse (on through incarnations), 403-404
consciousness soul, 220, 287, 333
communion, spiritual, 252
concentration, 49, 94, 154, 172, 185, 207, 216, 224, 226-228, 249, 288
concepts/conceptual, 49-50, 52, 54, 63, 105, 129-130, 132, 137-139, 163, 167, 208, 222, 373, 382
conscience, 172, 281-283, 324
voice of, 281-282
contemplation, 23, 26, 47, 49, 51, 77, 113, 118, 126-127, 140-141, 177, 180, 260, 267, 282
constellations, 95, 262, 271
cosmic/cosmos, 25, 27, 32-33, 35-38, 40-41, 44-46, 58, 60-62, 66, 71-72, 75, 82,-83, 85, 96, 107-109, 111-112, 115, 126, 179-180, 183, 205, 207, 212, 219, 242, 245, 252, 265, 270, 281-282, 289, 301, 303, 306, 312, 322, 324, 326, 370, 384, 388, 409-411, 415-417, 419, 421, 441
macrocosmic, 151
Word, cosmic, 303, 306
cosmic midnight, 158
cowardice, 176, 179, 184
Creative Word. *See* Mysteries of the Creative Word
Crookes, William, 151, 153
Crusaders, 475
crystal (quartz), 413
crystallize, 331, 390
Cusanus, 147

daily review, backward, 77
dance on stage (with chairs), 210
Darwin, 194
Der Kommender Tag (The Coming Day), 372, 394
destiny, 41, 379, 383, 389, 419, 421

Deussen, 187
devachan, 158
develop the grips, 399
devotion, 35-38, 41, 58-60, 65, 75, 77, 84, 140, 160, 166, 185-186, 288, 380, 398, 408, 430
devout/devoutness, 37, 60-62, 66, 69, 77, 223, 267-268, 324
disciples, 175
double, (the human double), 87, 90, 92, 94
double (seeing), 90-92, 94

Eckhart, Meister, 140, 147-148
eggshell (as aura), 163-165, 168-170, 174
egotism/egotistic, 27, 90, 96, 126-127, 147, 159-161, 163, 168, 171, 189, 191, 206, 228, 243, 249, 268, 322, 411
Egyptian, 104
elemental
  beings, 137-139, 210, 216, 261-265, 267-271, 418
  forces, 330
  world, 136, 155, 158, 210, 227-228, 244, 249
elements, 96, 316
elohim. *See* spirits of form (elohim)
embryo, 410
Empedocles, 152
Esoteric School (Steiner's), 295, 335, 385, 436
  Cognitive-Ritual Section, 297
  as First Class, 325
Esoteric Youth Group, 329, 335, 337-338, 359-363, 381, 403, 416
Essenes/Essene Order, 23-24, 27-28, 30-31, 44, 46, 58, 78-79, 84, 127
etheric, 65, 70, 92-93, 210, 218, 237, 269, 285, 301
  body, 24-25, 31-33, 45-46, 59, 61, 67, 71, 87-89, 91-94, 107, 152, 154, 156-161, 172, 174, 192, 194-196, 198, 202, 209-211, 213, 215-216, 218-219, 224, 226, 231, 235-236, 241-242, 248-249, 253, 260, 263-265, 267-268, 270, 288-289, 313, 319, 324, 400, 409, 433

loosening of, 160
new etheric body, 289
force, 96, 411
ethers, 199, 203, 208
   chemical (tone), 199, 208, 219, 324
   cosmic, 219, 324
   life, 199, 208, 219, 324
   light, 199, 208, 219, 324
   warmth, 199, 206, 208, 219, 324
Event in Palestine, 304
every active Anthroposophist is a priest, 360
evil, (as nourishment for seeds of good), 238, 243, 251, 275
Ex Deo nascimur, 24-26, 28, 31-32, 40-41, 47-48, 59, 61, 66-67, 71, 74-76, 79, 84, 93, 96, 99, 106, 110, 113, 118, 123, 128, 143, 164, 182, 188, 190, 201, 205, 207-208, 217, 221-222, 225, 230-233, 236, 239, 245, 251, 259, 262, 265, 277, 279, 287, 291, 311, 410, 412
Executive Council, 335, 340, 347-348, 350
eye illness, 88, 91, 93

faith, 254
Fall, the, 162-164, 167, 170
farmer-philosophy, 200, 204, 221
Father. *See* God
fear/fearful, 78, 83, 88, 92-93, 125-126, 157, 166, 170, 331, 413
feel/feeling, 7, 19, 21, 24, 26, 30, 32-33, 75, 77, 80-81, 83, 91-94, 98, 109, 111-112, 115, 131, 134, 141, 144-146, 148-149, 166-167, 172-173, 179-180, 182, 196-197, 199, 201, 204, 208, 215, 217, 220-226, 234-235, 237-238, 240-241, 246-247, 251, 254-256, 261-262, 265-267, 270, 272, 278-279, 285-288, 301-303, 306, 316, 347, 369, 387, 415-417, 419-420, 430, 441
   feeling-mysticism, 148
   feeling nature, 222
   perceptive (sensation), 7, 9
   sacramental, 29
fickle person, 185
Finckh, Helene, 296-297, 306

First Class. *See* Esoteric School (Steiner's), as First Class
fishers as seekers, 374, 395
force centers (what our organs become), 45
force-group, 365-366, 389
freedom, 96-98, 127, 286, 289, 291, 331, 358, 374, 380, 384-385, 398, 410
Friend of God from Oberland, 333-334, 391
fruits of communities, 368

Gabriel, Archangel, 377-378
Geering, Rudolf, 343
Gemut (spirit/mind), 138, 167
General Anthroposophical Youth Movement, 329
germ, of good (soul/spirit), 19, 27, 113, 121, 134, 144, 180, 187, 225, 228, 243-246, 249-251, 255, 266, 273-275, 278, 299, 301
glandular system, 208
God (Father), 36-37, 44, 47, 50-51, 53, 61, 74, 96-98, 118, 128, 153, 156-158, 169, 183, 200, 204-206, 211, 221-222, 263, 282, 334, 374, 410, 429
   as Creator Word, 17
   Father forces, 410
   as Great encompassing Spirit, 3, 5, 7, 9, 11, 13, 15, 17
   as Godhead, 58-59, 61-62, 83-84, 96-97, 165, 188, 268, 282, 304
Goethe, 99, 142, 148, 156, 366, 393
Goetheanum,
   First, 329, 337-338, 353, 398
Golgotha, 33, 275
Gospels, xv, 172
Gotte, Fritz, 361, 414, 417
grace, 32, 37, 54, 106, 108, 117, 212
gratitude, xix-xx, 36, 38, 47, 60, 65-66, 73, 78-79, 84, 104-105, 108-109, 112
gravity, 407-412, 417
Greeks, 25, 29, 36
   Greek Tragedies, 33
Grimm, Hermann, 366, 393, 420
Grone, von, Jurgen, 297
Groot, Georg, 338

group soul, 41
  conscious, 378, 397
guardian angel. *See* angel, guardian angel
Guardian of the Threshold, xxi, xxiii, 78, 129, 133, 210, 262, 299, 418-419, 421

Haeckel, 129, 136-137
Hahn, Herbert, 339, 355, 362, 390, 404
Hansen, C. Brumberg, 362, 399
Haptmann, Gerhard, 157
head, 400, 433
headache, 89-90, 93
heart, 46, 281-285, 288, 290, 298, 303, 320, 323, 407
Hegel/Hegelianism, xiv, xvi, 137, 139
herb gatherer, 421
Hierarchies/hierarchical beings, xix, xxiii, 3, 35, 64-66, 109, 137, 139, 160, 165, 169-170, 199, 201, 203, 205, 234, 244, 250, 256, 261, 264, 271, 274-275, 377, 396
  appear in blue-violet, 77-78, 80, 82
  appear in red-yellow, 77-78, 80
  as cosmic spirits, 72
  as Deus, 28, 31
  as divine beings, 64, 76
  as gods, 25, 28, 31-33, 36, 41, 44, 46-47, 58, 69-71, 73-75, 80, 82-83, 85, 98, 108, 122, 126-127, 150, 157, 162, 167, 211, 213-214, 217, 265, 283-284, 286-287, 290, 304, 443
  as high beings, 38, 69
  as spirits, 30, 79-80, 324, 421
higher self. *See* "I" (ego), higher "I"
Holy Decad, xvii
Holy Tetraktys, xviii
Holy Spirit, xvi, xviii-xix, 3, 5, 7, 9, 11, 13, 15, 17, 26, 29, 33, 37, 45, 47, 51, 74, 85, 99, 118-119, 128, 169, 183, 190, 206, 247, 252, 263, 265, 287, 305, 310, 411, 429
  as messenger of Christ, 85
  as Spirit of Truth, 206

House Hansi (Dr. Steiner's home in Dornach), 297
humility, xxi, 29, 41, 137, 157-158

"I" (ego), xxi, xxiii, xxvi, 17, 21, 24, 32, 35, 37, 40, 42, 45, 58-61, 67-68, 71, 74, 91, 95, 97-99, 102, 106-109, 111-112, 115-120, 122-123, 152, 154, 157-158, 162, 168, 170, 174, 178, 186, 192-193, 196, 198-199, 202-203, 205-207, 211, 217-218, 223, 230-231, 233, 235-237, 239-241, 246, 251, 257, 260-264, 267-271, 276-277, 279, 291, 301, 304-306, 310, 320, 380, 398, 407, 410-412, 429-430, 433
  divine "I", 60, 62
  higher "I", xix, xxvi, 26, 33, 35, 75, 109
  "I"-being, 97, 240, 261
  "I"-consciousness, 61, 101-103, 111-112, 118-119, 155-157, 178, 181, 183-184, 267, 270, 407
  "I"-experience, 37, 301
  "I"-feeling, 71, 74
  "I"-forces, 95, 98, 105, 122
  "I"-gendering, 123
  "I"-sense, 261, 264, 268
  luminous "I", 21, 258, 277, 279, 291
  spiritual "I", 211
  true "I", 407, 412, 237
I am, 64, 69, 72, 82
Ibsen, 377
  his "Gespenster" (Ghosts), 377
illumination, 428-429
imagination/imaginative, xx, 28, 49, 59, 64, 69-70, 72, 77-78, 80, 82, 86, 88, 91-92, 140, 152, 154, 157-158, 166, 170, 178, 195, 203, 208, 220-221, 227-228, 281-283, 301, 373
In Christo morimur, xvi-xvii, xix, xxvi, 26, 29, 31, 33, 40-41, 47-48, 59, 62, 67, 71, 74-76, 79, 85, 93, 97, 99, 106, 110, 113, 118, 123, 128, 143, 164, 169, 177, 180, 182, 188, 201, 205, 207, 217, 221-222, 225, 230-232, 236, 239-240, 246,

251, 259, 262, 265, 277, 279, 284, 287, 291, 311, 411-412
incorporation (in a body), 378, 396
Independent Anthroposophical Society, 339, 356-358
Independent School for Spiritual Science, 330, 332, 338, 353, 436
Independent Waldorf School (Stuttgart), 296, 347, 353
India/Indian, 326, 412-413, 417, 430. *See* also Sanskrit
   wisdom, 417
initiate/initiation, 106, 110, 120, 169, 177, 196, 282, 401
   initiative exercise, 224
   modern initiation, 403
inspiration, xxvii, 116-117, 120, 141, 146, 148, 194, 207, 277, 281-283, 295, 370, 377, 388
intellectual (mind) soul, 220
intuitions, 17, 207, 281-283
I think, I feel, I will. *See* thinking, feeling, willing
It thinks me, It weaves me, It works me, 35-38, 40-41, 51, 53-55, 58, 60-61, 65-66, 68-71, 73-74, 80, 83, 242, 248

Janus head, 371
Jesuits, 305-306
Jesus of Nazareth, 30-31, 44, 177, 183, 304
Job, book of, 36
John, St, gospel of, 143, 146-149, 160, 199, 204
John-baptism, 177
Judaism, 369, 387
   as Zionism, 395
Judge, William T., xii, 30
Julian the Apostate, 106, 110, 113, 117, 120
Jupiter, 13, 97, 105-106, 109, 114, 116-117, 120
Jupiter, New, epoch, 262, 264, 269-271, 285-291
Justinian, 314

Kali Yuga, xxvii, 330, 418-419
kamaloca, 192
Kant, 141, 176, 179, 181, 184

karma, xiii-xiv, xxi, xxiii, xxv, 30, 35-38, 41-42, 53, 77, 89-91, 93, 126, 136, 153, 168, 221-222, 287, 289, 299, 383, 419
Kieser, Luise, 343
Knauer, Vincinz, 421
Know thyself, 125
Koch, Else, 343
Kolisko, Eugen, 355
Kolinsko, Lili, 362, 428
Kristamurti, xv
Kubler, Fritz, 332-333

language, 168
   initiate developed, 58, 60
   proto-language, 168
larynx, 288
Leadbeater, 27, 30, 34, 40, 287
Legend of the Dog, 211
Lauer, Hans E, 325, 343
Lehrs, Ernst, 332-339, 359-363, 366, 385-386, 390, 393-398
Leibniz, 129, 136-137, 152
Leinhas, Emil, 355
Lempp, 297
Lemurian epoch, 281, 283
Leonardo da Vinci, 50, 53, 55-56
Lerchenfeld, von, Otto, 297
life-communities, 357
light, 13, 17, 19, 37, 106, 116-117, 132, 134, 144, 151, 163, 178, 181, 187, 199-200, 203-208, 225, 263, 266, 278, 304, 321, 324, 407-412, 430, 433
   force, 109
   light-filled, 68
   light-form, 175-176, 178, 181, 183, 271, 279, 318, 320-323, 421
   light-knowledge, 201
   light-roses, 206
   spirit/spiritual, 21, 105, 117, 160, 230-231, 233, 236, 239, 246, 251, 257, 259, 276, 279, 291, 420
lightness (force of), 408-412
lightning, 409
Light Age, 418, 420
living stream (in body), 298
Lord's Prayer, 160
lotus blossom (chakra), xxvi, 50, 57,

118, 411-413
love, xx, 19, 23, 29, 50, 52-56, 76, 95, 98, 102, 105, 113-114, 120, 126-127, 134, 144, 147, 200-201, 211, 225, 243, 266, 278, 321, 375, 396, 417, 419-420, 430
  divine, 53
  egotistical, 27
  as life, 201
lovelessness, 282-283
loyal/loyalty, xxv, 27, 367, 380, 398
Lucifer, xxi-xxii, 64-65, 68-70, 72-73, 75, 78, 81-83, 85, 95-99, 124, 126-127, 129-133, 138-143, 145-149, 155-158, 162-165, 168 171, 186-187, 189, 196, 200-201, 205, 208, 228, 244, 250, 256, 262-263, 265, 268, 270-271, 275, 281-283, 287, 289, 377
  Lucifer thinks in me, 64-65
luciferic, 65, 82-83, 98, 124, 126-127, 131, 135-139, 145-149, 168, 191, 200, 204, 206, 208, 235, 238, 244, 249, 275, 282, 377
Luke, St, gospel of, 23, 31

Maeterlinck, 142, 145, 192
Maikowski, Rene, 339, 366, 390
manas. *See* spirit self
Mani (phonetic expression), 413
Maria the Jewess, xviii
  as legendary sister of Mose, xviii
  as Maria the Prophetess, xviii
Mars, 9, 97, 105-106, 109, 113-114, 116-117, 120
Masters of Wisdom and the Harmony of Feelings, 26, 30, 45, 71, 74, 83, 113, 266
materialism/materiality, 24, 30, 44, 82-83, 96, 99, 107, 126, 129, 141, 145, 149, 155, 174, 176, 179, 181-182, 184, 194, 197, 202, 253-254, 295, 368, 376, 396
maya (illusion), xx, 46, 50, 56, 63-66, 69, 72-73, 83, 170, 262
  maya-idea, 69
meditant/meditation, xiii, xvi-xxi, xxv-xxvi, 34-35, 40, 43, 49-50, 52-54, 56-59, 61-64, 66, 69-7, 72-73, 77, 79-80, 82, 84, 86-87, 89-90, 92-95, 113, 124, 127, 130-132, 140, 143, 148-149, 152, 154, 158-161, 163-168, 170-172, 177-178, 180, 183, 185, 187, 189, 191-192, 195, 197-200, 202-209, 214, 216, 219-220, 223-224, 229, 231, 234-235, 239-240, 242, 244, 247-250, 256, 258, 260, 262-263, 265-266, 270, 276, 282, 285, 288-290, 297-299, 311, 321-322, 334-335, 373-376, 379-380, 395-398, 400-402, 406-408, 413, 420
  community meditation, 401-402
  meditative verses, 1-22, 68, 118, 128, 133-134, 144, 182-183, 189-190, 225, 229-231, 229-231, 233-234, 237, 239, 345-246, 250-251, 256-258, 276-279, 301-303, 305-306, 326, 408-413, 415, 417-422, 426-427, 430-445
mediums/mystics, 140-141, 145-146, 148, 150
  mediumistic, 145-146, 148
  in Middle Ages, 148
melancholic (temperament), 28, 31-32, 43, 176, 178, 181-184, 402
memory (pictures), 64-65, 72, 89, 101, 108, 117, 150, 154, 167, 178, 186, 189, 206, 213-215, 274-275, 279, 403. *See also* pictures (imaginative images), memory pictures
memory tableau, 274
mendaciousness, 159
Mephistopheles, 156
Mercury (planet), 11, 95, 97-98, 104-106, 108-109, 112, 114, 116-117, 119-120, 123
metamorphosis. *See* transform/ transformation
Meyer, Rudolf, 355
Michael/Michaelic, 311, 376-378, 400
  as Archangel, xv, xxii
  as guiding spirit (time spirit), 375-376

as Patron /Guardian of
   Anthroposophy, xxii
as Regent of the Age, xxii
Michelangelo, 286, 289
   his "Last Judgment", 286, 289-290
middle path, xxi, 143
mineral kingdom, 228, 238, 244,
   250, 275, 413
mirror image, as reality, 156-157,
   168, 226, 232, 235, 242, 249, 254
Molt, Emil, 355
monism. *See* unity
Moon, 7, 95-99, 103-106, 108, 112,
   114, 116-118, 120, 122, 163, 169
Moon, Old, epoch, xix, 35, 38, 44,
   59, 61, 64, 79, 82, 84, 221, 228,
   235, 238, 244, 250, 256, 262, 271,
   275, 285-286-290
moral/morality, 77, 95-99, 114, 196,
   214, 219, 223, 324
   force, 401
   impulse, 95, 97
   moral being, of cosmic ether, 324
Moses, xviii, 282, 284
Movement for the Threefold Social
   Organism, 329
Mucke, Joanna, 428
multiplicity, of the body, 130, 135-
   139, 145
Mysteries of the Creative Word, 17,
   71, 74
Mysteries, old, 148
Mystery Dramas. *See* Rudolf Steiner,
   his mystery dramas
Mystery of Golgotha, xvii, xix, xxi,
   xxiii, 25-27, 29, 33, 36, 38-39,
   41-42, 45, 47, 106, 109-110,
   117, 175, 177, 180, 182-184,
   193, 206-207, 299
   as turning point of time, xix
mysticism, 148

Nathan Jesus, 23
nature (plants), 50, 70, 73, 96, 111,
   130
nerves/nervous system, 49, 52, 54,
   56, 202, 208
new brooms sweep well, 399
Nietzsche, 187, 370-371, 388
nothingness, 227, 232, 236, 241-242,
   245, 248, 251, 255, 258, 274, 276
Novalis, xvi

O Human Being, Know Thyself, xxiii,
   xxvi, 125, 303, 306, 311, 325, 415,
   421, 441
observation, 149, 191, 213, 267
Order of the Golden Dawn, xii
Order of the Star, in the East, xv
Origenes, 315

pain. *See* suffering
Palestine, 27, 42
Palmer, Otto, Jr., 330
Paracelsus, xiv, xvii
patience, 52, 54, 56, 77, 158, 213,
   217, 259
Paul, St, 36, 106, 109
Pentecost, xv
Per Spiritum Sanctum revivicimus,
   xvi-xvii, xix, xxvi, 26, 29, 31, 40-
   41, 47-48, 60, 62, 71, 74-76, 79,
   85, 93, 97, 99, 106, 110, 113,
   118, 123, 128, 143, 164, 182, 188,
   190, 205, 207, 217, 222, 224-225,
   230-232, 234, 236, 239-240, 247,
   252, 259, 262, 265, 277, 279, 283,
   291, 311, 411-412
perception, 174, 226, 232, 281, 283,
   304, 416
persevere/perseverance, 89, 93
Persian, 104
Pfeiffer, Ehrenfried, 331-332, 343,
   346, 348, 351
phantom (body), 161
philosophers/philosophy, 129, 135,
   136-139, 152, 196, 226, 254
pictures (imaginative images), 64, 171,
   174, 199, 202, 207, 213, 215,
   221. *See also* memory (pictures)
   shadow picture, 249
piety, 83
pineal gland (and mucous glands),
   286, 288, 290
Piper, Kurt, 297
Plato, 97-98
Polzer-Holditz family, 295
Polzer-Hoditz, Ludwig, 325-326,
   355, 436, 444
pondering, 279

Post-Atlantean cultural epochs
  Fourth, 45, 59, 61
potentize/potentization, 379, 397, 401
pralaya, 262, 269
prayer, 289, 275, 396
  prayerful/prayerfulness, 58, 76
preconception, xxi, xxv
psychologists, 197, 202
  in Middle Ages, 197, 202
Pythagorus, xviii, 105, 109, 113
  Pythagorean theorem, 113, 116, 120

Raphael, 50, 53, 55-56
Rath, Wilhelm, 334-338, 340, 362, 366, 377-378, 385-386, 389-392
rays, 116, 187, 206, 416-417, 420, 430, 433
realism, 157
reason/reasoning, 101, 104, 109, 119, 134, 144, 266, 278
reincarnate, 403
reproduction, 95-98, 103, 108, 112, 121-123
resurrected/resurrection, 26, 164, 188, 190, 252, 304-305. *See also* Christ, His Resurrection
reverence, xix-xx, 36, 38, 41, 47, 58, 60, 62, 66, 70-71, 73-74, 76, 79, 83-84, 108, 224, 243, 367-368, 413
review of the day, 276
Rittelmeyer, Friedrich, 297, 355, 381-382
robber stories, 192, 194
Romanus (in mystery drama, "The Soul's Awakening"), 131
Roschl, Maria, 297, 339, 360, 362, 405, 414, 423
Rosicrucians/Rosicrucianism, xii, xiv, xvi-xvii, xix, xxi-xxii, 32, 47, 99, 110, 117-118, 201, 205-206, 208, 384, 436
  Brotherhood, xvii
  Fama (announcement), xvii
  mantra, xvi,32, 36, 45, 47-48, 51, 66, 71, 74-75, 79, 84, 93, 113, 118, 127-128, 143, 177, 180, 182, 189, 221, 224-225, 230, 232, 247, 252, 266, 277, 291, 380
  ten words of (tenfold nature of humans), 67, 74, 79, 81, 180. *See also* Holy Decad
  Rose Cross, xvii, 106, 110, 113, 120, 158, 295
  light roses, 118, 120, 206
  seven light roses (7 cosmic forces), 118, 120
  theosophy, 45
  Trinitarian meditation, xvi-xviii, xxii, xxvi. *See also* Ex Deo nasimur, In Christo morimur, Per Spiritum Sanctum revivicimus
  wisdom, 96
Rosenkreutz, Christian, xvii, 295
  his "Chymical Wedding", 295
rubber ball, 179, 181, 184
Rudolf Steiner Archive, xxviii, 338, 386
Ruysbrock, 140, 145

sacredness, 47
sacramental, 29
sainfain, 368-369
Sanskrit, xxvi-xxvii, 412-413, 417, 430. *See also* India/Indian
Saturn, 3, 97, 105-106, 109, 113-114, 117, 120
Saturn, Old, epoch, xix, 24-25, 28, 33, 35, 38, 44, 59, 61, 79, 84, 153, 158, 188, 221
Scheidegger, Walter, 343
Schelling, xiv, xvi
Schem, Baal, 371, 388
Schiller, 157, 366, 393
  his "Wilhelm Tell", 157
School of Athens, 314
Schopenhauer, 187
self-consciousness. *See* consciousness, self-consciousness
selfless, xix
Selling, Clara, 340
Selling, Karin, 335, 339
Selling, Wilhelm, 335, 339
Senn, Otto, 343
senses (twelve in humans), 261, 264, 268-271
sentient soul, 220

Sermon on the Mount, 147, 160
shame, 78
Sivers, von, Marie. *See* Steiner, Marie
skeletal system, 317
Smit, Emma, 339
soul (spiritual) organs, 241, 248, 253, 255
soul substance, 42, 47
soulless/soullessness, xxiii, 41-42, 299
 bodies, 299
speech, 411
Spinoza/Spinozian, 129, 137, 139
Spira, Maria, 340, 387
Spirit. *See* Holy Spirit
spirit self, 212, 217-218
spiritual science. *See* anthroposophy
spiritualists. *See* mediums/mystics
spirits of form (elohim), 28, 163, 228, 244, 250, 256, 261, 263-264, 267, 269, 271, 275, 281-284, 290
spirits of motion/movement (dynamis), 78, 261, 263-264, 267, 271
spirits of personality (archai), 188-189
spirits of will (thrones), 188-189
spirits of wisdom (kyriotetes), 261, 264, 267, 271
Spitteler, 370-371, 388
star (Earth as), 416-417
star-gaze, 384
Steffen, Albert, 297
Stein, Walter Johannes, 355
Steiner, Marie, xii-xiii, 295, 297, 337-338, 340, 376, 378, 381, 406, 413-414, 428
Steiner, Rudolf
 his "Appeal to the German People and Cultural World", 352
 as Arch Warden, xiii
 his book, *Autobiography*, xiii
 his Esoteric School, xii, xviii, xxii, xxviii
 his book, *Fifth Gospel*, 160
 his book, *From the History and Contents of the Esoteric School, 1904-1914*, xiii, xxvii
 his mystery drama, "The Guardian of the Threshold", 50, 53, 55
 his book, *How to Know Higher Worlds*, xiv, xvi, 228
 his lecture, "Life Questions of the Riddles of Death", 114
 his mystery dramas, 49
 his book, *Mystics after Modernism*, 334
 his book, *An Outline of Esoteric Science*, xiv, xvii, 201, 205, 258, 391
 as a Rosicrucian, xvii
 his mystery drama, "The Soul's Awakening", 130-131, 143, 158
 his mystery drama, "The Soul's Probation", 36, 40
 his "Temple Legend", 325
 his book, *Theosophy*, xiv, 132, 138-139
 his book, *Towards Social Renewal*, 352
stomach, upset, 87, 91, 94
Strohschein, Albrecht, 340
suffering (pain), 26, 89-90, 93, 96, 99, 166, 170-171, 192-193, 209, 211, 216-218, 224, 255, 268, 402
suicide, 176, 180, 182
surrendering, 6
Sun, 5, 23, 25, 28, 30-32, 44, 47, 58, 79, 84, 95-97, 99, 103, 105-106, 108-109, 111-112, 114, 116-120, 122, 127, 150, 163, 169, 174, 177, 198, 207, 271, 274, 279, 318, 421
 living, 9, 11
 spiritual, 25, 98, 105-106, 109, 113, 117, 120
Sun, Old, epoch, xix, 24-25, 28, 33, 35, 38, 44, 59, 61, 79, 84, 221
Suso, 140, 147-148
Swan, stage of, 212
sweating (during meditation), 159-161
Swedenborg, 141, 146, 148
sympathetic/sympathy, 23, 101-102, 107, 112, 115, 119, 132, 344
 soul-sympathy, 384

Ten Commandments, 282, 284
theosophical/Theosophy, xiii, xiv-xv, 45, 47, 72, 88, 91, 101, 107, 111, 124-126, 131, 139, 160, 172-174,

182, 192-193, 195, 223, 254-255, 261, 264, 272, 279, 285-286, 288, 290, 301-303, 306, 332, 347, 349, 373, 415-417, 419, 422, 430, 441, 443
theosophical-anthroposophical, xiv
Theosophical Movement, xii, 34, 383
Theosophical Society, xii-xiii, xv, 34, 287, 289
  Esoteric School of, xii-xiii
  German section, xii-xiii, xv
  London lodge, xii
thread, burning, 420-421
threshold, at the, 304
thinking, xix, xxvii, 34-35, 37, 40, 47, 52, 54, 64-65, 69, 77, 82-83, 87, 104, 109, 116, 124, 132, 147, 150-151, 153, 165-166, 168, 170, 185, 188, 194, 197-198, 201-202, 209, 212, 214-215, 220, 222, 226, 232, 235, 238, 240, 242, 247-248, 253
  concentrated, 197, 202, 216, 218
  intellectual, 283
  objectless, 202
  ordinary thinking, destruction of, 166
thinking, feeling, willing, xxvii, 51, 64-65, 69-70, 72-73, 82-83, 197, 202, 205, 207-208, 220, 242, 248, 268, 272, 416, 419-420
Thirty-Years War, 295
thought, xx, xxvi, 21, 23, 25-27, 32-38, 40, 46, 49, 51-52, 54, 56, 59, 61, 64, 69, 72, 82-84, 86-87, 89-90, 92, 94, 99, 105, 108-109, 113, 116, 120, 124-125, 127, 141, 150, 160, 166-167, 171, 173, 185-186, 188, 191, 193-194, 196-197, 199, 204, 206-207, 209, 212, 226, 228, 230-231, 235-237, 241, 243-244, 248-249, 251, 254-256, 258-259, 261, 264, 268, 272, 275-277, 286, 291, 314, 316-317, 319, 370, 380, 384, 416, 418, 422, 442
  cosmic, 35, 37, 40
  forces, 33, 165
  shadow-thoughts, 232, 242-243, 249
  thought-life, 237
  thought-pictures, 151-152
threefold human being, xxii
Threefold Movement, 352-353, 356
Threefold Social Order, xxii, xxiv
Tower of Babel, 168
transform/transformation, xiv, xvii-xviii, xx, 30, 46-47, 56, 182, 184, 216, 226, 228, 232, 241-242, 248-249, 288, 372, 374, 395
truth, 21, 23, 34, 39, 47, 82, 124, 159, 168-170, 193, 196, 213-214, 217, 223, 230-231, 233-234, 239, 245-246, 251, 257-258, 277, 279, 290-291, 305, 345, 417, 419, 422, 442
Turning Point of Time, xix

Uehli, Ernst, 354
Unger, Carl, 355
untruth/untruthfulness, 27, 34, 161-162, 170, 213,-214, 223
Upanishads, 430

Valentine, Basil, xvii
Vancano, von, Harriet, 297
Venus, 15, 95, 98, 104-106, 109, 113-114, 116-117, 120
Venus, New, epoch, 291
virtual time (related to meditation), 400
Vreede, Elisabeth, 297

Wachsmuth, Gunther, 297
Wachsmuth, Wolfgang, Mr. & Mrs., 297
Wachsmuth-Lerchenfeld Group, 297
Waldorf schools, xxii, 338-339, 346, 371, 389
Waldorfschule, Freie, 343
Wallace, 194
Wallach, Robert W., 341-343
Wallen, Oda, 69, 72
Walther, Kurt, 335, 340
Wandervogel Youth Movement, 330, 369, 387
warmth, 17, 105-106, 113, 120, 152, 158, 163, 199-201, 203-206, 208, 219, 223-224, 253, 261,

263-264, 268, 282, 288, 367, 409, 419
two kinds of warmth, 200, 204
warmth-love, 419
warmth sphere, 200, 203
Wegman, Ita, 297, 338, 414
Werbeck, Ludwig, 355
where two or more are gathered in my name, 37, 41
Whitsun Congress, 1907, xiii, xiv, xvii
will, xix, 17, 19, 25, 36, 58, 70, 86, 90, 92, 94, 134, 141, 144, 147, 167, 185, 187, 197, 201, 209, 211, 216, 219-220, 224-226, 266, 278, 301-302, 316, 318, 349, 352, 375, 377, 390, 396, 399, 411, 416-417, 420
  freewill, 222, 304
  initiative will, 210
  will-denial, 187
  will impulse, 66, 70, 83, 87, 94, 216
  will-nature, 148-149, 219
  will power, 166, 185
willing, xix, xxvii, 21, 40, 67, 91, 210, 230-231, 233-234, 246, 251, 257, 272, 276, 279, 291, 302, 332, 430
wisdom, 19, 23, 30, 32, 66, 96, 109, 114, 116, 120, 126, 134, 144, 180, 200, 212, 225, 244, 266, 278, 417
  wisdom-water, 201
withering/wilting, 98, 238, 240-241, 248
Wohlbold, H., 355
Woloschin, Margarita, 297
Word, cosmic. *See* cosmic, cosmic Word
word-sense, 261
world of bliss (of forms), 50
worldview, 45, 129, 141, 150, 342, 353-354, 357

Yahweh, 167, 201, 238, 287-290
  as Godhead, 288-289
  as Moon God, 287, 289
Yahweh-Elohim, 228, 244, 250, 285, 298

youth (as post Kali Yuga soul), 423
Youth Movement, xxiv-xxv, 329-331, 341, 369, 371, 387-388

Zionist Youth Movement, 369, 374, 387, 395
zodiac, 262, 264, 269-271

In memory of
VERA MARTHA STARKEY
January 6, 1942 – December 13, 2010

Faithfully
I will follow your soul
Through the gate of death
Into the light-engendering
time-places —
With love, I will ease spirit coldness for you
With knowing, I will untangle spirit light for you,
With thinking, I will linger with you.

(From CW 261, for Gertrud Noss, on the death of her son
Fritz Mitscher, February 1915)

www.ingramcontent.com/pod-product-compliance
Lightning Source LLC
Chambersburg PA
CBHW030558230426
43661CB00053B/1767